Caner Tekin
Debating Turkey in Europe

Caner Tekin

Debating Turkey in Europe

Identities and Concepts

Dissertation, Fakultät für Geschichtswissenschaften der Ruhr-Universität Bochum
Datum der Disputation: 29.11.2016

ISBN: 978-3-11-077706-2
e-ISBN (PDF): 978-3-11-061467-1
e-ISBN (EPUP): 978-3-11-061191-5

Library of Congress Control Number: 2019949239

Bibliographic information published by the Deutsche Nationalbibliothek
The Deutsche Nationalbibliothek lists this publication in the Deutsche National-
bibliografie;detailed bibliographic data are available on the Internet at http://dnb.dnb.de.

© 2021 Walter de Gruyter GmbH, Berlin/Boston
This volume is text- and page-identical with the hardback published in 2020.
Cover Image: © Jacques-Louis David: The Coronation of Napoln (detail), Halet Efendi Druck
und Bindung: CPI books GmbH, Leck

www.degruyter.com

Preface and Acknowledgments

The prominent British sociologist Gerard Delanty commented about European identity in 1995: 'The discourse of Europe is ambivalent in that it is not always about unity and inclusion, but is also about exclusion and the construction of difference based on norms of exclusion'.[1] Europe, even in its most hopeful times for peace and integration, remained a nebulous concept instrumentalised by the sides of power politics in relation to what they see as 'other'. The nation-states of Western Europe after the Second World War had found the occasion to blow this haze with a new integration project. Based on undecided European geography in the East, the EU materialised its political meaning in time in an attempt to define, with the yardstick of the accession criteria, what is European and what is not in peaceful and democratic terms.

The EU's uneasy relationships with Turkey evolved throughout the association and candidature phases bear significance concerning which binaries emerged in defining European and non-European despite the accession criteria's leverage. If one factor structuring Turkey's accession process is some democratic criteria, the other has inherently been the interests shaped in national politics, and the preoccupations with religion, welfare, and migration almost always led the contestations over Turkey's EU bid. Furthermore, particularly for conservative camps of continental Europe the conflictual history of the Ottoman Empire has so far become a weapon with which to question Turkey's compatibility with Europe. In brief, the way the EU comes to terms with Turkey's accession bid reveals how contested Europe as a concept is. Europe is a notion into which nation-states and their political camps fit their own stories. Although Turkey's accession to the EU is a far-fetched prospect today, contemporary history reveals the stakes involved in the understandings of the co-existence between Europe and Turkey.

With these questions in mind, I undertook my doctoral research at the Ruhr-University Bochum between 2013 and 2017, which originated the present book. The trajectories of the transforming relationships between Turkey and Europe are the subject of history, but the final period of Turkey's candidature is addressed by various disciplines. At the intersection between history, politics and international relations, the book has conceptual and methodological shortcomings that are entirely of my own doing.

A number of people helped me in this book with their intellectual breadth and motivations. I am first and foremost grateful to my very dear friend Stefan

---

1 Gerard Delanty, *Inventing Europe* (London: Palgrave Macmillan, 1995),1.

Berger, my first supervisor, who raised me to my current academic maturity with great concern. I owe him a debt of gratitude for his company and, most importantly, for his patience. Professor Markus Koller lent his support in the second and third chapters, and I am thankful to him specifically for his support for my post-doctoral activities. Seda Gurkan read and improved the first draft with her critics. *Fazit Stiftung*, foundation of Frankfurter Allgemeine Zeitung, accepted to fund the printing costs. As earlier models of inspiration, Professor Corinne Gobin and Professor Canan Balkir, with whom I had the chance to work in Brussels and Izmir, believed in me and helped me reach my early academic network. During my adventures in Brussels and Bochum, two very special people emerged on my path and touched my life. Especially during my early struggle with the obstacles of my research, Jasmina became a confidant and tutor bringing me up in social life and helping me hold onto my aspiration. Finally, but most importantly, I am indebted to my partner Isabel for her faith in me, as she never gave up on me even in my most discouraging moments and was the real strength of endurance throughout the entire process.

To close this section, the book's cover demands explanation, as it is relevant for Turkey's controversial position central to European debates over being a 'partner', 'aggressor', and 'sick man'. Commissioned by Napoleon Bonaparte, Jacques-Louis David painted his famous coronation and represented the participants of the ceremony held in the Notre Dame Cathedral of Paris in 1804. The present cover image is a detail of this renowned painting and features Halet Efendi, Ottoman ambassador in the Napoleonic age, as standing in the corner and watching the coronation behind the vast crowd. Such a detail draws questions regarding whether the spot reserved for an Ottoman diplomat mirrored the long-term place of Turkey in Europe. In any case, Halet Efendi had been given an insignificant position in the event despite relatively improving relations with France since Napoleon waged his unsuccessful invasion in Egypt 10 years ago, an offensive that expanded the orientalist literature about the Ottoman realm. From the turn of the 19th century onwards the image of the Turk saw its long evolution, with which this book deals in depth.

Contents

1 **Introduction and Conceptual Clarifications** —— 1
   European Identity and Turkey: An Intellectual Debate —— 7
   Conceptual Clarifications —— 32
   Plan of the Book —— 38

2 **Relations between Europe and Turkey in Modern History** —— 41
   European and Ottoman Images during the 18th and 19th Centuries —— 45
   Portraying the Ottomans: Instances from British and French Literatures —— 49
   Ottoman/Turkish Modernisation in the Eyes of Europeans —— 61

3 **Relations between Europe and Turkey in Contemporary History** —— 69
   Relations between the European Union and Turkey until the 1990s —— 74
   The EU's Political Integration and Its Accession Criteria —— 80
   Relations between the EU and Turkey before the Membership Negotiations —— 84
   Roles of the European Conservative and Far-right Camps in Turkey-EU Relations —— 91
   Conclusion —— 96

4 **Coming to Terms with Turkey's EU Bid: Evidence from the European Parliament** —— 97
   Common Political Values Derived from the EU's Accession Criteria —— 100
   European Values conceptualised by pan-European Parties —— 102
   Judging Turkey's Democratic Performance through the Prism of the Accession Criteria? —— 116
   Religious Concepts —— 123
   Geographical Concepts —— 127
   Conclusion —— 130

5 **Between the Constitutional Referendum and Leadership Contest: French Debates over Turkey's EU Bid in 2005** —— 132
   French Politics in 2005: the EU Constitution and Turkey —— 142

The EU and Turkey according to the French Media and Politics —— 147
Conclusion —— 157

6 **'Is it all about Welfare?' German Debates over Turkey's EU Bid in 2005** —— 159
The EU and Turkey according to the German Media and Politics —— 171
Conclusion —— 187

7 **The Struggle against European Political Integration: British Debates over Turkey's EU Bid in 2005** —— 189
The EU and Turkey according to the British Media and Politics —— 196
Conclusion —— 212

8 **Conclusion** —— 214

Bibliography —— 228
Documents of European Institutions —— 228
Election Programmes and other Documents of pan-European and National Political Parties —— 231
Debates in the European Parliament —— 232
Speeches —— 233
Opinion Polls —— 233
Other Documents —— 233
Bibliography —— 234
News Media —— 260

Index of subjects —— 267

1 Introduction and Conceptual Clarifications

Europe has been, and still is, home to many societies. It is a common roof, but one lacking a commonly accepted definition. The disagreements over what Europe is and which values define Europeanness emerged extraordinarily in the 2000s, as Turkey, which had been perceived to be Europe's antithesis for many centuries, was now knocking the EU's door as a candidate for membership. In 2005, at a time when the accession talks between Ankara and Brussels were finally commencing, essentially different understandings of Europe and its past were clashing in a political debate about Turkey's EU bid. Although today the future of the accession talks is unknown, and the notion of an authoritarian Turkey having a place in Europe is perceived to be far-fetched, these early years still bear importance, since they reveal many dichotomies over European identity in European and national politics. Building on this standpoint, the present book examines the link between historical conceptions of Europe and the contestations over the definition of Turkey in relation to the European Union (or vice versa) in the 2000s.

During the 2000s, the understanding of Europe and its common values was at the centre of political debates surrounding EU enlargements. The EU's bureaucrats were depicting the organization as the strongest representative of common liberal values, and they were presenting its enlargements ahead as part and parcel of a civilizational mission of promoting these values outside, a historical mission inherited to the contemporary Europe.[1] 'European values' became a piece of EU legislation (Acquis communautaire) as the Treaty on European Union (amended by the Treaty of Lisbon in 2009) employed this term often in order to refer to the EU's shared democratic rights, freedoms, and principles. The question between European political camps yet remained whether these 'formal' values of the European Union represented the whole European identity for these camps, parties and actors represented at European and national levels. This is still a relevant issue today, since the contemporary conceptions of 'common values' are questioned not only in the case of Turkey's compatibility with Europe, but also concerning how the Central and Eastern European countries conform to the EU.

Specifically at three levels the EU's identity policies, or, in other words, the policies to promote formal 'European values' develop: the EU's internal affairs, foreign affairs, and enlargement affairs. The third one became increasingly im-

---

[1] See, Romano Prodi, Speech in the European Parliament: 2000–2005: Shaping the New Europe, European Parliament, Strasbourg, 15 February, 2000, SPEECH/00/41.

portant in the 2000s as the former president of the European Commission expressed at the turn of the decade that enlargement was crucial if their aim was to 'spread peace, stability and shared values throughout the continent.'[2] The connection between the enlargement and the representation of values has political and cultural importance also in present Europe. Even today, when the EU's next enlargement is proclaimed to be a long-term outcome concerning the accession of Turkey and the remaining Balkan countries, the phenomenon of 'enlargement' means more than widening the Union's borders. This book therefore primarily concerns itself with the field of enlargement, particularly the debate about the EU's enlargement with Turkey and history's role in it.

It is widely argued that the European Union's supranational institutions work to reflect a collective and normative image of Europeanness that takes precedence over national politics.[3] The European Commission is the leading responsible body that embodies this state of affairs and promotes European political values.[4] For one example, the Commission's Directorate for Education and Culture has on many occasions sought to define the boundaries of European identity. In general, the civic values enshrined in the founding treaties create the baseline on which the European Commission maintains an institutional language that elevates Europeanness over national politics. Yet this is an only one aspect of the EU's identity representation. As Antony Smith remarks, 'at the conceptual level ... the contradiction between a European identity and existing national identities may be more apparent than real'.[5] The EU's identity construction then is not uniform; it is in fact merely a political construct, in which various identity conceptions from EU legislation and national politics encounter each other.

The EU's language about enlargement affairs is a similar case, in which the European Commission also plays a central role. It leads the EU's enlargement vision and is inspired by the well-known motto, 'united in diversity', which implies

---

2 Ibid.
3 Richard Hermann and Marilynn B. Brewer, 'Identities and Institutions: Becoming European in the EU', in *Transnational Identities: Becoming European in the EU*, eds. Richard Hermann, Thomas Risse-Kappen, and Marilynn B. Brewer (Lanham: Rowman& Littlefield Publishers, 2004), 2–3; Juan Diez Medrano, 'The Public Sphere and the European Union's Political Identity', in *European Identity* eds. Jeffrey T. Checkel and Peter J. Katzenstein (New York: Cambridge University Press, 2009), 106.
4 See Oriane Calligaro, *Negotiating Europe: Promotion of Europeanness since the 1950s* (New York: Palgrave Macmillan, 2013).
5 Anthony Smith, 'National Identity and the Idea of Unity', *International Affairs, (Royal Institute of International Affairs 1944-)* 68, no.1 (1992): 56, doi: 10.2307/2620461.

promoting unity on certain rules and values whilst also preserving the cultural diversity between member states.⁶ Still, the EU's enlargement involves other European and local actors too. Political camps represented in the European and national parliaments have a say during the accession process of a candidate, and they do question its compatibility with the European Union in political or other terms. As such, alongside the EU's collective approach, competing categorizations about the European Union and its outsider have emerged during the candidature process of the Balkan countries and also Turkey. One graphic example illustrates these dichotomies. In order to promote the enlargement vision of the EU, the European Commission televised a video in 2012 that has been characterised as scandalously racist.⁷ In the video, three 'non-European-looking' warriors, evocative of ethnic minorities of Europe, as well as historic rivals like Turkey, intercept and dare to intimidate a 'European' white woman disguised as 'the Bride' of the famed movie, 'Kill Bill'. 'The Bride' shows no fear, spreads her arms wide, and replicates herself twelve times (no doubt inspired by the twelve stars of the EU flag). The replicas then surround these fearsome warriors and lead the encircled three 'non-Europeans' to go down on their haunches and begin to peacefully communicate. The video ends with the message that reads: 'The more we are, the stronger we are'. The mixed messages within the video exemplify the paradoxes within the current enlargement discourse of the EU, specifically: who poses a challenge to whom under what influences?

The contrasting characteristics of Europeanness evoked in the video raise a number of questions and the relevance of history: Is there any uniform representation of Europe or being European? What values officially maintain Europeanness? What are their historical origins? ⁸ From which sources are they justified today? (Are their sources of justification at the level of Europe or nation-states?) How significant were Europe's historic rivals during the construction of these values? The European Commission partially addressed these questions in the

---

6 Andrea M. Geddes, *Promoting Unity, Preserving Diversity? Member-State Institutions and European Integration* (Oxford: Lexington Books, 2006).
7 'European Commission Criticized for Racist Ad', *The Guardian*, May 6, 2012.
8 It is important to remember that most ancient figures used to promote the idea of Europe are antithetically eastern in origin. The Phoenician Prince 'Europa', after whom the continent is named, Aeneas, the ancient founder of Rome, and Jesus of Nazareth, the Christian prophet and perhaps the strongest figure in the European idea, are of Asian origins. Anthony Pagden, 'Europe: Conceptualizing a Continent', in *The Idea of Europe: From Antiquity to the European Union*, ed. Anthony Pagden (New York: Cambridge University Press, 2002), 35.

mid-2000s. Its Directorate-General for Research specified that the historical dichotomies between European values are binding:

> The fundamental dilemma of European foreign policy is the tension between the logic of peace and the logic of cohesion. Europe sees itself as both a zone of peace and a community of values. This dilemma cannot be solved a priori. There is no essence of Europe, no fixed list of European values. There is no 'finality' to the process of European integration ... In principle this has been the case throughout Europe's history.[9]

The Commission reminded that the European identity is in a state of flux. The logic of Europeanness, the foremost constituent of the post-national thinking in the present-day EU, alters between normative political arguments that are in fact predicated on the images of Europe and its rivals forged in history. At the turn of the 21th century these arguments came to a firm shape in coming to terms with Turkey's EU bid.

The present book has two objectives. The first is to discuss the historical images and conditions that lie behind Turkey debates. Here the study explores how these long-term historical factors spanning from modern European history influence the contemporary and normative arguments about Turkey, a candidate for membership of the European Union and yet arguably Europe's historic archrival. Such a historical approach should be able to grasp the relationship between long-term enmity and the contemporary perceptions of Turkey within the EU. The second objective is to highlight political debates at European and national levels and to locate the tension of Turkey-specific national and European parties (mostly conservatives) with EU legislation concerning enlargement. As shown below, the European Union's language about Turkey as a candidate is not consistent: mainstream political camps both in national and transnational networks frequently challenge it.[10] A number of studies have demonstrated the engagements between European and national elites within the European Commission's committees in certain policy fields.[11] The book concerns itself with dis-

---

9 Kurt Biedenkopf, Bronislaw Geremek, and Krzysztof Michaleski, *The Spiritual and Cultural Dimension of Europe: Reflection Group Concluding Remarks* (Luxembourg: Office for Official Publications of the European Communities, 2005), 12.
10 Peter Kraus, *A Union of Diversity Language, Identity, and Polity-Building in Europe* (New York: Cambridge University Press, 2008), 66.
11 Neil Fligstein, *Euro-clash: the EU, European Identity, and the Future of Europe* (New York: Oxford University Press, 2008), 40–41. For the influences of supranationalist and nationalist policies over the Commission's Comities, see George Tsebelis and Geoffrey Garrett, 'The Institutional Foundations of Intergovernmentalism and Supranationalism in the European Union', *International Organization* 55, no.2 (Spring 2001), http://www.jstor.org/stable/3078635; Jorerges Christian and Jurgen Neyer, 'Transforming Strategic Interaction into Deliberative Problem-Solv-

cussions in the European Parliament over Turkey's performance throughout the candidate's membership negotiations with the EU and how national perspectives engage the process. The textual data produced within the European Parliament demonstrate the interplays between deputies' pan-European ideological constraints and their national backgrounds. More specifically, the EP's plenary debates and annual reports about Turkey expose how historical conceptions of Europe influence the debates over the past, current, and potential relationships between Turkey and Europe. In addition to the EU's supranational institutions, significant examples of contextualizing local identities, European identity, and distinctively Turkish identity are obvious in national debates that appear in the media. National actors, as reflected by the media, discuss Turkey not only to address its compatibility with the European Union but also to justify their own representations of European values.

The rest of the present chapter presents the main research question and the subsidiary ones, and it links them into an overview of the current literature. Then, it clarifies the key concepts employed throughout the study. Adopting a semantic approach, it explains how these concepts dovetail with the methodological framework. It later critically elaborates the existing methods of analysing documents and justifies its adherence to a historical-reflectivist approach and to a practice of conceptual reading. Finally, the chapter sets out the structure of the rest of the book.

The central question addressed in this study is: *How and by what historical values did the European political camps conceptualise Turkey in relation to the European Union during the accession talks (or membership negotiations) in the 2000s?* 'Historical values' here describe the moral principles involved in the arguments about Turkey's compatibility with the European Union and henceforth will be referred to as the political, religious, and geographical terms of conceptualising the European Union and Turkey. The chapter justifies these subdivisions in detail under the section 'Conceptual Clarifications'. Next, the term 'political camps' describes the wide range of actors who have a constitutionally defined engagement in EU politics. In the present study, political camps are limited to pan-European parties represented in the European Parliament and their

---

ing: European Comitology in the Foodstuff's Sector', *European Journal of Public Policy* 4, no.4 (1997), doi: 10.1080/135017697344091; Gijs Jan Brandsma and Jens Blomhansen, 'The EU Comitology System: What Role for the Commission?', *Public Administration* 88, no.2 (2010), doi: 10.1111/j.1467–9299.2010.01819.x; Sarah Lieberman and Tim Gray, 'The so-called "Moratorium" on the Licencing of New Genetically Modified (GM) Products by the European Union 1998– 2004: A Study in Ambiguity', *Environmental Politics* 25, no.4 (2006), doi: 10.1080/09644010600785218.

national constituents. This main research question therefore focuses on the linkage between historical values and contemporary thinking over the categorisation of the European Union in the context of Turkey.

Three subsidiary questions help contextualise the main research theme. The first one addresses how the terms of Europeanness from the 18th century onwards determined Europe's relationship with the Ottoman Empire and later with the modern Turkey. The historical relationship between European political actors and the Ottomans suggests how divergent terms, in political, religious, and geographical realms, were applied and evolved into a number of cultural perspectives about Europe and Turkey. The study thus historically examines the changing viewpoints that European actors adopted throughout their relationship with the Ottoman Empire. It shows that normative arguments derived from different European values alternately stereotyped Turkey as a realm of 'infidels', a political ally, the source of oriental mystery, and 'the sick man of Europe'. A second element of this sub-question is to explore the terms of discussing Europe in connection with Turkey that are legitimised under EU legislation (which encompasses the EU's accession criteria) and national politics. Here the aim is to grasp how the earlier versions of these terms have evolved in the previous centuries, especially in Western Europe. Various traditions of discussing Europe, embedded in EU legislation and national politics, today draw distinct pictures of the EU and Turkey. The other sub-questions then address the depictions of common European values within the contemporary political debate about Turkey at European and national contexts.

The second subsidiary question explores how the EU and Turkey are represented in European politics, particularly in the European Parliament. It asks how and by what historical values the political camps in the European Parliament conceptualised the European Union and Turkey during the 2000s, especially in the context of the candidate's negotiation process. The European Parliament is accepted as an arena where European and national politics meet, and Turkey arguments justified under EU legislation and national politics thus overlap or clash at the parliamentary level. From this standpoint, the study initially examines the plenaries about Turkey convened in the European Parliament and particularly in its AFET (the Committee on Foreign Affairs or *Affaires étrangères*) from 2005, when the candidate entered its accession negotiations. It also examines AFET's annual reports on Turkey and parliamentarians' proposals to amend them. AFET consists of members that represent mainstream political parties. As such, AFET's reports on Turkey demonstrate members' positions informed by both European and national contexts. In short, they provide a framework to understand various conceptualisations of the European Union and Turkey in political, religious, and geographical terms that are justified in terms of EU legislation and/or national politics.

Finally, the third sub-question discusses representations of the EU in connection with the candidate in Germany, France, and Britain and takes into consideration the national peculiarities that underpinned the debates held in 2005 over the EU's enlargement with Turkey. It explores which structural (country-based) factors and which historical values the leading political parties of the three countries used to represent national, European, and Turkish identities. Here the study is limited to the research of media coverage in a short period from September to early October 2005. This was a key period featuring lively debates in politics and the media, as it immediately predated the beginning of Turkey's accession negotiations, on 3 October 2005.

In the light of these questions, the book explores the traces of history in the contemporary debate about Turkey's compatibility with the EU in the European Parliament and national politics. The following section further contextualises these questions with the literature on contemporary European history and Turkey-EU relations, and makes specific reference to the relationship between European historical values and current identity debates.

European Identity and Turkey: An Intellectual Debate

Stating that 'communities are distinguished ... by the style in which they are imagined', Benedict Anderson notes that elites are and will remain the principal actors of imaginary identities within national contexts.[12] The project of an imagined community in the European context is but more complicated given the leverage of European legislation and its post-national institutions. Then, the departure point is that in contemporary European politics there are two principal sources, which political elites make use of in order to legitimise identities: EU legislation and national politics.[13] On the one hand, EU legislation looms

---

[12] Benedict Anderson, *Imagined Communities: Reflections on the Origin and Spread of Nationalisms* (New York: Verso, 1991), 6.
[13] Jeffrey T. Checkel and J. Peter Katzenstein, 'Politicization of European Identities', in *European Identity*, eds. Jeffrey T. Checkel and J. Peter Katzenstein (New York: Cambridge University Press, 2009), 11–12. Checkel and Katzenstein coin two concepts, 'cosmopolitan' and 'partisan' arguments, in order to denote those justified under EU legislation and national politics respectively. Yet it is highly important to remind that these concepts symbolise legislation and politics, not actors. For examples, see Erik Oddvar Eriksen, 'The EU: A Cosmopolitan Polity?', *Journal of European Public Policy* 13, no.2 (2006), doi: 10.1080/13501760500451683; Ian Manners, 'The Nor-

large as a source of legitimisation shaped by elites. EU legislation sets civic values in stone and is the result of EU elites constructing a post-national European identity.[14] In other words, the EU is fundamentally constructed on cosmopolitan values, common values oriented to rights and liberties, which eventually frame nation states' interests.[15] On the other hand, national politics has never lost importance or become a secondary consideration, and essentialist values from within national politics maintain their significances as alternative ways of describing the European and the non-European. Arguments derived from national politics can be in conflict with EU legislation as much as they can conflict each other.[16] Economic and refugee crises following the Lisbon Treaty reveal that political elites on really rare occasions give up their principal roles of following their national interests, and this has been a common case also in altering European or national identities within the EU.[17] The short history of the EU has been rife with tension between these two forms of identity constructions.

Over the last decades, identity politics at the European and national levels have been strongly influenced, in several respects, by the emergence of post-Cold War Europe. First, the end of the bipolar international rivalry opened the

---

mative Ethics of the European Union', *International Affairs* 84, no.1 (January 2008), doi:10.1111/j.1468–2346.2008.00688.x.

14 Jonna Johanson, *Learning to be a Good European, A Critical Analysis of the Official European Union Discourse on European Identity and Higher Education* (Linköping: Linköping University Press, 2008), 63.

15 Jurgen Habermas and Jacques Derrida, 'February 15, or What Binds Europeans Together: A Pleas for a Common Foreign Policy, Beginning in the Core of Europe', *Constellations* 10, no.3 (2003): 294, doi: 10.1111/1467–8675.00333.

16 Andrew Moravcsik, 'Reassessing Legitimacy in the European Union', *JCMS: Journal of Common Market Studies* 40, no.4 (November 2002): 603–624, doi: 10.1111/1468–5965.00390; Dario Castiglione, 'Political Identity in a Community of Strangers', in *European Identity*, eds. Jeffrey T. Checkel and J. Peter Katzenstein (New York: Cambridge University Press, 2009), 44; Thomas Risse, 'A European Identity? Europeanization and Evolution of a Nation-State Identities', in *Transforming Europe, Europeanization and Domestic Change*, eds. Maria Green Cowles, James A. Caporaso, and Thomas Risse-Kappen (Ithaca: Cornell University Press, 2001), 202; Bahar Rumelili and Didem Cakmakli '"Culture" in EU-Turkey Relations', in *Culture and External Relations: Europe and Beyond*, eds. Jozef Bátora and Monika Mokre (Burlington: Ashgate, 2011), 101.

17 Sergio Fabbrini, 'Constructing and De-constructing the European Political Identity: the Contradictory Logic of the EU's Institutional System, *Comparative European Politics*, 1–14, doi: 10.1057/s41295–019–00171–8; Roberta Capelo, 'Cohesion Policies and the Creation of a European Identity: The Role of Territorial Identity', *Journal of Common Market Studies* 56, no. 3 (2018): 489–502, doi: 10.1111/jcms.12611; Martin Marcussen, Thomas Risse, Daniela Engelmann-Martin, Hans-Joachim Knopf, and Klaus Roscher, 'Constructing Europe? The Evolution of Nation State Identities', in *The Social Construction of Europe*, eds. Thomas Christiansen, Knud Erik Jørgensen, and Antje Wiener (London: Sage Publications, 2001), 101–120.

way for political camps to orient themselves to local cultures and their local politics more than before.[18] In Eastern Europe, governments swiftly turned to nation-state policies and became instrumental in the rise of conflictual nationalisms.[19] In Western Europe, the post-Cold War EU rather emerged as an upholder of certain values that have developed with new summits and treaties.[20] The Laeken Summit held in 2001 was one of the first meetings that called for the EU to position itself as a global actor representing its political values and filling the power vacuum within the fragmented post-Cold War international order.[21] With this aim in mind, the European Union initiated the European Neighbourhood Policy in 2004 as an instrument for promoting its 'shared values' in Europe's hinterland.[22] In addition, with the Lisbon Treaty taking effect in 2009 the EU re-formulated the legal ground of its value-driven foreign policy by introducing the External Action.[23] Since then the EU has built its documents on international cooperation on the representation and promotion of its official values, in particular human rights, democracy, and the rule of law.[24]

As the second way in which the Cold War's end influenced identity representations, the removal of the 'iron curtain' at the heart of Europe revived populist arguments derived from national politics in favour of European enlargement and identity. In the 1990s, European politicians adorned a potentially unified Europe

---

18 Samuel Huntington, *The Clash of Civilizations and the Remaking of World Order* (New York: Simon & Schuster, 1996), 125.
19 Gerard Delanty, *Formations of European Modernity: A Historical and Political Sociology of Europe* (Cham: Palgrave Macmillan, 2019), 305–340, https://doi.org/10.1007/978-3-319-95435-6.
20 Ronald Holzhacker and Marek Neuman, 'Framing the Debate: The Evolution of the European Union as an External Democratization Actor Democracy Promotion and the Normative Power Europe Framework' in *The European Union in South Eastern Europe, Eastern Europe, and Central Asia*, ed. Marek Neuman (Cham: Springer, 2019), 13–36, https://doi.org/10.1007/978-3-319-92690-2; Hanns W. Maull, 'Europe and the New Balance of Global Order', *International Affairs* 81, no.4 (July 2005): 775–799, doi: 10.1111/j.1468–2346.2005.00484.x.
21 Stephen Weatherill, *Cases and Materials in EU Law* (Oxford: Oxford University Press, 2012), 15; Ali Tekin, 'Future of EU-Turkey Relations: A Civilizational Discourse', *Futures* 37, (2005): 289, doi: 10.1016/j.futures.2004.07.008.
22 Päivi Leino and Roman Petrov, 'Between "Common Values" and Competing Universals—The Promotion of the EU's Common Values through the European Neighbourhood Policy', *European Law Journal* 15, no.5 (September 2009): 654–671, doi: 10.1111/j.1468–0386.2009.00483.x.
23 Morten P. Broberg, 'Don't Mess with the Missionary Man! On the Principle of Coherence, the Missionary Principle, and the European Union's Development Policy', in *EU External Relations Law and Policy in the Post-Lisbon Era*, ed. Paul James Cardwell (Hague: T.M.C. Asser Press 183, 2012), 183.
24 Stephan Keukeleire and Tom Delreux, *The Foreign Policy of the European Union* (Basingstoke: Palgrave Macmillan, 2014), 135–155.

with religious and geographical terms. This began with the withdrawal of the Soviet influence from Eastern Europe, as politicians in national politics celebrated the 'return of the East to the European home'.[25] François Mitterrand, the French President at that time, spoke emotionally on this topic: '(Europe) is returning to its history and its geography like one who is returning home'.[26] Helmut Kohl, the former German Chancellor, and famously referred to as 'the architect of the modern Europe',[27] similarly stated in 1994: 'The Poles, the Czechs, the Slovaks, the Romanians, the Bulgarians and the Hungarians are our European brothers ... and need to attain their European rights.'[28] Indeed, metaphors such as 'home' or 'family' were indispensable in like-minded populist statements during that time.[29] The 1990s showed that the EU enlargement developed through similar metaphors, which were actually coined for national politics. Using these metaphors, European politicians expanded the political conception of Europe to include a religious and geographical fictional unity. At the same time, 'Eastern Europe', the term that once described the backward part of the continent, received a new significance in Western Europe during the 1990s.[30] In brief, the sense of solidarity with Eastern European countries was part of a civilizational rhetoric in national and transnational politics and was reminiscent of moral judgements that were invoked prior to Greece's accession in 1981.[31] Scholars agree that this solidarity gave momentum to the accession processes of the Eastern European Countries (which were referred to as the Central and Eastern European Countries) in the 2000s.[32] Further, the religious side of European politics much fav-

---

[25] Lászlo Kürti, 'Globalization and the Discourse of "Otherness" in the New Eastern and Central Europe', in *The Politics of Multiculturalism in the New Europe: Racism, Identity and Community*, eds. Tariq Modood and Pnina Werbner (New York: Zed Books, 1997), 30–31.
[26] Jacques Derrida, *The Other Heading: Reflections on Today's Europe* (Bloomington, Indianapolis: Indiana University Press, 1992), 8–9.
[27] Michael Gehler, *Europa: Von der Utopie zur Realität* (Innsbruck-Wien: Haymon Taschenbuch, 2014), 237.
[28] Rainer Hülsse, 'Imagine the EU: The Metaphorical Construction of a Supra-nationalist Identity' *Journal of International Relations and Development* 9, no.4 (2006): 407, doi:10.1057/palgrave.jird.1800105. 407.
[29] Ibid, 408–410.
[30] J. Hagen, 'Redrawing the Imagined Map of Europe: The Rise and Fall of the Center', *Political Geography* 22, no.5 (2003): 492–494, doi: 10.1016/S0962-6298(03)00030–1.
[31] Susannah Verney, 'Justifying the Second Enlargement: Promoting interests, Consolidating Democracy or Returning to the Roots?', in *Questioning EU Enlargement: Europe in Search of Identity*, ed. Helene Sjursen (New York and London: Routledge, 2006), 32.
[32] Helene Sjursen, 'Introduction: Enlargement and the Nature of the EU Polity', in *Questioning EU Enlargement: Europe in Search of Identity*, ed. Helene Sjursen (New York and London: Routledge, 2006), 10–14; Diez, 'Europe's Others', 319–335. Frank Schimmelfennig, 'The Community

oured solidarity with the East. In his Easter speech in 2004, Pope Paul stated that the Eastern European countries 'by culture and tradition were and felt European' and that only by turning back to its Christian roots could the new Europe sustain peace and prosperity.[33] This sense of solidarity based on representations of Europe in religious and geographical terms raises the question of how political actors would deal with candidates emerging from different historical conditions, such as Turkey.[34]

Third, the gradual rise of national populisms in national and European politics intensified cultural representations of Europe and nation states as well as oppositions to the EU's integration and enlargement during the 2000s.[35] The consequences of European enlargement to Eastern Europe, ever-closer European integration, and international migrations to Western Europe contributed significantly to the rise of the conservative right and populist radical right in this period.[36] Against a changing Europe, conservative and nationalist camps characterised the continent as a cultural fortress against outsiders, as they still do today in the face of similar realities.[37] At the same time, Turkey's EU candidature additionally ignited discussions in European and national politics about Europe's

---

Trap: Liberal Norms, Rhetorical Action, and the Eastern Enlargement of the European Union', *International Organization* 55, no.1 (2001): 68–69, doi: 10.1162/002081801551414; Klaus Eder. 'Remembering National Memories Together: The Formation of a Transnational Identity in Europe', in *Collective Memory and European Identity: The Effects of Integration and Enlargement*, eds. Klaus Eder and Willfried Spohn (Aldershot: Ashgate, 2005), 197.

33 Peter D. Sutherland, 'Europe: Values and Identity', *Studies: An Irish Quarterly Review* 99, no.396 (Winter 2010): 426, doi: http://www.jstor.org/stable/27896508.

34 Helene Sjursen, 'Why Expand? The Question of Legitimacy and Justification in the EU's Enlargement Policy', *JCMS: Journal of Common Market Studies* 40, no.3 (2002): 504, doi: 10.1111/1468–5965.00366; Thomas Risse, *A Community of Europeans? Transnational Identities and Public Spheres* (Ithaca: Cornell UniversityPress, 2010), 6.

35 Fennema Meindert, 'Some Conceptual Issues and Problems in the Comparison of Anti-Immigrant Parties in Western Europe', *Party Politics* 3, no.4 (October 1997): 473–492, doi: 10.1177/1354068897003004002; Wouter Van der Brug, Anthony Mughan, 'Charisma, Leader Effects and Support for Right-wing Populist Parties', *Party Politics* 13, no.1 (2007): 29–51, doi: 10.1177/1354068806071260.

36 Paul Hainsworth, *The Extreme Right in Western Europe* (London and New York: Routledge, 2008), 70–77. Dietrich Thränhardt, *Europe, a New Immigration Continent: Policies and Politics in Comparative Perspective* (Munster: LIT Verlag, 1996), 118–119; Andrew Geddes, The Politics of Migration and Immigration in Europe (London: Sage, 2003).

37 Anton Pelinka, 'Right-Wing Populism: Concept and Typology', in *Right-Wing Populism in Europe: Politics and Discourse*, eds. Ruth Wodak, Majid Khosravinik, and Brigitte Mral (London: Bloomsbury Academic, 2013), 15–16; Gerard Delanty, 'Fear of Others: Social Exclusion and the European Crisis', *Social Policy & Administration* 42, no.6 (December 2008): 676–690, doi: 10.1111/j.1467–9515.2008.00631.x.

cultural orientations.³⁸ By way of example, during the EU's constitutional referenda in 2005, national populism in France used Turkey's membership scenario as one argument against the EU Constitution.³⁹ Although it is outside the timeframe of the study, it is important to note that a very similar case happened in Britain few years ago, ahead of the Brexit referendum in 2016. In their leave campaign against the EU, the Brexiteers manipulated the bogeyman of Turkey's accession with their false argument that the candidate would join the EU very soon.⁴⁰ But specifically in the previous French example, Turkey's potential accession to the European Union sparked normative arguments that sometimes categorised the European Union as the 'cradle' of European civilization and the candidate as a cultural threat to the EU and its values.⁴¹

All these aspects of the post-Cold War Europe suggest that European political elites have drawn on history and tended to stereotype, positively or negatively, the European Union, Eastern Europe, and Turkey when discussing further enlargement.⁴² They have established a vision of a European civilization that is imbued with a sense of nostalgia, and which harks back to its earlier history.⁴³ The so-called cultural values of Europe that were constructed in the past still

---

38 Bo Strath, 'European Identity: To the Historical Limits of a Concept', *European Journal of Social Theory* 5, no.4 (November 2002): 397, doi: 10.1177/136843102760513965; Mirela Bogdani, *Turkey and the Dilemma of EU Accession: When Religion Meets Politics* (London: Tauris, 2011), 47.
39 Beyza Tekin, 'The Construction of Turkey's Possible EU Membership in French Discourse', *Discourse & Society* 19, no.6 (November 2008): 727–763, doi: 10.1177/0957926508095891; Hakan Yilmaz, 'Turkish Identity on the Road to the EU: Basic Elements of French and German Oppositional Discourses', in *Turkey's Road to European Union Membership: National Identity and Political Change*, eds. Susannah Verney and Kostas Ifantis (London and New York: 2009), 90.
40 Paul Levin, 'Who Lost Turkey? The Consequences of Writing an Exclusionary European History', in *History and Belonging: Representations of the Past in Contemporary European Politics*, eds. Caner Tekin and Stefan Berger (New York: Berghahn Books, 2018), 167.
41 Iver, B. Neumann, 'European Identity, EU Expansion, and the Integration/Exclusion Nexus', in *Constructing Europe's Identity: The External Dimension*, ed. Lars-Erik Cederman (Colorado and London: Lynne Rienner Publishers, 2001), 158; Thomas Diez, 'Europe's Others and Return of Geopolitics', *Cambridge Review of International Affairs* 17, no.2 (2004), dio: 10.1080/0955757042000245924; Bilgin, 'A Return to the Civilizational Geopolitics', 275; Gulnur Aybet and Meltem Muftuler Bac, 'Transformations in Security and Identity after the Cold War: Turkey's Problematic Relationship with the EU', *International Journal* 55, no.4 (Autumn, 2000): 569, doi:10.2307/40203501.
42 Kevin Robins, 'Interactive Identities: Turkey/Europe', in *Questions of Cultural Identity*, eds. Stuart Hall and Paul du Gay (London: Sage Publications, 1996), 81.
43 Derrida, *The Other Heading*, 8–9. This quote from Hobsbawm seems timely here: 'The past is a permanent dimension of the human consciousness, an inevitable component of the institutions, values and other patterns of human society.' Eric J. Hobsbawm, 'The Social Function of the Past: Some Questions', *Past & Present*, no. 55 (May, 1972): 3, doi:10.1093/past/55.1.3.

have their bearing on contemporary contestations over Turkey's accession to the EU.[44] This poses a question concerning the historical margins of Europe and the Ottoman Empire/Turkey.

In the 18th and 19th centuries, Western Europe experienced significant socio-economic and political changes that substantially altered the language of politics. The works of Eric Hobsbawm and Francois Furet trace many of these changes to revolutions and the transition from colonialism to imperialism, which together introduced a new republican and nationalist vocabulary into politics and literature.[45] This novel vocabulary presented 'civilization' during the 18th and 19th centuries as a concept that implied Western supremacy over the East.[46] The West, where political revolutions and ground-breaking socio-economic developments happened, came to define itself as European, as opposed to the Orient, which then included much of Eastern Europe.[47] The mass of 'orientalist literature', the narrative product of the shifting European political language, therefore emerged in Europe during the 19th century. Victor Hugo celebrated this wave: 'During the time of Louis the 14th we were Hellenists, now we are orientalists'.[48] According to Edward Said, since then the orientalists' attitudes towards the East have been accompanied by a sense of European pride. Orientalism came to symbolise a set of thinking that limited the 'East' to cultural, in particular religious and geographical, categories (something that continues to this day).[49] European romantics often compared Europe with its backward Eastern rivals, in an age marked by the Western dominance and colonialism.[50] Although

---

[44] James H. Liu and Denis J. Hilton, 'How the Past Weighs on the Present: Social Representations of History and Their Role in Identity Politics', *British Journal of Social Psychology* 44, no.4 (2005): 537–556, doi: 10.1348/014466605X27162; Thomas Banchoff, 'German Policy towards the European Union: The Effects of Historical Memory', *German Politics* 6, no.1 (1997): 60–76, doi: 10.1080/09644009708404464.
[45] Eric J. Hobsbawn, *The Age of Revolution: 1789–1848* (New York: Vintage Books: 1996), 53–54; François Furet, *Penser la Révolution française* (Paris: Gallimard, 1983), 71.
[46] Larry Wolf, *Inventing Eastern Europe: The Map of Civilization in the Minds of the Enlightenment* (Stanford, Stanford University Press, 1994), 12–13; Gerard Delanty, *Inventing Europe* (London: Palgrave Macmillan, 1995), 94.
[47] Bo Strath, 'Insiders and Outsiders: Borders in 19th Century Europe', in *A Companion to the 19th Century Europe*, ed. Stefan Berger (Oxford: Blackwell Publishing, 2006), 7.
[48] Catherine Clémentin-Ojha and Pierre-Yves Manguin, *A Century in Asia: The History of the École Française D'Extrême-Orient, 1898–2006* (Singapore: Editions Didier Millet, 2007), 31.
[49] Edward Said, *Orientalism* (New York: Vintage Books, 1978), 6, 240–241. Also see, Edward Said, 'The Clash of Ignorance', *The Nation*, October 22, 2001.
[50] Pratima Prasad, *Colonialism, Race, and the French Romantic Imagination* (New York: Routledge, 2009); Filiz Turhan, *The Other Empire: The British Romantic Writings about the Ottoman*

the extensive orientalist literature was not completely uniform in how it presented the East, a common feature between writings was the contrast between Western supremacy and Eastern backwardness.[51] In this case, the orientalist arguments on the Ottomans were structured mostly, but not entirely, by the image of a waning, inferior empire. Towards the 19th century's end, European diplomacy, which had previously proclaimed the Ottoman Empire to be a part of the European balance of power on very few occasions, such as short-term alliances with France and/or Britain, also came to presume on this image.

With the changing vocabulary of Europeanness, intellectuals came to define the Ottoman Empire and Turkey in terms of a broad set of characteristics, which also included political conditions. Writings of the European diplomatic, intellectual, and commercial visitors informed the understanding of the Ottoman culture.[52] Throughout this process, the image of the Ottomans/Turks as 'infidels' evolved to a source of mystery, but the one also lacking European civil values.[53] European writers either excluded the Ottoman authoritarianism from European civilisation or argued that the empire should be aligned with European values by means of European (colonial) powers.[54] As Serif Mardin records, the concept of 'Eastern despotism', which provided political and cultural critiques of the Ottoman realm, and particularly focussed on the Empire's 'restricted minorities', became a central theme in the orientalist literature and thus justified western interventions.[55] European states were approaching the Ottoman Empire with similar interventionist arguments. As Kramer and Reinkowski reminded, European powers would not emphasise humanitarian intervention in the post-Ottoman period as often as they did until the early 20th century.[56] Eventually, the rise of Euro-

---

Empire (New York and London: Routledge, 2003); Paul T. Levin, *Turkey and the European Union: Christian and Secular Images of Islam* (New York: Palgrave Macmillan, 2011).

51 Asli Cirakman, *From the 'Terror of the World' to the 'Sick Man of Europe': European Images of Ottoman Empire and Society from the Sixteenth Century to the Nineteenth* (New York: Peter Lang Publishing, 2005), 31; Geoffrey Nash, 'New Orientalisms for old Articulations of the East in Raymond Schwab, Edward Said, and the Nineteenth-century French Orientalists', in *Orientalism Revisited: Art, Land and Voyage*, ed. Netton Richard (New York: Routledge, 2013), 90.

52 Suraiya Faroqhi, *Approaching Ottoman History: An Introduction of Sources* (Cambridge: Cambridge University Press, 2004), 112–128; Fatma Müge Göçek, *East Encounters the West: France and the Ottoman Empire in the 18th Century* (New York: Oxford University Press, 1987).

53 Cirakman, *From the 'Terror of the World' to the 'Sick Man of Europe'*.

54 Mohammed Salama, *Islam, Orientalism, and Intellectual History: Modernity and the Politics of Exclusion since Ibn Khaldun* (London: Tauris & Co Ltd, 2001).

55 Serif Mardin, *Religion, Society, and Modernity in Turkey* (Syracuse, New York: Syracuse University Press, 2006), 28–29.

56 Heinz Kramer and Maurus Reinkowski, *Die Türkei und Europa: eine wechselhafte Beziehungsgeschichte* (Stuttgart: W. Kohlhammer, 2008), 77–78.

pean 'civilization' left its imprints over the way that Europeans saw themselves vis-à-vis the Ottomans and the Turks.[57]

In time, the fame and prosperity of European 'civilization' also inspired Ottoman/Turkish statesmen to embark on a long and progressive project of modernisation. Roughly in the early 19th century, when the very survival of the Ottoman state was at stake, Ottoman bureaucrats implemented a series of reforms to avoid the empire's further disintegration, and they laid the foundations of an emerging nation-state.[58] Modern Turkey remarkably rose from the ashes of the Ottoman Empire largely due to ongoing modernisation driven by the desire to follow European civilisation.[59] In contemporary history Turkey's modernisation goal was comparably in parallel with the country's prolonged relations with, and plan to join, the European Union.[60] Feridun Cemal Erkin, the Turkish diplomat presented in the signing of the Ankara Association Agreement between Turkey and the European Economic Community (1963) stated the state's official viewpoint: 'This is a phase which recorded Turkey as a country with the aim of becoming a part of Europe and which is full of promises in the way towards wealth and peace.'[61]

The arguments about European civilisation mostly conveyed a post-national conception of Europe. Despite that, and unsurprisingly, throughout the history of Europe's relations with the Ottomans/Turks, European categorisations of Turkey were mostly structured by national thinking.[62] With the rise of nation states,

---

[57] Patrick Pasture, *Imagining European Unity since 1000 AD* (Basingstoke: Palgrave, 2015), 43–44

[58] Stanford J. Shaw and Ezel Kural Shaw, *History of the Ottoman Empire and Modern Turkey, Volume II: Reform, Revolution, and Republic, The Rise of Modern Turkey 1808–1975* (New York: Cambridge University Press, 1977), 305; Bernard Lewis, *The Emergence of Modern Turkey* (New York: Oxford University Press, 1968), 235–237; Kemal Karpat, *The Politicization of Islam: Reconstructing Identity, State, Faith, and Community in the Late Ottoman State* (New York: Oxford University Press, 2001), 12; Inalcik, *Turkey and Europe*, 145; Donald Quataert, *The Ottoman Empire: 1700–1922* (New York: Cambridge University Press, 2005), 65.

[59] Arnold Toynbee, *A Study of History: Volume I: Abridgement of Volumes 1–6 by D. C. Sommerwell* (New York: Oxford University Press, 1947), 519.

[60] Meltem Muftuler Bac, 'Turkey's Political Reforms and the Impact of the European Union', *South European Society and Politics* 10, no.1 (2005): 25, doi:10.1080/13608740500037916; Ilber Ortayli, *Avrupa ve Biz* (Istanbul: Türkiye İş Bankası Yayınları, 2000), 2; Mehmet Dosemeci, *Debating Turkish Modernity: Civilization, Nationalism, and the EEC* (New York: Cambridge University Press, 2013).

[61] 'Ortak Pazar Antlasmasi Imzalandi', *Milliyet*, September 13, 1963.

[62] Stefan Berger, 'National Historiographies in Transnational Perspective Europe in the Nineteenth and Twentieth Centuries', *Storia Della Storiografia*, no.50 (2006), 10; Rogers Brubaker, *Na-*

pragmatic discussions occurred over what Europe essentially meant or should mean. As such, relations with the Ottoman Empire were driven by the influence of Europe's different political sovereigns. Perhaps one the most explicit examples was found during the 'Eastern Question', the struggle between European powers to take advantage of the slow disintegration of the Ottoman Empire.[63] Consider the Paris Peace Conference in 1856, which declared the Ottoman State 'European' when it was confronted by the existing Russian aggression.[64] A century later, the perception of the Soviet threat was also providing a strong rationale to European powers for establishing close contacts with Turkey. These pragmatic categorisations still survive in today's narratives.[65] As long as nation states exist, the influences of national politics will probably continue to shape the discussions about Turkey's EU membership.

That being said, what the EU represents today as its values are quite different from the practices of nation states. Given that the EU recognises a number of civic norms and values through its legislation, the *Acquis communautaire*, or EU legislation, plays a principal role in the promotion of European values. Initially, the values and norms that the European Union stands for are studied by reviewing the relevant EU policies, since, for example, the EU's foreign policy manifests the political dimension of Europeanness under codified European values.[66] First inspired by the pioneering essay of Francois Duchêne written in 1972, scholars have discussed the extent to which the EU can use foreign policy to spread civic values within its periphery.[67] Since then the EU's external policy has built a normative character, which is largely based on an implicit 'civilising' dimension along with a number of civic values that shape the political condition

---

tionalism Refrained: Nationhood and the National Question in the New Europe (Cambridge: Cambridge University Press, 1996), 3.
[63] C. D. Clayton, *Britain and the Eastern Question: Missolonghi to Gallipoli* (London: University of London Press, 1971), 9–10.
[64] Augustus Oakes and R. B. Mowat, eds., *The Great European Treaties of the Nineteenth Century* (London: Oxford University Press, 1918), 158.
[65] Said, *Orientalism*, 240–241.
[66] Sonia Lucarelli and Ian Manners, eds., *Values and Principles in European Union Foreign Policy* (London and New York: Routledge, 2006).
[67] Francois Duchêne, 'Europe's role in world peace', in *Europe Tomorrow: Sixteen Europeans Look Ahead*, ed. R. Mayne (London: Fontana, 1972). Also see Ian Manners, 'Normative Power Europe: A Contradiction in Terms?', *JCMS: Journal of Common Market Studies* 40, no.2 (2002): 235–258, doi: 10.1111/1468–5965.00353; Maull, 'Europe and the New Balance of Global Order', 775–799; Neumann (ed), *The European Union in South Eastern Europe, Eastern Europe, and Central Asia.*

of European identity today.⁶⁸ The literature identifies these values as generally consisting of civic rights and liberties, as distinguished from cultural values such as language, religion, ethnicity, and their historical remembrance.⁶⁹ While all of these overlap considerably, the common civic values were perhaps the last to emerge in Europe through the construction of EU legislation. Anthony Smith explains why: 'in the absence of a stress on the vernacular education of ethnic members, the civic element plays a greater role exactly because of the weight placed on training for citizenship in territorial nations.' ⁷⁰ This is essential if the EU is to gather societies from different local levels around a civic and political framework of values. To give a recent example, Article 1.a of the Treaty of Lisbon enshrines civic values, defining them as 'human dignity, freedom, democracy, equality, the rule of law and respect for human rights, including the rights of persons belonging to minorities'. ⁷¹ From this statement one might infer that the EU's institutions have the central role of reflecting the principal norms and values of Europe. The involvement of civic values in the official formation of European identity denotes a nexus between the EU, and Europeanness as a kind of transcendental logos.⁷²

---

68 Michael Bruter, *Citizens of Europe: the Emergence of a Mass European Identity* (Hampshire and New York: Palgrave Macmillan, 2005); Thomas Diez, 'Constructing the Self and Changing Others: Reconsidering "Normative Power Europe"', *Millennium-Journal of International Studies* 33, no.3 (2005): 627–628, doi:10.1177/03058298050330031701; Thomas Diez and Ian Manners, 'Reflecting on Normative Power Europe', in *Power in World Politics*, eds. Felix Berenskoetter and M.J. Villiams (London, New York: Routledge, 2007), 184; Ian Manners, 'The Constitutive Nature of Values, Images and Principles in the European Union', in *Values and Principles in European Union Foreign Policy*, eds. Sonia Lucarelli and Ian Manners (London and New York: Routledge, 2006), 33–41; Sonia Lucarelli, 'European Political Identity, Foreign Policy, and the Other's Image: an Underexplored Relationship', in *The Search for a European Identity: Values, Principles, and Legitimacy of the European Union*, eds. Furio Cerutti and Sonia Lucarelli (London and New York: Routledge, 2008), 23–42; Manners, 'The Normative Ethics of the European Union', 46; Florian Pichler, 'Cosmopolitan Europe: Views and Identity', *European Societies* 11, no.1 (2009), doi: 10.1080/14616690802209697.
69 Bruter, *Citizens of Europe*, 103. For a thematic explanation of European values, see Robert Clifford Ostergren and Mathias Le Bossé, *The Europeans: A Geography of People, Culture, and Environment* (New York: The Guilford Press, 2011).
70 Anthony D. Smith, *National Identity* (London: Penguin Books, 1991), 119.
71 Article 1.a of the Treaty of Lisbon cites these values as 'human dignity, freedom, democracy, equality, the rule of law and respect for human rights, including the rights of persons belonging to minorities'. *Treaty of Lisbon amending the Treaty on European Union and the Treaty establishing the European Community*, Official Journal of European Union C 306, December 13, 2007, 11.
72 Checkel, Katzenstein, eds., *European Identity*. Cerutti, Lucarelli, eds., *The Search for a European Identity*.

Be that as it may, European values are mostly presumed to be the socio-political results of historical experiences.[73] These were constructed during turbulent periods, and it is crucial to remember that they predate EU legislation. For example, the EU's law, the legal source of jurisdictions that is applicable across the union, primarily originates from Roman civic traditions.[74] Alongside this, the state and nation building phases of Western Europe after the 18th century played an important historical role in forming European political identity.[75] Historical thinking then concludes that the construction of EU legislation plays a significant role in defining and systematising only some of Europe's norms and values.[76] There exist other values, then, which are mentioned rarely or never in EU legislation, and are maintained by local and national traditions. Perhaps the most noteworthy example is Europe's religious legacy.[77] Europe has extensive and long-lasting Christian religious traditions, and many essentialist arguments have tried to attribute the cultural dimension of European identity to the intellectual wealth of Christendom, rather than the EU's secular framework.[78] In national politics, arguments about Turkey that make use of the term 'European civilization' can carry a religious character. In these arguments, Turkey's Islamic tradition and practices represent the antithesis of European values.[79] In 2004 former French President Valery Giscard d'Estaing stated that the Turkish candidate was a threat to the 'European historical heritage' that was founded and devel-

---

[73] Delanty, *Inventing Europe*.

[74] Peter Stein, *Roman Law in European History* (Cambridge: Cambridge University Press, 1999), 130.

[75] Bruter, *Citizens of Europe*, 168 Also see, Mark Juergensmeyer, *The New Cold War? Secular Nationalism Confronts the Secular State* (Berkeley and Los Angeles: University of California Press, 1993).

[76] Smith, 'National Identity and the Idea of Unity', 70–71; Lucarelli, 'European Political Identity, Foreign Policy, and the Other's Image', 28.

[77] Lavinia Stan and Lucian Turcescu, *Church, State, and Democracy in Expanding Europe* (New York: Oxford University Press, 2011), 7–8.

[78] Peter Katzenstein, 'Multiple Modernities as Limits to Secular Europeanization?', in *Religion in an Expanding Europe*, eds. Timothy Byrnes and Peter J. Katzenstein (New York: Cambridge University Press, 2006), 1–2. Polish scepticism about the EU's secular politics is one instance of recent contradictions between the two sorts of value-representation: religious local politics and secular European politics. José Casanova, 'Religion, European Secular Identities, and European Integration', in *Religion in an Expanding Europe*, eds. Timothy Byrnes and Peter J. Katzenstein (New York: Cambridge University Press, 2006), 69. The recent refugee crisis of the European Union (2015) also exemplifies these contradictions dramatically. Farid Hafez, 'The Refugee Crisis and Islamophobia', *Insight Turkey* 17, no.14 (2015), 19–26.

[79] Meyda Yegenoglu, *Islam, Migrancy, and Hospitality in Europe* (New York: Palgrave Macmilla, 2012), 102, 186; Levin, *Turkey and the European Union*.

oped within Europe's religious cosmos.⁸⁰ The religious dimension of Europeanness finds currency also in academia, as many argue that throughout history Christianity has laid the foundations for the development of humanism and even secularism within Europe. To Arend Theodor van Leeuwen, the gap between European secular nationalism and Christianity is actually quite thin. In contemporary Europe, European secular nationalism, or constitutional patriotism, conceals political developments that happened within the Christian environment and vocabulary.⁸¹ Europe's shared religious experiences have resulted in a transition towards the secular dimension of contemporary European identity. Similarly, it is sometimes claimed that Christian tenets are still the most important reservoir of European values today.⁸² From this perspective, the idea of European federalism can only be achieved through the universal values of Christianity.⁸³ According to José Casanova, an identity project that solely relies on the Greco-Roman law and Enlightenment philosophy neglects historical upshots that have long endured within Christendom.⁸⁴ That is to say, European values that are entirely aligned with the current secular and political dimensions of the European Union might disclose a construction different from that which religious values underpin in everyday life. Inevitably, the division between Europe's religious and secular values becomes explicit when Europeans use them to define Europe's identity, civilisation, and others.⁸⁵ In the case of the EU's enlargement with Turkey, political camps will continue to represent these dichotomous values, both of which influence the identity debates surrounding the candidate's compatibility with Europe.

If there is a tension between secular and religious representations within European and national politics, debates over European enlargement feature this tension in Turkey's case. First and foremost, the European Union's enlargement policy is based on a legal stand and this stand frames pro and contra debates categorically.⁸⁶ The EU has established a number of codified and commonly ac-

---

80 Thomas Risse, 'Identity Matters: Exploring the Ambivalence of EU Foreign Policy', *Global Policy* 3, no.1 (2012): 93, doi: 10.1111/1758–5899.12019.
81 Juergensmeyer, *The New Cold War*, 18.
82 The conservative politician and former European Commissioner Peter Sutherland represents this argument. Sutherland, 'Europe', 425.
83 Ibid, 420.
84 José Casanova, 'Religion, European Secular Identities', 82.
85 Atsuko Ichijo and Willfried Spohn, 'Introduction', in *Entangled Identities: Nations and Europe*, eds. Atsuko Ichijo and Willfried Spohn (Aldershot: Ashgate, 2005), 11–12.
86 Frank Schimmelfennig, 'Liberal Identity and Postnationalist Inclusion: The Eastern Enlargement of the European Union', in *Constructing Europe's Identity: the External Dimension*, ed. Lars-

knowledged norms and values that guide the accession process of new candidates.[87] The prime concern of the enlargement policy is then to export these values and principles to candidate countries.[88] In essence, these values and standards are made concrete through the Copenhagen political criteria, which set out the democratic responsibilities of candidates as well as EU members.[89] Normative arguments that adhere to the Copenhagen political criteria (henceforth the Copenhagen criteria or the accession criteria) accentuate the issues of applicant countries regarding democracy, the rule of law, and the implementation of human and minority rights.[90] The annually released candidate reports by the European Commission and Parliament adhere to similar principles. Among these principles, article 49 of the Treaty on European Union initially ruled that any country from the European geography that respects a set of rights and liberties may apply to join the European Union. In addition to this specific article, the Copenhagen criteria were established in 1993 and became a direct part of EU legislation with the amendments of the Amsterdam Treaty in 1997.[91] In this way, the European Union's political normative background, validated under its legislation, has become the primary source for justifying the EU's enlargements during the 2000s. Judging from these enlargements, Sjursen, following Habermasian logic, argues that 'the arguments and reasons provided in favour of enlargement have to be of a type that others can support'. [92] In brief, any candidate's concep-

---

Erik Cederman (Boulder, Colo: Lynne Rienner Publishers, 2001), 165–186; Medrano, 'The Public Sphere and the European Union's Political Identity', in *European Identity*, 106.

87 Frank Schimmelfennig and Ulrich Sedelmeier, 'Introduction: Conceptualizing the Europeanization of Central and Eastern Europe', in *The Europeanization of Central and Eastern Europe*, eds. Frank Schimmelfennig and Ulrich Sedelmeier (New York: Cornell University Press, 2005), 18–19; Ulrika Mörth, 'Europeanization as Interpretation, Translation, and Editing of Public Policies', in *The Politics of Europeanization*, eds. Kevin Featherstone and Claudio M. Radaelli (New York: Oxford University Press, 2003).

88 Meltem Muftuler Bac, 'Turkey's Political Reforms and the Impact of the European Union', 18; Georgeta Pourchot, 'EU's "Eastern Empire"', in *Revisiting the European Union as an Empire*, eds. Hartmut Behr and Yannis A. Stivachtis (Abingdon and New York: Routledge, 2016), 22; Sandra Lavenex and Frank Schimmelfennig, *EU Democracy Promotion in the Neighbourhood: From Leverage to Governance?* (Abingdon: Routledge, 2013).

89 Peter Van Elsuwege, *From Soviet Republics to EU Member States, A Legal and Political Assessment of the Baltic States' Accession to the EU* (Leiden: Martinus Nishoff, 2008); Christophe Hillion, 'The Copenhagen Criteria and their Progeny', in *EU Enlargement: A Legal Approach*, ed. Christophe Hillion (Oregon: Hart Publishing, 2004), 1–22.

90 Eric Faucompret and Jozef Konings, *Turkish Accession to the EU: Satisfying the Copenhagen Criteria* (London and New York: Routledge, 2008), 151.

91 Christophe Hillion, 'The Copenhagen Criteria', 3.

92 Sjursen, 'Introduction', 8; Sjursen, 'Why Expand?', 493.

tualisation by an EU actor must be legitimate, and in line with the EU's legislation and other actors' preferences.

This leaves the question of interplay between political camps within the EU's enlargement discourse, which is principally guided by EU legislation. In the 2000s, seminal scholar of European studies Frank Schimmelfennig famously remarked on how different actors came to agreement during previous enlargement rounds despite some member states being opposed to enlargement. For him, the explanation lay in the potency of the values and norms that are enshrined in EU legislation. The increasing political validity of European norms and values allowed stake-holding members to manipulate EU legislation according to their self-interests, and led the rest of the EU to approve the Central and East European (CEE) enlargement.[93] If this is the case, the discursive genres generated by EU legislation were of importance since they constrained EU actors' statements and eventually their choices.[94] Indeed, before the accession talks with Turkey, the other candidates from Central and Eastern Europe were anchored in the accession process from the moment they began their membership negotiations. EU candidates in Central and Eastern Europe (including Cyprus and Malta) had started the negotiations with a crystal-clear roadmap to membership and even with a date of accession. That was the source of the famous assumption in academia that any accession process, once started, would lead to a happy ending almost automatically due to its legally and rhetorically binding nature.

The question remains then of how Turkey overcame the opposition to its application and managed to get its accession bid to gather pace in the first half of the 2000s. According to the same logic of 'rhetorical action', before the negotiations started in 2005 EU members could not put up a firm opposition to the beginning of the accession negotiations because the Turkish government was keenly fulfilling part of its political reforms.[95] Schimmelfennig therefore further argued that as long as Turkey fulfilled the entire number of democratic standards required for accession, the members of the EU that were opposed to Turkey's membership on cultural grounds would not be able to resist the candidate's membership bid, as they would have been entrapped by the existing enlargement rhetoric.[96] In other words, if Turkey lived up to the EU's political norms and values, the arguments made in national politics would not carry enough weight against the case for enlargement. Yet history showed how strong the na-

---

93 Schimmelfennig, 'The Community Trap', 47–80.
94 Sjursen, 'Why Expand?', 500.
95 Frank Schimmelfennig, *Entrapped Again: The Way to EU Membership Negotiations with Turkey*, UCD Dublin European Institute Working Paper, August 8, 2008.
96 Ibid, 113.

tional oppositions to Turkey were and that the potency of the enlargement rhetoric was limited. Before the membership negotiations commenced, there was certainly concern on the part of German and French conservative politicians about a positive outcome of Turkey's EU accession. This granted, automatic nature of the accession talks witnessed in previous cases had alerted the Turkey-sceptic politicians about a similar outcome for the candidate. Therefore, before the negotiations commenced, a number of member states began to impose their political agendas on Brussels and rendered Turkey's accession conditions somewhat different than those set for the previous enlargements.[97] First, the beginning of the membership negotiations featured a number of strategies by these Turkey-sceptic governments, such as making the accession talks open-ended, or some unilateral decisions such as freezing a number of chapters, as France and Cyrus did.[98] Second, if Turkey ever implemented the reforms necessitated by the accession talks with the EU, its membership would still need to be ratified through parliamentary or popular vote after a successful negotiation process. That attests that the ways that EU actors from different levels categorise Turkey within the enlargement language are of immense importance.[99]

With respect to the roles played out by national and European actors and their interplay on Enlargement issues, the European Parliament has become one significant platform.[100] Its part in generating the EU's enlargement language is of more relevance to this study than its part in making or revising EU legislation. The European Parliament's initial stand on the candidate first emerges in parallel with EU legislation and with the European Commission and its country reports.[101] Votes and amendments of political camps in the European Parliament

---

97 Beken Saatcioglu, 'The EU's 'Rhetorical Entrapment' in Enlargement Reconsidered: Why Hasn't it Worked for Turkey?', *Insight Turkey* 14, no.3 (2012): 173.
98 Levin, 'Who lost Turkey?', 165.
99 Sjursen, 'Why Expand?', 501; Fuat E. Keyman and Ziya Öniş, 'Helsinki, Copenhagen and beyond Challenges to the New Europe and the Turkish state', in *Turkey and European Integration: Accession Prospects and Issues*, eds. Mehmet Ugur and Nergis Canefe (London: Routledge, 2004), 174–175; Kraus, A Union of Diversity Language, 66; With regard to the impacts of national politics on Enlargement issues, although Turkey is to be held directly responsible for the present-day problems within the accession talks with the EU, some Turkey-scepticism in European nation states has still a lot to do with this de facto standstill. Levin, 'Who Lost Turkey?', 152–173.
100 Seda Gürkan, 'The Role of the European Parliament in Turkey-EU Relations: A Troublemaker or a Useful Normative Actor?', *Southeast European and Black Sea Studies* 18, no.1 (2018): 107–125, doi: 10.1080/14683857.2018.1431515; Fligstein, *Euro-clash*, 19–20.
101 Richard S. Katz, 'Representation, the Locus of Democratic Legitimation, and the Role of the National Parliaments in the European Union', in *The European Parliament, the National Parliaments, and European Integration*, eds. Richard S. Katz and Bernhard Wessels (Oxford: Oxford UniversityPress, 1999), 24–25.

to adopt any report are still decisive for this stand, as MEPs give the final shape to the Parliament's official language. The European Parliament's affairs mostly develop within parliamentary groups, and the European Parliament's politics is a form of transnational party politics that is, in all other respects, 'like any other democratic parliament'.[102] But this transnational approach only holds to a certain degree. As several studies demonstrate, parliamentarians presenting opinions in the European Parliament are preoccupied at the same time with their profile and future in their national politics.[103] In summary, MEPs simultaneously represent transnational and national politics and, through this mechanism, national politics infiltrate the European Parliament. The discussions about the Turkish candidate within the European Parliament illustrate this ambiguity.

European integration achieved during the previous decades provides important insights into how European and national identities were politicised.[104] To explain the consequences of this integration between European and national politics, a study by Michal Kryzanowski identifies three key factors: public discussions about specific EU policies, the individualisation of European politics, and media involvement.[105] Political parties working in the post-Cold War EU began to demonstrate their own political identities on EU policies and, in this context, the EU's enlargement policy became highly relevant to national politics.

---

[102] Simon Hix, Abdul Noury, and Gérard Roland, 'Dimensions of Politics in the European Parliament', *American Journal of Political Science* 50, no.2 (April 2006): 509, doi: 10.1111/j.1540–5907.2006.00198.x.

[103] Pieter de Wilde and Tapio Raunio, 'Redirecting national parliaments: Setting Priorities for Involvement in EU Affairs', *Comparative European Politics* 16, no.2 (2018): 310–329, doi: 10.1057/cep.2015.28; Sven-Oliver Proksch and Jonathan B. Slapin, 'Position Taking in European Parliament Speeches', *European Union Politics* 11, no.3 (2009): 587–611, doi:10.1017/S0007123409990299; Jonathan B. Slapin and Sven-Oliver Proksch, 'Look Who's Talking: Parliamentary Debate in the European Parliament', *European Union Politics* 11, no.3 (2010): 333–357, doi: 10.1177/1465116510369266.

[104] Richard K. Herrmann, Thomas Risse, and Marilynn B. Brewer, eds., *Transnational Identities: Becoming European in the EU* (Lanham: Rowman Littlefield Publishers Inc., 2004); Frank Schimmelfennig and Hanno Scholtz, 'EU Democracy Promotion in the European Neighbourhood: Political Conditionality, Economic Development and Transnational Exchange', *European Union Politics* 9, no.2 (2008): 187–215, doi: 10.1177/1465116508089085. Europeanization literature significantly deals with the relationship between national and transnational networks, Cowles, Caporaso, and Risse-Kappen, eds., *Transforming Europe*. Featherstone and Radaelli, eds., The Politics of Europeanization. Schimmelfennig and Sedelmeier, eds., The Europeanization of Central and Eastern Europe.

[105] Michal Krzyzanowski, *The Discursive Construction of European Identities: A Multi-level Approach to Discourse and Identity in the Transforming European Union* (Bern: Peter Lang, 2010), 13.

Second, national and transnational party networks developed in accord with politicians' behaviours and statements. Perhaps surprisingly, individual politicians became able to build their public profile by speaking out for or against the enlargement policy. Finally, and connected with the previous factors, the mass media was a key instrument in legitimising the language of political elites.[106] Politicians in the 2000s used media coverage to establish their identity perspectives in debates over controversial issues, such as Turkey's accession to the EU.[107] Leading political figures from domestic politics provoked these debates through their a priori assumptions about European and Turkish identities. By way of example, Beyza Tekin, in one of the first monographs about Turkey's representation in European politics (in France), examines how President Sarkozy expressed opposition to Turkey's EU accession while in office between 2007 and 2012, and how he employed the exclusions of the candidate as a strategic instrument to appeal to the political right.[108] The present study also concerns itself with Sarkozy's early opposition to Turkey as part of his campaign for the presidential election.

That is to say, the activity of political camps in both national and transnational networks increasingly politicized the debates over Turkey's EU bid during the 2000s. At this point, the literature has already given important insights into the general motivations of European political camps for 'othering' or welcoming Turkey. Europe's political camps represented the candidate in two main ways: the one closely related to EU legislation and the other to national political agendas. The first type involves civic European values, particularly those embodied within the Copenhagen criteria and the political accession criteria. Here the political camps generally (but not necessarily) shape their representation of Turkey along the lines of the candidate's compliance with EU legislation, and particularly concern themselves with a democratic deficit in areas such as human and minority rights.[109] The EU's collective identity constructions, which were reflected in the progress reports of the European Commission and Parliament, al-

---

[106] Paul Statham, 'What Kind of Europeanized Public Politics?', in *The Making of a European Public Sphere: Media Discourse and Political Contention*, eds. Ruud Koopmans and Paul Statham (New York: Cambridge University Press, 2010), 300.
[107] Bouza Louis Garcia, 'European Political Elites' Discourses on the Accession of Turkey to the EU: Discussing Europe through Turkish Spectacles?', *European Perspectives – Journal on European Perspectives of the Western Balkans* 3, no.2 (October 2011): 70.
[108] Beyza, C. Tekin. *Representations and Othering in Discourse: The Construction of Turkey in the EU Context* (Amsterdam: John Benjamins Publishing Company, 2010), 79.
[109] Harun Arikan, *Turkey and the EU: An Awkward Candidate for Membership?* (Hampshire: Ashgate Publishing Limited, 2006), 5; Tekin, *Representations and Othering in Discourse*, 124–130; Eric Faucompret and Jozef Konings, *Turkish Accession to the EU*.

most exclusively focused on this kind of categorization. European civic values that were internalised in European and national politics provide the primary source of categorising the EU and Turkey under this first group. Empirical studies demonstrate that the EU's civic and political values have wide public support in Europe. Eurobarometer surveys, which have been carried out since 1973, have explored European attitudes towards European identity and towards modern social and political life. One survey conducted in 2008 found that European citizens mostly think that the common characteristics of European identity are the modern (Enlightenment-driven) values that were covered by the concepts of human rights, peace, and democracy.[110] These European civic values derived from the European Union's changing political dimension are broadly shared among EU citizens and provide a new basis for delineating who is European and who is not.[111] In parallel, scholarly opinions relying on European civic rights and liberties are likely to conceptualise the EU's changing distance to Turkey as an issue of political modernity, something of a temporal nature in the face of the candidate's democratization.[112]

European civic values are mainly represented at elite level and their acknowledgment in public is strongly linked to the popular strength of European institutions. It is a commonplace argument that until the 2000s European elites worked more on the legislative-republican nature of Europeanness rather than its social dimension, at least until the failure of the EU's Constitution.[113] This idealism led to a growing gap between the elite language and public opinions about what the EU's enlargement with Turkey signified. A very significant case that demonstrated this growing difference was the French ratification of the EU Constitution in 2005.[114] In France, the ethno-political arguments against the EU's first constitution were also against Turkey's EU membership. The French opposition partially argued during the constitutional campaigns that approving the

---

[110] European Commission, *Eurobarometer 69: 1. Values of Europeans*, November 2008.
[111] Dimitris N. Chryssochoou 'Civic Competence and Identity in the European Polity', in *Making European Citizens: Civic Inclusion in a Transnational Context*, eds. Richard Bellamy, Dario Castiglione, and Jo Shaw (London and New York: Palgrave Macmillan, 2006), 225–227. José Casanova, 'The Long, Difficult and Torturous Journey of Turkey into Europe and the Dilemmas of European Civilization', *Constellations* 13, no.3 (2006): 234–247, doi: 10.1111/j.1351–0487.2006.00453.x; Diez, 'Europe's Others and Return of Geopolitics', 2004.
[112] Delanty, *Formations of European Modernity*, 104.
[113] Medrano, 'The Public Sphere and the European Union's Political Identity', 82.
[114] Furio Cerutti, 'Why Political Identity and Legitimacy Matter in the European Union' in *The Search for a European Identity: Values, Principles, and Legitimacy of the European Union*, eds. Furio Cerutti and Sonia Lucarelli (London and New York: Routledge, 2008) 13–14.

EU Constitution also implied approving the new European Union with Turkey.[115] 11 years later during Brexit discussions in Britain, very similarly, Turkey's membership was held up as a bogeyman by the Leave campaign in Britain, as though voting to stay in the EU also meant accepting Turkey's membership.

The second mainstream categorisation of Turkey draws more on religious and geographical characteristics. It is a fact that the European Union's accession criteria already reflect a territorial condition, of being European, which Turkey as a candidate essentially fulfils. But further religious and geographical terms that were derived from national politics generated stereotypes. In the 2000s, many of these stereotypes were repeatedly expressed through a 'civilizational' paradigm dominating the post-Cold War political thinking, something that saw Europe as a cultural cosmos forged on civilizational traits such as a common geography and religion.[116] Politicians inspired by this paradigm inherently rejected Turkey's application under the assumptions that the candidate was not geographically European and was not of, or did not respect, Europe's Judeo-Christian values.[117] Those who conceptualised Turkey in these geographical and religious terms constructed an image of Europe in which there was no room for an Asian and Islamic Turkey.[118] Conservative parties in Germany and France arguably fell within this group during the 2000s.[119]

On the other hand, these geographical and religious aspects of defining the relationship between the EU and Turkey could work in the candidate's favour. This is especially the case where the term 'bridge' was used in order to highlight

---

[115] Paul Hainsworth, 'France Says No: the 29 May 2005 Referendum on the European Constitution', *Parliamentary Affairs* 59, no: 1 (January 2006): 104–105; Tekin, *Represantation and Othering* in Discourse, 92–97; Hakan Yilmaz, 'Turkish Identity on the Road to the EU: Basic Elements of the French and German Discourses', *Journal of Southern Europe and the Balkans* 9, no.3 (December 2007): 304, doi: 10.1080/14613190701689993; Hainsworth, *The Extreme Right in Western Europe*, 84; Medrano, 'The Public Sphere and the European Union's Political Identity', 106.

[116] Pinar Bilgin, 'A Return to "Civilisational Geopolitics" in the Mediterranean? Changing Geopolitical Images of the European Union and Turkey in the Post-Cold War Era', Geopolitics 9, no.2 (2004): 269–291, doi: 10.1080/14650040490442863; Diez, 'Constructing the Self and Changing Others'.

[117] Meltem Muftuler-Bac, 'The European Union's Legitimacy Crisis and the Final Frontiers of Europe', in *European Integration from Rome to Berlin, 1957–2007: History, Law and Politics*, eds. Julio Baquero Cruz and Carlos Closa (Brussels: Peter Lang, 2009), 265–266; Rumelili and Cakmakli '"Culture" in EU-Turkey Relations', 104–105.

[118] Bahar Rumelili, 'Negotiation Europe: EU-Turkey Relations from an Identity Perspective', *Insight Turkey* 10, no.1 (2008): 108.

[119] Senem Aydin-Duzgit, *Constructions of European Identity, Debates and Discourses on Turkey and the EU* (Basingstoke: Palgrave Macmillan, 2012), 168.

the candidate's geostrategic location between religious and geographical domains.¹²⁰ Some actors at European and national levels had used this 'bridge' to affirm Turkey's strategic location.¹²¹ Even so, we should note that politicians who conceptualised the candidate in this way did not necessarily accept it as an essential part of Europe.¹²² Samuel Huntington thus admitted the dichotomy in the common usage of bridge, along with his understanding of the candidate: 'a bridge, however, is an artificial creation reflecting two solid entities but is part of neither'.¹²³ How and through what argumentations European political elites make use of the 'bridge' function of Turkey today remain in question. The bridge discussion is also likely to continue with the changing conceptions of the geographies surrounding Turkey: Europe, the Middle East, the Mediterranean, etc.

Negatively categorising Turkey's compatibility with Europe in religious and geographical terms is largely derived from national politics, rather than the European Union's legislation. In fact, the validity of this kind of argumentation became open to question in the 2000s with the growing sense of 'democratic Islam' in Turkey. During this period, Turkey took steps toward a democratic vision, albeit under the rule of a so-called pro-Islamist government, and this posed a challenge to the Islamic stereotypes maintained by those culturally opposed to Turkey's accession to the EU. ¹²⁴ In the 2000s, British political elites in particular recognised and gave credit to Turkey's democratisation under a 'pro-Islamist' government. However, towards the end of the decade Turkey's democratic credibility began to dwindle, as its 'modernisation venture between Islam and democracy' did not always progress as expected.¹²⁵ It gave (and still gives) space for the religiously and geographically Turkey-sceptic arguments to flourish.¹²⁶ Furthermore, today the rising Islamic fundamentalism within Europe

---

[120] Ali Ihsan Aydin, 'Imagining the EU in the Turkish Mirror', in *Turkey's Accession to the European Union: An Unusual Candidacy*, ed. Constantine Arvanitopoulos (Berlin and Heidelberg: Springer, 2009), 177–180.
[121] Aylin Guney, 'Imagining "Europe as an Empire": Competing/converging Geopolitical Imaginations and EU Enlargements', in *Revisiting the European Union as an Empire*, eds. Hartmut Behr and Yannis A. Stivachtis (Abingdon and New York: Routledge, 2016), 105–106.
[122] Aydin-Duzgit, *Constructions of European Identity*, 32, 35.
[123] Huntington, *The Clash of Civilizations and the Remaking of World Order*, 149.
[124] Rumelili, 'Negotiation Europe', 106–107.
[125] Kürşad Ertuğrul and Öznur Akcalı Yılmaz, 'The Otherness of Turkey in European Integration', *Turkish Studies* 19, no.1 (2018): 48–71, doi: 10.1080/14683849.2017.1396895.
[126] Ranier Fsadni, 'The Debate's Impact on Europe', in *Turkey's Accession to the European Union: An Unusual Candidacy*, ed. Constantine Arvanitopoulos (Berlin and Heidelberg: Springer,

is a major concern for Europeans and contributes to the popularity of the essentialist argument against Turkey's EU membership.[127] Religious terror in present-day Europe enables some political camps, especially populist right-wing factions, to manipulate the fear of Islam and call for an 'Islam-free Europe'.[128] Under these circumstances, the candidate's compatibility with the European Union on religious and geographical grounds remains a controversial issue, unlike the previous eastern enlargements.[129] This, then, leads us to examine the national thinking about the European Union and Turkey during the 2000s.

Perceptions in Germany, France, and Britain over what the EU signifies significantly underpinned the direction of Turkey's EU prospect.[130] National thinking in Germany has been perhaps most open to the idea of supranational Europeanness, as the success of European integration is often seen as the key stimulus for the reconstruction of the post-war German identity.[131] As a result, the leading political camps have mostly shared a strong commitment to European integration.[132] The country also has a huge number of Turkish residents, more than any other EU state, who, along with Turkey-centred lobbies, have expressed

---

2009), 166–167; Bogdani, *Turkey and the Dilemma of EU Accession*, 127–146; Aydin-Duzgit, *Constructions of European Identity*, 172–175; Tekin, *Represantation and Othering* in Discourse, 92–97.
127 Bogdani, *Turkey and the Dilemma of EU Accession*.
128 Ayhan Kaya and Ayse Tecmen, 'Europe versus Islam?: Right-Wing Populist Discourse and the Construction of a Civilizational Identity', *The Review of Faith & International Affairs* 17, no.1 (2019): 49–64, doi: 10.1080/15570274.2019.1570759.
129 Meltem Müftüler-Baç, 'Turkey's Accession to the European Union: The impact of the EU's internal dynamics', *International Studies Perspectives* 9, No.2 (2011): 201–219, doi: http://10.1111/j.1528–3585.2008.00327.x; Aydin-Duzgit, Constructions of European Identity, 67–77. Ebru Canan-Sokullu S., Cigdem Kentmen, 'Public Opinion Dimension: Turkey in the EU? An Empirical Analysis of European Public Opinion on Turkey's 'Protracted' Membership', in *FiftyYears of EU-Turkey Relations: A Sisyphean Story*, ed. Armagan Emre Cakir (Oxon: Routledge, 2011), 124–125; Also see Lauren M. McLaren, 'Explaining Opposition to Turkish Membership of EU', *European Union Politics* 8, no.2 (2007), doi: 10.1177/1465116507076432.
130 See Seen Carey, 'Undivided Loyalties: Is National Identity an Obstacle to European Integration?', *European Union Politics* 3, no.4 (2002): 387–413, doi: 10.1177/1465116502003004001.
131 Thomas Risse, 'Nationalism and Collective Identities: Europe versus the Nation-state?', in *Developments in West European Politics* 2, eds. Paul Heywood, Erik Jones, and Martin Rhodes (Basingstoke: Palgrave Macmillan, 2002), 77–93; Marcussen et al. 'Constructing Europe', 109–111.
132 Stefan Berger, *Inventing the Nation: Germany* (London and New York: Bloomsbury, 2011), 242; Christoph Egle, 'The SPD's Political Preference on European Integration: Always One Step Behind?', in *Social Democracy and European Integration: The Politics of Preference Formation*, ed., Dionyssis G. Dimitrakopoulos (London and New York: Routledge, 2011), 23; Michael Gehler, *Europa: Von der Utopie zur Realität* (Innsbruck-Wien: Haymon Taschenbuch, 2014), 237–248.

their open support for Turkey's EU membership and sought to influence Germany's relationship with the candidate.[133] During the 2000s German political camps came to grips with many aspects of an identity debate in the context of the Turkish community, such as Germany's dual citizenship.[134] Between the two EU enlargements of 2004 and 2007, protecting the German labour market and welfare levels were vital political concerns in the country.[135] In France the European identity project had followed a more gradual course, which was once marked by François Mitterrand's office, alongside the European supra-nationalism.[136] This is partially explained with the common perception that the French public opinion tends to see European identity as a mirror-image of their country.[137] Since French national identity was (and still is) replete with strong cultural traditions,[138] part of the French public opinion saw Turkey, with its very different cultural image, as a diluter of French and European identities. In 2005, when the French rejected the EU Constitution and threw their country into what was called to be an 'identity crisis', the conservative camps in particular argued forcefully against Turkey's would-be EU membership for reasons of identity.[139] In a very different way, the idea of a sovereign Britain meant that the British people distanced themselves from European supra-nationalism unequivocally. British

---

[133] Sabine Ruß-Sattar, 'Building Borders on a Bias: The Culturalist Perception of Turkish Migrants in France and Germany and the Debate', in *New Border and Citizenship Politics*, eds. Helen Schwenken and Sabine Ruß-Sattar (New York, London: Palgrave Macmillan, 2014), 65; Ziya Öniş, 'Luxembourg, Helsinki and Beyond: towards an Interpretation of Recent Turkey-EU Relations', *Government and Opposition* 35, no.4 (October 2000), 272, 274.

[134] Jeffrey T. Checkel 'The Europeanization of Citizenship', in *Transforming Europe, Europeanization and Domestic Change*, eds. Maria Green Cowles, James A. Caporaso, and Thomas Risse-Kappen (Ithaca: Cornell University Press, 2001), 196; William Rogers Brubaker, *Citizenship and Nationhood in France and Germany* (Cambridge, Massachusetts, Harvard University Press, 1992), 172–176; Ruth Mandel, *Turkish Challenges to Citizenship and Belonging in Germany* (Durham NC: Duke University Press, 2008); Ayhan Kaya, 'Citizenship and the Hyphenated Germans: German Turks', in *Citizenship in a Global World, European Questions and Turkish Experiences*, eds. Fuat Keyman and Ahmet Icduygu, (London and New York: Routledge, 2005), 219–241.

[135] Sanna Inthorn, 'What Does It Mean to Be an EU Citizen? How News Media Construct Civic and Cultural Concepts of Europe', *Westminster Papers in Communication and Culture* 3, no.3 (2006): 76, doi: http://doi.org/10.16997/wpcc.60.

[136] Marcussen et al. 'Constructing Europe', 105–108.

[137] Risse, 'Nationalism and Collective Identities', 77–93.

[138] Krishan Kumar, 'Themed Section on Varieties of Britishness: English and French National Identity: Comparisons and Contrasts', *Nations and Nationalism* 12, no.3 (2006): 427, doi: 10.1111/j.1469-8129.2006.00247.x.

[139] Tekin, 'The Construction of Turkey's Possible EU Membership in French Discourse', 730–731.

public opinion almost always saw Europeanness as a rather novel, loosely structured, and insignificant concept compared to their own national identity, and the literature used the term Euroscepticism that captures this state of affairs.[140] In the face of the migration emanated from the EU's enlargements during the 2000s, Euroscepticism rose gradually and resulted in the country's complete breakaway from the European Union in 2016 Brexit referendum. Back in 2005, British mainstream parties were similarly upholding different levels of Euroscepticism, in a range from leaving the EU to empowering the national parliaments inside the Union. The way British parties approached Turkey's EU membership during the 2000s was undoubtedly a result of their European policies revolving around Euroscepticism.

In the 2000s, German, French, and British elites were bringing slightly different perspectives to European integration, which led to major policy changes. Until the beginning of Turkey's candidature for EU membership, in 1999, maximising European integration was part of the political rationale in Germany, the French aimed at integration through the control of their state and their republican regime, and Britain's European policy was rather to minimise integration.[141] It is no wonder that these alternate perspectives on the EU shaped the discussions on Turkey's accession bid in the 2000s, which have already been explored to some extent in earlier studies. It is noted elsewhere that, when discussing Turkey's accession to the EU, French political camps emphasised the virtue of public opinion, German political camps concerned themselves with immigration, and British camps prioritised the existing Eurosceptic foreign policy.[142] As the history of European integration showed, EU members that are fully engaged in the project of European political integration are more likely to internalise a European identity. By contrast, in the countries with opt-outs in certain fields of integration, national identity dominated European identity to a far greater extent.[143] Furthermore, as public opinion about European integration became

---

140 Risse, 'A European Identity?', 216. Marcussen et al. 'Constructing Europe', 111–114. Anthony Forster, *Euroscepticism in Contemporary British Politics: Opposition to Europe in the British Conservative and Labour Parties Since 1945* (London: Routlege, 2002); Andrew Geddes, *Britain and the European Union* (Basingstoke: Palgrave Macmillan, 2013).
141 Wolfgang Rudzio, *Das politische System der Bundesrepublik Deutschland* (Springer VS, 2015), 447.
142 Nathalie Tocci, 'Report Unpacking European Discourses: Conditionality, Impact and Prejudice in EU-Turkey Relations', in *Conditionality, Impact and Prejudice in EU-Turkey Relations*, ed. Nathalie Tocci, IAI-TEPAV Report July 2007, 25.
143 Neil Fligstein, Alina Polyakova, and Wayne Sandholtz, 'European Integration, Nationalism and European Identity', *JCMS: Journal of Common Market Studies* 50, no.8 (March 2012): 118–120, doi: http://10.1111/j.1468–5965.2011.02230.x.

more favourable, opposition to Turkey's membership could increase.[144] In the 2000s French politics similarly saw a lively polemic, which revived arguments about the Turkish 'threat' to the 'French-driven' European civilization.[145] The Turkish candidacy for EU membership emerged as a subject of civilizational discussions from different value-based (leftist and rightist) perspectives in France.[146] Perhaps a greater cleavage on these matters was seen in Germany. The Social Democrats affirmed Turkey's contributions to the European Union whereas the Christian Democrats argued that the candidate was religiously and geographically not European.[147] Divergent opinions about Turkey's Europeanness continued to drive political discussions amongst German political and religious communities.[148] Although Germany did not completely block Turkey's negotiations with the EU in later years, the Turkey-scepticism of the conservatives overall did not change.[149] In point of fact, the German and French public opinions in the 2000s went hand in hand with the opinions of conservative political elites in their rejection of Turkey's accession to the EU.[150] In Britain, on the other hand, an almost complete consensus over Turkey's EU membership seemed to emerge despite the essentially geographical and religious arguments about the candidate.[151]

---

[144] Katinka Barysch, *What Europeans Think about Turkey and Why* (London: Centre for European Reform, 2007), 3.
[145] Tekin, *The Construction of Identity in Discourse*
[146] Ibid. Catherine Macmillan, *Discourse, Identity and the Question of Turkish Accession to the EU: Through the Looking Glass* (Surrey: Ashgate, 2013), 134–137; Nicolas Monceau, 'French Perceptions', in *Turkey Watch: EU Member States' Perceptions on Turkey's Accession to the EU*, eds. Sait Aksit, Ozgehan Senyuva, and Cigdem Ustun (Ankara: Zeplin Iletisim, 2010), 16–20.
[147] Constanze Stelzenmüller, 'Turkey's EU Bid: A View from Germany', in *Conditionality, Impact and Prejudice in EU-Turkey Relations*, ed. Nathalie Tocci, IAI-TEPAV Report July 2007, 111–112.
[148] Katrin Bottger and Eva-Maria Maggi, 'German Perceptions'. Aksit, Senyuva, and Ustun, *Turkey Watch*, 22–33.
[149] Inthorn, 'What Does It Mean to be an EU Citizen?', 76.
[150] Müftüler-Baç, 'Turkey's Accession to the European Union', 201–219.
[151] Macmillan, *Discourse, Identity and the Question of Turkish Accession to the EU*, 112–114; Inthorn, 'What Does It Mean to be an EU Citizen?'. Thomas Koenig, Sabina Mihelj, John Downey, and Mine Gencel Bek, 'Media Framings on the Issue of Turkish Accession to the EU, a European or National Process?', *Innovation: the European Journal of Science Research* 19, no.2 (2006), doi: 10.1080/13511610600804240.

Conceptual Clarifications

Having explored the ways in which European political camps came to terms with Turkey in national and transnational networks, this section explains the main concepts employed throughout the present study. The first are two interconnected terms repeatedly used in the literature: the European 'self' and 'other'. The European subject and its 'other', its rival or outsider, are largely connected to the value-driven discussions of 'European civilization'. The self-other coexistence has been a focus of different disciplines. On the one hand, the fields of international relations and political science contain many, mostly Euro-centric studies that theorise the construction of the European Union's 'self' and 'other' at institutional and societal levels.[152] In these domains the leading work has sought to associate European identity with the relationship between the European subject and its contrary. On the other hand, studies from philosophy and history highlight the importance of the 'other' within civilizational debates and the arguments surrounding the many cultural stereotypes of Europe.[153] Notwithstanding the increasing emphasis on the categorizations of the 'self' and 'other', identity studies have so far had a relatively limited interest in the influence of history over cultural categorizations.

The concepts of the 'European' and 'non-European' are not categorical, nor are they ahistorical; they remain temporally and co-existentially related to each other.[154] In social theory it is widely accepted that the subject comes to terms

---

[152] Philip Schlesinger, 'On National Identity: Some Conceptions and some Misconceptions Criticised', *Social Sciences Information* 26, no. 2 (1987): 219–264, doi: 10.1177/053901887026002001; Richard C.M. Mole, *Discursive Constructions of Identity in European Politics* (Hampsire and New York: Palgrave Macmillan. 2007); Checkel and Katzenstein, eds., *European Identity*. Louiza Odysseos, *The Subject of Coexistence, Otherness in International Relations* (Minneapolis, London: University of Minnesota Press, 2007); Teun A. Van Dijk, ed., *Discourse Studies: A Multidisciplinary Introduction* (London: Sage Publishing, 2011).

[153] Gerard Delanty and Chris Rumford, *Rethinking Europe: Social Theory and Implications of Europeanization* (London: Routledge, 2005), 55; Amin Malouf, *In the name of Identity: Violence and the Need to Belong* (New York: Arcade Publishing, 2001); Edward Said, *Orientalism* (New York: Vintage Books, 1979); Jacques Derrida, *The Other Heading: Reflections on Today's Europe* (Bloomington, Indianapolis: Indiana University Press, 1992); David Campbell, *National Deconstruction: Violence, Identity, and Justice in Bosnia* (Minneapolis, London: University of Minnesota Press, 1998); Iver B. Neumann, *Uses of Other: The East in European Identity Formation* (Minneapolis: University of Minnesota Press, 1999).

[154] Ian Manners, 'The European Union as a Normative Power: A Response to Thomas Diez', *Millennium* 35, no.1 (2006): 178, doi: 10.1177/03058298060350010201; Odysseos, *The Subject of Coexistence*.

with 'the other' in order to reveal and confirm its difference.[155] Similarly, identity studies on Europe note how the European subject ceaselessly defines who is European according to who is not.[156] Because these definitions are articulated by European political actors, verbally and in written forms, it follows that the constructions of the 'self' and 'other' are not independent of the European Union's official language.[157] And finally, we should also examine the (possibly changing) motivations of the 'self' in defining the 'other'. Constructivist scholars postulate that a conscious entity constructs knowledge through a cognitive process that combines ideational and interest-ridden motivations.[158] Taking this on board, values, norms, and beliefs need to be considered as making a significant contribution to shaping the conceptualisation of the European Union and its contrary.

Another concept that requires clarification is 'values'. First of all, the European Union uses this concept, especially with the Treaty of Lisbon (2009), to refer to its democratic rights, freedoms, and principles. As the subsequent chapters demonstrate, the term 'European values' is part of the EU's official terminology. The second reason is linked to the present study's methodological viewpoint. Although some scholars recommend separating value-based and norm-based dimensions when studying the EU,[159] the components of European culture are not so easy to separate. It is clear that both values and norms arise from historical subjectivities, through which political camps have differentiated the European Union from Turkey. An explanation is required here. Norms are encom-

---

[155] David Campbell, *Writing Security: United States Foreign Policy and the Politics of Identity* (Manchester: Manchester University Press, 1992), 100. William E. Connolly., *Identity/Difference: Democratic Negotiations of Political Paradox* (Minneapolis: University of Minnesota Press: 1991), 64; Stuart Hall, 'Introduction: Who Needs identity?', in *Questions of Cultural Identity*, eds. Stuart Hall and Paul du Gay (London: Sage Publications, 1996), 5; Stuart Hall, 'Ethnicity: Identity and Difference', in *Becoming National: A Reader*, eds. Geoff Eley and Grigor Suny (New York: Oxford University Press, 1996); Jacques Derrida, 'Différance', in *Identity: A reader*, eds. Paul Du Gay, Jessica Evans, and Peter Redman, (London: Sage Publications, 2000); Charles Taylor, 'The Politics of Recognition', in *Multiculturalism: Examining the Politics of Recognition*, ed. Amy Gutmann (Princeton: Princeton University Press, 1994).
[156] Delanty and Rumford, *Rethinking Europe*, 51; Hall, 'Ethnicity', 4–5.
[157] Ernesto Laclau and Chantal Mouffe, *Hegemony and Socialist Strategy* (Verso, 2002); Neumann, *Uses of Other*, 209–214; Manners, Ian, 'The European Union as a Normative Power', 179.
[158] Jacob Ole Sending, 'Constitution, Choice and Change:Problems with the Logic of Appropriateness and its Use in Constructivist Theory', *European Journal of International Relations* 8, (2002): 447, doi: 10.1177/1354066102008004001.
[159] Sjursen, 'Why Expand?', 508. 'The European Union between Values and Rights', in *Questioning EU Enlargement: Europe in Search of Identity*, ed. Helene Sjursen (New York and London: Routledge, 2006), 203–215; Macmillan, *Discourse, Identity and the Question of Turkish Accession to the EU*.

passed by international law, in the present situation, by EU legislation.[160] Values, however, extend further than this. In his pioneering work, Clifford Geertz states that values are essential components of culture.[161] Although Geertz mostly makes use of culture to explain a broad group of human activities within ethnicities, his extensive usage of the term inspires this study to explore what is sometimes referred to as the EU's value-based cosmos. In other respects, values and norms are not synonymous, but values can confine norms within a cultural framework. Once a political norm – for example, about minority rights – is internalised by society, it then reaches an ethical level and becomes a part of society's democratic values. The EU's membership criteria are examples of embedding democratic and humanitarian values in legislation. From such a broad cultural perspective, European actors conceptualise the European Union and Turkey according to the values they advocate, which are justified with reference to two primary cultural sources: EU legislation and national politics. In summary, the term 'values' in the present study covers a wide array of beliefs and moral principles.

Nevertheless, the concept of 'values' needs to be made more concrete. Geertz writes about individual elements of values, i.e. ethnicity, language, geography, religion, and customs,[162] and in our context we can identify three types classified according to their relevance to the contemporary arguments about the nature of Europe and the European Union. The first is the political terms involved in the notion of Europeanness, the roots of which lie in earlier political revolutions and intellectual accumulation. For example, if republicanism in Europe initially stems from the Roman political tradition, its shape further evolved with the French Revolution and the Enlightenment. Human rights are certainly central European political values. One should also add the economic principles of the common market as another European political value. In the European Union's framework, these political conditions have been set in stone through EU legislation, as discussed in later chapters. The second type of values is linked to the religious aspect of Europeanness and refers to the influential role that Christianity has played in the construction of the European Union. The third type of apparent values in European descriptions stems from a common geography and describes Europe as having a shared territory. The religious and geographical terms are more circumstantial than the political values of Europe, and the legitimacy of

---

[160] Thomas Kappen Risse, Stephen C., Ropp, and Kathryn Sikkink, eds., *The Power of Human Rights: International Norms and Domestic Change* (Cambridge: Cambridge University Press, 1999).
[161] Clifford Geertz, *The Interpretation of Cultures* (New York: Basic Books, 1973), 50–51.
[162] Ibid, 261–263.

applying them as criteria, when discussing Turkey's compatibility with European values, is questionable. To take one example, the Treaty on European Union (1993) affirms that any 'European' country with certain political characteristics is able to apply for accession, although it, unsurprisingly, did not clarify the Eastern borders of Europe. Although the EU confirmed that it accepted Turkey to be geographically 'European' by accepting its membership application, many European actors continue discussing whether the country is part of the shared European territory. Another example is when Turkey is discussed in religious terms. EU legislation has enshrined only essentially political virtues that are linked to religious terms, such as the freedom of belief, rather than a common religion. According to EU legislation, political arguments about religious freedom in a country are legitimate. Others, including whether a candidate country's religious past is compatible with European values, remain controversial. As one can see, political, religious, and geographical ways of conceptualising Europe in connection with Turkey are not mutually exclusive but overlap considerably.

Against the backdrop of these conceptual explanations, this book takes as its basis a historical-reflectivist approach and a conceptual reading practice. Recent studies have postulated that contemporary categorizations of Europe and Turkey have been influenced by historical subjectivities constructed in earlier periods. Among them, Paul Levin's historical study mainly suggests that European political camps debate whether Turkey conforms to their historical constructions.[163] This sets a benchmark for this study concerning the historical influences on European actors' discussions over Turkey. From this starting point, this study first aims to understand the historical limits of conceptualising Europe and the Ottoman Empire, and subsequently Turkey, with specific reference to the period between the 18th and 20th centuries. Therefore, the first task is to address the historical construction of European values. The second task is to sketch out these values in contemporary European and national thinking about the European Union and Turkey.

On that account, the present research focuses on European values embodied in three groups of documents. The first group is the plenary sessions of the European Parliament that are annually convened to discuss Turkey's progress throughout the negotiations with the EU. The second group is also from the EU's official discourse and its debates at parliamentary level; it covers the reports that are annually released by the European Parliament and deputies' speeches and proposals for amendments to these reports. For both these two groups of documents, the period under investigation starts at the beginning of

---

163 Levin, *Turkey and the European Union*.

the negotiation process in the 2000s. The final group involves the media coverage in France, Germany, and Britain. It covers political leaders' statements about Turkey as reported by the news media in three leading European countries between September and October 2005, shortly before the beginning of the EU's membership negotiations with the candidate, 3 October 2005.

The research questions and documents within the present research framework entail a historical-conceptual approach.[164] Conceptual history basically comprises analytical approaches to the historical changes in the semantic field of any given term. Reinhart Kosselleck's *Begriffsgeschichte* has been leading these approaches, and it suggests that concepts should be studied with their semantic fields, namely through their connections with other concepts. Only when semantic changes of a concept are scrutinised in relation to any pertinent concept can the researcher offer analytical insights into understanding the underlying paradigms behind these conceptions. In parallel, researchers should study concepts in relation to their antonyms in a given historical period in order to understand their relevance to group identities.[165] The present study then concerns itself with a number of concepts used within the historical debate over Turkey and Europe and semantic relations between them.

---

[164] The conventional research purpose here is to understand conceptualizations of EU actors. The present study is inspired by the libraries of historicism as well as the conceptual approaches. To name but few inspiring works, see Stefan Berger, *In Search of Normality: National Identity and Historical Consciousness in Germany since 1800* (New York: Berghahn Books, 2003); Kathrin Maurer, *Visualizing the Past, the Power of the Image in German Historicism* (Berlin: Walter de Gruyter, 2013); Leopold Von Ranke, *The Secret of World History: Selected Writings on the Art and Science of History*, ed. trans. Roger Wines (New York: Fordham University Press, 1981); Reinhart Kosselleck, *Begriffsgeschichten* (Frankfurt: Suhrkamp Verlag, 2006); Reinhart Kosselleck, *The Practice of Conceptual History: Timing History, Spacing Concepts*, trans. Todd Presner (Stanford, Stanford University Press, 2002); Finally, Mark Bevir's criticisms of linguistic approaches to historical cases are pertinent. Mark Bevir, 'The Contextualist Approach', in *The Oxford Handbook of the History of the Modern Philosophy*, ed. George Klosko (New York: Oxford University Press, 2009); 'The Errors of Linguistic Contextualism', *History and Theory* 31, no.3 (1992), doi:10.2307/2505371; 'The Role of Contexts in Understanding Explanation', *Human Studies* 23, (2000), doi: 10.1023/A:1005636214102; 'Contextualism: From Modernist Method to Post-Analytic Historicism', *Journal of the Philosophy of History* 3, (2009), doi: 10.1163/187226309X461506.

[165] Jan Ifversen, 'About Key Concepts and How to Study Them', *Contributions to the History of Concepts* 6, no.1 (2011): 65–88, doi: http://dx.doi.org/10.3167/choc.2011.060104; Jan Ifversen, 'Text, Discourse, Concept: Approaches to Textual Analysis', *Kontur*, no.7 (2003): 67; Reinhart Kosselleck, *The Practice of Conceptual History*, 25, 208–217; Niels Åkerstrøm Andersen, *Discoursive Analytical Strategies: Understanding Foucault, Kosselleck, Laclau, Luhmann* (Bristol: The Policy Press, 2003), 38–48.

How helpful is the present approach in reading documents? The research preceding this book essentially reviewed the texts through a group of interconnected main and subsidiary keywords from their semantic fields.[166] This practice involves a number of key steps. Through a preliminary reading, readers first learn about the semantics of the given document. Then, they establish a conceptual framework using keywords captured from the text. If necessary, the readers add supplementary keywords taken from the contextual background. Finally, they construe the document through the established conceptual framework. For a general example, the idea of Europeanness as a semantic field of texts might unravel itself via concepts such as 'European values', 'European standards', 'market (economy)', or 'democracy'. The reader might add new terms even if the target texts do not contain them. The key aim is to understand as much as possible information about European contexts. In a particular example, understanding the semantic field of defining Europeanness entails taking account of the concepts critical to European identity, such as 'human rights', 'democracy' or 'market', even if they are not present in the target text. These concepts suggest the EU's contemporary social and political context governed by an ideology. As such, a semantic approach that is au fait with the historical contexts of the documents seems justified in order to grasp the conceptualizations contained within the texts. In our example, in which our aim is to understand conceptualisations of Europe and Turkey that have been swayed by historical values of Europeanness, the texts are confined to documents and minutes (plenary sessions) of the European Parliament and statements raised by national political elites to debate Turkey's EU bid. The terms framing the language of discussing Turkey in relation to Europe involve, but are not limited to, 'Europe', 'European Union', 'Enlargement', 'Integration', 'Turkey', 'Copenhagen Criteria', 'accession criteria', 'European values', 'modernization', 'Ottoman', 'bridge', 'democracy', or 'Islam'. True, this conceptual logic introduced here does not stand for a particular method, and rather than rely on technical strategies, a heuristic approach is adopted: the reader's cognition is the only way of understanding the texts. Still, the approach is systematic and analytical, as the documents held in the present study constitute coherent examples of the same semantic background. Programmatic statements by deputies in the European Parliament and statements by political leaders in national politics show contemporary

---

[166] Reinhart Koselleck, *The Practice of Conceptual History*, 25, 208–217; Ifversen, 'About Key Concepts and How to Study Them'; Ifversen, 'Text, Discourse, Concept: Approaches to Textual Analysis'.

and comparative cases. As such, the present conceptual approach is framed to be reasoning over a systemic documentation.

Plan of the Book

Very briefly, the second and third chapters explore the historical construction of European values and the changes in the conceptualisations of Europe and Turkey in European diplomacy and literature from the 18th century. The fourth one focuses on the plenary sessions reserved in the European Parliament to discuss Turkey's progress towards accession and scrutinises their documents and minutes. The subsequent three chapters discuss, respectively, the political representations of Turkey in politics and the media in France, Germany, and Britain, and they explore news sources, along with the literature. The eighth chapter draws conclusions, and also mentions the study's limits in addressing the identity issues involved and raises topics for further research.

The second and third chapters have a glance at the historical trajectories of defining Europe and then the European Union, and the Ottoman Empire and then modern Turkey. Primarily drawing on scholarly sources, the second chapter reviews several aspects of the Ottoman/Turkish image in Europe. European history, especially the post-Westphalian period, saw the flowering of many intellectual movements that have influenced national and post-national thinking in today's Europe. Through the rationalist and romantic counter trends of enlightenment, the historical genres between the 18th and 20th centuries will be thematically explored. Here, main contemporary sources on historical movements are mostly taken as a guide.[167] Although the name 'Europe' is derived from the ancient Greek, these sources postulate, discussions about Europeanness were mostly stimulated by the flourishing intellectual movements of mod-

---

[167] April Carter's book on the idea of universalism inherited from the European ancient and Kantian philosophy is a good example. April Carter, *The Political Theory of Global Citizenship* (London and New York: Routledge, 2001). For the particularist and orientalist genres in history Laclau's useful article on the universalist and particularist genres in European history, and Adorno and Horkheimer's critical work on the limits of enlightenment are, again, useful sources. Ernesto Laclau, 'Universalism, Particularism and the Question of Identity', in *The Politics of Difference, Ethnic Premises in a World of Power*, eds. Edwin Wilmsen and Patrick McAllister (Chicago and London: The University of Chicago Press, 1996), 45–58; Max Horkheimer and Theodor W. Adorno, *Dialectic of Enlightenment: Philosophical Fragments*, ed. Gunzelin Schmid Noerr, trans. Edmund Jephcott (Stanford: Stanford University Press, 2002).

ernity, which were connected with the processes of state and nation-building.[168] From this inspiration, the study traces the visions of the European and outsider using the political vocabulary that has evolved since the late 18th century. The chapter takes the diplomatic relationship between Europe and the Ottoman Empire as the main historical axis and mentions the monoliths of the idea of Europe, in this period, that sometimes contradict, or blend into, each other.

European identity has been discerned to be a historical metaphor that was born as a cultural subject and evolved to a political dimension.[169] The third chapter reviews the construction of this political dimension in the 20th century, with a specific reference to the relationship between Turkey and the European Union as well as to the birth of the accession criteria. It continues with the changing terms of categorizing Turkey in the eyes of Europeans under the influence of the turbulent Cold War era, the EU's prolonged enlargement and, in parallel, its promotion of a common identity. Within these courses, the main stress is laid on the contestations over Turkey's accession process aligned with the accession criteria.

The fourth chapter is confined to be a critical reading of the Turkey statements raised in the European Parliament during the 2000s, especially after 2005, the date of the negotiations' beginning. Throughout this period, the deputies of the European Parliament and the members of the Committee on Foreign Affairs (AFET) paid increasing interest in showing their opinions about the situation of new candidates, especially Turkey. The reports published in AFET and the plenaries convened in the Parliament suggest a number of assumptions. First, although parliamentarians conceptualised the EU in connection with Turkey between national and European politics, they mostly framed their arguments according to the EU's legislation, or, in particular, the accession criteria. But this does not mean national politics to have had not any say in the making of statements in the European Parliament. During the mentioned period deputies linked their Turkey arguments, which found origins in the national context, with the accession criteria. In parallel, parliamentarians could also 'hide' their religious and geographical stereotypes about the Turkish candidate within their statements oriented to the accession criteria. The radical right in this case provides signifi-

---

168 The Lexicon entitled 'Geschichtliche Grundbegriffe' led by Koselleck demonstrates that political concepts until the 19th century had conveyed semantic characteristics inherited from the Roman political culture. The 19th century marked by the earlier French Revolution changed this tradition. Novel meanings of the European political vocabulary loomed large in this way. Holge Jordheim, 'Against Periodization, Koselleck's Theory of Multiple Modernities', *History and Theory* 51, (2012): 170, doi: 10.1111/j.1468–2303.2012.00619.x.
169 Delanty, *Inventing Europe*, 4.

cant examples. In summary, in the 2000s political actors in the European Parliament represented not only European contexts but also their national politics largely through a political language that was legitimised by EU legislation.

The fifth, sixth, and seventh chapters discuss political leaders' statements over Turkey reported in the news media of France, Germany, and Britain between September and early October 2005. In this short period until the beginning of the membership negotiations (3 October 2005), the media reported on lively debates about national identity, the EU, and Turkey. The main parallelism between the three cases is that a number of long-term factors from the countries' earlier histories appeared to influence national thinking about the European Union and Turkey. In France, long-established republican norms were used to justify the importance of public opinion. Following the French public's rejection of the EU Constitution in 2005, French politicians repeatedly emphasised the importance of public opinion when discussing Turkey. In Germany, alongside other structural factors, economic concerns linked to the country's long welfare tradition were obvious in politicians' statements. In Britain, the main prism through which political leaders viewed Turkey's EU bid was the country's traditional scepticism towards European political integration. The long-term Eurosceptic inclinations of British political camps structured their policies about Turkey's accession talks with the EU and were the primary reason why the British Conservatives put up a Turkey-friendly foreign policy in contrast to their Turkey-sceptic counterparts in Europe.

2 Relations between Europe and Turkey in Modern History

The second chapter explores the historical trajectories of Europe's relationships with the Ottoman Empire and early modern Turkey. It remarks on the structural shifts in the European terms of defining Europe in relation to the country throughout the political transformations of both sides. In Europe, particularly in Western Europe, foreign relations in the post-Westphalian period, Enlightenment debates, and political movements inspired by the French Revolution and its aftermath preceded a new language of defining European politics. At the turn of the 18th century, this language was particularly evident in the relations of European powers with the Ottoman Empire and modern Turkey. On the Ottoman and Turkish side, however, the peculiar and long reformation project that impacted on bureaucratic administration and the governance of minorities contributed to the country's image in Europe dramatically. The Ottoman/Turkish modernisation, therefore, became a common concept connecting European descriptions at different times of history.

The section follows some methodological lines mentioned in the introduction. First of all, it reviews the mainstream definitions of Europe and Turkey made by intellectuals and diplomats of the period. In a nutshell, it begins with an overview of the early contacts between Europeans and the Ottomans and then explores mainstream European perceptions until the mid-20th century. The chapter then tells the history of ideas without delving into every detail, and reminds the reader of the most critical developments from the 18th century onwards. To this end, it is guided by the historical themes that earlier academic sources put forward.[1] The chapter finally is about the historical background of European relations with the Ottoman Empire and Turkey, and a semantic approach is crucial to bridge gaps between historical contexts – contexts that exist-

---

[1] To name but a few, see the editions entitled Stefan Berger, ed., *A Companion to the 19th Century Europe* (Oxford: Blackwell Publishing, 2006); Stefan Berger, ed., *Writing National Histories: Western Europe since 1800* (London: Routledge, 1999) and the monographs Eric Hobsbawm, *The Age of Revolution: 1789–1848* (New York: Vintage Books, 1996); Reinhart Koselleck, *Critique and Crisis: Enlightenment and the Pathogenesis of Modern Society* (Cambridge, Massachusetts: MIT Press, 1988); April Carter, *The Political Theory of Universal Citizenship* (New York: Routledge, 2008); Bernard Lewis, *The Emergence of Modern Turkey* (New York: Oxford University Press, 1968); Halik Inalcik, *Turkey and Europe in History* (Istanbul: Eren, 2006); Bernard Lewis, *A Middle Eastern Mosaic* (New York: Random House, 2000); Suraiya Faroqhi, *Approaching Ottoman History: An Introduction to the Sources* (Cambridge: Cambridge University Press, 2004).

ed within different timeframes. The practice of conceptual reading introduced earlier seeks to understand historical milieus with dominant conceptualisations.[2] The chapter thus alludes to some of the most important references to the Ottoman Empire and modern Turkey in history and highlights key concepts from these references.

A brief overview of the early encounters between Europeans and Ottomans is important to understand the later period. By the time the Muslim Turks first appeared at their Eastern gates, Europeans had for ages been living under Christian influence and defining outsiders primarily in religious terms.[3] From the 11th century, first the Seljuk Turks and then the Ottomans progressively broke into the Christian realm, and the latter turned out to be Europe's main rival at the time of Constantinople's conquest(1453).[4] Until connections between the two sides increased, Europeans depicted the Ottomans initially in terms of militancy and heresy,[5] and insecure conditions allowed very few travellers to make expe-

---

2 Reinhart Koselleck, *Begriffsgeschichten* (Frankfurt: Suhrkamp Verlag, 2006), 99–102. Explaining structural trends that swayed over social events has been critical to historical writing and analysis. Fernand Braudel, 'Histoire et Science Sociales, la longue durée', *Annales. Économies, Sociétés, Civilisations* 13, no.4 (1958): 725–753. Javiér Fernández Sebastian and Juan Francisco Fuentes, 'Conceptual History, Memory, and Identity: an Interview with Reinhart Koselleck', *Contributions to the History of Concepts* 2, no.1 (2006): 99–127. The changing structural trends after the 18th century impacted on the historical evolution of European politics and generated a novel political language. Reinhart Koselleck, *The Practice of Conceptual History: Timing History, Spacing Concepts*, trans. Todd Samuel Pressner and Others (Stanford: Stanford University Press), 4–5. In the present study cultural categories cover a broad perspective and mostly correspond to the explanation by Clifford Geertz. Clifford Geertz, *The Interpretation of Cultures* (New York: Basic Books, 1973), 50–51.
3 Illustrated in the 'City of God' of St Augustine (426), the European realm was to welcome the barbarians, only on the condition that they embraced the Christian doctrine. Saint Augustine, *City of God*, trans. Marcus Dods (Massachusetts: Hendrickson Publishers, 2009), 9. The medieval political sovereigns had sought to legitimise themselves against the outsider through religion. Rosamond McKitterick, *Charlemagne: The Formation of a European Identity* (Cambridge: Cambridge University Press, 2008), 293.
4 Roderic H. Davison, *Essays in Ottoman and Turkish History, 1774–1923: The Impact of the West* (Texas: University of Texas Press, 1990), 3; Cemal Kafadar, 'A Rome of One's Own: Reflections on Cultural Geography and Identity in the Lands of Rum' in *History and Ideology: Architectural Heritage of the 'Lands of Rum'*, eds. Julia Bailey, Sibel Bozdoğan, Gülru Necipoğlu (Leiden: Brill, 2007), 8.
5 Daniel Goffman, *The Ottoman Empire and Early Modern Europe* (Cambridge: Cambridge University Press, 2002), 1–2. John Agnew, *Geopolitics: Re-Visioning World Politics* (London and New York: Routledge, 1998), 23.

ditions to the Ottoman realm until the late 17th century.⁶ Historian Richard Knolles, for example, wrote of the 'ruthless Turks', in his book 'the History of Turks' (1603), without visiting the Ottoman country or knowing Turkish.⁷ The information gathered by early travellers was essential to describe the Turks/Ottomans and their geography. Among these early visitors, Marco Polo stated as early as the 12th century that the Turks were 'rude people with an uncouth language of their own'.⁸ Geographical categories also became known back then; the Seljuk Turks described Anatolia as *Rumi* (Roman) while Marco Polo used the word *Turcomania*, the land of Turks.⁹ Similarly, Venetian sailors were calling the region *Turchia* during the 13th century.¹⁰

The Ottomans, moved by religious motives, conquered a huge territory in Eastern Europe until the peace of Karlowitz (1699) halted their expansion.¹¹ Their Islamic character was then provoking the European writing of the time that was already structured by Christian faith. As they appeared at the gates of Central Europe, Martin Luther declared them to be the 'servants of the devil', who were 'of the wrath of God.'¹² The British clergy similarly assigned the Ottomans to a religiously inferior class. The Anglican Book of Common Prayer (Good Friday, 1662) announced 'Have mercy upon all Jews, Turks, Infidels, and Hereticks', while the theologian John Wesley denounced the writer, Lord Chesterfield in similar terms: 'as absolutely void of virtue as any Jew, Turk or heathen that ever lived'.¹³ Religion was the decisive factor not only for clerical writings but also for philosophers. William Penn, to give one example, welcomed the Ottomans to his proposal of European confederation provided they were converted

---

6 Murphey Roads, 'Bigots or Informed Observers? A Periodization of Pre-Colonial English and European Writing on the Middle East', *Journal of the American Oriental Society* 110, no.2 (April-June 1990): 297–298.
7 Michael Curtis, *Orientalism and Islam: Thinkers on the Muslim Government in the Middle East and India* (New York: Cambridge University Press, 2009), 46.
8 Marco Polo, *The Travels of Marco Polo: The Complete Yule-Cordier Edition* Volume 1 (Toronto: General Publishing Company, 1993), 43.
9 Polo, *The Travels of Marco Polo*, 42.
10 Ion Grumeza, *The Roots of Balkanization: Eastern Europe C.E. 500–1500* (Lanham: University Press of America, 2010), 190.
11 Goffman, *The Ottoman Empire and the Early Modern Europe*, 8.
12 Athina Lexutt, Luther und der Islam, *Spiegel der Forschung*, no. 2 (2011), 63.
13 Lewis, *A Middle East Mosaic*, 13. I interpret this line from the Common Prayer from the Church of England, in 1662 as evidence that actually the Church had a sense of pity for Jews and Turks in the relevant passage. The words that Lewis cited – 'Jews, Turks, Infidels, and Hereticks' – does not show the whole message; John Wesley, *The works of the rev. John Wesley, Volume IV* (London: John Mason, 1829), 56

to Christianity.¹⁴ Although the secular and critical philosophy of the Renaissance thrived in this period and impacted on the religious ways of defining the outsiders,¹⁵ against the Ottoman aggression Renaissance scholars mostly remained faithful to the Christian conceptions of European cosmos.¹⁶ The Ottoman expansion in Eastern Europe strengthened the linkage between 'Europe' and Christendom.¹⁷

In political affairs, the centre of influence was shifting from the clergy to civic authorities, and the leverage of the Church of Rome was declining in mobilising Christian powers against the Ottoman Empire. After the Ottomans began their expansion in Europe, Catholic Europeans (except the French kings, who chose to ally with the Ottoman Sultan) had waged various crusades upon the call of the Pope. The last of these events was the Holy League putting an end to the Ottoman expansion in 1699.¹⁸ Reform movements against the Papal hegemony weakened this idea of fighting together under the Christian banner.¹⁹ Eventually, European powers prevented the Pope from attending diplomatic negotiations for the first time in 1648, during the arrangement and signature of the Treaty of Westphalia ending religious wars in Europe.²⁰ In the subsequent period, national interest prevailed over Rome's jurisdictions, and political authorities gradually became unitary sovereigns in diplomacy, legitimising their foreign policies under political and pragmatic motives.²¹ This shift allowed European actors to establish closer relations with the Ottomans. As Hugo Grotius, the pathfinder of modern international law, implied, Christian states were now free to

---

14 William Penn, *A collection of the works of William Penn. To which is Prefixed a Journal of his Life, with Many Original Letters and Papers not Before Published* (Volume 2) (London: J. Sowle, 1726), 747.
15 Spethen Greenblatt, *Renaissance Self-Fashioning: From Moore to Shakespeare* (Chicago: The University of Chicago Press, 2005), 256; Nancy Bisaha, *Creating East and West: Renaissance Humanists and Ottoman Turks* (Philadelphia: University of Pennsylvania Press, 2004), 43–45; Gerard Delanty, *Inventing Europe: Idea, Identity, Reality* (Basingstoke: Palgrave Macmillan, 1995), 89.
16 Robert Schwoebel, *The Shadow of the Crescent: The Renaissance Image of the Turk, 1453–1517* (New York: St Martin Press, 1967), 73.
17 Patrick Pasture, *Imagining European Unity since 1000 AD* (Basingstoke: Palgrave, 2015), 14–15, 20.
18 John France, *The Crusades and the Expansion of Catholic Christendom, 1000–1714* (London and New York: Routledge, 2005), 323.
19 Ibid.
20 Benjamin Strauman, 'The Peace of Westphalia as a Secular Constitution', *Constellations* 15, no.2 (2008): 173–188.
21 Derek Croxton, 'The Peace of Westphalia of 1648 and the Origins of Sovereignty', *The International History Review* 21, no.3 (1999): 569–591, http://www.jstor.org/stable/pdf/40109077.pdf?acceptTC=true.

found official contacts with infidels.[22] Finally, diplomatic and commercial relations with the Ottoman Empire, including the privileges that France and England respectively obtained to do business within the Ottoman realm, contributed to these contacts tremendously.[23] The Ottoman image then gradually changed from a source of fear to a subject of discovery in the eyes of European visitors until the 18th century.

European and Ottoman Images during the 18th and 19th Centuries

On the European side, the 18th and 19th centuries featured long-term confrontations between the traditional monarchical system and its counter-arguments, which were generated by the Enlightenment and then the political revolutions in Europe and Americas. As a consequence of this struggle, political terminology changed towards a new degree marked, if not dominated, by civic rights and liberties.[24] The age of the Enlightenment and revolutions thereby exerted formative influences on the terms of describing the Europeans vis-à-vis the Ottomans.[25]

The Enlightenment and revolutions in the 18th and 19th centuries demand brief attention at this point, although they are out of the present book's coverage. The early intellectual movements first formed in a socioeconomic lieu changed by the capitalist and early industrialist transition. The Enlightenment was a logical continuation of this mentality.[26] As a flock of fledgling arguments

---

[22] Iver B. Neumann and Jennifer Welsh, 'The Other in European Self-Definition: An Addendum to the Literature on International Society', *Review of International Studies* 17, no.4 (Oct 1991): 339, http://www.jstor.org/stable/20097270.

[23] Fatma Müge Göçek, *East Encounters the West: France and the Ottoman Empire in the 18th Century* (New York: Oxford University Press, 1987); Suraiya Faroqhi, *The Ottoman Empire and the World Around It* (London: Tauris, 2006), 2–3; Gabor Agoston and Bruce Masters, *Encyclopedia of the Ottoman Empire* (New York: Facts on File, 2009), 118, 224–225; L.T. Darling, 'Ottoman Politics through British Eyes: Paul Rycaut's "The Present State of the Ottoman Empire"', *Journal of World History* 5, no.1 (1994 Spring): 73, http://www.jstor.org/stable/20078582.

[24] François Furet, *Penser la Révolution française* (Paris: Gallimard, 1983), 71; Koselleck, *Critique and Crisis*, 62–75; Delanty, *Inventing Europe*, 92–94, 107–109; Fernand Braudel *A History of Civilizations*, trans. Richard Mayne (New York: Penguin Press, 1994), 4.

[25] It is essential to note in the beginning that the Enlightenment did not occupy one context and should be taken as a source of inspiration, rather than one uniform argument. J. G. A. Pocock *Barbarism and Religion, Vol. 5: The First Triumph* (Cambridge: Cambridge University Press, 2010), 9–10.

[26] The Enlighteners were from the middle classes, a product of this socioeconomic change. Hobsbawn, *The Age of Revolution*, 21–22. Still, it needs to mention the support of the econom-

questioning the state's authority in relation to the people, the Enlightenment context introduced individual political rights and liberties, prompted revolutions against sovereign states, and gave origins to the political ideologies presiding over contemporary European politics.[27] Among these beliefs, republicanism, liberalism, and even early socialism emerged against authoritarian regimes with their Enlightenment-inspired promises of individual rights, human progress, rationality and social equality.[28] As a response to these challenges, the conservative ideology took form and upheld the current status of political and religious institutions. It fundamentally differed from its counterparts through the assumption that society required a gradual development, rather than rapid and top-down changes in opposition to its sociopolitical traditions.[29] In the subsequent period nationalism also took root in Europe, and its paradigm that human progress could be best achieved within cultural communities underpinned ethno-religious approaches against outsiders.[30] To cut a long story short, the mainstream ideologies of Europe became known in the 18th and 19th centuries with their approvals and criticisms of certain aspects of the Enlightenment era.[31]

Social trends moved by these arguments preceded political revolutions in Western Europe.[32] Theoretically, revolutions could eventuate thanks to the encounters and exchange of views between the political domain of the sovereign and the private domain of subjects. Then it became possible for various groups and ideologies to publicly gather and exchange opinions thanks to the increasing social communication during the 17th and 18th centuries.[33] Dialogues between revolutionary groups put forth a group of claims that were gradually internalised

---

ically higher classes for the political revolutions in the 19th century. Pierre Joseph Proudhon, *General Idea of the Revolution in the Nineteenth Century*, trans. John Beverley Robinson (New York: Haskell House Publishers, 1969).

27 Edmund Neill, 'Political Ideologies, Liberalism, Conservatism and Socialism', in *A Companion to the 19th Century Europe*, ed. Stefan Berger (Oxford: Blackwell Publishing, 2006), 211.
28 Hobsbawm, *The Age of Revolution*, 244.
29 Ibid. Also see Edmund Burke's letters about his scepticism toward the French Revolution, Edmund Burke, *Further Reflections on the Revolution in France* (Indianapolis: Liberty Fund, 2012).
30 Elie Kedourie, *Nationalism* (Oxford and Massachusetts: Blackwell Publishing, 1993), 155; Hans Kohn, 'The Paradox of Fichte's Nationalism', *Journal of the History of Ideas* 10, no.3 (Jun. 1949): 343, doi:10.2307/2707040; F. M. Barnard, 'National Culture and Political Legitimacy: Herder and Rousseau', *Journal of the History of Ideas* 44, no.2 (April-June 1983): 231, doi:10.2307/2709138.
31 Neill, 'Political Ideologies, Liberalism, Conservatism and Socialism', 212.
32 Carter, *The Political Theory of Universal Citizenship*, 55
33 Sharif Gemie, 'Revolutions and Revolutionaries: Histories, Concepts, and Myths', in *A Companion to the 19th Century Europe*, ed. Stefan Berger (Oxford: Blackwell Publishing, 2006), 134.

in Western Europe. Initially, the French Declaration of the Rights of Man and Citizen proclaimed preliminary civic rights that were presumed to be universally applicable. It briefly stated that men in any nation were equal in social and political rights, and legitimised political sovereignty with their own will.[34] The revolutionary process in France introduced equal rights to the attention of European societies through constitutional citizenship. In other words, the French shaped their revolution with an emphasis on the French citizen as the core of political and national consciousness.[35] Consequently, revolutionary movements in France between 1789 and 1848 led to regime changes and the institutionalisation of political norms such as national sovereignty and universal suffrage. In Britain, an evolutionary progress widened the franchise during the 19th century as a result of political movements and the empowerment of the working and middle classes. In Germany, however, it was the bureaucratic reformers who had the prime role in promoting political rights, as they, following their triumph over the Napoleonic France, went on to adapt French political novelties, especially constitutionalism with limited franchise.[36] Despite the flowering of individual rights, the revolutionary wave in Western Europe did not impact on women's rights immediately. To give a notorious example, the historical documents of the French Revolution explicitly excluded women from the political sphere, and so caused backlashes and a feminist struggle that would last for centuries.[37]

In the end, intellectuals and social movements of the period redefined European politics and equally enriched the vocabulary of defining Europe and its contraries. The diplomatic and scholarly narratives from the 18th century portraying the Ottoman realm in relation to the changing political forms of Europe attest this enrichment remarkably.

Despite these changes on the European side, Ottoman history from the 18th century is commonly presented as the period of decline, marked by defensive

---

34 'The Declaration of the rights of Man and of the Citizen'.
35 Stefan Berger, Mark Donovan, and Kevin Passmore, 'Apologias for the Nation State in Western Europe since 1800', in *Writing National Histories: Western Europe since 1800*, eds. Stefarn Berger, Mark Donovan, and Kevin Passmore (London: Routledge, 1999), 5.
36 Jorn Leonhard, 'The Rise of the Modern Leviathan, State Functions and State Features', in *A Companion to the 19th Century Europe*, ed. Stefan Berger (Oxford: Blackwell Publishing, 2006), 142.
37 Shirley Elson Roessler, *Out of Shadows: Women and Politics in the French Revolution, 1789–1895* (P.Lang, 2006), 108; Peggy Watson, 'Eastern Europe's Silent Revolution: Gender', *Sociology* 27, no.3 (August 1993): 477–478, http://www.jstor.org/stable/42855234; Joan Wallach Scott, 'French Feminists and the Rights of 'Man': Olympe de Gouges's Declarations', *History Workshop*, no.28 (1989): 17–18; Eric Hobsbawm, *The Age of Empire 1875–1914* (New York: Vintage Books, 1989), 198–201.

wars against Russia and alliances with Western European powers.[38] In 1774, the Russian aggression famously led by Catherine the Great, who had pledged to 'drive Turks out of Europe,'[39] led to a set of issues emanating from the slow disintegration of the Ottoman Empire, famously called 'the Eastern Question', which remained on the agenda of European powers until the Empire's breakdown.[40] European actors until then approached the Ottomans with the pertinent matters related to the Eastern Question, in particular, territorial losses and the status of the minorities in the realm. At the beginning of this period the Ottomans had allied themselves with France, but after this alliance lay shattered with a short-term French occupation of Egypt (1798), the Sublime Porte, the Ottoman Government in diplomatic language, turned to Britain. Eventually, British-Ottoman relations culminated in the declaration of the Ottoman state to be 'European' and a part of the Concert of Europe in the peace congresses in Vienna (1815) and Paris (1856). In the eyes of the Europeans, what commercial privileges the Ottomans granted to Britain and to other Western European powers and which social rights they conferred on their minorities indicated the 'Ottoman determination to comply with the European standards'.[41] The 'Europeanization' of the Ottoman country in the 19th century should be conceived in this way: by empowering minorities, the Ottomans sought European shelter against the Russian threat. The *Tanzimat* period of reform (1839–1876), which resulted in the Empire's first constitution, provided Ottoman subjects with civic rights, land rights, and finally political rights.[42] The so-called balance of power that the Ottomans could benefit was yet to change with the involvement of the German Empire and the Kingdom of Italy in European power politics. As Winston Churchill once noted, the European camps squabbling over the spoils of the Ottoman Empire's continuous disintegration resulted in the outbreak of the Great War.[43]

---

38 Faroqhi, *The Ottoman Empire*, 29–30.
39 John T. Alexander, *Catherine the Great: Life and Legend* (New York: Oxford University Press, 1989), 242.
40 J. A. R. Mariott, *The Eastern Question: An Historical Study* (Oxford: Clarendon Press, 1917), 6.
41 Fikret Adanir, 'Turkey's Entry into the Concert of Europe', *European Review* 13, no.4 (2005): 407, doi:10.1017/S1062798705000530.
42 Serif Mardin, 'Power, Civil Society and Culture in the Ottoman Empire', *Comparative Studies in Society and History* 11, no.3 (June 1969): 258–281, doi:10.1017/S0010417500005338.
43 Winston S. A Churchill, *History of the English-Speaking Peoples: The Great Democracies* (New York: Dodd, Mead, 1958), 26. Mariott, The Eastern Question, 15–16.

Portraying the Ottomans: Instances from British and French Literatures

In the shadow of these power-relations and a declining Ottoman influence, European scholars and diplomats portrayed the Ottoman realm in an orientalist fashion. First, the French invasion of Egypt in the late 18th century directed the attention of the French literature to the Ottomans' Eastern territories.[44] Recruitments of language experts as a result of the increasing diplomatic relations had a prime role in early studies.[45] French linguists continued to be at the forefront of the Western intelligentsia exploring the Ottomans. Translators and translation offices in France opened the Ottoman cultural life to the Western readers.[46] The first Turkologists from *l'Institute nationale des langues et civilizations* in Paris raised the earliest scholars representing the Orientalist mainstream in Europe.[47] Commercial relations between the Ottomans and Western Europe further contributed to the European portrayal of the Ottoman Empire. Diplomats, scholars, and merchants from these countries wrote about their observations and comparisons and remarked on how the leadership shifted from the East to the West.[48]

Orientalism and the notion of Ottoman despotism were also born within this practice, as fixed patterns to identify the social and political lives under the Ottoman realm.[49] In the most moderate terms, the Orientalists, a group of thinkers guided by the emerging European values and enchanted by Eastern territories, showed an appetite for discovering the socioeconomic sphere governed by the Ottoman despotism.[50] Victor Hugo mentioned this curiosity: 'During the time of Louis the 14th we were Hellenists, now we are Orientalists'.[51] Orientalist narratives then depicted Eastern despotism as an echo of the rivalry between ancient Greece and Persia, and associated Ottomans with the latter. They employed the term 'civilisation' to refer to the Europeans and employed 'culture' and 'barbar-

---

44 Said, *Orientalism*, 122.
45 Roads, 'Bigots or Informed Observers', 297–298.
46 Inalcik, 'Hermenötik, Oryantalizm, Turkoloji', 27.
47 Ibid., 29, Also see, Halil Inalcik *Turkey and Europe in History*, and Fatma Muge Gocek, *East Encounters West: France and the Ottoman Empire in the Eighteenth Century* (New York: Oxford University Press, 1987).
48 Curtis, *Orientalism and Islam*, 39–40. Roads, 'Bigots or Informed Observers?'.
49 Serif Mardin, 'Oryantalizmin Hasıraltı Ettikleri' *Dogu Bati*, no.20 'Oryantalizm-1' (2005): 118–119, Serif Mardin, *Religion, Society, and Modernity in Turkey* (Syracuse, New York: Syracuse University Press, 2006), 28–29.
50 Mardin, *Religion, Society, and Modernity in Turkey*, 29.
51 Catherine Clémentin-Ojha and Pierre-Yves Manguin, *A Century in Asia: The History of the École Française D'Extrême-Orient, 1898–2006* (Singapore: Editions Didier Millet, 2007), 31.

ism' to judge the Ottomans.⁵² The following part highlights a number of stereotypes from the Orientalist language. Among them, the narratives of Baron de Montesquieu and Edmund Burke in the 18th century preceded the Orientalist writing about the Ottomans and the Ottoman despotism. To give examples, some romantic scholars, like Ernest Renan and John Henry Newman, came to reduce the Ottoman 'backwardness' to race and religion.⁵³ Yet their connections between despotism and backwardness were rather insignificant and generally lacked an economic explanation.⁵⁴ On the other hand, scholars like Alphonse de Lamartine, Gerard Nerval, or James Porter showed a more benign attitude towards the Ottomans and argued that tolerance and the rule of law were intrinsic to the Islamic culture.

Colonial expansions of Britain and France provided a huge enthusiasm for depicting the underdeveloped Ottoman country in these writings. The official motive of colonialism was generally justified in terms of exporting libertarian values to the societies living under Ottoman despotic rule.⁵⁵ Still, British and French narratives showed nuances. According to the British literature, the 19th-century image of Turkey was linked to whether the Ottoman Empire would manage to survive with its unsettled minorities.⁵⁶ In addition, the Ottoman governance was comparable to the French one; the British scholarship on political theory at times chose the Ottoman despotism and backwardness as an argumentative object to question the new republican politics of France following its rev-

---

52 Delanty, *Inventing Europe*, 94. Braudel, *A History of Civilizations*, 4. Curtis, *Orientalism and Islam*. Mardin, *Religion, Society, and Modernity in Turkey*, 29.
53 Ernest Renan is counted within the term's romantic scholarship, Richard M. Chadbourne, *Ernest Renan* (New York: Twayne Publishers, 1968), 38.
54 It also needs to be mentioned that these scholars' contemporaries, such as Karl Marx and Max Weber in the 19th century, strived to explain the despotism and backwardness with their economic and political arguments. Lockman Zachary, *Contending Visions of Middle East: The History and Politics of Orientalism* (New York: Cambridge University Press, 2010), 48, 86–87. For a modern analytical perspective to the linkage between despotism and economic backwardness see, Manfred Hildermeier, *Geschichte der Sowjetunion 1917–1991: Geschichte der Sowjetunion 1917–1991. Entstehung und Niedergang des ersten sozialistischen Staates* (Munich: C.H. Beck, 1998), 17–18, 36–37, 63.
55 Egypt was an important case in which Britain and France sought to justify their interventions, Mohammed Salama, *Islam, Orientalism, and Intellectual History: Modernity and the Politics of Exclusion since Ibn Khaldun* (London: Tauris & Co Ltd, 2001), 18, 162. Consider, for example, the French historiography that sought to justify the French conquest of Tunisia: Whilst France governed Algeria and Morocco, how could be Tunisia left alone to the anarchical Ottoman regime? Donald Vernon Mckay, 'The French in Tunisia', *Geographical View* 35, no.3 (July 1945): 374.
56 Filiz Turhan, *The Other Empire: The British Romantic Writings about the Ottoman Empire* (New York and London: Routledge, 2003), 10.

olution.⁵⁷ British scholars then mainly discussed the Ottomans using European civic values that they called British values. On the other hand, French intellectuals perceived the Ottomans through the lens of terms adopted after the revolution. In particular, French romantics were interested in how the Ottomans lacked the civil characteristics that were prospering in Western Europe thanks to the French Revolution. The term 'civil' was essentially coined for urban society but was also employed by European civilizational arguments against the Ottomans. French scholars deliberately attributed the concept 'civilisation' to the human development in Western Europe.⁵⁸ Marquis de Condorcet, for instance, asked whether all nations could in the end acquire 'the state of civilisation reached by the most enlightened, most free, most unprejudiced peoples, such as the French and the Anglo-Americans'.⁵⁹ The ideas of civilisation, racism, and colonialism met in the French romantic writing about the Ottomans.⁶⁰

Despite these small-scale disagreements in portraying the Ottoman realm, British and French scholars of the 18th and 19th centuries employed the words 'Turk' and 'Turkey' together, in order to designate the Ottoman country and Muslim communities distinctively. They also chose the word 'European' in referring to the Ottoman territory in the European continent. Examples varied. Montesquieu mentioned the 'European part of Turkey' in his Persian Letters⁶¹, as Adolphus Slade, the English diplomat and scholar, referred to 'European Turkey' in his writings.⁶² The Annual Register, the British reference book partially edited by Edmund Burke, used 'Turkey' in 1758 to depict the Ottoman political authority.⁶³ Although ethnic Turks made up less than 45–50 percent of the entire Ottoman population, European intellectuals traditionally opted for the word 'Turk'.⁶⁴ Throughout centuries, 'the Turk' had become an essential term to refer to the Muslim societies under the Ottoman rule. As Nerval mentioned in his writings,

---

57 See Edmund Burke's comments below.
58 Larry Wolff, *Inventing Eastern Europe: The Map of Civilization in the Minds of the Enlightenment* (Stanford, Stanford University Press, 1994), 12–13.
59 Ibid., 13.
60 Pratima Prasad, *Colonialism, Race, and the French Romantic Imagination* (London and New York: Routledge, 2009), 8.
61 Montesquieu, *Persian* Letters, trans. Margaret Mouldon (New York: Oxford University Press, 2008), 149.
62 Adolphus Slade, Adolphus Slade, *Turkey, Greece and Malta* Volume 1 (London: Saunders and Otley, 1837), 222, 240, 312; Lewis, *A Middle East Mosaic*, 430.
63 *The Annual Register or a View of the History Politics and Literature of the Year 1758*, Ninth Edition (London: R. and J. Dodsley, 1758), 58.
64 William Hale, *Turkish Foreign Policy: 1774–2000* (London: Frank Cass Publishers, 2000), 15.

once adhered to the Islamic community any Ottoman subject was called 'Turk' regardless of his ethnic origin.[65]

Political considerations on the Ottoman/Turkish despotism can be first connected to the writings of a British diplomat. Paul Rycaut drew on his observations made during his mission in Istanbul and compared British and Ottoman political cultures in his book entitled *The Present State* (1686), in which he particularly used the concept 'tyranny' to introduce Ottoman absolutism.[66] To Rycaut, the Ottoman Sultan was perfectly legitimate because his tyranny was based on the blind obedience of the masses.[67] Next, John Locke, Rycaut's contemporary, visualised a benign image of the Ottomans. One of the pathfinders of the British Enlightenment, Locke believed that fundamental political traditions enabling social relations and property rights were prerequisites for political legitimacy.[68] Since tyranny began 'wherever law ended',[69] Locke's conception of tyranny did not correspond to the Ottoman rule built on a legal system. Further, his 'Letter Concerning Toleration' also reflected on the Ottoman realm. Although the Ottomans and Europeans were distinct religious communities, they all were governed by the same nature of political authority. In his view the Ottomans provided a legal system of religious tolerance and a model to the 17th-century Europe, where Christians had fought each other.[70]

From the 18th century, however, the term 'Eastern despotism' mostly signified the Ottoman absolutist administration over the backward territories.[71] Guided by Rycaut, Montesquieu's imagination of the Ottoman country exemplified the common view about Eastern despotism in the following century.[72] In his *Persian Letters* (1721), a collection of fictional correspondences between two Persian

---

65 Gerard M. Nerval, *Voyage en Orient*, Troisième Édition (Paris: Charpentiere Libraire Éditeur, 1851), 152–153.
66 Curtis, *Orientalism and Islam*, 42–43.
67 Cirakman, *From the 'Terror of the World'* 203–204.
68 Cohen, 'Structure, Choice, and Legitimacy', 143–166.
69 John Locke, *Two Treaties of Government* (London: Harvard College Library, 1824), 249.
70 'Will any man say that any right can be derived unto a Christian church over its brethren from a Turkish emperor? An infidel, who has himself no authority to punish Christians for the articles of their faith, cannot confer such an authority upon any society of Christians, nor give unto them a right which he has not himself. This would be the case at Constantinople; and the reason of the thing is the same in any Christian kingdom. The civil power is the same in every place', John Locke, *A Letter Concerning Religious Toleration, and Other Writings*, ed. Mark Goldie (Indianapolis: Liberty Fund, 2010), 22.
71 Asli Cirakman, 'From Tyranny to Despotism: The Enlightenment's Unenlightened Image of the Turks', *International Journal of Middle East Studies* 33, no.3 (2001): 49.
72 Ibid., 117, 204.

aristocrats, Montesquieu put forth noteworthy prejudgments about the Ottomans. Even though France was ruled by a comparably absolutist administration in his time, in Montesquieu's view the Ottoman despot was the real issue. His words were grave: 'there one could find families where, from father to son, nobody has laughed since the foundation of the monarchy.'[73] Jean Bodin's trace was also visible in this stance, as, Bodin had explained the absolutist character of the East with local weather conditions two centuries earlier. In a similar vein, Montesquieu associated the Ottoman uncivil absolutism with climate and religion.[74] His Persian character commented: 'for the French do not suppose that our climate can produce civilised men; however, I must admit that they are well worth putting right.'[75] In brief, Montesquieu's depiction of the Ottoman despotism was one of the first systematic models constructed with presumptions.[76]

Montesquieu claimed that Eastern despotism existed due to particular conditions of the East. Contrary to him, Edmund Burke, the prominent British conservative, refuted the rationales that had been taken for granted. He rather claimed that political traditions caused Eastern authoritarianism, for which the lack of property ownership was the key pre-condition.[77] Because they restricted property rights and hindered the flowering of political traditions, despotic authorities like the Ottoman Empire were not legitimate. As the revolutionary French regime was similarly undermining political traditions, Burke made analogies between the new France and eastern empires. In the following excerpt from his work entitled 'Reflections on the Revolution in France…', he made reference to the Ottoman despotism in order to illustrate his opinions about the changing French political regime:

> To hear some men speak of the late monarchy of France, you would imagine that they were talking of Persia bleeding under the ferocious sword of Taehmas Kouli Khan, or at least describing the barbarous anarchic despotism of Turkey, where the finest countries in the most genial climates in the world are wasted by peace more than any countries have been worried by war; where arts are unknown, where manufactures languish, where science is extinguished, where agriculture decays, where the human race itself melts away and perishes under the eye of the observer. Was this the case of France … Facts do not support this resemblance. [78]

---

73 Montesquieu, *Persian Letters*. 44.
74 Cirakman, *From the 'Terror of the World'*, 117.
75 Ibid., 59.
76 Curtis, *Orientalism and Islam*, 100–101, 305.
77 F.P. Lock, *Edmund Burke: Volume II* (Oxford: Clarendon Press, 2006), 172.
78 Edmund Burke, *Reflections on the Revolution in France: And on the Proceedings in Certain Societies in London Relative to that Event* (London: J. Dodsley, 1790), 189. Also see *The Works*

Burke made use of the Ottoman example in an explicit way. At first, he contended that the monarchy in France, as of the 18th century, was not as despotic as the Persian and Ottoman regimes. Within the entire argument, the Ottoman Empire was an auxiliary case next to the Persian militancy. In other words, he used the Ottoman and Persian cases to underpin his apology of the French monarchy. To him, Ottoman Turkey was so underdeveloped and uncivil that the finest conditions were wasted in there. He principally pointed to Greece in regard to the suffering civil countries under the Ottomans.[79] But, in his judgmental arguments, Burke did not limit the Ottoman backwardness to race, geography, or religion. In the following passage, he reveals more details about his argumentation:

> I do not recognize, in this view of things, the despotism of Turkey. Nor do I discern the character of a government, that has been, on the whole, so oppressive, or so corrupt, or so negligent, as to be utterly unfit for all reformation. I must think such a government well deserved to have its excellencies heightened; its faults corrected; and its capacities improved into a British constitution.[80]

The Ottoman regime was too corrupt, authoritarian, and unaccountable, Burke wrote, to change itself with slight political improvisations. Even in such a negative portrayal, though, he chose to employ solely political terms. Eventually, Ottoman authorities had to take the example of British legal and political traditions. In his overall argumentation, Britain was superior to the Ottoman Empire and also to the post-revolution France.

Montesquieu and Burke thus became two of the first scholars opting for the term 'Ottoman despotism'. They yet put forth distinctive explanations about the political nature of the Ottoman Empire. Taking the above-mentioned instances into consideration, it emerges that Montesquieu categorised Ottoman despotism with given cultural and geographical constructs while Burke explained it with political conditions. As the following section discusses, the 19th-century romantics by and large depicted the Ottomans between the lines that these scholars previously set out through essentially geographical, religious, and political arguments. Further, Romantics contested the great powers that took, although partially and shortly, the Ottoman Empire as part of Europe. The examples below also revealed this dichotomy between culturalist approaches to the Ottomans within

---

of the Right Honourable Edmund Burke: with a Portrait and Life of the Author (London: Thomas M'lean Haymarket, 1823), 233–234.
79 Turhan, *The Other Empire*, 6.
80 Burke, *The Works of the Right Honourable Edmund Burke*, 240, *Reflections on the Revolution in France*, 195.

the 19th-century literature and the rationalist foreign policy that predominated European balance of power.

The 19th century began with the aggression of Napoleonic France to – as they saw it – liberate Europe from traditional European monarchies. After the French fallback, monarchs in a counter movement intended to restore the political order with a broad depiction of Europe, which additionally included the Russian and Ottoman Empires. Thus, the Congress of Vienna (1815) conceptualised Europe in international political terms, rather than religious and geographical.[81] It also meant that the Ottoman state in its demise could be represented within European institutions. Of course, the Europeanness of the Ottomans was merely a result of the power politics on the continent. The dissolution of the Ottoman Empire was a matter of the highest importance, one over which European actors' interests clashed in the 19th century.[82] European balance of power took many forms according to various political developments concerning the Ottoman Empire's decline. And, as Winston Churchill also stated, many alliances emerged in this period to take advantage of the Empire's disintegration and this eventually led to the First World War.[83]

Romantic scholars contested such a Europe principally defined by international relations. For the first example, once the Congress of Vienna guaranteed the territorial integrity of the Ottoman Empire, Francois-Rene de Chateaubriand, the French romantic historian and diplomat, fiercely objected the decision and the Empire's compatibility with Europe. Instead of the Greeks fighting for liberation, in his opinion, the Congress falsely proclaimed the tyrannical Ottoman rule to be European. He put into words:

> the Porte will be deeply surprised to know that something is guaranteed for her (territorial guarantees by the Congress of Vienna)... The Sultan reigns by the Koran and sword; that already gives doubt to recognise these rights, it is supposed that he does not have full commitment, in an arbitrary regime the law is offence or crime, according to the legality of the action ... it should be allowed at least to claim for the victims of Muslim tyranny, the freedom that one might ask for the subjects of his Catholic Majesty ... It (Ottoman State) does not recognize the political rights of Europe, it is governed by the code of the peoples of Asia ... [84]

---

81 Ibid., 73–74. Pasture, *Imagining European Unity*, 51–52.
82 Hobsbawm, *The Age of Revolution*, 100, 104.
83 Churchill, *History of the English-Speaking Peoples*, 26.
84 M. Le Vicomt, Chateaubriand, *Itinéraire de Paris à Jérusalem*, Volume I (Paris: Libraire de Firmin Didot Freres, 1852), 37–38. The translation is mine.

'Koran', 'tyranny', 'despotism', 'Catholicism', 'regime', 'law', and 'Asia' were the concepts Chateaubriand used to exclude the Ottoman Empire from Europe. He built his opposition on religious and geographical reflections, and justified the state of war with the Ottomans through his mention of Islam: 'the law of war among the Turks is not the law of war among Christians: it carries death in defence of slavery in the conquest.'[85] In fact, some of his contemporaries, like Gerard Nerval, whose views were introduced below, believed that the Islamic slavery observed in the Ottoman rule had been more humane than that of the early Christianity. In Chateaubriand's assertion, religion was the ultimate handicap for the Ottoman civilisation as he stated: 'all things showed, the right of sovereignty under the Crescent can not be seen as identical as it is under the empire of the Cross'.[86]

Whilst the Ottoman Empire was continuously losing territory to the seceding Balkan nations in the 19th century, Europeans gave vocal support to ethnic unrest under its rule, such as the secessionist movement of Greece, which represented to many the cultural cradle of European civilisation. During the Greek revolts, several romantic scholars approached the country as a part of Europe under the control of the Ottoman historic rival. In Chateaubriand's view the absolutist Ottoman regime had remained the sole bulwark against the Greek and European prosperity:

> I must say more: free Greece, its army as Christian people, that is fortified and relaxed by engineers and gunners borrowed from foreign countries, destined to become promptly, by his ability, a naval power. Greece despite its small extent, better covers the east of Europe than the vast Turkey, and form a useful counterweight in the balance of nations.[87]

He drew attention to a possible Greek counter-force against the Ottoman hegemony in the region and called on the Europeans to interfere in Ottoman affairs in favour of the independence of Greece, which he deemed European. In like-minded romantic narratives, British intellectuals were highly enthusiastic about an intervention on the side of Greeks.[88] For instance, Lady Craven gave the British with the task of liberating Greeks and re-civilising them through British political traditions.[89] Throughout the era of the Greek secessionist movement until 1832,

---

85 Ibid., 41
86 Ibid., 42.
87 Ibid.
88 Churchill, *A History of the* English-Speaking Peoples, 25.
89 Turhan, *The Other Empire*, 35–36.

poets like James Skene and Lord Byron visualised Greece as a female figure, chained by the Ottomans, awaiting her British saviours.[90]

John Henry Newman, or Cardinal Newman of the Church of England, in his 'History of the Turks' (1851), argued that societies without belief were deemed to be barbarous. From his perspective, the Turks/Ottomans were equal to Spartans, the fierce rivals of the Athenian democracy. While Newman wrote his book, Britain was nevertheless backing its Ottoman ally during the Crimean War against Russia, which was in fact presumed by him to be the potential liberator of the Greek heritage.[91] This British-Ottoman alliance that Newman contested came to a head in the Paris Peace Conference, three years later, where the Ottoman country was declared 'European', once again. Apparently, British foreign policy during the 19th century at time conflicted with the traditional categories that the then romantic writings represented.

In other respects, the romantic thinkers of the time approached the Ottomans in ethnic terms. Ernest Renan gave suggestive examples as he attributed racial and Islamic inferiorities to the eastern world. Renan's theory principally had a linguistic origin. From a linguistically genetic perspective, he presumed that world languages found their ways from one source. Language families then were evidences of ethnicities and their religious practices.[92] In his lecture *L'islamisme et la science*, he justified his argument accordingly:

> Philosophy is abolished in Muslim countries ... Soon the Turkish race will take the hegemony of Islam, and its total lack of philosophical and scientific spirit will prevail everywhere. It is not my intention to reduce the role of this great science called Arab that marks a milestone so important in the history of the human spirit ... This science called Arab, what did it show that was Arab in reality? The language, nothing but the language ... among the philosophers and the scholars called Arabs, there is only one, al-Kindī, who was originally Arab ... Not only they are not from Arab blood, but they have nothing of the Arab mind ... Arab philosophers and scholars generally are poor writers ... This science is not Arab. Is it at least Muslim? Islam, in reality, has always troubled science and philosophy. Islam ... gave in to the Tatars and Berber races, races that are coarse, brutal, and without intellect.[93]

---

90 Churnjeet Kaur Mahn, 'The Sculpture and the Harem: Ethnography in Felicia Skene's Wayfaring Sketches', in *Women Writing Greece: Essays on Hellenism, Orientalism and Travel*, eds Vassiliki Kolocotroni and Eftepri Mitsi (Amsterdam: Editions Rodopi B.V., 2008), 102–103.
91 Robert Pattison, *The Great Dissent: John Henry Newman and the Liberal Heresy* (New York: Oxford University Press, 1991), 180–181.
92 Said, *Orientalism*, 150.
93 Ernest Renan, *L'Islamisme et la science; conférence faite à la Sorbonne, le 29 mars 1883* (Paris : C. Levy, 2005), 15–17.

Renan chose to justify his repudiation of Islamic progress and heritage with central concepts of religion and race. The Ottoman/Turkish dominance entirely ended the scientific progress in the Middle East that had been already in a difficult situation under Arab influence. He therefore argued that race and religion in the Middle East had been the biggest barriers to scientific development, and, therefore, to the survival of civilisations. The Ottoman/Turkish leadership in the Islamic world was apt to bring even more illiteracy, as Renan delivered. His argument was similar to Newman's negative portrayal of Turks. In parallel with Renan, John Henry Newman saw the Tartars as representative of the pre-Islamic state of the Turks.[94] For Newman, the Turks could not civilise themselves after the Tartar age because they clung to false beliefs. Their Islamic character was the structural problem before any civilised level, unlike the Christian path to progress.[95]

Newman and Renan's contemporary, the British statesman and opposition leader William Ewart Gladstone was also credited with his disapproval of the British policy on the territorial integrity of the Ottoman Empire. In that period, the Britain-allied Ottoman government was struggling with secessionist revolts in the Balkans and, consequently, receiving harsh reactions from European actors. During the Bulgarian separatist movement (1876) Gladstone wrote his pamphlet 'Bulgarian Horrors', and used this reactionary, yet orthodox, language against the Ottoman Empire:

> Let me endeavour very briefly to sketch, in the rudest outline, what the Turkish race was and what it is. It is not a question of Mahometanism simply, but of Mahometanism compounded with the peculiar character of a race. They are not the mild Mahometans of India, nor the chivalrous Saladins of Syria, nor the cultured Moors of Spain. They were, upon the whole, from the black day when they first entered Europe, the one great antihuman specimen of humanity. Wherever they went, a broad line of blood marked the track behind them; and, as far as their dominion reached, civilisation disappeared from view. They represented everywhere government by force, as opposed to government by law.[96]

In this excerpt, a very extreme language of marginalising Islam and the Ottoman/Turkish culture hence went beyond the criticisms of a suppressor government. The Ottoman case, in Gladstone's terms, was a combination of religious and racial offences against humanity. He, in other respects, presented the

---

94 Newman, *History of the Turks*, 74
95 Pattison, *The Great Dissent*, 181–185.
96 Right Hone W. E. Gladstone, *Bulgarian Horrors and the Question of the East* (London: J. Murray, 1876), 9.

known European viewpoint in favour of the self-determination principle, the fundamental right that Balkan nations possessed against the unjust Ottoman government.

In contrast to these arguments, a number of romantic scholars in the 19th century reflected on more positive aspects of the Ottomans. They firmly refuted the prejudgments found in Montesquieu's oriental despotism and in the subsequent romantic mainstream. By way of example, Alphonse de Lamartine stated that Islam could not be a motive for the Eastern despotism because the Ottomans/Turks were a tolerant culture.[97] Unlike the fierce opposition to Islamic civilisation seen so far, he claimed that the authentic Turkish culture was compatible with European civic values. Pierre Loti similarly questioned the traditional marginalisation of the Ottomans in religious terms, and further claimed that Turkish culture had superiorities over European values in certain instances. Despite the general emphasis on Eastern despotism, he concluded that the adoption of European political systems by the Ottoman Empire would dilute its cultural cosmos.[98] In this, he contrasted with the romantic thinkers of the 19th century, who largely implied that the Ottoman Empire should be aligned with European values by means of the colonial Western European powers.[99]

In a similar vein, Gerard Nerval, in his book entitled 'Voyage en Orient', pointed out the civic characteristics emanating from Ottoman culture. He, in one instance, compared the forms of slavery in the Ottoman Empire and European colonies and concluded that the former system was more humane.[100] He also proposed to comprehend social life under Ottoman rule with its own contexts, as people of Orient were not raised in the same conditions of their Western contemporaries, and under Ottoman despotism they had not any awareness to lay claim to their inherent rights:

> in order to understand the influence of despotism in the Eastern political life, you need to know these people ... if you slash them they ignore if you have this right ... but you show your pride, and you assume a great attitude that affects their simplicity. The East never questions: everything is possible.[101]

---

97 Alphonse de Lamartine, *A Pilgrimage to the Holy Land, Comprising, Recollections, Sketches, and Reflections, Made During a Tour in the East in 1832–1833, Volume 2* (London: Rayner and Hodges, 1835), 30.
98 Ibid., 52.
99 Hélène de Burgh, *Sex, Sailors and Colonies: Narratives of Ambiguity in the Works of Pierre Loti* (Bern: Peter Lang, 2005), 144.
100 Nerval, *Voyage en Orient*, 154, 352–353.
101 Ibid., 309.

Nerval questioned the influences of Eastern despotism on its people, observing a strict relationship between the Ottoman despotism and human behaviour in social life. In this, he adhered to the scholarship characterising the Ottoman Empire in political terms, instead of the other constructions merely structured by religion and geography. Likewise, Anquetil Dupperron drew political conclusions about the nature of Ottoman social life. He took a stand against Montesquieu's view that Eastern societies were lawless and lacked property rights. Based on observations from his journey to the Eastern geography, he wrote that property rights and the rule of law were common points with the West.[102] British diplomat James Porter added to this viewpoint that the Koran was a source of law restricting the Ottoman despotism and it provided the background of the rule of law.[103] The *Ulema*, the group of scholars responsible for the compatibility of the Sultan's decrees with the Koran, had the mediating function between the commons and political authority.[104] Porter then brought the Ottoman Empire's backwardness into focus, again with political explanations: 'Turks have laws to regulate property, and secure commerce ... It is not the Turkish law, but the corrupt administration, the flagitious venality of the judges'.[105]

In brief, European diplomacy and literature in the 18th and 19th centuries, at a time impacted by colonialism and political movements across Western Europe, featured a repertoire of ways to define the Ottoman Empire, as 'European civilisation' and 'Ottoman despotism' were products of a changing terminology. Yet, although the common inclination was debating the Ottomans in civic terms, the diplomatic and scholarly sources retained tensions about the nature of the Ottoman despotism. In foreign affairs, the slow disintegration of the Ottoman Empire in the face of Russian aggression led Western European powers to reproduce Ottoman images with a rational and secular foreign policy motivated by their interests in the European balance of power and the emerging colonial system. As a consequence, Western European powers proclaimed the Ottoman Empire to be European for a brief while. In literature, on the other hand, intellectuals revealed their diverse misgivings about the Ottoman Empire's compatibility with Europe in political, geographical, religious, and, sometimes, ethnic terms. They also subscribed to the colonialist rhetorics of their home countries

---

102 F. Whelan, 'Oriental Despotism: Anquetil-Duperron's Response to Montesquieu', *History of Political Thought* 22, no.4 (2001): 619–647.
103 James Porter, *Turkey: Its History and Progress* (London: Hurst and Blackett Publishers, 1854), 257.
104 Lock, *Edmund Burke*, 172.
105 Porter, *Turkey*, 256–257.

while discussing the Ottomans.¹⁰⁶ In diplomacy and literature, the modernisation attempts of the Empire, including the improvements in administrative and minority affairs, became increasingly relevant. In other words, the Ottoman/Turkish modernisation was the common concept between European descriptions of Turkey at different times of history. In the following century, the trend of practically approaching the Ottoman Empire and modern Turkey with a broad terminology remained, and in this state of affairs, Turkey's modernisation venture always had a significant value.

Ottoman/Turkish Modernisation in the Eyes of Europeans

The modernisation venture from the late Ottoman age was critical to the changing Ottoman/Turkish image in Europe. The textual examples from the 18th and 19th centuries given above were comments on a slowly disintegrating empire. The Porte then went to take a series of measures to avert its ultimate destruction. Most of these measures fell into the attempts to modernise the Ottoman administration. At the outset, the Western influence on the Ottomans was visible in military and early industrial artisanship.¹⁰⁷ Against the Russian march into South in the 18th and 19th centuries, the Ottoman modernisation had to turn to military reforms.¹⁰⁸ Military personnel were systematically sent to France, where they acquired the revolutionary norms of 19th century Europe. The Ottoman civil bureaucracy also acquired a European education, and especially the Ottoman official translators received foreign degrees. Eventually, European knowledge proved important to the civil and military bureaucracy, who considered the western way of modernisation to be the key to saving the Empire.¹⁰⁹

The following *Tanzimat* (reform) era lasted in a period from the *Tanzimat* Act (1939) on the recognition of civil rights to the Empire's first constitution (1876), which introduced a legislative assembly to Ottoman governance. The reforms undertaken in this era impacted on bureaucratic and governmental traditions of the Empire and bestowed certain rights on citizens, including non-Muslims. Europeans in return questioned these novelties' implications and their effects on the

---

106 Said, *Orientalism*, 240–241.
107 Inalcik, *Turkey and Europe*, 145.
108 *The Annual Register, or a View of the History, Politics, and Literature of the Year 1826* (London: Pater-noster-row Press, 1827), 353.
109 Donald Quataert, *The Ottoman Empire: 1700–1922* (New York: Cambridge University Press, 2005), 62–63.

quality of minority lives. On the declaration of the new penal code in 1840, the British news media stated:

> A penal code has since been published; but what is a book of law without men to enforce it? and whence are these men to come? From the barbarous clans who occupy the Ottoman provinces, and who scarcely know what law and government mean? or from the corrupt habitues of the old system?[110]

The rationale of Ottoman bureaucrats was primarily to improve the corrupt state institutions and minority rights according to European political standards and therefore to secure the recognition and protection of the Empire's territorial integrity by its European allies. In 1856, through the same ambition, the Sublime Porte released the Reform Act, which gave preliminary social and political rights to religious minorities. The Act was seen as indispensable in the run-up to the Paris Peace Conference held the same year, the gathering of European actors on whether to take action against the Russian invasion in Ottoman territories. The Ottoman country in the end was recognised as a European power and part of European law.[111] In the subsequent decades, the Ottomans gave further political rights to minorities and diplomatic-commercial privileges to Europeans to maintain their 'privileged' position in Europe.[112] In this regard, the modernisers of the late 19th century, like Tevfik Fikret and Abdullah Cevdet, understood replicating European powers to be the sole means to Ottoman survival.[113]

Among the modernisation attempts, the Ottoman bureaucrats first intended to underpin the conception of 'Ottomanism' with certain rights of Ottoman subjects, which were salient in the Reform Act and Paris Peace Conference in 1856.[114] This initial term had involved the equality and solidarity between Ottoman subjects preserved by the law regardless of religious differences. As this strategy failed and the non-Muslim minorities in the Ottoman Balkans continued to secede from the Empire, modernisers sought to bring some core values forward. The Berlin Peace Treaty (1878) concluding the last Turco-Russian war before the turn of the 20th century, which resulted in massive territorial losses in Bal-

---

110 'The Turkish Empire', *Spectator*, November 28, 1840, 13.
111 Augustus Oakes and R. B. Mowat, eds., *The Great European Treaties of the Nineteenth Century* (London: Oxford University Press, 1918), 158.
112 Ibid., 159
113 Stanford J. Shaw and Ezel Kural Shaw, *History of the Ottoman Empire and Modern Turkey, Volume II: Reform, Revolution, and Republic, The Rise of Modern Turkey 1808–1975* (New York: Cambridge University Press, 1977), 305; Lewis, The Emergence of Modern Turkey, 235–237.
114 Kemal Karpat, *The Politicization of Islam: Reconstructing Identity, State, Faith, and Community in the Late Ottoman State* (New York: Oxford University Press, 2001), 12.

kans, was a turning event, after which the Ottomans resorted to the essentialist definitions of the Ottoman society that were Islam and Turkish ethnicity. After 1878, Sultan Abdulhamid officially employed his Caliphate status and the policies of pan-Islamism to keep the remaining Ottoman territory as a whole.[115] This also meant the abolition of some Western-type political institutions, including the constitution, by the Sultan, although massive bureaucratisation continued. The breakdown of Abdulhamid and the re-establishment of the Constitution in 1908 led to the final era of the Empire under the tutelage of civil and military bureaucrats. The new authority instituted policies to nationalise Ottoman subjects in tandem with the typical evolution of European nation states.[116] The Young Turk political movement, which mobilised themselves under the Committee for Union and Progress (CUP) and seized power in 1908, found a territorially shrinking empire with a densely Turkish population.[117] On gaining independence from the Ottomans, the new Balkan countries had ousted millions of Muslims. The flow of Turks to Anatolia was so immense that when the World War began, at least one-fourth of the population in the country were Balkan immigrants.[118] Therefore, the 'European Turkey' mentioned by Adolphus Slade a century ago had almost entirely disappeared, and Anatolia with Eastern Thrace remained the land of the Turks. Under changing conditions, Young Turks adopted a particular nationalistic vision by shifting the state's emphasis from Turkishness to Turkism.[119] Their enterprise was a modernisation with the goal of a secular nation state, rather than imperial cosmopolitanism. August Compte's positivism, which saw scientific progress as the key to modern civilisation, influenced theorists such as Ahmed Riza, and Young Turks considered technical achievements to be more important than Western lifestyle, unlike the view of scholars of the *Tanzimat* period. In particular, Ziya Gökalp, the pioneer theoretician of the movement, was suggesting a modernist drift from Ottoman traditions to European nation states, but not in cultural terms.[120] The CUP in this direction partially ex-

---

115 Ibid., 12–13; Quataert, *The Ottoman Empire*, 68.
116 Stefan Berger and A. Miller, 'Nation-Building and Regional Integration, C. 1800–1914: The Role of Empires', *European Review of History: Revue Europeenne d'Historie* 15, no.3 (June 2008): 318.
117 Ibid., 320–321; Eric Zürcher, *The Young Turk Legacy and Nation Building* (London: Tauris, 2010), 118–120; Suraiya Faroqhi, *Geschichte des Osmanischen Reiches* (Munich: C.H. Beck Verlag, 2000), 106–107.
118 Hale, *Turkish Foreign Policy*, 11; Eric Zürcher, *Turkey: A Modern History* (London: Tauris, 2004), 117; Rogers Brubaker, *Nationalism Refrained: Nationhood and the National Question in the New Europe* (Cambridge: Cambridge University Press, 1996), 152–153.
119 Kemal Karpat, *The Politicization of Islam*, 356.
120 Lewis, *The Emergence of Modern Turkey*, 231; Inalcik, *Turkey and Europe*, 145.

cluded the sultanate from state affairs, de-religionised Turkish politics, further modernised bureaucracy, and therefore paved the way for modern Turkey. However, the Young Turk years also stood for military dominance over politics, which was justified by wartime conditions – the Ottoman participation in the Great War.[121] An ultra-nationalist, secular, and totalitarian modernisation at the hands of the Turkish officers came to the forefront. The CUP's modernisation enterprise even turned out to bring unfavourable consequences for non-Muslim minorities in Anatolia and met with serious condemnation at the European level. In particular, the incident resulting in the vast massacre of Armenian subjects under the Ottoman Realm from 1915 was, and still is, condemned by the European Union as the Armenian Genocide.

The Ottoman state's reorganisation according to Turkism had a price to pay for the minorities. Towards the final breakdown of the Ottoman Empire, Europeans held the Turks solely responsible for the growing atrocities between ethnicities in the region. According to Europeans, ethnic conflicts and the unjust governance of the CUP regime had made Western intervention a necessary outcome. To take one example, British historian William Miller wrote in 1913, two years before the Armenian tragedy:

> most races, emancipated from the Turks, become discontented when they had time to forget the great evil of Turkish rule. A generation ... which does not remember the joy of the British flag was welcomed there. Education has made Christians more inclined to regard the British occupation.[122]

British historian J.A.R. Mariott similarly wrote in 1917, before the complete fall of Ottomans: 'If it be true that in its dealings with the Near East Western Europe has in the past exhibited a brutal and callous selfishness, the Near East is indeed avenged.'[123] In the eyes of most Europeans, after all these centuries of tyranny, the Ottomans deserved their defeat at the end of the Great War. Europeans then also utilised the allegations directed at the Ottoman Government in order to sustain their interventions in the East.[124] The Allies of the Great War were exchanging letters, for one example, about 'the setting free of the populations subject to the bloody tyranny of the Turks; and the turning out of Europe of the Otto-

---

[121] Quataert, *The Ottoman Empire*, 65.
[122] M. A. Miller, *The Ottoman Empire: 1801–1913* (Cambridge: Cambridge University Press, 1913), 469.
[123] Mariott, *The Eastern Question*, 17.
[124] Ibid., 442.

man Empire as decidedly foreign to Western civilisation'.[125] Therefore, the minority issues in Anatolia had provoked furious backlashes similar to the late 19th century claims against the Ottoman rule in Balkans. Amidst these allegations, the Ottomans lost the World War to the allied powers of Western Europe. As Mariott remarked, the Eastern question would yet remain unresolved as long as the Turkish rule in the Balkans and Near East continued.[126]

Then the Turkish modernisation took a new form in a completely revolutionary spirit. As the Ottoman Empire was breathing its last, a Turkish general named Mustafa Kemal (Ataturk) mobilised a number of military and civil bureaucrats and met the post-War European occupiers. In 1920, the Sublime Porte accepted the Treaty of Sevres, which de-facto ended the Ottoman sovereignty. Montesquieu had proclaimed in his 'Persian Letters' (1721) that the despotic empire would be conquered in less than two centuries.[127] Indeed, the empire was coming to an end in 1920. Comparable to the Treaty of Versailles concluding the war with Germany, the Peace Treaty of Sevres was a death sentence for the Ottomans.[128] In truth, the Porte was aiming at a British guarantee of its survival, as it had sought to ensure its territorial integrity with a similar alliance a century ago. The Empire had to surrender its sovereignty this time. A novel movement upheld by Ottoman civil and military bureaucrats, called the 'Kemalists', then defied this draconian decree and waged a series of battles, at the end of which the Lausanne Peace Treaty (1923) was signed. With this final treaty, the European approach to Turkey drastically changed. As an example, a British Journal announced the authorisation of Lord Curzon to discuss the peace terms with Turkey at the Lausanne Conference: 'he represents the views of the vast majority of Englishmen who are not indeed anti-Turkish but who dread the return of the Turkish influences to countries which have been relieved of them.'[129] After the centuries of Ottoman withdrawal, a preoccupation with the return of Turkish influence to Eastern Europe was entirely novel for Europeans. The media was also tolerant when categorising modern Turkey. The new American Journal *Time*, during the negotiations in Lausanne, acclaimed 'the emancipation of Turkey' through its headline featuring the portrait of Mustafa Kemal. It implied: '(he) is one of the great figures in contemporary history. He stands now against the

---

125 Correspondence between the Allies to the US President Woodrow Wilson, January 10, 1917, cited in Mariott, *The Eastern Question*, 442.
126 Ibid., 443–444.
127 Montesquieu, *Persian Letters*.
128 Lewis, *The Emergence of Modern Turkey*, 247.
129 'Lord Curzon's Mission', *The Spectator*, September 22, 1922, 5.

forces of Western civilisation, determined to hold what Turkey has won.'[130] The Lausanne Treaty and the foundation of the Republic opened a new era of Turkish modernisation that received highly benign reactions at that moment. As the subsequent sections will demonstrate, however, this era would additionally come in for critical remarks much later, during Turkey's candidature for European Union membership.

Although the Ottoman Empire had officially ceased to exist and the power of the Young Turks had also come to an end with the foundation of modern Turkey, most of the bureaucrats from the late Ottoman years continued in their positions in the early Republic. A study estimates that 93% of the military bureaucracy and 85% of the civil bureaucracy of the late Ottoman state continued in early modern Turkey.[131] The republican ideology therefore took hold of these bureaucratic cadres under the leadership of Ataturk. The abolition of the Sultanate in 1922 was followed by the foundation of the Republic the next year. The building of Modern Turkey started with the abolition of the caliphate, the Act on the Unification of Education, and the new constitution in 1924, to which the principle of laicism was introduced in 1927. Turkish social life further modernised with novelties including the Swiss-inherited civil law (1926), the revolution in the writing system (1928), and women's suffrage (1930). The Europeans noted all these attempts with sympathy. To mention one example, a French observer, Berthe Georges Gaulis, wrote in 1924: 'Turkish action will remain in history as a kind of prodigy accomplished in a superhuman exaltation'.[132] Although the new political regime was not a democracy in current terms, it was bound up with a constitution and parliament. It was still a kind of dictatorship, Arnold Toynbee stated, but a kind that progressively aimed at the modernisation of Turkish nation through European values.[133]

It was mentioned earlier that the Ottoman/Turkish bureaucrats equated modernisation with westernisation, which entailed a process of interiorising the Western-European institutions of political and social life. Ataturk was no different in seeking to connect Turkish modernism to the common values of Euro-

---

[130] Time, 'Mustafa Kemal Pasha', *Time* 1, no.4, March 24, 1923.
[131] Dankwart A. Rustow, 'The Military: Turkey', in *Political Modernization in Japan and Turkey*, eds. Robert E. Ward and Dankwart Rustow (Princeton: Princeton University Press, 1964), 388.
[132] Berthe Georges Gaulis, *La Nouvelle Turquie* (Paris: Colin, 1924), 271, cited in Turhan Feyzioglu *Un Libérateur et Un Modernisateur Génial: Kemal Atatürk* (Ankara: Centre des Recherches Atatürk, 1987), 109.
[133] Arnold Toynbee, *A Study of History: Volume I: Abridgement of Volumes 1–6 by D. C. Sommerwell* (New York: Oxford University Press, 1947), 519.

pean civilisation.¹³⁴ European scholars in return welcomed the western legislative traditions introduced to Turkey.¹³⁵ Granting women's rights perhaps was one of the most extraordinary cases.¹³⁶ In her book entitled 'Turkey: Today'(1928), for instance, British journalist Grace Ellison enthusiastically backed the 'liberation of women' by the new Turkish regime.¹³⁷ Toynbee wrote in 1938 about the new Republic that 'this Turkish people's strength has been doubled by the emancipation of the women'.¹³⁸ Indeed, women in Turkey now was highly empowered in the family and public life, compared even to some of their Western contemporaries.¹³⁹ Alfred Lyttelton wrote: 'What this may eventually mean to Europe is … the spectacle of an Eastern nation slowly being transmuted into a Western one with the help of its women.'¹⁴⁰ In brief, Europeans had begun to characterise modern Turkey with the rights and freedoms that the new regime granted to its society.

Next to the developments within the country, western narratives concerning modern Turkey in the 20th century were less subjective than 19th-century orientalism. The American literature had a role in this. With the weakening of British and French colonial powers, the US rose to fill the power vacuum in international affairs. Analysing the East still continued to be the prime rationale in the age of the Atlantic supremacy. Scientific scholarship improved, and area studies became distinguished thanks to American expertise.¹⁴¹ Then, especially in the second half of the 20th century, the Western intellectual view of Islam and the East gained a highly academic character. Although the Anglo-Saxon academic language about the new Turkish regime was by no means uniform, scholars largely approved of Turkey's modernisation attempts. In their common view, the country's Islamic traditions formed barriers within its modernisation path. To Alexander Rosskeen Gibb, the seminal historian on Orientalism, Islamic society did not develop challenging practices against dominant theological institutions, unlike the Western case. Islam did not raise rational individuals that could rea-

---

134 Lewis, *The Emergence of Modern Turkey*, 267.
135 Faroqhi, *Approaching Ottoman History*, 209.
136 Francess Ruth Woodsmall, *Women in the Changing Islamic System* (Delhi: Bilma Publishing House, 1936), 254, 406; Reina Lewis, *Rethinking Orientalism: Women, Travel, and the Ottoman Harem* (Rutgers University Press, 2004), 50–51.
137 Ibid., 42–43.
138 Arnold Toynbee, 'The Savior of Turkey', *The Spectator*, November 18, 1938, 18.
139 Jenny, B. White, 'State Feminism, Modernization, and the Turkish Republican Woman', *NWSA Journal* 15, no.3 Gender and Modernism between the Wars, 1918–1939 (Autumn, 2003): 145–159.
140 Alfred Lyttelton, 'Women at Istanbul', *The Spectator*, May 2, 1935, 11.
141 Zachary, *Contending Visions of Middle East*, 111.

son 'in scientific terms'.[142] Therefore, Islamic communities like Turkey had to realise cultural revolutions embracing human rationality in order to reach the western level of development.[143] Bernard Lewis also stated that the Islamic culture was distinct from Western values in that it was submissive to authoritarianism in character.[144] In parallel, Toynbee was advocating European influences over the East and giving time to Turkey for a gradual change. After all, they assumed, it was not plausible to embrace European civilisation straight away.[145]

Between all these approaches the common point was that Islamic countries in the East lacked institutions that could prompt the rational development of society. The Turkish secular modernisation, commonly acknowledged as a transition from Islamic traditions to European institutions, was becoming a highly fascinating case for the academics. To Lerner, the changing cultural milieu in Turkey was a sign of the successful application of classical modernisation methods.[146] To Lewis, Ataturk's modernisation project was essentially the familiar European path to prosperity.[147] Toynbee similarly claimed Ataturk's plan 'to extricate the Turkish nation from the ruins of the Ottoman Empire, and to set this nation on its feet again by putting it through a 'totalitarian' conversion from a hereditary Islamic to a new-fangled Western way of life.'[148]

To put the early 20th century in a nutshell, the Turkish modernisation played the most significant role in the radical transition to a just, sovereign Turkish state. Owing to the republican part of this reformation period, Turkey could break free from the limits imposed by its earlier image of Ottoman despotism in Europe. Advancements in objective historiography and area studies additionally took a part in the changing European narrative about Turkey. The country's modernisation continued after the death of Ataturk, but later policies and perceptions on modern Turkey were rather shaped by external factors, such as the waning Western European colonialism and the increasing Soviet aggression. Following the Second World War, the Turkish nation state took a stand on the Western side of the Cold War geography and aligned itself with the emerging European institutions, with which the next chapter deals.

---

142 Hamilton A. R. Gibb, *Studies on the Civilization of Islam* (Boston: Beacon Press, 1968), 192.
143 Lockman, *Contending Visions of the Middle East*, 119. Said, *Orientalism*, 117.
144 Lockman, *Contending Visions of the Middle East*, 133.
145 Elie Kedourie, 'Islam and Orientalists: Some Recent Discussions', *The British Journal of Sociology* 7, no.3 (Sep. 1956): 223, doi:10.2307/587993.
146 Zachary, *Contending Visions of Middle East*, 139.
147 Lewis, *The Emergence of Modern Turkey*, 291, 267–268.
148 Toynbee, *The Savior of Turkey*, 18.

3 Relations between Europe and Turkey in Contemporary History

Following the long, turbulent period of Europe's state of affairs with the disintegrating Ottoman Empire, the 20th century witnessed two important phenomena changing the pace of the relations between two camps, on which the previous chapter remarked. First, a group of the Ottoman civil and military bureaucracy sworn to advance the late Ottoman modernisation founded the Turkish Republic and progressively adopted part of European political and civic values led by republican and secular principles. The republican turn by the Kemalist bureaucratic movement within the Ottoman/Turkish modernisation venture played a big part in positively shifting the Turkish image in Europe. Second, the decline of colonialist Western Europe and the rise of the Soviet Union in the global power struggle rendered modern Turkey critical to the West in security terms. Under these conditions, and in the Cold War's shadow, the official relationship between Turkey and the European Union began. The third chapter explores European attitudes towards the country in the second half of the 20th century, during the transition to the European Union.

It wouldn't be wrong to assume that the striking 'other' of Europe was the Soviet Union for most of the 20th century. In addition, Europeans marginalised extreme nationalist movements in a new political context following the Second World War (WWII). Turkey, in the meantime, categorically corresponded to neither of these types; if anything, it emerged as an important security partner of Europe. The Russian expansion in the 19th century had caused the erstwhile Eastern Question. A century later, the rise of the Soviet threat was rendering Turkey's geography vital, in the eyes of the Europeans, in security terms. Turkey was then being conceptualised primarily in the light of its security contribution to the Western faction of the Cold War. The country was a founding member of the United Nations (1945), and in the face of the emerging Soviet threat it chose to align its regime (and its economy) with the United States and Western Europe, as it embraced a multiparty system (1946) and joined the Council of Europe (1949) and the North Atlantic Treaty Organisation (1952). US statesmen considered Turkey essential for the security architecture of the Middle East.[1] In 1956, *Life* magazine commended the country as 'the most modernised of the old nations in the

---

[1] Melvyn P. Leffler, 'Strategy, Diplomacy, and the Cold War: The United States, Turkey, and NATO, 1945–1952', *The Journal of American History* 71, no.4 (1985): 807–825, doi:10.2307/1888505.

Middle East. It is a member in NATO and, because there is no record of colonialism but a substantial record of U.S. aid, Turkey is the best Middle Eastern friend'.[2] With this rationale, the US had inaugurated the Marshall Plan to help European countries recover from war-time structural losses, and included Turkey within this group. The Organisation for European Economic Cooperation, the framework for the distribution of Marshall aids, additionally involved Turkey as a European country. It was later reformed to an institutional version named the Organisation for Economic Cooperation and Development with the European founding countries inclusive of Turkey. The country also co-initiated the Conference for Security and Cooperation in Europe, in 1973, to deal with security and conflict matters, human rights promotion, and democratic consolidation. In parallel, in 1959, Turkey acknowledged the European Court of Human Rights (ECHR), the Council of Europe's judicial division, and agreed to its jurisdictions on human rights violations committed by states against individuals – until 2016 the country was found guilty of human rights offences in 16% of the entire ECHR judgments.[3]

If Turkish history in the 20th century featured the country's swift orientation towards Western standards in political and legal terms, it also witnessed a number of structural issues emanating from the country's transition. These instabilities fall within Turkey's democratic deficits and its tensions with its neighbours, which the institutions of the European Union broadly address today. The present chapter does not explain them in detail but pinpoints the historical connections between the country's modernisation and European criticisms of contemporary Turkey. These issues can be listed as authoritarianism and illiberal practices observed in the fields of civil-military relations, Islamisation of politics, implementations of minority rights, and, in addition, problems related to international politics, particularly Turkey's relationship with Greece, Armenia, and Cyprus.[4]

To begin with civil-military relations, it is common to link the transformation of Turkish military and civil bureaucracy to the Ottoman modernisation from the 19th century.[5] As illustrated in the previous chapter with a number of examples,

---

[2] 'A Prized Area Divided Within, Beset from without and Jealous of its Own Heritage', *Life*, March 26, 1956, 23.
[3] See, 'Overview ECHR 1959–2016', European Court of Human Rights Public Relations Unit, March 2017, available from www.echr.coe.int/Documents/Overview_19592016_ENG.pdf (12.08.2017).
[4] Meltem Muftuler-Bac, 'The Never-Ending Story: Turkey and the European Union', *Middle Eastern Studies* 34, no.4 (October 1998): 240–258, http://www.jstor.org/stable/4283976.
[5] Handan Nezir Akmese, *The Birth of Modern Turkey: The Ottoman Military and the March to WWI* (New York: Tauris, 2005), 1–9; Richard L. Chambers, 'The Civil Bureaucracy: Turkey' in *Po-*

modernisation in the late Ottoman Empire normally stands for the policies to partially liberalise social and political life of the Ottomans, as well as the attempts to recruit a mass bureaucracy in civil and military affairs. From the second half of the 19th century, in an empire territorially shrinking and being home to fewer and fewer minorities, the burgeoning bureaucratic cadres mostly adhered to the nascent Turkish nationalism and increasingly interfered in governmental affairs. The military-dominated governments of the Community of Union and Progress (CUP) were even reportedly involved in criminal activities against ethnic minorities during the Empire's final years. The Armenian issue, the deportation and eventual ethnic cleansing of a massive number of Armenian subjects after 1915, remained the most severe case of the years of the CUP's power. From the late 20th century many western countries in their national parliaments recognised the event as genocide, and the European Parliament also asked Turkey to face up to this tragic event, henceforth the 'Armenian Genocide', for the first time in 1987.[6]

Although the new Turkish Republic forbade military officers to participate in politics, and even Mustafa Kemal Ataturk officially set his military role aside during his presidential office, in the following period the removal of the military bureaucracy from civil politics was only partially achieved. The military bureaucracy emerged or 'took responsibility' throughout the 20th century when it deemed the secular-republican regime to be in question. Turkish history witnessed several military coups, as a result of which officers seized political power in 1960 and 1980, or coerced civil governments into resigning in 1971 and 1997.[7] Sources acknowledge the military to have attempted to dominate civil politics in 2007, one final time, to put pressure on the parliament before it elected a new president.[8] Among these instances, in 1997 and 2007 the Turkish armed forces had defied the authority of political parties representing the Islamic

---

litical Modernization in Japan and Turkey, eds. Robert E. Ward and Dankwart Rustow (Princeton: Princeton University Press, 1964), 301–327; Dankwart A. Rustow, 'The Military: Turkey', in *Political Modernization*, eds. Ward and Rustow, 352–388.

6 See The European Parliament, Resolution on a Political Solution to the Armenian Question, Official Journal of the European Communities, Doc. A2, July 7, 1987, 33/87.

7 In 1997, the chief generals of the Turkish armed forces asked the prime minister to resign, in an ordinary gathering of the National Security Council, and caused a change of government. Ever since, it has generally been acknowledged as a military intervention. For example, see Erik Zurcher's usage of 'military interference', Erik J. Zurcher, *Turkey: A Modern History* (London and New York: I.B. Tauris, 2007), 300–301.

8 See the pertinent comments given by the European Parliament or its deputies in the next chapter.

legacy of Turkish society, to regulate politics in favour of the secular regime.⁹ As an overall response, the dichotomy in the civil-military relationship always remained a subject of criticism by the European Union and its political camps, as the military tutelage introduced with the 1980 takeover had led to a halt in relations throughout the accession process.

Second, the public and political representations of religions and the freedom of belief in society came to light as contested subjects in modern Turkey. Kemalist bureaucrats had to confront the religious legacy of Turkish society in order to dismantle the Islamic state tradition, which stirred debates as early as the first years of the republic. Sir Evelyn Wrench wrote of the 'Godless Turkish country', in 1935: 'I wondered if Ataturk ever has time to think of the spiritual future of his people … Ataturk is not the first, nor will he be the last, who has sought to create a civilisation in which there is no place for God, but the divine spark in man cannot be thus easily quenched.'¹⁰ These structural disagreements between the religious legacy of the Ottoman/Turkish society and Turkish modernizers surfaced with the transition to a fully multi-party system, as electoral behaviours became exposed to the influences of political camps standing for traditional values of society from the first multi-party election in 1946. In some contemporary instances, European public opinion affirmed religious representations in politics to contribute to Turkey's liberalisation. During the 2000s, Turkish political elites revolutionised the use of religious symbols in public and politics, and they famously removed the headscarf ban for women in public institutions. In return, Europeans at first credited these practices with continuing modernisation. Nevertheless, when Turkish statesmen systematically resorted to Sunni Islam to legitimise their growing authoritarianism in the following period, the EU began to question the Islamisation of Turkish politics and regarded this as a rather novel problem of Turkey. In brief, tensions between different approaches to religious representation and freedom of belief (e.g. secular, liberal, Sunni-Islamist) have marked Turkish contemporary history and have been equally observed by Europeans.¹¹

The third issue that originated in Turkey's modernisation course was the problematic representation of minorities and minority rights. As mentioned above, the classical Ottoman regional governance was based on the *Millet* system, the administration of religious groups through local laws,¹² in which

---

9 Gareth Jenkins, 'Continuity and Change: Prospects for Civil-Military Relations in Turkey', *International Affairs* 83, no. 2 (2007): 339–355, https://doi.org/10.1111/j.1468-2346.2007.00622.x.
10 Evelyn Wrench, 'A Country Without God', *The Spectator*, November 22, 1935, 8.
11 Carter Vaughn Findley, Turkey, *Islam, Nationalism, and Modernity: A History, 1789–2007* (New Haven and London: Yale University Press, 2010), 418–421.
12 Hale, *Turkish Foreign Policy*, 15–16. Davison, *Essays in Ottoman and Turkish History*, 103.

'Turk' was a term of a broader usage that encompassed the Muslim ethnic groups. In the Treaty of Lausanne (1923), which officially concluded the World War and the subsequent war with Turkey, and also recognised the new Turkish authority, the tradition of limiting minorities to non-Muslim groups was maintained. Other ethnic groups were considered 'Turkish'; however, later these groups began efforts to develop their own their identities. The ethnic group that is best known for long-term identity struggle and insurgency is the Kurds, as they engaged in various armed and unarmed campaigns from the early 1920s. Despite the high election threshold, they could also represent their community in the Turkish Parliament, particularly from the 1990s. The religious *Alevi* minority as a faith community distinct from the dominant Sunni belief also continued their strife for the acquisition of religious rights, including their own supreme institution for religious affairs. The representations of the ethnic Kurdish and religious *Alevi* minorities consequently remained on the EU's agenda of debating Turkish democracy and its compatibility with Europe.

Fourth, the issues that emanated from Turkey's relations with its neighbourhood, i.e. conflicts with Greece and Cyprus, are not directly connected with Turkey's modernisation attempts. Still, they are major issues concerning the country's relationship with the European Union during its candidature and have historical causes. The conflict in Cyprus can be traced back to the late 19th century, when the British Empire had taken it over as a protectorate, in a secret agreement with the Ottomans in 1878, in return for its support for Ottoman territorial integrity in Balkans against Russian aggression. Britain annexed the island in 1914 when the Ottomans entered the World War against the Allied powers. As a consequence of declining British colonialism, the British transferred the authority to the joint administration of local Greeks and Turks established in 1960. However, the British withdrawal added to the existing tensions between the two communities. Turkey, one of the guarantors according to the founding agreements signed in 1960, unilaterally intervened in the conflicts and twice landed soldiers on the island in 1974. Although the international community generally regarded the first operation as legal, the second one stretching the occupied territory drew strong reactions and an US-invoked embargo on Turkey.[13] Today, the island is still divided, although Cyprus under the Greek authority joined the EU in 2004. The borderline between the Greek and Turkish Cypriot ter-

---

[13] Fiona B. Adamson 'Democratization and the Domestic Sources of Foreign Policy: Turkey in the 1974 Cyprus Crisis', *Political Science Quarterly* 116, no.2 (2001): 295–296, 297, doi:10.2307/798062.

ritories was recognised by the European Council as an 'interior boundary', which also signified that the island is only represented by the Greek government.[14] The EU today repeatedly calls on Turkey to recognise the Cypriot state and, on the basis of the 'good neighbourly relations' principle (one of the accession criteria stipulated to Turkey), officially raises objections to the deployment of Turkish armed forces on the island. Apart from the Cyprus issue, there are problems arising from the sea frontier between Turkey and Greece, which are mostly linked to maritime law.[15]

Today the European Union addresses these subject matters extensively. In discussing Turkey's democratic reforms in line with the accession criteria, European actors are in fact dealing with the side-effects of Turkey's long-term modernisation venture. The early period of the relationship between Turkey and the EU, which the section below discusses, did not refer to these issues systematically, not least because the European Economic Community did not have any clear political criteria for membership from its foundation (1958) until the Copenhagen Summit (1993). Still, this phase featured the critical steps the EU took to achieve European integration and materialise its accession criteria, and was also accompanied by Turkey's emerging membership prospect.

Relations between the European Union and Turkey until the 1990s

Modern Turkey adapted to the new international system after the Second World War and joined the western camp of the Cold War rivalry. In regard to its changing security policy, Turkey's relationship with the European Union, or at first the European Economic Community (EEC), was initially a practical case. In 1959, Turkey followed its Greek opponent in the Mediterranean and applied to create an association with the EEC. Relations between Europe and Turkey hence proceeded formally and gradually. At the outset, the EEC planned its partnership with Turkey to be an economic process without a clear membership perspective, sim-

---

14 The Council of the European Union, *Corrigendum to Council Regulation (EC) No 866/2004 of 29 April 2004: on a regime under Article 2 of Protocol 10 to the Act of Accession*, Official Journal of the European Union, L 161 (30.04.2004), 51.
15 The major disagreements between two countries might be grouped as the continental shelves, territorial waters, air-space related problems, and finally the legal status and armament of Greek islands. Deniz Bolukbasi, *Turkey and Greece: the Aegean Disputes: A Unique Case in International Law* (London: Cavendish Publishing, 2004), 68–69.

ilar to what it arranged as its association with Greece in 1962.[16] The Ankara Agreement (1963) named Turkey an associate, proclaimed a specified transition period to harmonise the country's economy with the EEC's common market, and its Additional Protocol (1970) set out the systemic reduction of tariffs within the process. At the end of this phase a customs union with Brussels was envisaged (the final stage reached in 1995). Economic formalities aside, the Ankara Agreement did not involve a direct reference to membership but a weak statement; in the conclusion of a successful transition process, the sides were going to 'examine the possibility of the accession of Turkey to the Community'.[17]

Initially, Turkey's vital security role oriented to the West was a stimulus for the European Economic Community to start an association with the country. It is argued elsewhere that there were few differences between the accession possibilities specified for Turkey and the other Mediterranean applicants at the beginning of their association periods.[18] In other words, the conditions until the 1970s suggested that Turkey was not estranged more than the democratically week Spain, Portugal, and Greece. Instead, some signals of convergence have been discerned between the EEC and Turkey within the context of the Cold War.[19] However, a series of developments in Turkey changed this relatively positive situation. The Turkish intervention in Cyprus in 1974 and its continuous military deployment on the island substantially damaged its image in the West. The US also turned against Turkey and laid a military and economic embargo on the country until 1978. The country's economy declined, and its international reputation faded partially, and it consequentially fell short of the developing Mediterranean countries.[20] In these decades Turkish politics also remained under the firm influence of the armed forces. By way of example, the military coup in 1980 was the biggest event in the Turkish army's intervention history and provoked a backlash from Europe. Eventually, Turkey's association with the EEC was suspended until 1986.

---

16 Thomas Diez, 'Ethical Dimension: Promises, Obligations, Impatience and Delay: Reflections on the Ethical Aspects of Turkey-EU Relations', in *Fifty Years of EU-Turkey Relations: A Sisyphean Story*, ed., Armagan Emre Cakir (Oxon: Routledge, 2011), 168.
17 The European Community, *Agreement Establishing an Association between the European Economic Community and Turkey,* (signed at 12.09.1963), Official Journal of the European Communities, vol.16.c113, December 24, 1973, 7.
18 Ziya Öniş, 'Luxembourg, Helsinki and Beyond: Towards an Interpretation of Recent Turkey-EU Relations', *Government and Opposition* 35, no.4 (2000): 467, doi: 10.1111/1477–7053.00041.
19 Atila Eralp, 'The Role of Temporality and Interaction in the Turkey-EU Relationship', *New Perspectives on Turkey*, no. 40 (2009): 151– 153, doi:10.1017/S0896634600005252.
20 Ibid., 468.

From the 1970s the European integration project took yet another turn, and the political description of Europe gradually transcended the traditional relations based on nation-states. The EEC had started off as an initiative in economic affairs, but it also had a political vision of unification. It launched its Political Cooperation aligned with a common foreign policy in 1970. Three years later, when the EEC held its first enlargement with the UK, Ireland, and Denmark, the European Commission's President Malfatti reminded that the EEC members had to 'be measured by the immense hopes that are raised by the idea of European unity'.[21] There existed a strong emphasis on the will of attaining economic integration and political union, with the strengthened term, 'political unification'. The later declarations of the European Council on identity (1973) and democracy (1978) shared the same political prospect.

The Declaration on European Identity tabled by the Copenhagen Summit was the first of the documents on European values. It argued that the EEC had to represent certain values in its relations with the countries outside. The common ground to trace or re-construct European values was marked with the terms 'common heritage' and the 'dynamic nature of the European unification'.[22] A strong language associated Europe with 'common values', the elements of which were yet unspecified. The declaration emphasised the EC's role in upholding the principles of democracy, the rule of law, social justice, and human rights. Any other European country respecting these principles would be welcomed to the integration project. Through these emphases, the nine foreign ministers of the EEC suggested a distinct European image but still something that was in close proximity to the United States in economic and security terms. Finally, the document reiterated Europe's historical connection with the Middle East and Africa emanating from its colonial period, as this relationship obliged the member states to assist countries of these regions,[23] an echo of the historical role of civilising the Orient. Five years later, the Declaration on Democracy set in another Copenhagen summit (1978) similarly stated 'the cherished values of their legal, political and moral order' with democratic principles given as repre-

---

[21] Speech by the President Malfatti, President of the European Commission, at the Signing of the Acts of Accession. Brussels, 22 January 1972. Bulletin of the European Communities, The Enlarged Community: Outcome of the Negotiations with the Applicant States, Supplement 1, 1972, 7.
[22] 'Document on the European Identity Published by the Nine Foreign Ministers, Copenhagen, 14 December 1973', European Political Cooperation Fifth Edition (Bonn: Press and Information Office, 1988), 48.
[23] Ibid., 52.

sentative democracy, the rule of law, social justice, and human rights. It pointed to the commitments of member states to democratic principles, which, additionally, indicated a set of criteria for candidates.[24] It hence made an introduction to the accession criteria: 'respect for and maintenance of representative democracy and human rights in each Member State (were) essential elements of membership in the European Communities'.[25] Finally, the wording of the declaration aimed to precede the first European Parliament directly elected by European societies. Parliamentary elections were held next year, and, thereby, European public opinion began to appear in the European political scene.

Meanwhile, Spain, Portugal, and Greece turned into parliamentary regimes and were considered eligible for the accession to the European Economic Community. Their applications collided with the EEC's objectives to further its political dimension.[26] The Community then was developing a political dimension of its foreign policy predicated on its 'common values'.[27] The idea that these countries were cultural parts of European civilisation provided a motivation for the southern enlargement. In this case, Greece's entry to the EEC had a noteworthy political significance. When the country turned its military rule into a parliamentary regime in 1974 and applied to join the EEC next year, many welcomed it on the grounds of the traditional Greek image, the ancient culture and cradle of European civilisation. The European Commission's emphasis in its recommendation report for the Greek application was striking:

> It is the first time that the European Community has been presented with an application for full membership from a country with which it already has close contractual links. This relationship is defined in the Association which was created between the EEC and Greece in 1962, covering not just trade policy but a whole series of steps that were to be undertaken to ensure Greece's progressive integration into the entire fabric of Community life. In particular, the Athens agreement was explicitly aimed at paving the way for eventual full membership ... Given the avowed aims of the Community in establishing the Association, and Greece's return to a democratic form of government, there can be no doubt, in the view

---

24 Ulrich Sedelmeier, *European Enlargement, Identity, and the Analysis of European Foreign Policy: Identity Formation through Policy Practice*, Robert Schuman Centre for Advanced Studies, no.2003/13. 2003, 10.
25 European Community, Declaration on Democracy, Bull. EC 3–1978, 6.
26 Susannah Verney, 'Justifying the Second Enlargement: Promoting interests, Consolidating Democracy or Returning to the Roots?', in *Questioning EU Enlargement: Europe in Search of Identity*, ed. Helene Sjursen (Oxon: Routledge, 2006), 29.
27 Ibid., 32.

of the Commission that the Community must now give a clear positive answer to the Greek request.²⁸

The Commission had interpreted the Association Agreement's unclear membership perspective in favour of Greek integration to the Community. In accord with the Commission's recommendation, the European Council considered the Greek membership to be an opportunity to add a new function to the EEC's political meaning. Although the Commission in fact suggested a delay, the European Council eventually ruled to start the accession negotiations with the applicant in 1976. In the absence of any clear accession criteria, the adhesion of Greece (1981), Spain, and Portugal (1985) relied merely on the territorial condition, Article 237 of the Treaty of Rome stating that any European country was capable of application for membership.²⁹

The EEC maintained its economic and political integration at a steady pace during the 1980s, at a time when Turkish politics was under firm military influence. New declarations by European bureaucrats marked this period. The Solemn Declaration on the European Union (1983) initially called on the member states to cooperate and 'to affirm the awareness of a common heritage as an element in the European identity'.³⁰ The concept 'common heritage' yet remained hollow. Two years later, the Adonnino Report recommended further action with value-bearing social symbols such as a European passport, flag and anthem, and cultural institutions and events like common visa regulations (initiated the same year through the Schengen Agreement), social programs, and Euro competitions that would play a role in building a sense of belonging.³¹ Next, the Single European Act introduced fundamental measures in 1987 in order to establish a single economic market by 1992. The single market was planned to co-occur with other political institutions including a common visa regime and European citizenship. New voting procedures additionally authorised the European Parliament in some areas in relation to the European Commission and Council of the European Union (Council of the European Community). Following the Single European Act, the Parliament's consent became essential for the ap-

---

28 Commission of European Communities, Opinion on Greek application for membership (transmitted to the Council by the Commission on 29 January 1976, Bulletin of the European Communities, no.2, February 1976, 7.
29 Verney, 'Justifying the Second Enlargement', 22.
30 European Council, *Solemn Declaration on European Union*, Bulletin of the European Communities, no.6 June 1983, 24–29.
31 Pietro Adonnino, *A People's Europe, Reports from the Ad Hoc Committee*, Bulletin of the European Communities, no.7, 1985.

proval of fundamental agreements and new members' accessions.[32] During the enlargements from the 1990s the European Parliament held the primary position along with the Council.

Meantime, Turkey was struggling to re-consolidate its democracy and improve its external image after the short but impactful military intervention. Following the end of the three-year military rule and the subsequent elections held in 1983 and 1984, the European Economic Community decided to resume the association process with Turkey in 1986. The following year, Turkey officially applied for membership. Once requested by the Council of the European Union, the European Commission's opinion (1989) was one of the first direct assessments about the country's current distance from Europe in economic and political terms. The Commission remarked on the current situation, which was not too favourable to Turkey's accession:

> In order to take an informed decision on the opening of accession negotiations, the Community will have to engage in in-depth political consideration of the implications for the architecture of an enlarged Europe and the functioning of the Community ... The Commission believes that any decision to open negotiations with a particular country must be based on a strong conviction that a positive conclusion is possible, indeed probable, within a reasonable period ... In the particular case of Turkey, these two aspects are all the more significant in that Turkey is a large country – it has a greater geographical area and will eventually have a bigger population than any Community Member State – and its general level of development is substantially lower than the European average.[33]

The European Commission thus suggested deferring any final decision on Turkey's application. Its opinion showed a picture of Turkey mostly in economic terms in tandem with the EEC's primary common market status. The EEC was accordingly in a transition process requiring a substantial capacity to accept new members, and the already-enlarged Community had to gather paces for the functioning of the single market with political institutions. A similar mention of transition would be repeated within the Commission's enlargement documents during the 2000s as the EU's 'absorption capacity' vis-à-vis the applicant countries, especially Turkey. In 1989, the European Commission was recommending that the EEC should not place Turkey on the agenda before improving its integration capacity. Had the EEC been capable of the following enlargement, Turkey would still not have been compatible with changing European standards in the short-

---

32 Christophe Crombez, 'Legislative Procedures in the European Parliament', *British Journal of Political Science* 26, no.2 (1996): 200.
33 Commission of the European Communities, Commission Opinion on Turkey's Request for Accession to the Community, SEC(89), 2290 final 1989.

run. Despite these opinions, the European Commission recommended the Council to keep its dialogue with Turkey on the level of the association process towards a customs union, which would be realized in 1996.

The EU's Political Integration and Its Accession Criteria

Following the end of the Cold War and the unification of Germany, international conditions were favourable for the European Union to internalise and uphold its political values.[34] In the early 1990s, the EU deepened its political integration on the basis of its emerging internal market; it introduced EU citizenship with certain rights and liberties, empowered the European Parliament further, and adopted the common accession criteria. The Maastricht Treaty (the Treaty on European Union – TEU), which turned the European Economic Community into the European Community (and unofficially the European Union) in 1993, became a cornerstone of political integration, as it elevated the post-national understanding of Europe through novel institutions. In parallel, the European Union set forth the admission standards with the TEU and with the Copenhagen criteria.

The TEU particularly designated the socioeconomic rights and liberties of European subjects under the title 'EU citizenship'. Former Belgian Prime Minister Leo Tindemans had proposed a common citizenship regime to his European associates in 1975.[35] The TEU put the EU citizenship into force after 18 years and made it the strength of the intended post-national political identity. Under the rights of EU citizens, the treaty re-institutionalised rights and liberties first set out by the Treaty of Rome, including the free movement of persons or Europe-wide franchise.[36] The legal ground of social integration was therefore underpinned. The Treaty of Lisbon in 2009 further consolidated the EU citizenship by updating the TEU with the Charter of Fundamental Rights, through which the offi-

---

[34] Chris Shore, 'Inventing the "People's Europe": Critical Approaches to European Community "Cultural Policy"', *Man* 28, no.4 (December 1993): 780, doi:10.2307/2803997.
[35] Considerations over a citizenship initiative through a set of communication technologies were already voiced in 1975, 'European Union must be experienced by the citizen in his daily life. It must make itself felt in education and culture, news and communications, it must be manifest in the youth of our countries, and in leisure time activities', Commission of the European Communities, European Union Report by Leo Tindemans to the European Council, Bulletin of the European Communities, Supplement 1/76, 1975.
[36] Chris Shore, *Building Europe: The Cultural Politics of European Integration* (London-New York: Routledge, 2000), 75.

cial connection between the EU citizenship and rights and liberties was strengthened.[37] The charter comprised them, under the title 'Freedoms', as a large range of norms including but not limited to the rights to liberty and security, property and private life, the freedoms of thought, conscience and religion.

In addition to EU citizenship the EU also officially attached the term 'European culture' to the European Union. Within the previous framework European culture had received fewer mentions. The Declaration on European Identity (1973), by way of example, referred to 'common heritage', as the Solemn Declaration (1983) allowed for 'cultural matters' without clarification. Correspondingly, the TEU sustained an unstructured vision of European culture with previously introduced concepts.[38] Further, the treaty encumbered member states with competencies to preserve and progress European identity and culture. According to Article 151 (former Article 128), the EU was to 'contribute to the flowering of the cultures of the Member States while respecting their national and regional diversity and at the same time bringing the common cultural heritage to the fore'[39]. The EU also put forth the new term 'respect and promotion of the diversity of cultures' in cooperation with the third countries and international organisations. Given the political institutionalisations on common citizenship and culture, Brussels was promoting a sense of post-national 'unity' through cosmopolitan traits, while acknowledging the diversity of particularistic elements in Europe.[40]

In addition to the EU citizenship and European culture, the common accession criteria for the EU's candidates for membership materialised during the 1990s under two initiatives: first, the political and territorial application conditions, and second, the Copenhagen criteria on the political and economic standards of accession. Before the TEU (1993), the European Union governed applications merely through Article 237 of the Treaty of Rome (1957), which set forth a territorial condition.[41] Meanwhile, the Copenhagen European Council (1978) had made its first reference to a common democratic ground between its members, with its Declaration on Democracy.[42] The TEU later structured the legal field

---

[37] See the Charter's Preamble, The Charter of the Fundamental Rights of the European Union, Official Journal of European Union 55, C326, 2012, 396–407.
[38] See the Declaration on European Identity and Solemn Declaration.
[39] Ronan McCrea, *Religion and Public Order in the European Union* (New York: Oxford University Press, 2010), 169.
[40] Monica Sasatelli, 'Imagined Europe: The Shaping of a European Cultural Identity Through EU Cultural Policy', *European Journal of Social Theory* 54, (2002): 439–440, 446, doi: 10.1177/ 136843102760513848.
[41] Verney, 'Justifying the Second Enlargement', 22.
[42] Peter Van Elsuwege, *From Soviet Republics to EU Member States, A Legal and Political Assessment of the Baltic States' Accession to the EU* (Leiden: Martinus Nishoff, 2008), 203–207; Chris-

of the new countries' accession and the application procedure in Article 49. The European Union presented the territorial and political conditions, together, pursuant to the TEU modified by the Treaty of Lisbon (2009):

> Any European State which respects the values referred to in Article 2 and is committed to promoting them may apply to become a member of the Union. The European Parliament and national Parliaments shall be notified of this application. The applicant State shall address its application to the Council, which shall act unanimously after consulting the Commission and after receiving the consent of the European Parliament, which shall act by a majority of its component members. The conditions of eligibility agreed upon by the European Council shall be taken into account.[43]

At first, Article 49 made a reference to the founding principles of the Union', which were enshrined in Article 2 as the 'values of the European Union'. [44] The EU's democratic, cosmopolitan principles that were previously cited in Article 6(1) thereby became 'European values' under Article 2:

> The Union is founded on the values of respect for human dignity, freedom, democracy, equality, the rule of law and respect for human rights, including the rights of persons belonging to minorities. These values are common to the Member States in a society in which pluralism, non-discrimination, tolerance, justice, solidarity and equality between women and men prevail.

European values hence covered a broad array of individual rights and liberties. Article 49 of the Treaty on European Union therefore spelled out 'Europeanness' in both territorial and political terms and also made reference to European civic values cited in Article 2.

The conditions of eligibility for accession, on the other hand, were founded as a separate document than the TEU to function as a yardstick to decide on the candidate's accession.[45] The European Copenhagen Council in 1993 officially materialised a set of political guidelines to formulate the Central and Eastern European applicants' transition to market-based democracy and eventually into accession. The Copenhagen criteria stood for the characteristics of: 'Stability of in-

---

tophe Hillion, 'The Copenhagen Criteria and their Progeny', in *EU Enlargement: A Legal Approach*, ed. Christophe Hillion (Oregon: Hart Publishing, 2004), 5.
43 Consolidated Versions of the Treaty on European Union, Official Journal of European Union 55, C326, 2012, 43.
44 The Amsterdam Treaty introduced Article 6(1), on the founding principles of the EU, to the TEU. Armin Von Bogdandy, 'Founding Principles of EU Law: A Theoretical and Doctrinal Sketch', *European Law Journal* 16, no.2 (March,2010): 96, doi: http://10.1111/j.1468–0386.2009.00500.x.
45 Hillion, 'The Copenhagen Criteria and their Progeny', 2–3.

stitutions guaranteeing democracy, the rule of law, human rights, respect for and protection of minorities, the existence of a functioning market economy, as well as the capacity to cope with the competitive pressure and market forces within the Union, and, the ability to take on obligations of membership including adherence to the aims of political, economic, and monetary Union'.[46] In addition, the Copenhagen European Council mentioned the EU's capacity to integrate new members to be 'an important consideration in the general interest of both the Union and the candidate countries'.[47] The EU's 'absorption capacity', the term famously employed in Turkey's accession context throughout the 2000s, therefore first appeared in 1993.

The political accession criteria eventually allowed the European Union to scrutinise candidate countries' democratisation. Throughout the Eastern enlargement, the European Commission made use of the Copenhagen criteria as the legal source of discussing candidates' compliance with EU legislation.[48] These conditions were never set in stone, as the concepts introduced therein were to change in time, in agreement with the EU's political and economic situation.[49] In other words, the way European elites discussed the membership candidates also depended on the European Union's current conditions.[50] An example was the EU's absorption capacity mentioned above, which was born along with the Copenhagen criteria but was not used during the Eastern European enlargement. Another example was an update to the Copenhagen criteria introduced in consequence of border problems among membership candidates and member states. The Helsinki European Council (1999), considering Turkey's problems with Greece and Cyprus and the conflicts between Balkan countries, therefore introduced a new condition entitled 'good neighbourly relations'.[51]

---

[46] Council of the European Union, Presidency Conclusions, Copenhagen European Council, 21–22 June, 1993, SN 180/1/93.
[47] Ibid.
[48] Hillion, 'The Copenhagen Criteria and their Progeny', 13–14; James Hughes, Gwendolyn Sasse, and Claire Gordon, 'Conditionality and Compliance in the EU's Eastern Enlargement: Regional Policy and Reform of Sub-National Government', *Journal of Common Market Studies* 42, no.3 (2004): 523–551, doi: http://10.1111/j.0021–9886.2004.00517.x.
[49] Heather Grabbe, 'European Union Conditionality and the "Acquis Communautaire"', *International Political Science Review / Revue Internationale De Science Politique* 23, no.3 (July 2002): 249–68, http://www.jstor.org/stable/1601310.
[50] Dimitry Kochenov. *EU Enlargement and the Failure of Conditionality*, (Kluwer Law International, 2008), 33.
[51] Constantine Arvanitopoulos, *Turkey's Accession to the European Union: An Unusual Candidacy* (Heidelberg: Springer Verlag, 2009), 112–113; Othon Anastasakis, 'The EU's Political Condi-

Throughout the Eastern enlargement that involved Central and Eastern European Countries, Malta, and Cyprus, the EU established substantial political dialogues with candidate countries based on certain financial and discursive incentives.[52] Through these close contacts, the EU provided the chief support for the CEE candidates in their transition.[53] In Turkey's case, the distance between the EU and the candidate was markedly different. With the terms of Mehmet Ugur, the already existing gap was growing from the late 1990s between Turkey being less of a credible candidate, and the EU being less keen to cooperate on admission.[54] In comparison with the Eastern enlargement, discussing Turkey's EU bid led to more ambiguous results, even with the same accession criteria.

Relations between the EU and Turkey before the Membership Negotiations

The accession of the Central and Eastern European (CEE) countries as well as Cyprus and Malta was a comprehensive process from the early 1990s, and the present section does not explain the entire period at length. Within the present identity context, the EU strived to orientate CEE countries into standardised European values with an encouraging language. Consider, for example, the association agreements the EU signed with Turkey and Poland. The Agreement signed with Turkey (1963) fundamentally aimed at 'strengthening of trade and economic relations between the Parties', as well as the prosperity of Turkish people.[55] The latter association agreement (1991) with Poland rather foresaw to achieve the 'development of close political relations between the parties' and 'an appropriate framework for Poland's gradual integration into the Community', as Article 1 stated. The document added: 'To this end, Poland shall work towards fulfilling

---

tionality in the Western Balkans: Towards a More Pragmatic Approach', *South East European and Black Sea Studies* 8, no.4 (December 2008): 368, doi:10.1080/14683850802556384.
52 Hughes, Gwendolyn, and Gordon, 'Conditionality and Compliance in the EU's Eastern Enlargement', 547–548.
53 Mehmet Ugur, *The European Union and Turkey: an Anchor/credibility Dilemma* (Aldershot Ashgate, 1999).
54 Mehmet Ugur. 'Testing Times in EU–Turkey Relations: the Road to Copenhagen and Beyond', *Journal of Southern Europe and the Balkans* 5, no.2 (2003): 165–183, http://doi.10.1080/1461319032000097923.
55 Agreement, Establishing an Association between the European Economic Community and Turkey (signed at Ankara, 12 September 1963), Official Journal of European Communities O.J. C113, December 24, 1973, 4.

the necessary conditions – to promote cooperation in cultural matters'.[56] In comparison with Turkey's association agreement centred on economic relations, the Europe Agreement signed with Poland involved a strong language favouring accession, through the concepts such as 'political dialogue', 'cultural matters', 'security and stability in the whole of Europe'.[57] In the early 1990s, the EU and almost the entirety of European politics had already acknowledged and welcomed the concept of enlarging towards Eastern Europe, as reflected by the enlargement language.[58] The European Commission had therefore proclaimed in 1990 that the principal objective for the association agreements was to integrate the Central and Eastern European countries to the European Union, whereas the European Parliament next year added that the measures should bridge the distance 'between the two halves of Europe'.[59]

The details of the relationship between the EU and Eastern European applicants are subject to further inquiry.[60] But at least three of the historically decisive Council meetings held in Luxembourg (1997), Helsinki (1999), and Copenhagen (2002) are crucial here. As a result of the applicant countries' increasing reforms, the Luxembourg European Council decided to start the accession negotiations with six of the applicant countries, the Czech Republic, Slovenia, Estonia, Hungary, Cyprus, and Poland. The second group of applicants were Malta, Bulgaria, Romania, Latvia, Lithuania, and Slovakia. The European Council also asked the Commission to prepare a pre-accession strategy for the Eastern enlargement based on the Copenhagen criteria.[61] The Commission was given the role of pro-

---

56 Europe Agreement Establishing an Association between the European Communities and their Member States, of the One Part, and the Republic of Poland, of the Other Part, Official Journal of the European Communities O.J. L348, December 16, 1991, 3.
57 Ibid., 3.
58 Thomas Diez, 'Europe's Others and Return of Geopolitics', *Cambridge Review of International Affairs* 17, no.2 (2004), doi: 10.1080/0955757042000245924.
59 Commission of European Communities, Communication from the Commission to the Council and the Parliament on the Association Agreements with the countries of Central and Eastern Europe, Com(90) 398 Final, August 27, 1990; European Parliament, Report of the Committee on External Economic Relations on a General Outline for Association Agreements with the Countries of Central and Eastern Europe. Session Documents 1991, A3–0055/91, March 13, 1991, 33.
60 For further reading about the CEE enlargement, see Frank Schimmelfennig and Ulrich Sedelmeier, eds., *The Europeanization of Central and Eastern Europe* (Ithaca: Cornell University Press, 2005).
61 The Council's related decision is cited in the Commission's report. European Commission. Commission of the European Communities, The 2004 Progress Report on Bulgaria's Progress Towards Accession, SEC(2004) 1199, October 6, 2004, 4.

viding regular reports on the annual progress of candidates on adopting and implementing EU legislation.⁶² Later, the European Parliament additionally began to release reports on candidate countries.

The Luxembourg European Council additionally expressed its opinion about Turkey's potential membership between the lines of the accession criteria. In its presidential conclusions the Council left this reference that Turkish elites did not find promising:

> The Council confirms Turkey's eligibility for accession to the European Union. Turkey will be judged on the basis of the same criteria as the other applicant States. While the political and economic conditions allowing accession negotiations to be envisaged are not satisfied, the European Council considers that it is nevertheless important for a strategy to be drawn up to prepare Turkey for accession by bringing it closer to the European Union in every field.⁶³

The Council did not declare Turkey as a candidate, but eligible for the accession. In so doing it considered official dialogues essential in order to bring the applicant closer to European standards. Once requested by the Luxembourg Summit and the following Cardiff Summit, the European Commission began to devise the pre-accession strategy for Turkey and also tabled annual reports about Turkey's compliance with EU legislation and the accession criteria. Although Turkish public opinion regarded the Luxembourg Summit as a dismissal of Turkey's EU bid,⁶⁴ European institutions were now formally and regularly expressing their common arguments about the applicant on the political basis established with the accession criteria.

Klaus Kinkel, the German Minister of Foreign Affairs and the Christian Democrat member, predicted in 1997 that Turkey would not be able to join the EU in the 'foreseeable future' due to its human rights violations.⁶⁵ In contrast, most EU actors in the late 1990s began to think that excluding Turkey would not serve the EU's interests.⁶⁶ Following the Luxembourg Summit, socialist parties successively came to power in Western European countries, except Spain, and impacted on

---

62 Council of the European Union, Presidential Conclusions, The Luxembourg European Council, December 12–13, 1997. See Article 28.
63 Ibid. See Article 31.
64 Öniş, 'Luxembourg, Helsinki and Beyond', 465.
65 Stephen Kinzer, 'Europeans Shut the Door on Turkey's Membership in Union', *The New York Times*, May 27, 1997.
66 Öniş, 'Luxembourg, Helsinki and Beyond', 470; Gunal Incesu, *Ankara-Bonn-Brusel: Die deutsch-türkischen Beziehungen und die Beitrittsbemühungen der Türkeiin die Europäische Gemeinschaft, 1959–1987* (Bielefeld: Transcript Verlag, 2014), 10–11.

the EU's language about Turkey.⁶⁷ Although the socialists had criticised Turkey's human rights records in the 1980s, now they were considering its membership to be an opportunity to disprove the popular argument that the EU was a Christian Club.⁶⁸ According to Joschka Fisher, the new German foreign secretary in the coalition between the Social Democrats and Greens, the European Union with Turkey would 'better integrate other cultures, gain in external stability, and have a bridge to the countries of the Middle East'.⁶⁹

With these considerations, the Helsinki European Council (1999) reckoned Turkey among the candidate countries and indicated the 13 applicants to be 'starting the accessions process on an equal footing'.⁷⁰ Nevertheless, concerning Turkey's relations with Greece and Cyprus, the Helsinki Summit introduced a new condition to the accession criteria. The Council called on the applicant countries to settle their important border disputes. The 'good neighbourly relations', along with the previous Copenhagen criteria, hence concerned the applicant countries, and especially Turkey.⁷¹ Still, the Helsinki Summit laid a stronger emphasis on Turkey's accession perspective than the Luxembourg Summit, with the references to 'political dialogue' and 'full membership'. Under changing conditions, Europeans elaborated Turkey's application this way:

> Turkey is a candidate State destined to join the Union on the basis of the same criteria as applied to the other candidate States. Building on the existing European strategy, Turkey, like other candidate States, will benefit from a pre-accession strategy to stimulate and support its reforms. This will include enhanced political dialogue, with emphasis on progressing towards fulfilling the political criteria for accession with particular reference to the issue of human rights, as well as on the issues referred to in paragraphs 4 and 9(a) ...⁷²

The Helsinki European Council was a turning event in Turkey's accession process on two occasions. At first, it gave a clear membership perspective to the candidate. Second, it defined the lines of the pre-accession strategy with a clear emphasis on Turkey's political transition. Put differently, Turkey's major task until the accession was considered to be its democratisation. The Helsinki European Council hence eased disappointments in Turkey caused by the previous Luxem-

---

67 Öniş, 'Luxembourg, Helsinki and Beyond', 470–471.
68 Ibid., 471.
69 Joschka Fischer, 'Turkey's European Perspective: The German View', *Turkish Policy Quarterly* 3, no.3 (Fall 2004).
70 Council of the European Union, Presidency Conclusions, Helsinki European Council, Press Release, Brussels, December 11, 1999, 0300/99.
71 Van Elsuwege, *From Soviet Republics to EU Member States*, 219
72 Council of the European Union, Presidency Conclusions, Helsinki European Council.

bourg Summit.⁷³ It gathered all applicants, the first six countries or the 'Luxembourg Group', the second group of countries, and Turkey, in one domain, and therefore refrained from discrimination. Instead, it signalled a clear perspective that it was going to give the green light to Turkey's accession provided that the candidate enacted the necessary political reforms. Nevertheless, it was still the fact that in its presidential conclusions the Council had detailed the future accessions of the CEE candidates with Cyprus and Malta but reserved only a brief mention for that of Turkey.

The post-Helsinki period showed a continuous development of these countries except for Turkey, in that in 2000 Turkey was the only candidate whose membership negotiations did not commence. The Copenhagen Summit (2002) welcomed the success of the candidates' negotiation processes and declared that the negotiations would be finalised on 1 May 2004. Along with the others, Cyprus joined the European Union before the resolution of its problems with Turkey. Bulgaria and Romania were also given their own roadmaps for accession. The EU and these two countries signed accession treaties in 2005 that entered into force in 2007. With the end of the CEE enlargement, the Western and Eastern parts of Europe were formally unified within the EU's framework.

In any case, Turkey's accession process based on its pre-accession strategy was underway. With the motivation stipulated by the Helsinki Summit, Turkish governments initiated a series of constitutional amendments to harmonise the national law with EU legislation. They generally concentrated political reforms on human and minority rights. In 2001, the Turkish Parliament amended the constitution on 34 points, perhaps most importantly on education and broadcasting in the vernacular, and the abolition of the capital punishment.⁷⁴ The Laeken European Council (2001) noted these reforms to be 'progress' and encouraged further reform. The Copenhagen European Council next year decided to open the negotiations provided Turkey fulfilled the Copenhagen criteria. Following the Commission's recommendation in 2004, which stated that Turkey met the criteria, the accession negotiations were scheduled to start on 3 October 2005.

Shortly before this presumed date, diplomatic bargaining between the EU's member states peaked. In September 2005, German conservatives, who rose to power in a federal election within that month, were already campaigning against Turkey, although the previous Social Democratic-Green coalition had earlier

---

73 Phil Gordon. 'Europe's Helsinki Summit: Now Make Turkey a Serious Offer', *International Herald Tribune*, October 12, 1999; Öniş, 'Luxembourg, Helsinki and Beyond', 476.
74 For a detailed view, see Ergun Ozbudun, 'Democratization Reforms in Turkey 1993–2004', *Turkish Studies* 8, no.2 (2007): 179–196, doi: 10.1080/14683840701312195.

paved the way for the negotiations' beginning. At this stage, the main barrier to the opening of Turkey's accession negotiations with the EU was Austria. In particular, the huge number of Turkish residents and the conservative ideology of the government resulted in Austria uncompromisingly rejecting the candidate. Austria was lobbying instead for the negotiations with Croatia, whose candidate status had been granted only a year earlier. In return, Turkey's key ally emerged as Britain. British statesmen known for their traditional scepticism of the EU were giving overt support to the beginning of the membership negotiations with Turkey, to turn, arguably, the course of European political integration to their advantage.[75] Britain, the term president of the Council of the European Union back then, managed to convince the Austrian delegation to remove their veto in exchange for abandoning London's veto of Croatia's membership negotiations.[76] As a consequence, the two candidates for the EU membership, Turkey and Croatia, became interlinked to each other on a hurried bargain between European powers over national interests. Eventually, these two could begin the accession negotiations on the same day.

The European Commission's 2004 report on Turkey had been critical to the official negotiations' opening. Fifteen years after its first, negative opinion on Turkey's application, the Commission had used relatively welcoming language on a circumstantial process for Turkey's accession:

> Turkey's accession would need to be thoroughly prepared in order to allow for a smooth integration which enhances the achievements of fifty years of European integration. This is an open-ended process whose outcome cannot be guaranteed beforehand. Regardless of the outcome of the negotiations or the subsequent ratification process, the relations between the EU and Turkey must ensure that Turkey remains fully anchored in European structures.[77]

Although Turkey sufficiently fulfilled the Copenhagen criteria, the Commission noted, the accession process would require an in-depth preparation of the candidate. The Commission hence suggested that the EU start the negotiations without an accession date. The term 'open-ended negotiations' co-occurred with the EU's ability to integrate the candidate, the current conception of its accession criteria, and the candidate's performance to accommodate itself with the current

---

[75] Antonio V Menéndez-Alarcón, *The Cultural Realm of European Integration: Social Representations in France, Spain, and the United Kingdom* (Westport: Praeger, 2004), 127.
[76] 'Turquie: les britanniques passent en force', Le Figaro, October 5, 2005.
[77] Commission of the European Communities, Recommendation of the Commission on Turkey's Progress Towards Accession, Com2004 0656, 2004, 2–3.

EU.⁷⁸ In the recommendation document the EU's capacity to integrate the candidate or its 'absorption capacity' therefore equally came to the fore. The next document structuring the future negotiations period, the official framework tabled by the Commission on 3 October 2005, repeated the absorption capacity along with the open-ended process and the significance of the Copenhagen criteria.⁷⁹ The next Pre-accession Strategy for Balkan states and Turkey (2006) also reaffirmed that the EU would drive the next enlargement in tandem with its 'institutional capacity'.⁸⁰ In regard to Turkey's foreseen open-ended accession negotiations and the EU's integration capacity, the Commission had underlined the institutional, demographic, and geographical impacts of the candidate's membership on the EU.⁸¹ As might be expected, these emphases did not motivate Turkish authorities throughout the subsequent negotiation process.⁸²

The literature argues two strictly interrelated facts to have determined the negotiations period during the 2000s. Turkish governments slowed down necessary reforms for the accession, and the European Union, increasingly dominated by conservative political parties, provided insufficient motivation and sent unclear signals to the candidate.⁸³ The problems on the Turkish side were particularly the slowed down political reforms and the stalemate on the Cyprus issue.⁸⁴ That Turkish governments later leant toward Islamism in national politics only

---

78 Mehmet Ugur, 'Open-Ended Membership Prospect and Commitment Credibility: Explaining the Deadlock in EU–Turkey Accession Negotiations', *Journal of Common Market Studies* 48, no.4 (2010): 968, doi: http://10.1111/j.1468–5965.2010.02082.x.
79 Commission of the European Communities, *Negotiating Framework*, Luxembourg, October 3, 2005, paragraph 2.
80 Michael Emerson, Senem Aydin, Julia de Clerck-Sachsse, and Gergana Noutcheva, 'Just What is this Absorption Capacity of the European Union?', *Center for European Policy Studies Policy Brief*, no.113 (2006): 33.
81 Commission of the European Communities, Recommendation of the Commission on Turkey's Progress Towards Accession, 8, 10.
82 Arvanitopoulos, *Turkey's Accession to the European Union*, 15; Beken Saatcioglu, 'Turkey-EU Relations from 1960s to 2012: A Critical Overview', in *Turkey's Accession to the European Union: Political and Economic Challenges*, eds. Belgin Akcay, Bahri Yilmaz (Lenham MD: Lexington Books, 2013), 12; Meltem Müftüler-Baç, 'Turkey's accession to the European Union: The impact of the EU's internal dynamics', *International Studies Perspectives* 9, No.2 (2011):212–214, doi: http://10.1111/j.1528–3585.2008.00327.x.
83 Ziya Öniş, 'Domestic Politics, International Norms and Challenges to the State, Turkey-EU Relations in the post-Helsinki Area', *Turkish Politics* 4, no.1 (2003): 28, doi: 10.1080/714005718; Philip Bohler, Jacques Pelkmans, and Can Selcuki, 'Who Remembers Turkey's Pre-accession?', *Centre for European Policy Studies Special Report*, no.74 (December 2012): 6.
84 Ibid., 2; See European Parliament, European Parliament Critical of Slowdown in Turkey's Reform Process, Press Service 20060922IPR10896, September 27, 2006.

worsened the candidate's declining membership prospects. On the European side, however, it was the rise of the conservative and far-right ideologies. Conservative parties gaining majorities in national parliaments and in the European Parliament, along with the far-right parties that also made significant headways from the late 1990s, caused an ambiguity in, if not obstruction of, the progress on the accession talks with the candidate.

Roles of the European Conservative and Far-right Camps in Turkey-EU Relations

It is justified to argue that political landscape after Luxembourg European Council (1997) turned in Turkey's favour partially because in many countries of Western Europe socialist parties rose to power. These parties had repudiated Turkey's EU bid during the 1980s on the basis of the applicant's nondemocratic aspect underpinned by military bureaucracy. In the late 1990s, they were against the EU's image of Christian club and inclined to emphasise the value of European multiculturalism through Turkey's membership perspective, and in the Helsinki European Council, they were led by the Socialist-Green coalition of Germany to give a green light to Turkey's candidature. Yet the power of socialist parties in Western Europe was short-lived, and, except in Britain, the conservative parties returned one by one by speaking to economic problems arguably caused by social policies as well as standing against the socialists' migration policy. They also opposed Turkey's accession bid on the grounds of their European conceptions excluding the candidate in religious and geographical terms, and European public opinion being already sceptical of Turkey –the opposition to the candidate in 15 EU countries rose from 46% (2001) to 55% at the beginning of the membership negotiations in 2005.[85]

According to Gerard Delanty, the term 'the people' was practically employed in the French Revolution to refer to civil society. It was then raised during the October Revolution to address the proletariat across the world. Similarly, contemporary populist movements finding origins in cultural thoughts of the earlier centuries often manipulated the term.[86] The present-day usage of 'people' re-

---

[85] See and compare, Eurobarometer 56.2: Radioactive Waste, Demographic Issues, the Euro, and European Union Enlargement, October-November 2001; Eurobarometer 56 Public Opinion in the European Union October-November 2001; Eurobarometer 64: Public Opinion in the European Union, Autumn 2005.
[86] Ibid., 153.

minds us of this last context. The post-Cold War conditions in Europe allowed the political right to pursue similar cultural policies of integration, unification or difference by employing the concepts of 'people', 'unity', and 'values' repeatedly. The European People's Party (EPP) constituted a prime example. Through its focus on religion and federalism, it kept European identity within the bonds of core values.[87] According to the party, these values stemmed from the Greco-Roman and Judeo-Christian roots of European civilisation, as well as the Enlightenment's philosophy.[88] The Christian Democrats therefore welcomed Eastern Europe, the geography of their same cultural kind, with the keywords 'unity' and 'home'.[89] The Socialist bloc's disintegration in Eastern Europe in the late 1980s and the German unification in 1990 set important milestones and also discursive metaphors for European integration, as German Chancellor Helmut Kohl stated: 'There is no going back on the road to European Union ... German unity and European unity are two sides of the same coin.'[90]

The Christian Democrats saw the EU as an instrument of European self-construction based on close geographical and religious proximity. Helmut Kohl similarly stated in 1994 about the Eastern enlargement: 'the Poles, the Czechs, the Slovaks, the Romanians, the Bulgarians and the Hungarians are our European brothers ... and need to attain their European rights.'[91] Turkey would thus dilute such a historic project of cultural unity; Kohl maintained that 'the European Union is a civilisation project, and within this project Turkey has no place'.[92] From the 1999 European elections, the EPP dominated the European Parliament and Commission and thus openly questioned Turkey's candidate status. Before the 2002 Copenhagen European Council, as an example, the Christian Democrats in Germany began their campaign against Turkey in geographical and religious

---

[87] Michael Gehler and Wolfram Kaiser, *Christian Democracy in Europe since 1945: Volume 2* (New York: Routledge, 2004), 169.
[88] For example, see European People's Party, EPP Action Programme: 2014–2019.
[89] László Kürti, 'Globalization and the Discourse of 'Otherness' in the New Eastern and Central Europe', in *The Politics of Multiculturalism in the New Europe: Racism, Identity and Community*, eds. Tariq Modood and Pnina Werbner (New York: Zed Books, 1997), 30–31.
[90] Helmut Kohl, Address given by Helmut Kohl to the Bundestag, Bonn, 13 December 1991, Centre Virtuel de la Connaissance sur l'Europe, http://www.cvce.eu/obj/address_given_by_helmut_kohl_on_the_outcome_of_the_maastricht_european_council_bonn_1 3_december_1991-en-12090399-dc71–42ee-8a3d-daf2420c0a9a.html (12.06.2014).
[91] Rainer Hülsse, 'Imagine the EU: The Metaphorical Construction of a Supra-nationalist Identity' *Journal of International Relations and Development* 9, no.4 (2006): 407, doi:10.1057/palgrave.jird.1800105.
[92] Chris Nuttall and Ian Traynor, 'Kohl Tries To Cool Row with Ankara', *The Guardian*, March 7, 1997.

terms, and warned the coalition of the Social Democrats and Greens not to give any promise to Turkey that the EU cannot keep in the future.[93] The Copenhagen Summit is therefore an illustration of how German Christian Democrats contrasted with the socialists, who during their power had shaped the previous Council meetings that paved the way for Turkey's candidacy.[94]

The French components of the Christian Democrats evinced a similar image of Europe that geographically excluded Turkey. The debates over whether to start Turkey's membership negotiations in 2005 had collided with the early efforts of Nicholas Sarkozy, the then minister of internal affairs, to promote himself for the presidential elections in 2007. In opposition to President Jacques Chirac, who backed giving the candidate a chance for the sake of its modernisation project and also European multiculturalism, Sarkozy had argued bluntly: 'I do not believe that Turkey belongs in Europe, and for a simple reason, which is that it is in Asia Minor ... What I wish to offer Turkey is a true partnership with Europe, it is not integration with Europe.'[95] His presidency for the next term often featured his attempts to dissolve the lengthy debate on whether Turkey's geography is European.[96] To take one suggestive example, in 2008 Sarkozy inaugurated a security zone in the Mediterranean region and added Turkey in as an Eastern associate.[97] The security and development organisation called the Union for the Mediterranean brought together the EU's members, other European coastal countries, and partners in the Middle East and North Africa. Under the French initiative, Turkey was given member status within the final non-European group.[98]

The Christian Democratic vision of European civilisation entailed a firm integration project excluding Turkey, and ahead of the accession talks with Turkey, the EPP and its German and French counterparts repeatedly stood against the

---

[93] Pinar Bilgin, 'A Return to 'Civilisational Geopolitics' in the Mediterranean? Changing Geopolitical Images of the European Union and Turkey in the Post-Cold War Era', *Geopolitics* 9, no.2 (2004): 276, doi: 10.1080/14650040490442863.
[94] E. Fuat Keyman and Ziya Önis, 'Helsinki, Copenhagen and beyond Challenges to the New Europe and the Turkish state', in *Turkey and European Integration: Accession Prospects and Issues*, eds. Mehmet Ugur and Nergis Canefe (London: Routledge, 2004), 188–189.
[95] Sedat Laçiner,'France, Asia Minor and Mind Minor', *Turkish Weekly*, September 22, 2007.
[96] Bernard Steunenberg, Simay Petek, and Christiane Rüth, 'Between Reason and Emotion: Popular Discourses on Turkey's Membership of the EU', *South European Society and Politics* 11, no.3 (2011): 449–468, doi: 10.1080/13608746.2011.598361.
[97] Bilgin, 'A Return to the Civilizational Geopolitics', 275.
[98] Steven Erlanger, 'Sarkozy's Union of the Mediterranean Falters', *New York Times*, June 6, 2008.

candidacy for identity reasons. Next, an extreme variant of the political right also ambitiously opposed Turkey's membership. Their disapproval of Turkey aside, the radical right was principally standing against the European Union's highly elitist integration project. As European integration peaked in the 1990s and the EU gradually took precedence over national sovereignties in certain fields, the parties of the extreme right found occasions to express their Euroscepticism and eventually to justify it by speaking to economic concerns and national fervour. The breakdown of Communist Europe, the unification of Germany, and finally the Eastern European enlargement stimulated international migration to Western Europe, which in return caused a social backlash.[99] Migrations from Middle Eastern countries, on the other hand, were at a steady pace and were only adding to the public discontent in Europe. Finally, economic crises gravely influenced social reactions against European integration. As Dietrich Thränhardt wrote, the conservative and far-right parties were describing the migrants as growing problems for Europe and made them an important part of their election propaganda as early as the 1990s.[100]

The French political landscape showed an explicit case, where the far-right manipulated nationalism and preoccupations with economic immigration in society. For part of the French public opinion, the 'Polish plumber' figure became a symbol of opposition to the Eastern workers officially engaging in the EU's market with the eastern enlargement.[101] The French far-right campaigned against the EU Constitution before its referendum (2005) by addressing similar economic and cultural concerns. Popular support for the EU's first constitution had reached 69% in the polls of 2004, shortly before the enlargement to Eastern Europe, but fell dramatically to 48% later.[102] Next to the economic side effects of the enlargement, the failure in the French constitutional referendum was also associated with reservations about Turkey's accession and the contentions that the constitution would facilitate Turkey's membership and the entry of future Turkish workers to France.[103] The national populism in France would later make its

---

99 Shore, 'Inventing the 'People's Europe', 780–781; Matheu Deflem and Fred C. Pampel, 'The Myth of Postnational Identity: Popular Support for Unification', *Social Forces* 75, no.1 (September 1996): 136, doi: 10.2307/2580759.
100 Dietrich Thränhardt, *Europe, a New Immigration Continent: Policies and Politics in Comparative Perspective* (Munster: LIT Verlag, 1996), 118–119.
101 Raphael Franck, 'Why did a majority of French voters reject the European Constitution?', *European Journal of Political Economy* 21, no.4 (2005): 1075, doi:10.1016/j.ejpoleco.2005.09.004.
102 Henry Milner, '"YES to the Europe I want; NO to this one." Some Reflections on France's Rejection of the EU Constitution', PS: *Political Science & Politics* 39, no. 2 (April 2006): 258, http://www.jstor.org/stable/20451732.
103 Yilmaz, 'Turkish Identity on the Road to the EU', 293–294.

biggest stride with the 2014 European elections. The radical 'National Front' came first, winning 25% of total votes, with their striking posters designed with an illustration of Joan of Arc and bearing the sloagan: 'No to Brussels, yes to France!'[104] In brief, economic pressures on EU countries that partially emanated from European integration and eastern enlargement aggravated cultural and welfare-oriented preoccupations with migrants in Europe, which in return would not favour Turkey's accession.[105]

The rise of the national populisms in Europe became a fact mostly after the period investigated by this book. In the following term, populist radical right parties manipulated the repeating economic crises and increasing refugee inflow, most notably the EU's Schengen crisis in 2015, and religious terrorism to strengthen their long march. They also did not fail to connect these problems, especially security issues, to Turkey's –fading- EU prospect and play to the fears of Europeans. The UK Independence Party, in its programme for the 2014 European elections, thus argued that the EU's enlargement with Turkey would mean losing control of British borders.[106] Ahead of the Brexit referendum, the UKIP still made false claims about Turkey's would-be EU accession, in an attempt to create a criminal, insecure aspect of the future Europe and mobilise masses for the leave cause. A relatively newer populist party in Germany, Alternative for Germany, in its basic programme rejected Turkey's EU accession for the security and cultural unity of European nation states.[107] As a very recent example, the Northern League in Italy, in its campaign devised for 2018 general elections, similarly expressed their rejection of Turkey's EU accession mainly on the grounds of migration, which would arguably impair Italy's security and identity. After the 2000s, apart from the developments intrinsic to Turkey's accession process, economic crises, terrorism and other security issues in Europe provided an arsenal available for the use of conservative and ultra-conservative political camps repudiating the candidate's EU bid.

---

104 Helga Zepp-La Rouche, 'The Empire is Crumbling: Future of Europe's Nations is with the Silk Road', *Executive Intelligence Review*, June 6, 2014, 23.
105 Ebru S. Canan-Sokullu and Cigdem Kentmen, 'Public Opinion Dimension: Turkey in the EU? An Empirical Analysis of European Public Opinion on Turkey's "Protracted" Membership', in *Fifty Years of EU-Turkey Relations: A Sisyphean Story*, ed. Armagan Emre Cakir (Oxon: Routledge, 2011), 124–125. Also see Lauren M. McLaren, 'Explaining Opposition to Turkish Membership of EU', *European Union Politics* 8, no.2 (2007): 252–278, doi. 10.1177/1465116507076432.
106 UK Independence Party, 'Create an Earthquake'. UKIP Manifesto 2014.
107 Alternative Für Deutschland, Programm für Deutschland. Das Grundsatzprogramm der Alternative für Deutschland, 34.

Conclusion

Turkey's accession case has been an unusual one for the European Union. Since its foundation, the EU elevated universal political values, adapted them to its legislation, and thus set out the accession criteria for candidates. The emerging European Union and its accession criteria therefore largely structured Europe's relationship with Turkey and led the European political camps to mainly approach the country in political terms. In general, European political camps were expected to discuss Turkey, like any other candidate, on the basis of the common accession criteria. Yet, religious and geographical terms for discussing Europe also retained their importance in national and transnational politics. In addition to the political standards, with the end of the Cold War, the conservative and nationalist political camps found a highly convenient political environment to raise their inherently geographical and religious constructions of Europe. As a continuation of these dichotomies on defining Europe and Turkey, European politics during the 2000s involved diverging arguments about the European Union in relation to the Turkish candidate in political, religious, and geographical terms. The next chapter delves into how the mainstream political camps represented in the European Parliament conceptualised the Turkish candidate and its compatibility with the EU during the 2000s, in particular after the beginning of the membership negotiations.

4 Coming to Terms with Turkey's EU Bid: Evidence from the European Parliament

The European Union entered the 21st century with the rising political right. The end of the Cold War, the EU's Eastern enlargement and its effects on immigration, and finally economic recessions facilitated the progress of conservative and nationalist parties. An essentialist genre of conceptualising Europe thus gained currency in European politics, instead of the earlier definition by universal political values. With respect to Turkey's emerging membership prospect, cultural debates about European identity were intensified. From the beginning of the accession talks in 2005, European politicians debated the applicant's accession to the EU with controversial concepts, which often carried the influences of European and Ottoman/Turkish histories. The present chapter explores the historical values and contexts with which European political camps conceptualised the European Union and Turkey in the 2000s. To this end, it scrutinises the plenaries held in the European Parliament (EP) to confer on Turkey's progress during the negotiations after 2005. These plenaries involve three types of textual data examined. The first type is the minutes of meetings assembled in the EP to discuss Turkey's reform process towards accession. The European Commission also attended most of these meetings. The second comprises the official Turkey reports annually tabled by the Committee on Foreign Affairs (AFET or *Affaires étrangères*) some time after the European Commission's annual progress reports. They demonstrate AFET's comments on Turkey's political reforms, in line with the Commission's technical reviews and criticisms about the candidate. The third is MEPs proposals to amend AFET's Turkey reports.

The concepts of European values and transnational politics precede the chapter's methodology. Culture, defined by Clifford Geertz as mentioned previously, covers a broad understanding of relations including politics, religion, and geography and also confines the term 'value' to refer to various traditions (belief systems, ideologies, or stereotypes) underpinning these relations.[1] But there is another and more significant reason for using the term in the European context. Earlier chapters note that the European Union declares its founding principles to be 'values' in the Treaty on European Union (Article 2 and Article 49), in its final version amended by the Treaty of Lisbon in 2009. Further, this chapter discusses at length that the term 'European values' today officially implies the EU's political-liberal standards and is also connected with the EU's ac-

---

1 Clifford Geertz, *The Interpretation of Cultures* (New York: Basic Books, 1973), 50–51, 261–263.

cession criteria. But not every political camp limits 'European values' to political terms, and their definitions mostly lead to disputes regarding the Turkish candidate's compatibility with Europe. The debates over the definitions of the EU's political accession criteria constitute a striking case, since, in the 2000s, the criteria were conceptualised not always in terms of political values and principles but sometimes with a view to religion and geography. In this period disagreements occurred between the uses of the accession criteria explored in this chapter: as the heart of European identity confined to fundamental rights and liberal democracy, as a product of the historical development underpinned by Christianity and thus only one component of European values, or as a legal ground on which European nation states cooperate so long as their interests match.

Transnational politics is also strongly related to the parliamentary debates over Turkey's EU bid. Conceptualisations of Europe and Turkey by mainstream political parties reveal two sorts of differences: among pan-European parties and between pan-European parties and their national constituents. The first group of differences has been evident in parliamentary discussions since, in general, traditional ideological lines at the European level and affiliations with European parties impact on parliamentarians' statements.[2] In a process following the Treaty on EU (1992), the European Parliament's leverage in European politics gradually increased, and political camps publicly discussed subject matters linked to the EU's integration and enlargement.[3] Generally speaking, the parties centred on the 'right' or 'centre-right' upheld a functioning free market and EU-led authority to control criminal and immigration issues, while the 'political left' cleft to the social policies, equality, and fundamental liberties.[4] That aside, in the 1990s and 2000s the three biggest European parties – the Party of European Socialists (PES), the Alliance of Liberals and Democrats for Europe (ALDE), and the European People's Party (EPP) – almost uniformly advocated European integration, disagreeing only about the social principles on which integration should be built, e.g. social equality and multiculturalism for Socialists, liberal values for liberals, and Christian history and ethics for Christian Democrats.[5] From

---

[2] Simon Hix, 'Legislative Behaviour and Party Competition in the European Parliament: An Application of Nominate to the EU', *Journal of Common Market Studies* 39, no.4 (November 2001): 663–688, doi: 10.1111/1468–5965.00326.
[3] Sergio Fabbrini, 'The European Union and the Puzzle of Parliamentary Government', *Journal of European Integration* 37, no.5 (2015): 571–586, doi: 10.1080/07036337.2015.1019877.
[4] Simon Hix, *The Political System of the European Union* (New York: Palgrave Macmillan, 2001), 167–68.
[5] Robert Ladrech, 'Political Parties in the European Parliament', in *Political Parties and the European Union*, ed. John Gaffney (New York: Routledge, 1996), 296.

the 2000s, the leading pro-European positions of these parties have been challenged by Eurosceptic conservative and far-right pan-European parties, as well as British conservative parties, which have gradually come to influence European politics with their growing public support.[6]

The second group of differences have rather stemmed from the respective natures and interests of national politics.[7] Since the foundation of the European Parliament, the politics of nation states infiltrate supranational parliamentary affairs in two primary ways. At first, members of the European Parliament (MEPs) are elected according to the election quotas reserved for their countries. Generally speaking, candidates for European elections aim at gaining electoral support in national milieus, even though they stand for pan-European parties.[8] The electorates also get to know pan-European parties through connections with their constituent national parties.[9] Consequently, the successes of European parties rely on their positions in national politics, and MEPs also represent their interests shaped in national contexts.[10] By way of an example, in the 2000s British members' statements in the European Parliament had strikingly demonstrated the linkage between national contexts and political behaviours at supranational levels. To summarize, from a transnational perspective any political member in the European Parliament is expected to act under the influence of his affiliation

---

[6] Although the effects of Eurosceptic and nationalist parties on Turkey debates were marginal in the 2000s, the end of this period marked by the European elections in 2009 showed the rise of these parties and their potential impacts on enlargement debates. Alexander H. Trechsel, 'How Much 'Second-order' were the European Parliament Elections 2009?', in *2009 Elections to the European Parliament, Country Reports*, ed. Wojciech Gagatek (Florance: European University Institute, 2010), 11; Wojciech Gagatek, Alexander H. Trechsel, and Fabian Breuer, 'Preface: Bringing the European Parliament Election Results Closer to the Citizens', in *2009 Elections to the European Parliament, Country Reports*, ed. Wojciech Gagatek (Florance: European University Institute, 2010), XI-XIII.
[7] Beate Kohler-Koch, *Organized Interests in the EC and the European Parliament, Social Science Research Network*, European Integration online Papers 1, no.9, http://ssrn.com/abstract=302669 (12.02.2015).
[8] Hix, *The Political System of the European Union*, 90; Simon Hix, Tapio Raunio, and Roger Scully, *An Institutional Theory of Behaviour in the European Parliament*, European Parliament Research Group Working Paper, No. 1 (1999): 8, http://personal.lse.ac.uk/hix/EPRG_Working_Papers/workingPaper1.pdf (12.10.2014); Jonathan B. Slapin and Sven-Oliver Proksch, 'Look Who's Talking: Parliamentary Debate in the European Parliament', *European Union Politics* 11, no.3 (2010): 352–353, doi: 10.1177/1465116510369266.
[9] Julie Smith, *Europe's Elected Parliament* (Sheffield: Sheffield Academic Press, 1999), 106.
[10] Hix, *The Political System*, 49; Slapin and Proksch, 'Look Who's Talking', 333–357.

with his pan-European Party, his own political interests, and his affinity with national politics.[11]

Disputes provoked by Turkey's EU bid throughout the 2000s betray the influences of the above-given factors dramatically. Party constraints, relationships with national politics, and finally different conceptions of common European values and the EU's accession criteria that are constructed in political, religious, and geographical terms led to the parliamentary deputies expressing contradictory images of Europe and Turkey. From this standing, the rest of the chapter unfolds in three sections subdivided by essentially political, religious, and geographical terms of debating Turkey in relation to the EU. The section on political attitudes explores, in a subsequent order, the European Union's common political values derived from its Accession Criteria, the depictions of European values by the European Parties, the preconditions stipulated to Turkey's EU membership, and finally discussions about Turkey's compliance with European democracy. The second and third sections elaborate on the religious and geographical aspects of the debates about Turkey's compatibility with the EU.

Common Political Values Derived from the EU's Accession Criteria

Before the Treaty of Lisbon (2009), principal documents of the European Union often made references to European values in political contexts, but only slightly conceptualised them. In one instance, the Declaration on Democracy by the Copenhagen European Council (1978) had embodied 'the cherished values of their legal, political and moral order' with the political terms of representative democracy, the rule of law, social justice, and human rights. Although the overall European legislation and its practices unquestionably contextualise the political rationale of the European Union, a functioning internal market and liberal democracy, the question remained if it fully embodied European moral standards. Amended by the Treaty of Lisbon (2009), the Treaty on European Union finally enshrined democratic principles and responsibilities in Article 2 under the term 'European values':

> The Union is founded on the *values* of respect for human dignity, freedom, democracy, equality, the rule of law and respect for human rights, including the rights of persons be-

---

[11] Liesbet Hooghe and Gary Marks, 'The Making of a Polity: The Struggle over European Integration', *Social Science Research Network*, European Integration Online Papers 1, no.4, http://ssrn.com/abstract=302663 (05.02.2015).

longing to minorities. These values are common to the Member States in a society in which pluralism, non-discrimination, tolerance, justice, solidarity and equality between women and men prevail.[12]

European values are also connected to the EU's enlargement policy with Article 49 of the Treaty on EU, which states: 'any European State which respects the values referred to in Article 2 and is committed to promoting them may apply to become a member of the Union.'[13] In parallel, the values referred to in Article 2 are widely mentioned in the Copenhagen criteria, a set of political and economic conditions stipulated to the EU's applicants and the official yardstick when discussing the congruence between candidate countries and the EU, since the Copenhagen European Council (1993).[14]

EU institutions principally orient any candidate's democratic developments to this set of principles, just as the European Commission has been the chief actor scrutinising the candidate countries' compliance with the EU's legislation through the accession criteria. The committees established under the European Parliament similarly table their country reports following the Commission's reports and proposals.[15] The Commission's progress reports are written in a technical language – being directly connected to issues from Turkey's annual performances – and precede the country reports of the European Parliament, or specifically those of Committee on Foreign Affairs. In other words, political camps represented in AFET form their arguments by taking into account, inter alia, the European Commission's progress reports. In the present case, right after the accession talks' beginning, the European Commission's annual progress report (2005) had noted Turkey's slowdown in its essential legislative reforms to conform to the accession criteria.[16] Next year, in 2006, the European Commission and Parliament together underlined in their reports Turkey's further downturn in

---

[12] Consolidated Versions of the Treaty on European Union, Official Journal of European Union 55, C326, 2012, 17.
[13] Consolidated Versions of the Treaty on European Union, Official Journal of European Union 55, C326, 2012, 43.
[14] The Council established them as: Stability of institutions guaranteeing democracy, the rule of law, human rights, respect for and protection of minorities, the existence of a functioning market economy and the capacity to cope with the competitive pressure and market forces within the Union, and the ability to take on obligations of membership including adherence to the aims of political, economic, and monetary Union. Council of the European Union, Presidency Conclusions, Copenhagen European Council, 21–22 June, 1993, SN 180/1/93.
[15] Hix, Raunio, Scully, *An Institutional Theory*, 24.
[16] Commission of European Communities, Progress report of Turkey, SEC(2005)1426, November 9, 2005, 137.

this matter.¹⁷ Their critical comments undoubtedly constituted a standpoint for subsequent political commentaries about Turkey.

Normally, political camps of the European Parliament are expected to acknowledge the accession criteria in the same way, as the common values of the European Union. Commissioner for the European Enlargement Oli Rehn therefore reminded the European Parliament several times during the 2000s that the EU was built on 'the basic values of democracy, the rule of law and human rights.'¹⁸ Yet the application of the accession criteria sparked debates at the beginning of Turkey's membership negotiations. To give a very brief introduction, the parties from leftist ideological spectrums largely limited European values to the accession criteria while discussing Turkey's compatibility with European values. The Party of European Socialists, the Alliance of Liberals and Democrats for Europe, the European Green Party, and the European Left, which can be referred to as the Socialists, Liberals, Greens, and the Communists, upheld an organisation principally defined with the Copenhagen principles. Between these camps, especially for the Socialists, Turkey's membership was going to enrich the 'values of multiculturalism' inside the EU.¹⁹ In comparison with these camps, the Christian Democrats, conservatives, and the far-right members were rather fragmented in the 2000s, as they embraced a broad range of values between the accession criteria and the other religious and geographical constructions.

European Values conceptualised by pan-European Parties

In general terms, to the European People's Party, common European values included but were not limited to the accession criteria. The party's 2001 Berlin congress, entitled 'A Union of Values', stated that the European common cultural heritage originated in 'Hebrew prophecy, Greek philosophy and Roman law ... the Christian message and Judeo-Christian values ... the Renaissance, and the

---

17 European Parliament, European Parliament Critical of Slowdown in Turkey's Reform Process, Press Service 20060922IPR10896, September 27, 2006.
18 Olli Rehn, Debate on Turkey's 2007 Progress Report, Strasbourg, May 21, 2008; Debate on Opening of Negotiations with Turkey – Additional Protocol to the EEC-Turkey Association Agreement, Strasbourg, September 28, 2005; Debate on Democratic Process in Turkey, Strasbourg, May 5, 2009.
19 Glenis Willmot's address, Debate on Turkey's Progress Towards Accession, Strasbourg, September 26, 2006.

Enlightenment' make political integration of Europeans a prerequisite.[20] Their manifesto for the European elections in 2009 implied that the Christian Democrats presented their conception of European values as a historical legacy, which unequivocally transcended the accession criteria and also enjoined Europeans to undertake the ambitious project of European integration.[21] With regard to the integrity of these promoted values, an unrestricted European Enlargement then could endanger European identity. The party's programme for the following elections stated: 'EPP favours judicious enlargement, while retaining the identity of the EU.'[22] In other words, the EU had to continue its enlargement, provided that European identity remained intact with the accession of new countries. This implied Turkey obviously. Pursuant to their party policy, the party's deputies equally expressed religious and geographical concerns in parliamentary plenaries about the candidate.[23] Martin Schulz, the former leader of the Party of European Socialists, therefore criticised the EPP's construction of European values and fierce opposition to Turkey before the negotiations' commence: 'I can tell ... that it does not want Turkey because Turkey is distant and Muslim, but that Croatia is acceptable on the grounds of being Catholic, conservative and close at hand.'[24] Independent members representing the extreme right raised arguments similar to those of the Christian Democrats; to them, Turkey's adoption of European values was only likely if the country left Islamic and 'Ottoman values' aside.[25] Despite that, the conservative members from Britain contrasted with the EPP, even though they were affiliated with it and sat in the same parliamentary group for most of the 2000s. The British conservatives in their arguments

---

[20] 'A Union of Values', Basic Document Adopted by the Fourteenth EPP Congress in Berlin on 11–13 January 2001, annexed by Thomas Jansen, Steven van Hecke, *At Europe's Service: The Origins and Evolution of the European People's Party*, (Centre for European Studies and Springer-Verlag Berlin Heidelberg, 2011), 336. Also see pages 20 and 22.
[21] 'United Europe's founding fathers were Christian Democrats. Their achievements were built on deep convictions rooted in Judaeo-Christian civilisation and the Enlightenment, emphasising freedom as well as responsibility, and the dignity of the human being. On the basis of these values, over the last 50 years the men and women of the European People's Party have been at the forefront of improving and successively expanding the Union as well as introducing the Euro.' European People's Party, 'Strong for the People', EPP Manifesto, European Elections 2009, 1.
[22] European People's Party, Why Vote for the Political Family of the European People's Party? EPP Manifesto, May 22–24, 2014, 14–15.
[23] Amendment 13 for recital C, Amendments 1–188 for the Draft Motion for Resolution, PE416.543v01–00, January 7, 2009, 8.
[24] Martin Schulz's address, Debate on Opening of Negotiations with Turkey – Additional Protocol to the EEC-Turkey Association Agreement (2005).
[25] Lydia Schenardi's address, Debate on Women in Turkey, Strasbourg, February 12, 2007. Mogens Camre's address, Debate on Turkey's 2007 Progress Report (2008).

about Turkey almost always expressed that the Copenhagen criteria reflected European values, and discussed the candidate only through the accession conditions that were already set by the EU's founding treaties. The British Conservative Party's manifesto for the European election in 2009 similarly pledged that their members would support the EU's enlargement with Turkey on the basis of the accession criteria.[26]

In complete contrast to the Christian Democrats and radical right, Socialists, Liberals, and Greens generally set forth a more inclusive construction of the European Union with the term 'multiculturalism', recalling the EU's universal political values, and they voiced in plenary meetings that the Copenhagen criteria should remain the sole yardstick for Turkey's accession.[27] Among them, the Party of European Socialists restated that the objective of the negotiations should be the accession provided that Turkey substantially fulfilled the Copenhagen criteria.[28] The party overtly expressed its backing in its manifesto for the 2009 elections, stating that its very principle of multiculturalism obliges the EU to continue the membership negotiations with Turkey based on the accession criteria.

> We believe that the EU should respect the fundamental rights of all peoples as well as supporting the multicultural and multi-religious nature of European societies. We support an open-ended process of negotiations with Turkey towards EU accession, based on clear criteria, and that both Turkey and the EU should fulfil their respective commitments.[29]

In 2009, almost four years after the beginning of the accession talks with Turkey that had already slowed down and been partially frozen, the Socialists were reminding the EU of its responsibilities in its relations with Turkey arising from its multicultural and multi-religious nature. They were thus in conflict with the Christian Democrats on the definition of European values and the scope of the accession criteria. For the Socialists, the accession criteria signified the universal

---

[26] Vote for Change, European Election Manifesto, Conservative Party European Election Manifesto, 2009.
[27] Amendments 17 and 18 for recital C., Amendments 1–162 for the Draft Motion for a Resolution, PE404.587v01–00, April 7, 2008, 9–10.
[28] Amendments 6 and 7 for recital A, amendment 28 for paragraph 1 and amendment 39 for paragraph 5, Amendments 1–243 for the Draft Motion for a Resolution, PE431.004v02–00, January 1, 2010, 5–6, 15, 19–20; Amendment 11 for paragraph 8, Amendments 1–207 for the Draft Motion for Resolution on the 2012 Progress Report of Turkey, PE504.377v01–00, February 12, 2013, 7.
[29] Party of European Socialists, Manifesto for Elections, June 2009.

applicability of European values whereas the Christian Democrats saw them as only partially suggestive of the historical construction of Europe-rootedness.

The Alliance of Liberals and Democrats for Europe and the smaller parties titled the European Green Party and European Left also generally differed from the Christian Democrats by discussing the European Union and its enlargement solely in terms of the accession criteria.[30] With regard to the political nature of the accession criteria, for the Liberals Turkey was unquestionably eligible to reach European values by implementing political reforms.[31] Although the Party's 2004 election programme stated that 'all European countries that fulfil the Copenhagen criteria should be welcome to join the European Union',[32] in the next election campaign it included the EU's integration capacity within their conception of the accession criteria. Prior to the elections in 2009, the party backed the realisation of 'the existing EU enlargement commitments for those countries fulfilling the Copenhagen EU accession criteria, which includes integration capacity as an important consideration.'[33] Possibly concerned by the impact of Turkey's future accession on the EU, the party therefore mentioned the integration capacity the first time. In addition, the European Green Party and the Party of European Left remained strictly entangled in the practice of approaching the EU and Turkey with the accession criteria. The Green Party's programme for the European elections in 2004 read the fundamental element of EU membership to be 'stable political institutions that guarantee democracy, justice and human rights.'[34] The Greens thus principally referred to the EU's Charter of Fundamental Rights as one primary source of European values.[35] The Communists also subscribed an understanding of European values restricted to the terms of the accession criteria, but they mainly emphasised European values to oppose the capitalist development of the European Union.[36] Finally, British national parties represented in the European Parliament predicated their argu-

---

[30] European Liberal, Democrat and Reform Party, European Liberals' Top 15 for EP Elections, Manifesto for the European Elections 2009, Adopted at the Stockholm Congress, October 31, 2008.
[31] Marios, Matsakis' address, Debate on Turkey's Progress Towards Accession (2006); Metin Kazak's address, Debate on Democratic Process in Turkey (2009).
[32] ELDR Manifesto, 2004 European Parliamentary Elections, Approved in Amsterdam, November 14, 2003
[33] European Liberals' Top 15 for EP Elections, ELDR Manifesto for the European Elections 2009.
[34] The European Green Party, Manifesto for the 2004 European Elections, Fourth European Greens Congress, Rome, 20–22 February, 2004.
[35] Ibid.
[36] Party of the European Left, United for a Left Alternative in Europe, European Left Election Manifesto, 2004.

ments about Europeanness and European Enlargement primarily on the accession criteria. Their national programmes for European elections, regardless of their ideological backgrounds, put forth the British parties' reliance on the Copenhagen criteria during the EU's enlargement process with Turkey.[37]

The majority of pan-European parties seemed to have laid certain emphases on the Copenhagen criteria as the sole basis of Turkey's accession to the EU, since the country was already promised a candidate status on an equal footing with the other applicants (CEE countries with Cyprus and Malta) in the Helsinki European Council (1999). Yet a number of external conditions in addition to the Copenhagen criteria arose individually from Turkey's particular case, which demanded attention at this stage. Although these conditions – the open-ended nature of the accession talks, the EU's absorption capacity, the principle of good neighbourly relations – mostly fell within political conceptions of the candidate in relation to the EU, the Turkey-sceptical parties arguably manipulated some of them with other motivations. Especially ahead of and shortly after the beginning of the membership negotiations, the MEPs entered heated debates on the applicability of these additional conditions in Turkey's case.

On 3 October 2005, the EU had started off an open-ended negotiation process with two candidates, Turkey and Cyprus, for the first time in its history, which meant that this period would not proclaim an accession date until all the requirements would be met and EU members would approve it in their parliaments or national polls. Apart from Croatia's accession talks, which took a relatively straight line towards accession, members of the European Parliament discussed whether these open negotiations should conclude in Turkey's full membership. For one very suggestive instance, at the very beginning of the accession talks a reference by the European Parliament to the Commission's earlier Turkey recommendation was highly contested by ideologically motivated MEPs. The European Commission had recommended the Council to launch the negotiations with Turkey in 2004 and presented a roadmap to the applicant, stating

> This is an open-ended process whose outcome cannot be guaranteed beforehand. Regardless of the outcome of the negotiations or the subsequent ratification process, the relations between the EU and Turkey must ensure that Turkey remains fully anchored in European structures.[38]

---

[37] The British Conservative Party, Vote for Change: European Election Manifesto, Manifesto for European Elections, 2009. Liberal Democrats, Stronger Together Poorer Apart.

[38] Commission of European Communities. Communication from the Commission to the Council and the European Parliament, Recommendation of the European Commission on Turkey's Progress towards Accession, COM(2004) 656 final. Brussels, October 6, 2004, 2.

The Parliament reiterated these terms almost yearly, but a draft report tabled in 2006 provoked debates and amendment proposals following this statement: 'regardless of whether or not negotiations are successfully concluded, relations between the EU and Turkey must ensure that Turkey remains fully anchored in European structures.'[39] A dichotomy then occurred among political members about the original text. To amend the statement, a Socialist member proposed to add 'the full commitment from the European Union to a successful outcome to the negotiations', and he evoked the EU's responsibilities within the accession process.[40] In contrast, a Christian Democratic member proposed to delete the adverb 'fully' from the original statement.[41] In parallel, a non-attached conservative member proposed to change the term in the original document, 'European structures', into 'friendly terms with EU member states', and therefore intended to diminish the extent of the EU's relationship with Turkey.[42] In opposition to these conservative figures, Geoffrey Orden, a member of the British Conservative Party who was affiliated with the European Democrats in the EP, stated in his proposal that Turkey should also stay anchored to the 'transatlantic structures'.[43] This deputy thus reflected the overall British view, which favoured the security partnerships among the EU, NATO, the US, and Turkey. He also proposed to remove from the text the terms 'regardless of whether or not negotiations are successfully concluded' to minimise the European Parliament's stress on any scenario other than the membership. Through his proposal, he echoed Britain's antecedent foreign policy favouring Turkey's accession to the EU.[44]

It would be quite justified to argue that the deputies of the PES, the Greens, and the European Left, as well as the British conservative deputies, sustained their long-term stand throughout the 2000s that the goal of the negotiations was the full membership of Turkey.[45] Among them, the Socialists in particular insisted that the period of the accession talks was a mutual responsibility be-

---

[39] European Parliament, Draft Report on Turkey's progress towards accession, PE 374.360v03–00, A6–0269/2006, September 13, 2006, 11.
[40] Amendment 230 for paragraph 36, Amendments 1–343 for Draft Report on Turkey's progress towards Accession 2006, PE 376.373v02–00, July 4, 2006, 79.
[41] Amendment 233 for paragraph 36, ibid., 80.
[42] Amendment 232 for paragraph 36, ibid., 79.
[43] Amendment 231 for paragraph 36, ibid., 79.
[44] Amendment 231 for paragraph 36, ibid., 79.
[45] See the proposals by the PES, Greens, and European Left in, Amendments 7–10 for recital A and amendment 234 for paragraph 22a, Amendments 1–236 for the Draft Motion for a Resolution, PE393.947v02–00, September 25, 2007, 3–4, 78; Amendments 10–11 for recital A, Amendments 1–162 for the Draft Motion for a Resolution, (2008), 6–7. Amendment 9 for recital A, Amendments 1–188 for the Draft Motion for Resolution, (2009), 12–13, 6.

tween the EU and the candidate by nature. Turkey then needed time throughout the membership negotiations, during which the EU should support the candidate systematically in the same way of previous enlargements.⁴⁶ Richard Corbett, PES member from British Labour Party, stated days before the beginning of Turkey's membership negotiations that there was 'no reason of principle why it should not be entitled to join the European Union.'⁴⁷ In contrast, the political camps sceptical of Turkey's accession regarded the candidate as having sole responsibility for modernising itself and taking steps ahead throughout the negotiations, regardless of the EU's attitudes towards the process.⁴⁸ To take one suggestive example, the Christian Democrats put forward a blunt amendment to the European Parliament's report on Turkey (2007) that the negotiations 'strengthen economic, social and political ties with Turkey but should not lead to Turkey's accession'.⁴⁹

Instead, Turkey-sceptic deputies often expressed the scenario of the 'privileged partnership' with Turkey as an alternative to the full membership.⁵⁰ A month after the European Commission's recommendation to the European Council (November 2004) on starting the accession talks with the candidate, that it 'would be an important model of a country with a majority Muslim population adhering to such fundamental principles as liberty, democracy, respect for human rights and fundamental freedoms and the rule of law'⁵¹, Hans-Gert Poettering, the Chairman of the Christian Democrats' parliamentary group, stated bluntly:

> Those in our group who either do not want negotiations or want them to tend towards a privileged partnership ... are gravely concerned that, should Turkey join the European Union, this enlargement might prove fatal and Europeans might lose their identity, that

---

46 See amendment 4 for paragraph 1 and amendment 8 for paragraph 1 a, Amendments 1–343 for Draft Report on Turkey's progress towards Accession 2006 (2006), 2, 4.
47 Richard Corbett's address, Debate on Opening of negotiations with Turkey – Additional Protocol to the EEC-Turkey Association Agreement (2005).
48 Amendment 18 for recital B, Amendments 1–236 for the Draft Motion for a Resolution (2007), 6.
49 Amendment 6 for recital A, Ibid., 2–3.
50 Amendment 205 for paragraph 32, Amendments 1–343 for Draft Report on Turkey's progress towards Accession 2006 (2006), 71; Amendment 250 for paragraph 35 a 2010, Amendments 1–315 for the Draft Motion for a Resolution, PE456.654v02–00, January 25, 2011, 133; Bernd Posselt's address, Debate on Turkey's Progress Towards Accession (2006); Daniel Hannan's address, Debate on Women in Turkey (2007). Amendment 250 for paragraph 40, Amendments 1–162 for the Draft Motion for a Resolution (2008), 136.
51 Recommendation of the European Commission on Turkey's progress towards accession, COM(2004) 656 final, October 6, 2004.

it might be detrimental to the sense of being 'us' on which solidarity in the European Union is founded.[52]

The reasons for Poettering's privileged partnership were more than pragmatic concerns, since he was presenting it as a remedy for a probable identity crisis in the EU in consequence of admitting Turkey, a country believed to be culturally different from the EU's existing members. Moved by these preoccupations, the Christian Democrats called on the EU authorities to 'live up to its many positive promises and statements concerning Turkey as a fully-fledged member of the EU', even after the accession talks commenced,[53] and repeatedly raised their privileged partnership proposal as an alternative to Turkey's accession.[54] Meanwhile, the far-right members used this term much more frequently than any other camp did in the 2000s.[55] These members held that Turkey already had a privileged partnership with the EU established through the Customs Union, and for identity reasons the candidate cannot and should not join the European project under any circumstances.[56] Turkey-sceptics aside, the concept of privileged partnership was entirely rejected in other political camps, who reiterated that full membership to be the only objective of the negotiations.[57]

The EU's absorption capacity was another key term individually employed in Turkey's case. The European Commission referred to the concept in its negotiating framework concerning Turkey (2005), as it had 'full regard to all Copenhagen criteria, including the absorption capacity of the Union.'[58] Although the EU's absorption capacity first came to view in 1993 with the Presidency Conclusions of

---

[52] Hans-Gert Poettering's address, Debate on Turkey's Progress towards Accession, Strasbourg, December 13, 2004.
[53] Amendment 205 for the paragraph 32, Amendments 1–343 for Draft Report on Turkey's progress towards Accession 2006 (2006), 71.
[54] For example, see Amendment 250 for paragraph 35a Amendments 1–315 for the Draft Motion for Resolution on Turkey's 2010 Progress Report (2011), 133; Bernd Posselt's address, Debate on Turkey's Progress Towards Accession (2006). Daniel Hannan's address, Debate on Women in Turkey (2007).
[55] See amendment 328 for paragraph 35a, Amendments 1–343 for Draft Report on Turkey's progress towards Accession 2006 (2006), 78; amendment 238 for paragraph 22a, Amendments 1–236 for the Draft Motion for a Resolution (2007), 78; amendment 250 for paragraph 40, Amendments 1–162 for the Draft Motion for a Resolution (2008), 136.
[56] For example, see Lydia Schenardi's address, Debate on Women in Turkey (2007).
[57] See Marielle De Sarnez's address, Debate on Opening of Negotiations with Turkey – Additional Protocol to the EEC-Turkey Association Agreement (2005); Emine Bozkurt's address, Debate on Turkey's Progress Towards Accession (2006).
[58] Commission of European Communities, Negotiating Framework, Luxembourg, October 3, 2005, Article 2.

the Copenhagen European Council,[59] it was not proclaimed to be one of the accession criteria until Turkey's membership negotiations. The Commission first expressed the term in 2005 regarding the later enlargements, and the Brussels European Council followed next year.[60] The European Parliament similarly included the term in its Turkey reports several times, and asked the Commission to table reports on Turkey's impact on the EU's capacity.[61] Before the accession talks' beginning, the European Commission published a summary of the legitimate concerns arising from Turkey's future economic burden on the EU in the case of its membership, without using the term absorption capacity. It underlined a possible migration inflow from Turkey specifically, assuming this either to add to the economic growth of Europe or to 'lead to disturbances in the EU labour market.'[62] The report mentioned the history of migration from Turkey to Europe and estimated further labour transfer to France, Holland, Austria, and Germany in the case of accession.[63] Except some conservative and nationalist deputies cautioning against a possible wave of Turkish workers, during the 2000s the EP did not debate possible migrant inflows as much as the candidate's political characteristics.[64]

Still, the EU's absorption capacity remained a controversial issue, partly because the Turkey-sceptic members of the European Parliament connected the term to their stereotypes. According to them, to say the least, Turkey was too 'different' for the EU to absorb. A member of ALDE denounced this conduct in 2009: 'what we are unhappy about is the fact that some of our fellow members seem to wish to use this notion of absorption capacity in order to postpone the accession

---

[59] Council of the European Union, Conclusions of the Presidency, Copenhagen European Council 21–22 June 1993, SN 180/1/93 Rev 1.
[60] Council of the European Union, Presidency Conclusions, Brussels European Council, 14/15.12.2006, 16879/1/06 REV 1 CONCL 3, Brussels, February 12, 2007.
[61] For one example, see European Parliament, European Parliament Resolution on Turkey's Progress towards Accession, P6_TA(2006)0381, Strasbourg, September 27, 2006, Article 79; European Parliament Resolution of 21 May 2008 on Turkey's 2007 Progress Report, P6_TA(2008)0224, A6–0168/2008 Strasbourg, May 21, 2008, Article 58.
[62] European Commission, 'Issues Arising from Turkey's Membership Perspective', Commission Staff Working Document, October 6, 2004, COM(2004) 656 final, 16.
[63] Ibid, 19.
[64] See Gerard Batten's address, Debate on Croatia: progress report 2008 – Turkey: progress report 2008 – Former Yugoslav Republic of Macedonia: progress report 2008, Strasbourg, 11 March 2009 and Charles Tannock's addresses, Debate on Turkey's Progress Towards Accession, Strasbourg, September 26, 2006

of new countries indefinitely. We do not approve of that.'⁶⁵ The representative of the European Council, Carl Bildt, addressed these members at the same meeting:

> I did notice that there were a number of – mainly – gentlemen from the Far Right up there who had their reservations on Turkey, to put it in the mildest possible terms. If I understood the argument, it was that Turkey is too large, too complicated and too Muslim. If you read Article 49 of the treaty, and that is what we have to base our policies on, it does not make any exceptions for big countries, it does not make any exceptions for complicated cases, and it has no religious criteria.⁶⁶

The Christian Democrats were also referring excessively to the EU's capacity to absorb Turkey. To them, Turkey's accession hinged on the full implementation of the Copenhagen criteria together with the EU's ability to absorb the candidate.⁶⁷ EPP members thus insistently referred to the Brussels European Council's conclusions (2006) on the EU's absorption capacity.⁶⁸ These members nevertheless did not repeat the term that much in their parliamentary reports about the candidates of Balkans or in their proposals to amend them. The amendments of the reports on the progress of the Former Yugoslav Republic of Macedonia in 2007 and 2008 did not involve the concept or any reference to the EU's capacity to absorb the candidate.⁶⁹ Similarly, political discussions to revise the Parliament's reports about Croatia in 2007 and 2008 had quite limited but positive mentions. To give an example, the Christian Democrats in the European Parliament welcomed the fact that Croatia would not be a burden on the EU's capacity for integration at the time of accession.⁷⁰ During the years considered, absorption capacity became a term in political discussions mainly destined to define the European side of the EU-Turkey negotiations. To the Christian Democrats, the EU had to mind the hazard of 'overstretching itself' by keeping a reference

---

65 Annemie Neyts-Uyttebroeck's address, Debate on Enlargement Strategy 2009 Concerning the Countries of the Western Balkans, Iceland and Turkey, Strasbourg, November 25, 2009.
66 Carl Bilt's address, ibid.
67 See amendment 21 for paragraph 4a and amendment 51 for paragraph 7 a, Amendments 1–149 for the Draft Motion for Resolution, PE430.291v01–00, November 9, 2009, 12–13, 30.
68 For an example, see amendment 20 for recital C, Amendments 1–236 for the Draft Motion for a Resolution (2007), 7.
69 Similar concepts were used only regarding the progress of the country and the stability and Association Process, See European Parliament, Amendments 1–156, for the 2006 Progress Report on the Former Yugoslav Republic of Macedonia, PE 388.550v01–00, May 11, 2007, and, Amendments 1–184, on the 2007 Progress Report on the Former Yugoslav Republic of Macedonia, 2007/2268(INI), February, 12, 2008.
70 Amendment 42 for paragraph 1b, European Parliament, Amendments, 1–151, on Croatia's 2006 Progress Report, PE 384.604v01–00, March 1, 2007, 3.

to its absorption capacity in its reports about Turkey.[71] Therefore, EPP members called on the European Commission to devise reports about the impact of Turkey's membership.[72] For them, the EU's capacity to absorb Turkey had to be a precondition to the candidate's accession, and it should be rigorously examined.[73]

Other parliamentarians sometimes made use of the EU's capacity, but from different perspectives. For one example, members of the European Left pointed to the need of building the EU's integration capacity for the enlargements ahead, including the 'preparation for the accession of Turkey'.[74] In a similar manner, PES members considered the absorption capacity to be a sort of institutional and financial preparation of the EU.[75] The Socialists thus welcomed the Lisbon Treaty (2009) enhancing the EU's capacity to cope with further enlargements.[76] To these members, absorption capacity was a necessity in order for the EU to enlarge with Turkey eventually. They remained critical of the usage of this term in direct relationship with the candidate, and instead they linked Turkey's accession only to the accession criteria.[77] For one instance, the Party of the European Left proposed to amend the Parliamentary Report in 2006 with this additional statement: 'No new barriers, such as the "absorption capacity", should be set

---

[71] Elmar Brok, Debate on Enlargement Strategy 2009 Concerning the Countries of the Western Balkans, Iceland and Turkey (2009).

[72] Ursula Stenzel's address, Debate on Progress towards Accession by Turkey, Strasbourg, April 1, 2004; European Parliament, Draft Report on Turkey's Progress Towards Accession 2006, Paragraph 72, 17.

[73] For EPP members, see Jacques Toubon's address, Debate on Turkey's Progress Towards Accession (2006); Alexander Lambsdorff and Werner Langen's addresses, Debate on EU-Turkey Relations, Strasbourg, October 24, 2007; Elmar Brok, Ioannis Kasoulides, and Francisco José Millán Mon's addresses, Debate on 2009 Progress Report on Croatia, 2009 Progress Report on the Former Yugoslav Republic of Macedonia – 2009 Progress Report on Turkey, Strasbourg, February 10, 2010; Eimar Brok's address, Debate on 2010 Progress Report on Turkey, Strasbourg, May 8, 2011. ALDE members also emphasised the EU's absorption capacity in their arguments although not in a manner against Turkey. For an example, see Siiri Ovir's address, Debate on 2009 Progress Report on Croatia, 2009 Progress Report on the Former Yugoslav Republic of Macedonia – 2009 Progress Report on Turkey (2010).

[74] Amendment 47 for recital Fc, Amendments 1–236 for the Draft Motion for a Resolution (2007), 14.

[75] Amendment 236 for paragraph 37, Amendments 1–343 for Draft Report on Turkey's Progress towards Accession 2006 (2006), 80–81.

[76] Amendment 11 for paragraph 2a, Amendment 1–149 for the Draft Motion for Resolution (2009), 7–8.

[77] Amendment 17 and 18 for recital c, Amendments 1–162 for the Draft Motion for a Resolution (2008), 9–10; Amendments 14 and 15 for citation 12, Amendments 1–200 for Draft motion for a resolution on the 2013 Progress Report on Turkey, PE526.229v01–00, January 13, 2014, 8–9.

up because it is not up to the incoming countries to take responsibility for the absorption but to the EU to prepare and provide for it.'[78] In another example, the Parliamentary report (2008) drafted by a Christian Democratic member stated the EU's absorption capacity to be an indispensable condition for the negotiations: 'Copenhagen Criteria and EU integration capacity, in accordance with the conclusions of the December 2006 European Council meeting, remain the basis ...'[79] The European Left proposed to amend this statement too; in their opinion, the accession criteria continued to be 'the sole basis for the accession to the EU', and the EU should not introduce 'no further or supplementary criteria.'[80]

The final two preconditions stipulated to Turkey, the recognition of the Armenian Genocide committed by the Ottoman Empire and the peaceful resolution of conflicts with Cyprus, also arose from the principle of good neighbourly relations, a condition presented by the Helsinki European Council (1999) to evoke Turkey's prolonged issues with its neighbours. In 1987, the European Parliament had already officially called on Turkey to acknowledge as genocide the massacres committed by Ottoman civil and military bureaucrats to the Armenian minority in 1915.[81] The Parliament revived the issue through its reports about Turkey's reform progress in 2004 and 2005, in which the candidate's recognition of the Armenian genocide was proclaimed to be a precondition to its accession. There was very little debate among the deputies on whether the recognition of the genocide should be a prerequisite this way. The members mostly agreed that facing history was an essential part of Turkey's compliance with the accession criteria, and it should also be discussed in line with the situation of the Armenian minority in the country.[82] Yet, once Turkey took steps towards the rap-

---

[78] Amendment 258 for recital c, Amendments 1–343 for Draft Report on Turkey's progress towards Accession 2006 (2006), 87.
[79] European Parliament, Report On Turkey's Progress 2007 Progress Report, PE 402. 879v02–00, A6–0168/2008, April 28, 2008. 3.
[80] Amendment 18 for recital c, Amendments 1–162 for the Draft Motion for a Resolution (2008), 10.
[81] The European Parliament, Resolution on a Political Solution to the Armenian Question, Official Journal of the European Communities, Doc. A2, July 7, 1987, 33/87.
[82] See and compare, Paragraph, 56, European Parliament Resolution on Turkey's progress towards accession P6_TA(2006)0381, paragraph 34; European Parliament resolution of 12 March 2009 on Turkey's progress report 2008, P6_TA(2009)0134, paragraph 44; European Parliament Resolution of 21 May 2008 on Turkey's 2007 progress report, P6_TA(2008)0224; Amendment 99, paragraph 20.a, amendment 13 for recital c, Amendments 1–188 for the Draft Motion for Resolution, PE416.543v01–00, January 7, 2009, 54/103; Amendment 104 for paragraph 19 a, amendment 185 for paragraph 32, Amendments 1–243 for the Draft Motion for a Resolution,

prochement with Armenia in 2008, debates on the case temporarily abated and parliamentarians rather focused on the normalisation of the relations between Turkey and its neighbour.[83]

The settlement of disputes with Cyprus was also acknowledged almost by every parliamentarian to be a precondition given the member status of Nicosia. Before the negotiations' opening, the European Commission commended Turkey's commitments to a peaceful resolution in tandem with the United Nations framework.[84] Nevertheless, the peace negotiations between the Turkish and Greek communities of the island did not meet with success, and Cyprus joined the EU in 2004 as the sole representative of the island, which meant that Turkey was then not recognising an EU member. This caused a very serious problem under the principle of the good neighbourly relations, as the Commission's progress report in 2005 noted.[85] Further, following the EU's enlargement Turkey was expected to modernise the Association Agreement and Additional Protocol signed with the European Economic Community in the 1960s. Updating the documents according to the new members would indicate the full recognition of Cyprus by Turkey. In return, the candidate declared that it was going to involve Cyprus in the agreements as soon as the EU ceased the isolation of the Turkish Cypriot Community on the island. Turkey's restrictions against Cyprus mostly in the field of transportation continued, at the expense of the membership negotiations coming to a standstill and, in this context, receiving quite adamant reactions in the European Parliament. In a manner heavier and more straightforward than that of the Commission, the Parliament's annual report argued that Turkey's refusal to recognise Cyprus set a serious barrier in the accession process.[86] It therefore linked the full implementation of the association documents and the recognition of Cyprus to Turkey's accession perspective. It added the Council

---

PE431.004v02–00, January 1, 2010, 55, 98/127; Amendment 372 for paragraph 31, Amendments 1 – 461 for the Draft Motion for a Resolution on the 2011 Progress Report on Turkey, PE478.719v01–00, February 1, 2012, 64. Also see the entire discussions in, Debate on Turkey's Progress towards Accession (2006) and Debate on EU-Turkey Relations (2007). Also see, Jacques Toubon's address, Debate on Opening of Negotiations with Turkey – Additional Protocol to the EEC-Turkey Association Agreement (2005). Ioannis Kasoulides' address, Debate on Turkey's Progress towards Accession (2006).

83 See the European Parliament's official reports on Turkey after 2007.
84 Commission of European Communities, 2004 Regular Report on Turkey's Progress towards Accession, Brussels, SEC(2004)1201, Brussels, October 06, 14.
85 Commission of European Communities, Turkey 2005 Progress Report, Brussels, SEC(2005) 1426, Brussels, November 9, 2005, 137.
86 European Parliament, European Parliament Resolution on Turkey's Progress towards Accession (2006), recital AB.

Resolution (2006) declaring this issue to be a precondition for Turkey's accession.[87]

The Cyprus conflict had in fact many other aspects, such as the presence of Turkish armed forces on the island and the isolation of the Turkish community in the north. The European Parliament had already criticised Turkish military existence in Northern Cyprus in its 2000 report, calling the armed forces to be 'occupation forces', and called for their withdrawal.[88] Following the negotiations' beginning, the European Parliament repeated its warnings against Turkey's military involvement in Cyprus, although it refrained from using the term 'occupation'. The early negotiation years then featured Cypriot and Greek members' joint participation in parliamentary debates on this subject. Among them, in 2006 and 2007 conservative members from Cyprus denounced Turkish military as the forces of occupation and colonization, and communist and liberal deputies from Greece and Cyprus also called for their immediate withdrawal. [89] Greek and Cypriot parliamentarians from different ideologies also together asked Turkey to end its veto against the accession of Cyprus to international organizations, implying its membership in NATO.[90]

While the Christian Democrats repeatedly declared Turkey's relations with Cyprus to be a precondition of its full membership, the Socialists, Greens, Liberals, and British Conservatives additionally asked the EU to take constitutive initiatives for the solution and to lift the sanctions imposed on Turkish Cypriots.[91] At times, the Socialists and Liberals also called on the Cypriot Greek Government to start new reforms and initiatives in order to advance the rapprochement be-

---

87 Ibid., recital AB. See, Council of the European Union, Enlargement: Turkey. Declaration by the European Community and its Member States, Document 12541/05, September 21, 2005.
88 European Parliament, Report on the 1999 Regular Report from the Commission on Turkey's Progress towards Accession, A5–0297/2000, 19 October 2000.
89 Amendments 206 and 207 for paragraph 19, amendment 217 for paragraph 19a, Amendments 1–236 for the Draft Motion for a Resolution PE392.298v02–00, PE393.947v02–00, 25.09.2007, 69–70, 73/79; Amendment 262 for recital Ca and amendments 179 and 186 for paragraph 30, Amendments 1–343 for Draft Report on Turkey's Progress towards Accession 2006, PE 376.373v02–00, 04.07.2006, 62–64, 88/115; Amendments 208, 213 and 214 for paragraph 19 and amendment 222 for paragraph 20, Amendments 1–236 for the Draft Motion for a Resolution PE392.298v02–00, PE393.947v02–00, 25.09.2007, 70–72, 75/79.
90 Amendment 173 for paragraph 29a, amendment 195 for paragraph 30a and amendments 201, 202 and 203 for paragraph 31a, Amendments for Draft Report on Turkey's Progress towards Accession 2006, PE 376.373v02–00, 04.07.2006, 60, 67–68, 70/115.
91 See, Warner Langen's address, Debate on Turkey's Progress towards Accession (2006); Amendment 22 for recital D, and amendments 181 and 184 for paragraph 30, Amendments 1–236 for the Draft Motion for a Resolution, (2007), 7, 61–62.

tween two societies.⁹² The British Conservatives notably challenged the EU's typical stand on the Cyprus issue. By way of example, Geoffrey Orden, from the British Conservative Party and the European Democrats, held the EU responsible for the solution process and for the isolation on the North of Cyprus.⁹³ Moreover, since the European Council did not relieve the Cypriot Turkish Community from international sanctions, Turkey's refusal to fully recognise Cyprus was 'justifiable' to him.⁹⁴ On the other hand, the members representing extreme-right ideologies made the most judgemental statements on Turkey's part in the Cyprus case.⁹⁵ They also disapproved of the European Union's prospective support for the Northern Cypriot authority including its financial incentives.⁹⁶ In contrast to the arguments of the Socialists and European Democrats (Eurosceptics), they contended that financial support to the Turkish Cypriot Community would infringe international law.⁹⁷

Judging Turkey's Democratic Performance through the Prism of the Accession Criteria?

Political camps of the EP highlighted several cases of Turkey's democratic progress and deficit through the prism of the Copenhagen political criteria. Although the progress reports of the European Commission had remarked on the slow pace of Turkey's democratisation, in the early years of the accession talks MEPs reflected a promising picture. First, many political actors were satisfied with the democratic course of elections in Turkey.⁹⁸ The representatives of the

---

92 Amendment 187 for paragraph 30, Amendments 1–343 for Draft Report on Turkey's progress towards Accession 2006, (2006), 65; Emma Bonino's address, Debate on Opening of Negotiations with Turkey – Additional Protocol to the EEC-Turkey Association Agreement (2005).
93 Amendment 216 for paragraph 19 Amendments 1–236 for the Draft Motion for a Resolution (2007), 73.
94 Amendment 331 for recital U, Amendments 1–343 for Draft Report on Turkey's progress towards Accession 2006 (2006), 111.
95 For example, see amendment 200 for paragraph 31, Amendments for Draft Report on Turkey's progress towards Accession, 69.
96 Amendment 177 for paragraph 30, Amendments 1–343 for Draft Report on Turkey's progress towards Accession 2006, (2006), 61, and amendment 220 for paragraph 19 Amendments 1–236 for the Draft Motion for a Resolution, (2007), 74.
97 For example, see amendment 221, Paragraph 20, Amendments 1–236 for the Draft Motion for a Resolution, (2007), 74.
98 See European Parliament resolution of 21 May 2008 on Turkey's 2007 progress report and on Turkey in 2007 and European Parliament resolution of 29 March 2012 on the 2011 Progress Re-

European Commission and Council in the European Parliament accordingly credited the free and fair elections held in 2007 to be the signs of democracy and stability in Turkey.[99] In spite of the military pressure on civil politics, the Socialists claimed, the elections had proved the will in Turkish politics and society to maintain the democratic track.[100] The Socialists and Christian Democrats also separately mentioned the rising participation of women in the Turkish Parliament at the end of the elections in 2007 and 2011.[101] That aside, political parties were generally concerned about the election threshold in Turkey, and, in particular, political rights and participation of Kurdish minority remained the gravest problem.[102] All in all, Turkey's political transition was believed to take time. In a speech in the EP in 2009, the Commissioner for Enlargement Affairs was noting the 'steady progress in Turkey' despite the slowing democratic reforms.[103] The Socialists, Liberals, and Greens were calling for a fair assessment of Turkey's situation as late as 2012; the country was accordingly still in the process of change towards European values.[104] To these members, the EU had to show a clear membership perspective to Turkey and 'take the Copenhagen criteria' seriously, so

---

port on Turkey. Olli Rehn, Manuel Lobo Antunes, and Maria Eleni Koppa's addresses, Debate on EU-Turkey Relations (2007); Amendment 92 for paragraph 3, amendment 96 for paragraph 3, Amendments 1– 461 for the Draft Motion for a Resolution on the 2011 Progress Report on Turkey (2012), 52.

99 Addresses of Oli Rehn and Manuel Lobo Antunes' addresses, Debate on EU-Turkey Relations (2007).

100 Amendment 51 for paragraph 1 a, amendment 55 for paragraph 2, and amendment 61 for paragraph 2 a, Amendments 1–236 for the Draft Motion for a Resolution (2007), 16–19; Maria Eleni Koppa's address, Debate on EU-Turkey Relations (2007); Amendment 92 for paragraph 7, Amendments 1–236 for the Draft Motion for a Resolution (2007), 30.

101 Amendment 54 for paragraph 2, Ibid,, 16–17; Amendment 96 for paragraph 3 and amendment 257 for 19 a, Amendments 1– 461 for the Draft Motion for a Resolution on the 2011 Progress Report on Turkey (2012), 52, 147.

102 European Parliament, European Parliament Resolution of 29 March 2012 on the 2011 Progress Report on Turkey, P7_TA(2012)0116, Brussels, March 29, 2012, Article 4; Amendment 57, 58, and 59 for paragraph 2, Amendments 1–236 for the Draft Motion for a Resolution (2007), 18; Amendments 46 for recital F b and amendment 58 for paragraph 2, Amendments 1–236 for the Draft Motion for a Resolution (2007), 14, 18; The Party of the European Left, Together for Change in Europe, Manifesto for European Elections, October 28, 2009.

103 Speech by Olli Rehn, Strategy Paper at EP Plenary, Strasbourg, November 25, 2009, Speech/09/555.

104 Richard Howitt, Emine Bozkurt, Franziska Keller's addresses, Debate on Enlargement report for Turkey, Brussels, March 28, 2012.

that the candidate could continue reforms in agreement with the accession conditions.[105]

For those who favoured Turkey's accession process, the candidate's credibility declined over time, and its democratic transition never returned to its pre-negotiations pace. As a Socialist member expressed in 2009, although Turkey had shown considerable development before the negotiations began, now it was somehow lagging behind.[106] The freedom of expression was perhaps the most critical among the fields requiring urgent reforms.[107] Certain articles of the penal code and anti-terror law in Turkey, especially article 301 of the constitution, the clause about insulting Turkishness that in fact justified many legal charges against journalists and authors, remained the subjects of criticism.[108] MEPs from broad ideological spectrums also disaffirmed the Turkish government's increasing authoritarianism against the popular movements and country-wide protests, as well as the corruption scandals that erupted in 2013.[109] The Christian Democrats stated that year that new chapters should not be opened, as the Turkish government was becoming more and more authoritarian.[110] The Liberals contended that the government in its recent authoritarian and corruptive condition was breaking away from European values.[111] For the pro-Turkish parliamentarians, it was a dramatic change of direction in Turkish politics within a short timeframe. Andrew Duff from ALDE stated his thoughts about the coun-

---

[105] Bastiaan Belder's address, Debate on 2009 Progress Report on Croatia – 2009 Progress Report on the Former Yugoslav Republic of Macedonia – 2009 Progress Report on Turkey (2010); Metin Kazak's and Helene Flautre's address, Debate Enlargement report for Turkey (2012); Amendment 4 for paragraph 1, Amendments 1–343 for Draft Report on Turkey's progress towards Accession 2006 (2006), 2.
[106] Vural Oger's address, Debate on Democratic Process in Turkey (2009).
[107] Alexander Lambsdorff's address, Debate on Democratic Process in Turkey (2009).
[108] Richard Howitt, Emine Bozkurt, Franziska Keller's addresses, Debate on Enlargement report for Turkey, Brussels, March 28, 2012; European Parliament, European Parliament Resolution of 9 March 2011 on Turkey's 2010 Progress Report, P7_TA(2011)0090, March 9, 2011, Articles 9, 10, and 27; Enlargement Report for Turkey, European Parliament Resolution on the 2011 Progress Report on Turkey, P7_TA(2012)0116 B7–0189/2012, March 29, 2012, Articles 15, 21, and 23.
[109] Mitro Repo, Claudette Abela Baldacchino's address, Debate on 2013 progress report on Turkey, Strasbourg, March 12, 2014; Roberta Angelilli, Anna Maria and Corazza Bildt's address, Debate on 2013 Progress Report on Turkey, Strasbourg, March 11, 2014; Stefan Fule, Richard Howitt, and Fransizka Keller's addresses, Debate on 2013 Progress Report on Turkey (2014).
[110] Markus Pieper and Peter Jahr's addresses, Debate on 2012 Progress Report on Turkey, Strasbourg, April 18, 2013.
[111] Guy Verhofstadt's address, Debate on Situation in Turkey, Strasbourg, June 12, 2013; Pino Ariacchi and Claudette Abela Baldacchino's addresses, Debate on 2013 Progress Report on Turkey (2014/2).

try in early 2013: 'Turkey has a great capacity to become the world's first liberal modern Muslim European country, and I rejoice at the events that are now in train.'[112] Following the corruption scandals and the signs of growing authoritarianism in the country, the same member revised his position in the same year, and stated that 'Turkey has ceased to fulfil the Copenhagen criteria sufficiently.'[113] The then prime minister's turning to authoritarian means of controlling society came under the most fire. He had to change his personal character, Hannes Swoboda from PES asserted, if he ever wanted to see Turkey inside Europe.[114] Pro-Turkey parliamentarians were additionally worried about the risk of the candidate's breaking off negotiations completely. The EU's Commissioner for Enlargement remarked in 2013 that the EU had to remain an anchor during the candidate's negotiations regardless of the current status of its democracy.[115] The negotiation procedure was thus a burden not only on Turkey's shoulders, and the EU should come to grips with the political situation in the country. Fransizka Keller, from European Green Party, reproached: 'if Member States did not always reject outright Turkey's accession no matter what, then we would have much more leverage.'[116]

While Turkey's credibility was declining, most British deputies, including the British Conservatives, seemed to have maintained their traditional support for Turkey's EU bid. In their opinion also, Turkey's democratic deficit was growing bigger, but even so the EU should stay committed to the candidate's expected political transition.[117] In the same way as Conservative Geoffrey von Orden, who argued that the EU should send positive messages to Turkey in order to keep the country on the democratisation track,[118] most of the British parliamentarians insisted on restoring relations with the candidate. William Dartmouth, from the UK Independence Party, countered this common British stand in the European Parliament: 'Turkey should be regarded as too big, too poor, too different and too authoritarian ever to become a member of the European Union. It is totally depressing that in this establishment UK political parties are all cheerleaders for Turkey to join the EU. They, and this House, should think again.'[119]

---

112 Andrew Duff's address, Debate on Situation in Turkey (2013).
113 Andrew Duff's address, Debate on 2013 Progress Report on Turkey (2014).
114 Hannes Swoboda's address, Debate on Situation in Turkey (2013).
115 Stefan Fuhle's address, ibid.
116 Fransizka Keller's addresses, ibid.
117 Charles Tannock's address, Debate on 2013 progress report on Turkey (2014/2).
118 Geoffrey Von Orden's address, Debate on 2013 Progress Report on Turkey (2014).
119 William Dartmouth's address, Debate on 2013 Progress Report on Turkey (2014).

Far-right deputies of the EP disfavoured Turkey's EU bid throughout the negotiations (until the early 2010s) repeatedly, regardless of the positive or negative changes in the candidate's democratic character. They entered the discussions over the candidate's democratic deficits according to their stereotypes. Even in the early, 'promising' years of the negotiations, far-right members were in disagreement with the European Commission and Parliament, which were together affirming that Turkey was fulfilling the Copenhagen criteria. In one instance, these members expected a halt in the negotiations by the EU authorities as early as 2007 because the country was blatantly violating fundamental human rights.[120] To the radical right, the Commission's progress reports were just disregarding two facts, that Turkish governments almost always violated human rights and Turkey's non-European nature was hindering any amelioration in its democracy.[121] To give one example, Laurence Stassen, non-attached member representing the Dutch Party for Freedom, proposed to amend the European Parliament's country report with these statements: 'Turkey is corrupt: according to Transparency International, in 2012 Turkey scored only 49 on a scale from 1 to 100; that means that it is highly corrupt.'[122] There were certain facts in these comments about Turkey, particularly about the freedom of expression. But the member's stereotypes hindered a fair evaluation of the country. In the above proposal, she highlighted Turkey's corruption performance (49 points) documented by the Transparency International in 2012. According to the same report, however, even EU members could sometimes fall behind Turkey's corruption score. In that year, indeed, Italy and Greece had hit only 42 and 36 points in their performances of fighting corruption.[123] This MEP hence dismissed the idea that Turkey would ever possibly democratise in the same way Europeans did. The same member bluntly argued: 'having regard to the fact that Turkey will never fully meet the criteria, or be able and willing to do so, and should therefore never accede to the EU...'[124] The main reason for the candidate's so-called failure to fulfil the accession criteria, consequently, was not its democratic progress, but rather its religious and geographical condition. She hence asserted that the applicant

---

[120] Amendment 19 for recital c and amendment 48 for paragraph 1, Amendments 1–236 for the Draft Motion for a Resolution (2007), 6, 15.
[121] Laurence J. A. J. Stassen's address, Debate on 2013 Progress Report on Turkey (2014).
[122] Amendments 208–415 for the Draft Motion for Resolution on the 2012 Progress Report of Turkey, Part II, PE.504.402v01–00, February 12, 2013, 103.
[123] Transparency International, Transparency International Corruption Perceptions Index 2012, 5.
[124] Amendment 18 for Citation 11, Amendments 1–207 for the Draft Motion for Resolution on the 2012 Progress Report of Turkey (2013), 10.

being 'highly Islamised and geographically outside Europe should never accede to the EU.'[125]

The issues related to women rights were also broadly discussed throughout these years, especially between the majority of the EP and far-right members. The European Commission pointed out in its 2005 and 2006 progress reports that women's participation in work life was the lowest in Turkey among the OECD countries.[126] Although the European Parliament welcomed the active female figures in Turkish public life, it also underlined the insufficient progress in the implementation of women's rights as well as the continuing problems of discrimination and violence against women.[127] Together, the deputies critiqued Turkey's inadequate progress in gender equality and the slow empowerment of women in public social and economic life. The far-right, however, chose to orient women rights to Islam and to blame the discrimination of women on the government of the Justice and Development Party (AKP). Philip Claeys thus opposed the European Parliament's emphasis that 'considerable number of women in Turkey held strong positions in the economy and in the academic world.' He proposed to amend: '(Turkish woman) are not only routinely subjected to violence and all kinds of discriminatory action but, since the AKP took power, are also finding life much harder in the increasingly Islamised administration and are under pressure to resign.'[128] The rise of the conservative AKP therefore preoccupied these members additionally as a women's issue, as Islam allegedly declared women 'inferior'. The situation of women was not to improve as long as Islam predominated Turkey, Frank Vanhecke held in the European Parliament at the beginning of the negotiations.[129] Roberto Fioere was similarly arguing that mos-

---

[125] Amendment 378 for Paragraph 26 a, Amendments 208–415 for the Draft Motion for Resolution on the 2012 Progress Report of Turkey (2013), 103.
[126] See Commission of European Communities, Turkey 2005 Progress Report, Brussels, SEC(2005)1426, Brussels, November 9, 2005, 33; Turkey 2006 Progress Report, SEC(2006) 1390, Brussels, November 8, 2006, 19.
[127] Women's participation in Turkish public sphere was commended. European Parliament, Motion for a Resolution on EU-Turkey Relations, PE 396.011v01–00, B6–0376/2007, October 15, 2007, Article 17; Also see Meglena Kuneva's address, Debate on Women in Turkey (2007). European Parliament, European Parliament resolution of 10 February 2010 on Turkey's progress report 2009, P7_TA(2010)0025, B7–0068/2010, February 10, 2010; Amendments 161–164 for paragraph 15, Amendments 1–236 for the Draft Motion for a Resolution (2007), 54–55; Emine Bozkurt's address, Debate on 2020 perspective for women in Turkey, Strasbourg, May 21, 2012; Amendment 54 for paragraph 2, Amendments 1–236 for the Draft Motion for a Resolution (2007), 16–17; Amendment 96 for paragraph 3 and amendment 257 for 19 a, Amendments 1–461 for the Draft Motion for a Resolution on the 2011 Progress Report on Turkey (2012), 52, 147.
[128] Amendment 160 for paragraph 15, ibid., 54.
[129] Frank Vanhecke's address, Debate on Women in Turkey (2007).

ques in Turkey were increasing in number, which somehow had a role in the oppression of females to a wider extent.[130] Through their arguments, these members leant towards Islamophobia, rather than mere Turkey-scepticism in political terms.

The influence of the Kemalist legacy on Turkish politics became another debatable matter linked to the application of the Copenhagen criteria. Parliamentarians representing different ideologies questioned Kemalism's compatibility with minority rights in Europe.[131] They tended to link Article 301 of the Turkish Constitution to the nationalist roots of the Kemalist legacy in Turkey.[132] According to this view, the recent authoritarianism in Turkey had its origins in the early Kemalist history of the country.[133] The British conservative members therefore contended that Kemalist traditions in Turkish politics should evolve to a more pluralistic political environment although for a long while they had served security cooperation between Europe and America well.[134] In their view, Turkey's Kemalist legacy at present was motivating nationalist opposition to European reforms stipulated to Turkey.[135] Turkish military was perceived to be one of these Kemalist-nationalist forces that were impeding Turkey's EU prospects.[136] These criticisms aside, some conservative and nationalist members also credited the modernist lines of Kemalism as essential for Turkey's reform process; Ataturk's reforms had to remain intact for a secular Turkey.[137] Some members considered Kemalism to be a source of enlightenment against political Islam. Gerard Batten from the right-wing populist party Europe of Freedom and Democracy (also representing UKIP in Britain) thus held: 'The reforms of Kemal Ataturk in the 1920s were to be applauded, as they sought to leave behind the antiquities of the Ottoman Empire and the worst of the Dark Age Islamic practices and to take Turkey forward into the 20th century.'[138] To the same member, it was a fact that Ataturk

---

130 Roberto Fiore's address, Debate on Democratic Process in Turkey (2009).
131 Bernd Posselt's address, Debate on Turkey's Progress Towards Accession (2006).
132 Alexander Lambsdorff's address, Debate on EU-Turkey Relations (2007).
133 Marios Matsakis' address, Debate on Democratic Process in Turkey (2009); Elmar Brok, Debate on Situation in Turkey (2013).
134 Charles, Tannock's address, Debate on Democratization in Turkey (2010).
135 Bastian Belder's address, Debate on Democratic Process in Turkey (2009).
136 Amendment 156 for paragraph 28 a, Amendments 1–343 for Draft Report on Turkey's Progress towards Accession 2006 (2006), 54; European Parliament, European Parliament Resolution on Turkey's Progress towards Accession (2006), Article 20.
137 Geoffrey Von Orden and Christiana Muscardini's addresses, Debate on Situation in Turkey (2013).
138 Gerard Batten's address, Debate on Democratization in Turkey, Strasbourg, January 20, 2010.

stood against and repelled radical Islam in Turkey.[139] Islamic extremism, which was already on the rise, would find opportune moments to advance further in the case of Turkey's EU accession because EU legislation would take precedence over Turkey's secular institutions.[140]

Religious Concepts

Religious and political concepts did overlap on two occasions in the 2000s: At first, parliamentarians discussed the candidate with regard to political rights and liberties associated with religious freedoms. The implementation of religious rights in Turkey was rated as 'insufficient' on the basis of the Copenhagen criteria, according to which the supreme institution regulating the state's religious services, entitled the Directorate for Islamic Affairs, represented only the Sunni faith despite the numerous Alevi community.[141] The growing religious fragmentation in the country also concerned political parties from a broad range, as they mentioned the divide between the secular and Islamic parts of Turkish society.[142] As ALDE member Alexander Lambsdorff recommended, secularism in Turkey had to survive during the reformation period if the country wanted to provide and preserve religious freedoms of different communities.[143] These comments aside, at least until the 2010s the European Commission's and Parliament's official Turkey reports largely lacked any argument on the Islamisation of Turkish politics, partially because they still considered the Justice and Development Party to be committed to fulfilling democratic reforms. Yet, religious clichés about Turkey continued to crop up in deputies' comments about the country's progress towards EU accession. On this occasion, MEPs from conservative and far-right origins revealed their Islamic stereotypes within parlia-

---

139 Gerard Batten's address, Debate on EU-Turkey Relations (2007).
140 Ibid.
141 European Parliament, European Parliament resolution of 10 February 2010 on Turkey's progress report 2009, Article 4; Amendment 243, 17 a, Amendments 208–415 for the Draft Motion for Resolution on the 2012 Progress Report of Turkey (2013), 26.
142 See Ria Oomen-Ruijten's Motion for Resolution, PE430.695v02–00, December 8, 2009; Amendment 94 for paragraph 16, Amendments 1–243 on the Draft Motion for a Resolution (2010), 50; Amendment 164 for paragraph 9 a and amendment 235 for paragraph 17a, Amendments for Draft motion for a resolution on the 2013 Progress Report on Turkey (2014), 98.
143 Alexander Lambsdorff's address, Debate on Turkey's 2007 Progress Report (2008).

mentary plenaries, as they oriented their religious prejudices to Turkey's democratic performance.

Despite being secular in practice, the European People's Party, especially its members from Germany and France, upheld their mono-culturalist perspective of Europe in the course of discussing Turkey's EU bid. Herman Van Rompuy, the first President of the European Council selected as an EPP member, spoke straight from the shoulder that Turkey was not European and would never be, and its membership would dilute the EU's Christian heritage.[144] This was equally raised by some Christian Democrats in the EP, who ascribed the country's recent authoritarianism to its 'Islamic devotion'. According to Zbigniew Zaleski, for one example, despite Turkey's European reforms its Islamic tradition and 'unwritten social codes' led it to diverge from European values.[145] The situation of Christian minorities in a culturally non-European country particularly concerned the Christian Democrats. Hans Gelt Poettering raised this issue at the very beginning of the membership negotiations with the candidate:

> We, in the Group of the European People's Party (Christian Democrats) and European Democrats, are all in favour of partnership, friendship and dialogue with the Islamic world, but that cannot be a one-way street. Islam, too – meaning, in this instance, the Turkish Government – must be willing to acknowledge the legitimate rights of Christians in Turkey and to give that practical expression.[146]

It was quite just to refer to the problems of Christian minorities in Turkey, since they at times faced religious and nationalist persecution as well as hate crimes. In Poettering's opinion, Turkey and the European Union were still two very distinct camps in religious terms, despite the start of the accession talks. This problematic language was much more evident in the opinions and amendments by far-right MEPs than those by the Christian Democrats. 'Turkish Islam', as named by them, was the main reason for the violence against Christian minorities,[147] and it also preceded the discrimination against women in Turkey.[148] As

---

144 'EU President: Herman Van Rompuy Opposes Turkey Joining', The Telegraph, September 19, 2009.
145 Zbigniew Zaleski's address, Debate on Turkey's 2007 Progress Report (2008).
146 Hans Gelt Poettering's address, Debate on Opening of Negotiations with Turkey – Additional Protocol to the EEC-Turkey Association Agreement (2005).
147 Philip Claeys and William Dartmouth's addresses, Debate on Enlargement Strategy 2009 Concerning the Countries of the Western Balkans, Iceland and Turkey (2009); Jim Allister's address, Debate on Turkey's Progress towards Accession, European Parliament, Strasbourg, 13 December 2004.

Mogens Camre from the Europe of Freedom and Democracy asserted in 2006 that, despite the accession talks' beginning, Turkey was not entirely adhering to European values and on the contrary was insisting on 'unacceptable Turkish and Islamic values'.[149] For an explicit example, far-right members were slamming Turkey for being affiliated with the Organisation of the Islamic Conference (OIC), whose declaration made use of the word 'Sharia' in its founding documents. Turkey's membership in the Organisation was arguably incompatible with 'the separation between the church and state in Turkey'.[150] However, the OIC was a legitimate establishment represented in the United Nations, and through its official Arabic language it inherently involved the term 'Sharia' that merely connoted the minimalist conception of Islamic humanitarian ethics.[151] According to the European conservatives and nationalists, even a moderate understanding of Islam apparently would not correspond to European values, as Charles Tannock contended: 'Turkey's membership of the OIC, where such common Western values as we all share in the European Union are not evident because the OIC cites Sharia law as a basis for human rights in the Islamic world.'[152] To summarise, aside from righteously questioning the freedom of religion in Turkey, in all these statements the common point was the act of conceptualising the country as a different, anti-civil, and anti-European entity. The Justice and Development Party's growing electoral support in and outside Turkey was a sign of Islamisation and an implicit menace to Europe.[153]

During the 2000s, political camps of the EP most often discussed Turkey's Islamic aspect in connection with its Ottoman past.[154] As such, the Ottoman history gave way to essentially two distinct sorts of arguments. According to the first one, from conservative and far-right camps, the Ottoman past was incongruent

---

148 Amendment 77 for paragraph 16 a, Amendments 1–343 for Draft Report on Turkey's progress towards Accession 2006, (2006), 27; Amendment 160 for paragraph 15, Amendments 1–236 for the Draft Motion for a Resolution (2007), 54.
149 Mogens N. J. Camre's address, Debate on Turkey's Progress Towards Accession (2006).
150 Amendment 378 for Paragraph 26 a Amendments 208–415 for the Draft Motion for Resolution on the 2012 Progress Report of Turkey (2013), 103; Amendment 84 for paragraph 18 a, Amendments 1–343 for Draft Report on Turkey's progress towards Accession 2006 (2006), 29.
151 See Cairo Declaration on Human Rights in Islam, August 5, 1990, U.N. GAOR, World Conference on Humanitarian Rights, 4th Session, Agenda Item 5, U.N. Doc. A/CONF.157/PC/62/Add.18, 1993.
152 Charles Tannock's address, Debate on Democratization in Turkey (2010).
153 Amendment 53 for paragraph 2, Amendments 1–236 for the Draft Motion for a Resolution (2007), 16.
154 See Paul T. Levin, *Turkey and the European Union: Christian and Secular Images of Islam* (New York: Palgrave Macmillan, 2011).

with European history and therefore rendered the candidate Europe's cultural antithesis and even an arch-rival by nature.[155] The second sort of argument found currency in liberal camps elaborating on the candidate's past in political terms, and instead conceived some features of the Ottoman Empire as an essential source of potential multiculturalism in Turkey. By way of a significant example, at the beginning of the accession talks the members of the European Green Party pointed at Turkey's cultural background and its diversity and called on the candidate to provide religious freedoms by acting on its Ottoman cultural and historical heritage:

> Respects the sensitivities that exist in a country where the large majority are Sunni Muslims but reminds Turkey of the important cultural and historic heritage handed down to it for safe-keeping by the multicultural, multiethnic and multireligious Ottoman Empire; also emphasises that the freedom for citizens to worship whichever religion or denomination they choose has to extend to giving them similar legal and administrative arrangements to practise their religion, organise their communities, hold and administer community assets and train their clergy ...[156]

The Greens implied an Ottoman heritage famously credited with the 'Millets', the Ottoman administration system based on autonomous religious groups, which preceded the modern-day conception of religious minorities in Turkey. These deputies construed parts of the earlier history as compatible with the expected freedoms in contemporary Turkey. The government then should find inspiration in the multicultural Ottoman past, where a 'Multicultural, multi-ethnic, and multireligious Ottoman Empire' bestowed various kinds of social rights on its subjects; so should the Turkish government.[157] The abolishment of the headscarf ban at Turkish universities that came into effect in 2008 was accordingly discerned as a significant step of providing religious freedoms in Turkey in harmony with the pluralist aspect of Ottoman history.[158]

---

[155] See Lydia Schenardi's address, Debate on Women in Turkey, Strasbourg, February 12, 2007; Mogens Camre's address, Debate on Turkey's 2007 Progress Report (2008).
[156] Amendment 76 paragraph 16 a. Amendments 1–343 for Draft Report on Turkey's progress towards Accession 2006 (2006), 26.
[157] Ibid.
[158] Ibid. Alexander Lambsdorff's address Parliamentary Debate on Turkey's 2007 Progress Report (2008).

Geographical Concepts

Throughout its integration history, the European Union had an intrinsically ambiguous territorial image. The earlier version of the Treaty of Rome (former Article 237) had spelt out a hazy territorial condition that countries from Europe could apply for the accession to the European Economic Community. The Treaty on European Union (TEU, 1992) enhanced this condition with civic responsibilities in Article 49. In its latest version, amended by the Lisbon Treaty in 2009, TEU enshrined European values and the territorial condition together: 'any European State which respects the values referred to in Article 2 and is committed to promoting them may apply to become a member of the Union.'[159] These clauses constitute the sole yardstick of the EU's territorial criterion today. The EU, whose enlargement policy was built more or less on a continental conception, put Turkey's accession request into operation in 1987 but also ruled out Morocco's application in the same year mainly for geographical reasons. Despite that, Turkey's Europeanness in territorial terms still remained a much-debated issue in the 2000s, as MEPs were inclined to discuss Turkey using controversial geographical concepts, such as being 'Asian' or forming a 'bridge' between the two continents.

Throughout its relations with Brussels since 1963, for the European political camps Turkey's primary benefit arose from its geostrategic position. It was a necessary ally in security terms of the Cold War years, and during the 2000s it was still deemed important in a Europe facing mass migration, conflicts, and religious terrorism. The European Parliament acknowledged in its 2006 report: 'a modern, democratic and secular Turkey... could play a constructive and stabilising role in promoting understanding between civilisations.'[160] As a socialist member remarked, strengthening the ties between the European Union and Turkey was therefore 'of fundamental importance for the EU, for Turkey and for the wider region.'[161] The Liberals, in line with the ALDE's traditional emphasis on the security aspect of Europe, noted that Turkey's membership would 'contribute greatly to the future development of EU common foreign, security and defence policy.'[162] Turkey-sceptic political camps also acknowledged the economic and

---

[159] Consolidated Versions of the Treaty on European Union, Official Journal of European Union 55, C326, 2012, 43.
[160] European Parliament, European Parliament Resolution on Turkey's Progress towards Accession (2006), Article 55.
[161] Amendment 42 for recital Fa, Amendments 1–236 for the Draft Motion for a Resolution (2007), 13.
[162] Amendment 324 for recital T, ibid., 108.

security benefits the EU was going to reap from closer relations with Turkey.[163] The young Turkish population could take a part in the solution to the ageing EU, and the cooperation with the country would secure Europe's energy supply.[164] But for the Turkey-sceptic members its geopolitical uses did not necessarily have to result in EU accession; the Union would also be able to profit the candidate's geo-strategic position through a privileged partnership.[165]

Most of these references to Turkey's strategic importance had an essentially geopolitical nature. Political camps generally explained Turkey's Islamic character and geopolitical location with its so-called connecting function between the West and East. In regard to Turkey's strategic contributions to Europe, geographical and religious categorisations blended into each other within the use of the term 'bridge'. For instance, the Christian Democratic statements conceptualising Turkey as 'a bridge between Europe and the Islamic world' disclosed an alternative definition of the EU in relation to the 'Islamic civilisation'.[166] The Communists, quite surprisingly, also made use of the 'bridge' metaphor while positioning Turkey 'between the East and West, Islam and Christianity.'[167] Unlike these suggestive mentions, Socialist members made perhaps more balanced comments about Turkey's potential role in regional contribution, as they stated that the candidate was a 'bridge' between 'the EU and its neighbours in the Middle East and with Islamic countries in the world.'[168] Turkey's partnership with Spain in the 'Alliance of Civilisations', the project launched in 2005 for improving multicultural and peaceful dialogue between European and Middle Eastern religions, was commended through the country's bridging function. Liberal and Socialist members lauded Turkey's role in this project and for showing 'its international commitment to bringing the West and the Arab and Islamic world closer

---

163 Amendment 318 for recital Ra and amendment 319 for recital Rb, Amendments 1–343 for Draft Report on Turkey's progress towards Accession 2006 (2006), 106–107; Hans-Gert Poettering's address, Debate on Turkey's Progress towards Accession (2004).
164 Amendments 1–343 for Draft Report on Turkey's progress towards Accession 2006, (2006), 107; Amendment 204 for paragraph 31 a, Amendments 1–343 for Draft Report on Turkey's progress towards Accession 2006 (2006), 70; Amendment 73, 77, 80 and 83 for paragraph 5, Amendments 1–236 for the Draft Motion for a Resolution (2007), 23, 25–27.
165 Amendment 228 for paragraph 35a and amendment 234 for paragraph 36a, Amendments 1–343 for Draft Report on Turkey's progress towards Accession 2006 (2006), 78, 80.
166 Amendment 329 for recital Ta, ibid., 110.
167 Amendment 43 for recital Fa, Amendments 1–236 for the Draft Motion for a Resolution (2007), 13.
168 Amendments 325 and 326 for recital T, Amendments 1–343 for Draft Report on Turkey's progress towards Accession 2006, (2006), 109. Also see amendment 42 for recital Fa, Amendments 1–236 for the Draft Motion for a Resolution (2007), 13.

together.'¹⁶⁹ In all these references, the ambiguity was Turkey's position: involved in one significant category, acknowledged as a common member between the overlapping Western, Islamic, and 'Arabic' (a misconception used to imply the Middle Eastern) worlds, or a country bestriding various regions but belonging to neither of them.

In the build-up to membership negotiations, a common argument among the conservative and far-right camps came into prominence that the candidate had no place in Europe geographically.¹⁷⁰ In Christian Democrat Zbigniew Zaleski's opinion, Turkey's distance from Europe was at variance with its orientation to the West, and for this reason the candidate was not able to accede to the European Union despite its westernised foreign policy.¹⁷¹ Also for the members of the European Freedom and Democracy Turkey's accession carried a geographical risk since it would entail the stretching of the EU's frontiers to Iran and Iraq.¹⁷² Turkey's membership was 'bizarre', given that only 3% of its territory was situated in Europe.¹⁷³ With respect to its geographical location, Turkey-sceptics also accentuated the candidate's positive relations with its authoritarian and war-torn neighbours in the Middle East and the likelihood of a future refugee inflow from these countries to Europe.¹⁷⁴ Laurence Stassen therefore reiterated in 2013: 'if Turkey accedes to the EU, the EU will have borders with Iran, Iraq and Syria; thus the EU's external borders will be even worse than they are already; Turkey is not a European country: geographically, 95% of Turkey is located out-

---

169 Amendment 180 for paragraph 43a, Amendments 1–188 for the Draft Motion for Resolution (2009), 98–99.
170 Michl Ebner and Véronique Mathieu's address, Debate on Progress towards Accession by Turkey (2004).
171 Zbigniew Zaleski's address, Debate on Turkey's 2007 Progress Report (2008).
172 William Dartmouth's address, Debate on Enlargement Strategy 2009 Concerning the Countries of the Western Balkans, Iceland and Turkey (2009); Lorenzo Fontana's address, Debate on 2009 Progress Report on Croatia – 2009 Progress Report on the Former Yugoslav Republic of Macedonia – 2009 Progress Report on Turkey (2010).
173 William Dartmouth's address, Debate on Enlargement Strategy 2009 Concerning the Countries of the Western Balkans, Iceland and Turkey (2009). The EFD members several times repeated their argument that only 3% of Turkish territory exists in Europe. See Magdi Christiano Allam's address, Debate on Enlargement Report for Turkey (2012), and William Dartmouth's address, Debate on 2013 Progress Report on Turkey (2014).
174 Niki Tzavela and Bastiaan Belder's addresses, Debate on 2009 Progress Report on Croatia – 2009 Progress Report on the Former Yugoslav Republic of Macedonia – 2009 Progress Report on Turkey (2010); Amendment 378 for Paragraph 26 a, Amendments 208–415 for the Draft Motion for Resolution on the 2012 Progress Report of Turkey (2013), 103.

side Europe.'[175] In this respect, Turkey's accession was believed to occasion a growth in the number of asylum seekers using the country as a bridge to arrive in Europe. Elmar Brok, MEP for the EPP and also representing the Christian Democratic Union of Germany, stated: 'we will have to examine ... whether Turkey can be regarded as a safe third country for the purposes of the asylum procedure, as Germany accepts more asylum seekers from Turkey than from any other country.'[176] Another Christian Democrat from Austria, Ursula Stenzel, brought her national perspective in the same plenary: 'Turkey is one of the countries producing the most asylum seekers, and Austria, for example, grants asylum to more Turks than to anyone else.'[177] These members expressed the common concern in Germany and Austria, whose governments later declared that they would veto the opening of the negotiations with Turkey on the chapters concerning free movements in EU premises.[178]

Conclusion

Through an overview of pan-European parties' election programmes and parliamentary statements about Turkey's compatibility with European values, this chapter concludes that European politicians in the 2000s justified their political, religious, and geographical categories of the European Union and Turkey primarily, but not entirely, with reference to the accession criteria. In this case, highlighting the documents through the subdivisions of political, religious, and geographical concepts sheds light on the ideological distances of mainstream political camps to the accession criteria while debating Turkey's EU bid. Given the election manifestos and statements of MEPs, the ideological camps taking the accession criteria as identical to European values, led by the Socialists, Liberals, Greens, Communists and British Conservatives, debated Turkey's compatibility with Europe in political terms. They also presumed Turkey's geographical location to be complementary to the European Union, which they emphasised with the famous 'bridge' concept. Within conservative thinking, the 'Asian', 'Middle Eastern', and 'Islamic' aspects of Turkey rather led to the country's exclusion

---

[175] Amendment 378 for Paragraph 26 a, Amendments 208–415 for the Draft Motion for Resolution on the 2012 Progress Report of Turkey (2013), 103.
[176] Elmar Brok's address, Debate on Progress towards Accession by Turkey (2004).
[177] Ursula Stenzel's address, Debate on Progress towards Accession by Turkey.
[178] Ahmet Insel, 'Boasting Negotiations with Turkey: What Can France Do?', in *Global Turkey in Europe*, eds. Senem Aydin Duzgit, Anne Duncker, Daniela Huber, E. Fuat Keyman, and Nathalie Tocci (Roma: Edizioni Nuova Cultura, 2013), 49.

from a Europe that did not limit European values to the EU's accession criteria but envisioned them additionally in religious and geographical terms. On the far right, furthermore, these exclusionary terms almost always predominated the discussions of Turkey. Therefore, many Christian Democratic and nationalist deputies repeatedly referred to the Union's insufficient capacity to absorb Turkey and remained the strongest advocates of the privileged partnership with the candidate instead of its full membership in the EU.[179]

Very remarkably, during the 2000s the parliamentarians from Britain raised almost uniform statements. Through their arguments about Turkey's compatibility with European values and its accession, major British parties merely relied on the accession criteria. British Conservatives in this context differed from their conservative counterparts in Europe, as they showed vocal support for the candidate's accession. An exception to this support was the members of the UK Independence Party, who marginalised Turkey in political, religious, and geographical terms. But on the whole, based on their election programmes and parliamentary discussions, mainstream British parties represented in the EP showed an agreement on Turkey's EU bid. At this stage one can only presume the main reason for their pro-Turkish statements to be linked to the overall British view critical of European integration – the traditional British state of affairs that the next chapters will discuss at length. In contrast to most of the British parliamentarians, the MEPs of European origin were mostly loyal to the integrationist agenda of their national politics. The connections between national politics, perceptions of European integration and identity, and Turkey's EU bid and its compatibility with Europe then become highly relevant to the debates held in a supranational framework. More specifically, the above-mentioned Turkey-sceptic arguments predicated on religious and geographical assumptions found origins in national politics during the 2000s, if not in the EU's accession criteria. Political discussions about Europe and Turkey in national contexts were, as the next chapters dwell on, not limited by the political accession criteria, which at least shaped the statements at the European level.

---

179 The EPP and far-right continued to raise the privileged partnership as an alternative to Turkey's membership. See Amendment 250 for Paragraph 35 a, Amendments 1–315 for the Draft Motion for Resolution on Turkey's 2010 Progress Report, 133; Amendment 80 for Paragraph 1 a, Amendments for the Draft Motion for Resolution on the 2012 Progress Report of Turkey (2013), 39.

5 Between the Constitutional Referendum and Leadership Contest: French Debates over Turkey's EU Bid in 2005

In an attempt to address the question of how political camps approached the European Union and Turkey in national politics, the rest of this book explores public debates in France, Germany, and the United Kingdom in a given time frame. As an opening, the present chapter delves into the contestations over Turkey's EU prospects in the French media and politics in 2005, with a focus on the debates held one month before the presumed date of the accession talks' beginning, 3 October. In this final short timeframe, Turkey's compatibility with Europe became a much-debated issue in the shadow of the French public's rejection of the EU Constitution in March 2005. Furthermore, the debates over Turkey also related to party and individual campaigns that began to be shaped two years ahead of the next presidential elections.

The first section reflects on a number of long-term factors underlying contemporary French opinions about Turkey vis-à-vis the European Union. These long-term conditions largely explain the discussions in French politics about the rejection of the EU Constitution and the beginning of Turkey's membership negotiations in 2005. In the light of these structural factors, the final section analyses political elites' conceptualisations of the European Union and Turkey. The period between the rejection of the EU Constitution on 29 May and Turkey's membership negotiations on 3 October saw a lively polemic in French politics, the sides of which disputed Turkey's compatibility with a France-led European Union. Shortly before the negotiations' beginning, the French socialists and communists approached the candidate mostly in terms of political categories, whereas the conservative and far-right parties (except President Jacques Chirac and a small group following him) excluded it from Europe with essentially geographical and religious arguments. That aside, some of the political elites voiced opinions about Turkey according to their political interests, and specifically Nicolas Sarkozy, the then minister of France, chose to instrumentalize Turkey-sceptical public opinion to enhance his popularity before the parliamentary election of 2007. Overall, French politicians justified their political, religious, and geographical arguments about Turkey's EU membership in terms of the republican principles the French regime promoted, and these actors, naturally, overemphasized the role of French public opinion in Turkey's accession process.

It is a commonplace argument that the historical trajectories of different regime types brought about contemporary party politics in Western Europe throughout history. According to Lipset and Rokkan, conflicts between various interest groups formed modern party systems over the course of the regime-building process in Western Europe.[1] In other words, contemporary national politics in Europe are marked by disagreements between social and political actors on the formation of the regime in earlier history. An accompanying argument in the European framework is that these sociopolitical disputes underlying regimes have shaped contemporary political camps' attitudes towards the idea of Europe. As Risse et al. argued, nation-state principles constructed in history today impact on the present-day party politics about European integration.[2] In summary, not only current national interests but also regimes in Western Europe have been historically relevant to contemporary political parties' European policies.

A striking case is the French regime, the significance of which can be found in the conception of the French state. Consider the term 'state', which, according to John Peter Nettl, might have different meanings in the French and English languages. The British usage might not represent the state's political meaning in the first instance; it rather conjures up the instrumental image of the government or dynasty. The British state is used in a functional meaning linked to law and traditions.[3] The French case suggests a different conceptual example; the French language employs the word 'state' as 'État', the first letter capitalised.[4] The state in the French context therefore signifies more than an apparatus but an active representative of a viewpoint.[5] France is the birthplace of the idea of the nation-state; the French state in the modern conception has been the prime subject integrating and representing the French nation.[6] In the subsequent centuries marked by the French Revolution, politics credited the state and nation to be the pillars of French civilisation.[7] Therefore, there is more than the state in

---

[1] Seymour Martin Lipset and Stein Rokkan, *Cleavage Systems. Party Systems, and Voter Alignments : Cross-national Perspectives* (New York : Free Press, 1967).
[2] Martin Marcussen, Thomas Risse, Daniela Engelmann-Martin, Hans Joachim Knopf, and Klaus Roscher, 'Constructing Europe? The Evolution of French, British and German Nation State Identities', *Journal of European Public Policy* 6, no.4 (1994): 614–633, doi: 10.1080/135017699343504.
[3] H. S. Jones, *The French State in Question: Public Law and Political Argument in the Third Republic* (Cambridge: Cambridge University Press, 1993), 7–8.
[4] J.P., Nettl, 'State as a Conceptual Variable', *World Politics* 20, no.4 (July 1968): 567, http://www.jstor.org/stable/2009684. Also see Jones' reference to the linguistic difference, Jones, *The French State in Question*, 9.
[5] Jones, *The French State in Question*, 13.
[6] Nettl, 'State as a Conceptual Variable'.
[7] Gordon Wright, *France in Modern Times: From the Enlightenment to the Present* (Chicago: Rand McNally, 1960), 48.

what the French state represents: there is the regime – the republican system and civic values within a historical continuum.

In a turbulent period following the French Revolution (1789), the republican regime generated the idea of the French nation through five structural conditions. First there emerged the idea that political power nested in sovereignty. As François Furet noted, the solemn principle of representing the French people predominated the regime's political language and became the instrument of legitimisation for political actors.[8] In 2005, it was also the prime factor underpinning the French discussions about Turkey vis-à-vis the European Union.[9] Second, the French republican regime, which was devised to promote the principle of national representation in Europe and the colonies, also entailed a citizenship system forged in political terms. Third, the French form of secularism entitled Laïcité was born in agreement with the regime's emphasis on political values and national sovereignty, entailed the state as the guarantor of religious rights and freedoms since 1905, and additionally restricted the conformist side of French politics. Fourth, the French regime in the post-revolution period promoted itself as the source of civilisation and therefore the origin of Europe. The regime in the end had undertaken the prime mission of civilising the Orient through its colonies. And fifth, geopolitics remained a concern for France until the foundation of the European Union. The significance of Schuman Declaration taking the roots of the contemporary project of European integration should also be attributed to this geopolitical concern. French political actors preoccupied with security thereby assumed the historical mission of uniting Europe in 1950.

The first decisive factor in French national thinking is the emphasis on French national will in politics. The pre-revolutionary history of France had seen the absolute rule of French kings, summed up in the well-known maxim (voiced by Louis the XIV in 1655), 'I am the state'. As 'L'etat c'est moi' and 'la grace de Dieu' heralded famously, the king was the sovereign by divine right.[10] In the following century, this absolutism lay shattered. At first, the En-

---

[8] François Furet, *Penser la Révolution française* (Paris: Gallimard, 1983), 71.
[9] It is argued elsewhere that education and immigration are the most significant French policy areas in which republican idealism seems manifest. Jeremy Jennings, 'Citizenship, Republicanism and Multiculturalism in Contemporary France', *British Journal of Political Science* 30, no.4 (October 2000): 575–598, http://www.jstor.org/stable/194286. It can be added that the French republicanism additionally limits discussions of European enlargement in French politics.
[10] Herbert H. Rowen, '"L'Etat c'est moi": Louis the XIV and the State', *French Historical Studies* 2, no.1 (Spring, 1961): 83, do: 10.2307/286184.

lightenment introduced the rudimentary notion of popular sovereignty.[11] As Jean-Jacques Rousseau argued long before the Revolution, society legitimated the government as long as the government reflected their general free will.[12] The revolution built on this thought; the disengagement of the French Assembly from the crown contributed to the modern and distinct representation of civil society.[13] Since then, the French Revolution was credited to have repositioned the state as the upholder of the French nation's civil aspect.[14] It served the unified conception of national sovereignty throughout modern and contemporary French politics.[15] Its historic document entitled the Declaration of the Rights of the Man and Citizen ruled that 'sovereignty resides in the nation' in Article III and designated the French Assembly to realise national sovereignty on behalf of the French civil society.[16] With these attempts, national sovereignty was given a central place in the political language. The representation of the French nation, ideally through public vote, increasingly became a norm. Later French governments continued to seek public consent, even so when they were in a tutelary form.[17]

Under these conditions, 19th-century France saw the contention between different forces claiming that they represented national will, and the successors of the National Assembly, the Directors, the French Consulate, and the Napoleonic Empire legitimised themselves through constitutional referenda.[18] Following Napoleon's failed war against the European powers, the Vienna Congress (1815) enthroned Louis the XVIII in France, but with limited rights against the legislation. The new constitution maintained a group of civic rights that were born with the

---

11 Scott Haine, *The History of France* (Westport: Greenwood Publishing Group, 2000), 67. Furet, *Penser la Révolution française*, 49.
12 Chimène J. Keitner, *The Paradoxes of Nationalism: The French Revolution and its Meaning for Contemporary Nation-Building* (Albany: State University of New York Press, 2007), 38.
13 Keitner, *The Paradoxes of Nationalism*, 25. Furet, *Penser la Révolution française*, 107. In the midst of an economic crisis, Louis the XVI decided to strengthen his legitimacy, re-convened the General Estates between clerics, notables, and commons, and triggered the revolutionary movement. The Third Estate then declared itself the only legitimate legislative body under the name National Assembly and set out to establish the French Republic.
14 Keitner, *The Paradoxes of Nationalism*, 26.
15 Eric Hobsbawm, *The Age of Revolution 1789–1848* (New York: Vintage Books, 1996), 59.
16 See article 3, l'Assemblée nationale, Déclaration des droits de l'homme et du citoyen du 26 août 1789.
17 Serge Velley, *Histoire constitutionnelle française de 1789 a nos jours* (Paris: Ellipses, 2009), 12–13
18 Furet argued that the actors of the French Revolution led by Jacobins tended to this second Hobbesian conception in the name of representing the nation. Furet, *Penser la Révolution française*, 52.

Revolution decades ago. The struggle for political power did not cease, however. Until 1870, the turn of the Third Republic, power changed hands between royalists and republicans acting on behalf of the French nation. Having seized the office with a landslide victory in presidential elections, Louis Bonaparte, Napoleon's nephew, chose to turn the French regime back into a monarchy with a referendum in 1852. His empire continued until 1871, when France surrendered to Prussia after a crushing defeat. The National Assembly then brought back the Republic through the constitutional changes in 1875. The idea of national representation has been a part of state ideology ever since. Only once, when the Nazi-established Vichy Government dominated France during the WWII, was the republican logic temporarily suspended.[19]

The second factor, the civic nature of citizenship in France, was born in line with the principle of national representation.[20] A sort of citizenship existed in the Ancien Regime and legitimised French nobility and their privileges over the commons.[21] The Revolution aimed to end this inequality. The National Assembly and its successors, henceforth the French Parliament, became the heart of the revolutionary practice and primarily represented the French national identity. Under their adjudications, national belonging was connected to political conditions, including language.[22] The parliament founded the first French constitution (1791), including the Declaration of the Rights of Man and Citizen in its preamble. The universal understanding derived from the Enlightenment philosophy, which positioned man without ethnic and religious constraints, was thereby attached to the primary French documents.[23] Since the law was substantially enacted in 1889, the political nature of citizenship has remained unchanged.[24] The emphasis on civic citizenship also remained in agreement with the country's colonial aspirations as well as its progressive national identity.[25]

---

19 Vichy France did not represent national sovereignty; it was an attempt without effect. The Provisional French Government of General Charles de Gaulle later passed a law, 'ordonnance', that all the Vichy Government's actions were void, as the Republic of France with its dignity had not ceased to exist. See the first three articles of the document: Le Gouvernement provisoire de la République française, Ordonnance du 9 août 1944 relative au rétablissement de la légalité républicaine sur le territoire continental, JORF (d'Alger), no. 65, August 10, 1944.
20 William Rogers Brubaker, *Citizenship and Nationhood in France and Germany* (Cambridge, Massachusetts, Harvard University Press, 1992), 182–185.
21 William Rogers Brubaker, 'The French Revolution and the Invention of Citizenship', *French Politics and Society* 7, no.3 (1989), 31.
22 Eric J. Hobsbawm, *Nations and Nationalism Since 1780: Programme, Myth, Reality* (Cambridge: Cambridge University Press, 1992), 20–21.
23 Wright, *France in Modern Times*, 60.
24 Brubaker, *Citizenship and Nationhood in France and Germany*, 14

In harmony with the ruling principle of national representation and political citizenship, France established the rigid separation between the church and state entitled Laïcité, the third factor underpinning contemporary debates over Turkey. It delimited the church's domain by turning the clergy into a governmental bureaucracy.[26] In the late 19th century, the famous Ferry laws set up a secularised education system in France in an attempt to create a secular and literate nation.[27] From the late 19th century, French citizenship also dissociated itself from religious conditions and evolved to the moral and civic tradition of secular patriotism.[28] The law of 1905 built on the previous Ferry laws and provided the neutrality of the state concerning religious affairs, the freedom of religious faith, and competences of the church, and it also forbade religious education in schools. This law remained in force and also preceded further laws, including the law of 2004 on the prohibition of religious symbols in schools except for universities. The significance of Laïcité framed contemporary political debates over Turkey consequently in two senses. First, it constrained the use of Christian terminology in expressing opposition to the candidate. Unlike the German case the next chapter dwells on, Turkey-sceptic political factions did not resort to religion as the prime source of repudiating the candidate. Second, it still occasioned some modernist arguments taking Islam as a submissive religion (particularly as regards women) and incompatible with French and European cultures.

The third historical factor underpinning French national thinking is the conception of the French regime as the centre of Europe and beyond. The Revolution played a vital part here: The French Declaration of the Rights of the Man and Citizen later turned out to be the manifesto for republicanism, including the right of self-determination within national frontiers, and encouraged the revolutionary cause in Europe.[29] At a time when it was Napoleon's instrument to 'liberate' nations, European powers at first were alienated from the idea of national sovereignty. Yet France later continued to promote national sovereignty and political citizenship both in the motherland and Europe. By way of an example, towards the end of the First World War the French Foreign Minister, in addition to US

---

25 Ibid, 76–77; William Rogers Brubaker, 'Immigration, Citizenship, and the Nation-State in France and Germany: A Comparative Historical Analysis', *International Sociology* 5, no.4 (December 1990), 398, doi: 10.1177/026858090005004003.
26 Wright, France in Modern Times, 60.
27 Ibid, 305; Haine, *The History of France*, 123.
28 Jennings, 'Citizenship, Republicanism and Multiculturalism' 578; Jean Paul Willaime, 'Religion et Politique en France: Dans le Contexte de la Construction Européenne', *French Politics Culture and Society* 25, no.3 (Winter 2007): 38, http://www.jstor.org/stable/42843513.
29 Wright, *France in Modern Times*, 90.

President Woodrow Wilson, was initiating the peace conditions centred on the self-determination of nations and the protection of minorities in Europe.[30] These revolutionary principles were impacting on the political thought in Europe throughout the 19th and 20th centuries.[31]

France additionally assumed a national mission outside Europe: liberating and civilising the Orient with political institutions. In the 19th and 20th centuries the country granted its colonies a certain number of republican rights.[32] As Historian Rudolph Winnacker commented in 1938, no other European colonialist power shared the French idealism of national representation. With the revolutions in 1789 and 1848, colonies were granted the right of representation in the French Parliament.[33] Yet the republicanism envisaged for French colonies was only a restricted form, distant from contemporary liberal conceptions. First, in colonies French authorities only allowed the local groups sharing republican ideology to send delegates to Paris.[34] Second, although the government granted French citizenship to the populations of the Caribbean Islands and Senegal, this privilege was limited in Algeria only to the 'European' society settled by the motherland.[35] In fact, Algeria was considered an integral part of France. Unlike the other colonies governed by the Foreign Ministry, the land was under the authority of the French Ministry of Interior Affairs. In other words, although the French were revolutionist primarily in Europe, they could turn out to be centralist and assimilative in colonial affairs.[36]

The French mission of civilising the Orient did not remain unopposed. The war in Algeria between 1954 and 1962 eventually showed the strength and limits of the French revolutionary identity. To give an example, Prime Minister Guy Mollet denounced the violent Algerian rebels and stated that France would not negotiate with them but only with the true representatives of the Algerian popula-

---

30 J. Samuel Barkin and Bruce Cronin, 'The State and the Nation: Changing Norms and the Rules of Sovereignty in International Relations', *International Organization* 48, no.1 (December 1994): 121, http://www.jstor.org/stable/2706916.
31 Ibid, 119; James Mayall, 'Sovereignty, Nationalism, and Self-determination', *Political Studies* 47, no.3 (1999): 476, doi: 10.1111/1467–9248.00213.
32 Hazareesingh, *Political Traditions in Modern France*, 162.
33 Rudolph A. Winnacker, 'Elections in Algeria and the French Colonies under the Third Republic', *The American Political Science Review* 32, no.2 (April 1938): 261, doi: 10.2307/1948669.
34 Ibid, 264.
35 Haine, *The History of France*, 135.
36 Ibid; Winnacker, 'Elections in Algeria', 263.

tion following free elections.³⁷ His speech to the French Parliament in 1957 further revealed the orthodox French view about the Orient:

> France began in 1830 to establish herself in what the man in the street called 'Barbary', a group of territories theoretically under Turkish domination where, in fact, anarchy reigned ... French settlement in Algeria has long been recognised by all powers and its legitimacy has never been questioned. Who could dispute the importance of French settlement in the country and the extent of France's achievements there: modernisation of the economy, safeguarding of the public health, increase in population?³⁸

The idea that France civilised the country had justified the French colonial settlement in Algeria. After all, the French had achieved modernisation in Algeria despite the unenlightened Turkish rule centuries ago. It was also worthy of note that in his speech Prime Minister Mollet did not mention national representation, the source of self-determination in Europe. National representation was rather an instrument of the French colonial argument against the rebels: They were not popular, therefore not legitimate. These claims turned out to be wrong when the Algerian referendum resulted in the colony's independence in 1962. However, although the separation of Algeria from France impacted on the civilising aspirations of the French national identity, it allowed the Republic 'to reshape the republican legitimacy, civil liberties, and the state' in home affairs, in Todd Shepard's words.³⁹ The French regime afterwards continued to represent its key ideas in Europe.

The fourth long-term factor has been the significance of European geopolitics for France. For most of the 19th and 20th centuries France set its European foreign policy in relation to its eastern rival, first Prussia then unified Germany. Military defeats against Germany until 1945 and insecure borders resulted in a proactive policy of France attempting to turn European geopolitics into its favour.⁴⁰ The country chose, consequently, to incorporate European security into its security policy via the foundations of the European Union. Whilst in Britain geographical realities led the country to distance itself from European integra-

---

37 Public disclosure to North Atlantic Organization: 'Statement by M. Guy Mollet On Algeria', Item RDC(57)15, January 10, 1957, 6.
38 Ibid, 3.
39 Todd Shepard, *The Invention of Decolonization: The Algerian War and the Remaking of France* (Ithaca: Cornell University Press, 2006), 3. Also see Pascal Blanchard, Nicolas Bancel, and Sandrine Lemaire, *La fracture coloniale: La société française au prisme de l'héritage colonial* (Paris: Editions La Découverte, 2006).
40 Hazareesingh, *Political Traditions in Modern France*, 126. Barkin and Cronin, 'The State and the Nation', 120.

tion, geographical interests of France compelled political elites to internalise the idea of European integration.[41] The French policy of initiating a firmly structured organisation in Europe, the final structural factor discussed below, should be read from this historical fact, the geopolitical concerns of the country. In 2005, French conservative political elites moved by similar concerns discarded Turkey's geographical compatibilities with Europe.

The historical mission of uniting Europe therefore emerged with geopolitical concerns. The Second World War, which ended the Third Republic's prosperous age, called forth the need of a proactive French foreign policy attentive to the political changes in Europe. The following Fourth Republic initiated the foundation of the European Union in an attempt to keep European politics under French control.[42] Diplomat Jean Monnet and Foreign Minister Robert Schuman thus delivered their proposal in 1950 to form the first step towards a 'European federation indispensable to the preservation of peace'.[43] Schuman wrote in *Foreign Affairs* (1953) that France aimed at introducing a common European interest over national politics through economic integration. Thereby nationalism and the other reasons for European wars would abate according to the French plan.[44] The emphasis was mainly laid on Germany. With this European initiative strongest of all, France predominantly targeted the containment and assimilation of its former German threat. The Schuman Declaration thus proposed the participants of the Coal and Steel Community to be 'France, Germany, and other member countries'.[45] In brief, Schuman's emphasis on European integration signified breaking away from the traditional nation-state model France principally promoted before. The mainstream principle of pro-Europeanism was finally taking root in French politics.

A contrary policy to the pro-Europeanism, however, emerged with Charles de Gaulle's office in the 1960s. The era of decolonisation in the 1950s eventually caused turmoil in France. During a political stalemate, General de Gaulle, the country's liberator during the Second World War, assumed the presidency at the parliament's invitation in 1958. He introduced the Fifth Republic, over which he presided with his impact on the policy of European integration. De Gaulle prioritised national interest in contrast to the pro-Europeanism that Monet and Schuman previously started. His France-centred vision of Europe excluded Britain, for a while, with the aim of holding it and the United States back

---

41 Consider the Schuman Declaration, Robert Schuman, Schuman Declaration, June 9, 1950.
42 Haine, *The History of France*, 173.
43 Schuman, Schuman Declaration.
44 Robert Schuman, 'France in Europe', *Foreign Affairs*, April, 1953.
45 Schuman, Schuman Declaration.

from European affairs. Until his office came to an end in 1969, France was disinclined either to assign greater authorities to European institutions or to approve Britain inside the EU.

All these developments implied two genres of European politics. In addition to the structural factors above, throughout the EU's history two trends in French politics formed the idea of Europe in France. The first trend emerged to be the liberal position Jeanne Monet and Robert Schuman first represented in order to fulfil French interests with European integration. The second trend instead remained faithful to the primacy of national interests and was aligned with Charles de Gaulle's political legacy.[46] Following de Gaulle's term, France turned to a more pro-European foreign policy. De Gaulle's influences lived on later, especially on the subject of the security relationship between the United States and the European Union. But Britain was not any more a 'trojan horse' to the Europe of France.[47] The following French leaders took the initiative of deepening and enlarging the European Community.[48] In the 1980s, François Mitterrand, the socialist leader of France, was enjoying the high level of pro-Europeanism in French public and legitimating his proactive role in European integration. Meanwhile, introducing novel economic and fiscal policies to the promising development of the European Community had become a strong option. The French President had then remained at a crossroads between the mainstream socialist principle of anti-capitalism and the supranational European Monetary System.[49] In agreement with the French public opinion, he chose, perhaps more willingly even than his German counterparts, to contribute to European integration.[50] In addition, Jacques Delors, the Head of the European Commission and Mitterrand's socialist colleague, devised the European Single Act and the Treaty of the European Union, which institutionalized the European internal market through supra-national institutions. French socialism, encouraged by the French public, fully embraced the idea of European integration in an attempt to initiate a European social economy.[51]

---

46 Menéndez-Alarcón, Antonio V. *The Cultural Realm of European Integration: Social Representations in France, Spain, and the United Kingdom* (Westport: Praeger, 2004), 25.
47 De Gaulle had seen Britain as a "Trojan Horse" of the United States in Europe, Haine, *The History of France*, 187.
48 Alice L. Conklin, Sarah Fishman, and Robert Zaretsky, *France and Its Empire Since 1870* (New York: Oxford University Press, 2011), 322.
49 Thomas Risse, 'A European Identity? Europeanisation and the Evolution of Nation-State Identities', in *Transforming Europe: Europeanisation and Domestic Change*, eds. Maria Green Cowles and James Carporaso (Ithaca: Cornell University Press, 2001), 216.
50 'Mitterrand Backs European Integration', *New York Times*, August 12, 1989.
51 Haine, *The History of France*, 207.

However, in the next decade this pro-European enthusiasm in French public began to turn down. Before the Treaty of the European Union (1992), public support for European integration was no less than 55%. Under the new conditions in French politics, Mitterrand thus decided to hold a referendum to seal the fate of the EU's founding treaty, for the first time in EC/EU history. In return, the treaty was approved only by 51%. Pro-European support in France has declined since then.[52] The growing resentment against immigration had a vital role there, as immigrants flowed to France from Western Europe's hinterland and fuelled nationalist reactions in the second half of the 20th century.[53] The EU's enlargement to Eastern Europe further added to these backlashes. As a consequence, thirteen years after the Treaty of the EU, at a time of Jacques Chirac's presidency, French people rejected the EU's first constitutional attempt by 55%. As France left the referendum behind, in 2005, French national interests had taken precedence over European integration. The beginning of the accession talks with Turkey coincided with such turmoil.

French Politics in 2005: the EU Constitution and Turkey

As a result, European integration became a subject of a vital debate between the French political camps. Before the referendum on the EU Constitution (2005), French politics had been shaped most notably by two chief parties, the Union for Popular Movement and the Socialist Party.[54] Both these camps actively promoted European integration in the early 2000s and sided with the EU's Constitution. The Union for Popular Movement (UMP) had dominated French politics since the 2002 legislative elections. The merger of two conservative parties from the political right, the Gaullist Union of the Democrats for the Republic and the Rally for the Republic, the UMP was founded at the helm of Jacques Chirac on a sizeable electoral basis. Alain Juppé became the first president and was followed by Nicolas Sarkozy in 2004. Despite its Gaullist nature, the party under the leadership of these names campaigned for the EU's Constitution in 2004.[55] Additionally, the party was one of the biggest constituents of the European People's Party, the integrationist pan-European party known for its party-wide scep-

---

52 Menéndez-Alarcón, *The Cultural Realm*, 25.
53 Hazareesingh, *Political Traditions in Modern France*, 126–127; Andrew Geddes, *The Politics of Migration and Immigration in Europe* (London: Sage, 2003), 71–74.
54 Menéndez-Alarcón. *The Cultural Realm*, 26.
55 'Se démarquant de Jacques Chirac, l'UMP prend position contre l'entrée de la Turquie dans l'UE', *Le Monde*, April 9, 2004.

ticism about Turkey's EU bid. The UMP would later reform itself, in 2015, under the name *Les Républicains* again in Sarkozy's leadership.

The main opposition in France in the 2000s and constituent of the Party of European Socialists in the European framework, the French Socialist Party (PS), had shared the pro-European stance with the UMP. The party lost the legislative election in 1993 and the presidential election in 1995 to the Rally for the Republic (which preceded the Union for Popular Movement). Since then, the PS continued to campaign for farther European integration through social policies.[56] Lionel Jospin, the party's leader back then, stated in 2001 that they were advocating a 'European constitution for the federation of European nation states'.[57] During the constitutional debate four years later, PS Secretary François Hollande thus urged socialists to vote 'yes' to further European integration.[58] On the contrary, Laurent Fabius' group inside the party opposed the EU Constitution and led a considerable amount of socialists to the rejection.[59]

The chief political parties of France saw the European Union as an instrument to realise national interests and promote French identity. Still, the constitutional referendum showed widespread support for the Eurosceptic cause against the EU. In 2005, the French public rejected the EU Constitution with a majority of 55 %, a consequence of the declining pro-European trend since the 1990s. Minorities from the UMP and PS aside, the communist and ultra-nationalist parties played essential roles in the countrywide campaign against European integration. Among them, the Communist Party of France (PCF) stood against the liberal European market and immigration to France.[60] The PCF additionally defended French independence and national sovereignty against the EU project. The National Front (FN) shared these postures with the Communist Party. The party opposed the market-oriented project of the EU and the migrant inflow to France. But unlike the Communist Party, the National Front entirely rejected the EU and defied its founding treaties.[61] In their opposition, the FN also presented

---

56 Christian Krell, *Sozialdemokratie und Europa: Die Europapolitik von SPD, Labour Party und Parti Socialiste* (Wiesbaden: Verlag für Sozialwissenschaften. 2009), 350–351, 364–366.
57 Pascale Robert Diard and Daniel Vernet, 'Lionel Jospin veut faire l'Europe de demain "sans défaire la France"', *Le Monde*, May 29, 2001.
58 Nicholas Watt, 'Early French Vote on EU Constitution', *The Guardian*, February 28, 2005.
59 'Le processus d'adhésion de la Turquie à l'UE avive les tensions au PS et à droite', *Le Monde*, September 30, 2005; Krell, *Sozialdemokratie und Europa* 368.
60 Ibid, 31.
61 Ibid, 32.

the EU Constitution as a step to facilitate Turkey's future EU membership without the French nation's consent.[62]

The rejection of the EU Constitution by the French popular vote revealed a new identity crisis in France, in which long-term structural factors clashed. On the one hand, according to the principal argument of French diplomacy, the country was the heart of European civilisation and pioneer of European integration. On the other hand, for centuries the republican regime had upheld the idea of national sovereignty in Europe and beyond, in other words, the decisive role of the national will over politics. Elitism and populism went hand in hand throughout European integration. French political actors largely remained committed to European integration as long as the French public consented to pro-Europeanism. But this changed in 2005. The arguments based on 'France of the nation' prevailed over the arguments based on 'France of Europe' at the end of the constitutional referendum in 2005. Then what was the role of Turkey, the EU's membership candidate, in this pessimistic context? Had the constitutional referendum and Turkey's negotiations not collided in 2005, perhaps European integration and Turkey's Europeanness would not have been so frequently discussed together. French politicians approached the constitution's rejection and Turkey's EU bid as the two sides of an identity debate. After all, the French were mostly against Turkey's EU membership. In 2003, polls showed that 46% considered Turkey's membership positively. As *Le Figaro* pointed out, Turkey fell into disfavour from that point on. After the constitutional referendum and shortly before the negotiations with the candidate were inaugurated, the general support for Turkey was only 35%.[63] According to another poll held shortly before the negotiations for the conservative weekly magazine *Valeurs actualles*, 40% of the French were in favour of Turkey's membership. Among the pessimists, rightwing voters were generally more reluctant to see Turkey inside the EU. The level of rejection was therefore 70% within the UMP and UDF, and 84% of the followers of the National Front. The political left also did not show a truly open support, according to the newspaper. Only 47% of Socialists approved Turkey's accession whereas this level was 49% for the communists.[64]

The French reservations about Turkey's membership stemmed from various reasons. *Le Figaro* counted them to be the country's geography, its Islamic reli-

---

[62] Paul Hainsworth, 'France Says No: the 29 May 2005 Referendum on the European Constitution', *Parliamentary Affairs* 59, no: 1 (January 2006): 104–105.
[63] 'Les Français réfractaires au processus d'adhésion de la Turquie à l'UE', *Le Figaro*, January 26, 2014.
[64] 'Les Français contre l'entrée de la Turquie', *Le Nouvel Observateur*, October 3, 2005.

gion, its massive population, its refusal to recognise the Armenian Genocide, and the risk of the European market's disintegration through its membership.[65] Some righteous critiques aside, stereotypes about the country impacted on *Le Figaro*'s coverage. Its editor, for one, had interpreted the polls as such: 'Europeans, in their majority, do not want a marriage with Turkey. They indeed preserve their culture.'[66] The European and French people, in the editor's opinion, did not see Turkey as a European country. France was arguably rejecting Turkey with the highest popular rate in Europe, on the ground that the candidate was not European in nature.[67] By way of an example, the former French President Valéry Giscard d'Estaing argued in 2002 that Turkey's membership would be the end of the idea of Europe because the country was originally Asian. (This was even before the AK Party, which would be later regarded as 'pro-Islamist', had come into power.) He stated: 'Its capital is not in Europe, 95% of its population is outside Europe, this is not a European country'.[68]

The conservatives and other representatives of the French political right asserted that Turkey was not inside Europe, its language was not European, and it had not made any positive contribution to the European heritage.[69] *Le Monde* was employing the term *hostilité* (hostility) to reflect on the negative postures of the French political right about Turkey's EU membership in 2005.[70] In addition to the UMP, the Union for French Democracy (UDF) of François Bayrou, the Movement for France (MPF) led by Philippe de Villiers, and the National Front were important representatives of Turkey-scepticism on the political right.[71] Among these camps, the radical right antagonised the candidate. For example, the leader of the ultra-nationalist National Front, Jean-Marie Le Pen, claimed that Turkey's accession 'would help to augment the Islamisation of Europe,

---

[65] Laurent de Boissieu, 'Europe: la Turquie cherche l'appui de la Francemardi', *Le Figaro*, July 20, 2004.
[66] 'Turquie en Europe: "le coût du mépris"', *Le Figaro*, October 7, 2005.
[67] Ahmet Insel, 'Boasting Negotiations with Turkey: What Can France Do?', in *Global Turkey in Europe* ed. Natalino Ronzitti (Roma: Edizioni Nuova Cultura, 2013), 49.
[68] 'Pour ou contre l'adhésion de la Turquie à l'Union européenne', *Le Monde*, November 8, 2002.
[69] Olivier Pognon. 'Simone Veil dit non à l'entrée d'Ankara dans l'Union européenne', *Le Figaro*, May 12, 2005.
[70] Christiane Chombeau and Philippe Le Coeur, 'La droite affiche son hostilité à l'adhésion de la Turquie', *Le Monde*, September 30, 2005; Béatrice Gurrey, 'La droite française, hostile à l'entrée de la Turquie, en fait un enjeu présidentiel pour 2007', *Le Monde*, October 3, 2005.
[71] Chombeau and Le Coeur, 'La droite affiche'.

which would lose its nature, its roots and culture.'[72] He then added: 'Turkey did not meet the Copenhagen criteria anyway'.[73] The extreme right also emphasised the impacts of Turkey's EU membership on the French economy. Before the negotiations with Turkey began, the National Front publicly raised the spectre of how France was going to suffer the aftermath of Turkey's future accession to the EU. As *Le Monde* observed, Le Pen's disapproval of Turkey had similar grounds to his earlier opposition to the Eastern migrants in France, especially the Polish workforce.[74] In complete contrast to these Turkey-sceptics, the French socialists and communists were principally against the religious and geographical arguments raised against Turkey's accession. They opposed the EU's image as a Christian Club.[75] They rather approached Turkey directly with the EU's common accession criteria as mentioned below.

Turkey's economic impact on France in fact did not seem a giant hurdle before its accession to the EU. First of all, the European Commission did not anticipate such a huge immigrant influx as Le Pen claimed. According to *Le Figaro*'s coverage, to the Commission there were already 3 million Turks living without any problem in Europe, and the EU was going to benefit from more, high-skilled workers with the candidate's accession.[76] As Olli Rehn, the Commissioner for Enlargement, wrote in *Le Monde*, Europe needed Turkey in economic, political, and many other terms.[77] The optimistic picture that the European Commission drew in return came in for criticism from *Le Figaro*. According to one commentary published in the newspaper, the Commission was taking into consideration neither the rejection of the EU Constitution in France and the Netherlands nor the widespread discontent with Turkey's membership in Europe. France had arguably little influence in changing the course of events leading to the beginning of the negotiations with the candidate. The socialist governments in Germany and Britain were rather shaping the agenda, and the Commission was 'hiding behind the European Council's conclusions', a correspondent concluded.[78] Accordingly, Brussels was 'playing down' the consequences of Turkey's accession.[79] But a French

---

[72] Avril, Pierre, 'Pour ou contre l'adhésion: cinq questions en débat', *Le Figaro*, December 16, 2004.
[73] Ibid.
[74] Jean-Baptiste De Montvalon, 'La tentation du populisme', *Le Monde*, July 19, 2005.
[75] 'La candidature turque à l'UE a-t-elle des chances d'aboutir?', *Le Monde*, October 3, 2005.
[76] Alexandrine Bouilhet, 'La Commission fait l'éloge de l'adhésion turque', *Le Figaro*, October 1, 2004.
[77] Olli Rehn, 'Donnons sa chance à la Turquie', Le Monde, September 1, 2005.
[78] Alexandrine Bouilhet, 'Bruxelles garde le cap avec Ankara', *Le Figaro*, June 29, 2005.
[79] Alexandrine Bouilhet 'Bruxelles dédramatise l'adhésion de la Turquie', *Le Figaro*, September 29, 2004.

expert in economics shared this optimism too. Before the beginning of the negotiations, the French companies doing business with Turkey were the prime upholders of the candidate's membership. Jean-Antoine Giansily, President Chirac's close associate and the leader of the French Economic Mission in Turkey, was, in the words of Le Figaro, a 'tireless advocate' of Turkey's accession for economic reasons. The chief French companies he represented also showed their support for the candidate.[80]

To French conservatives, Turkey's entry to the EU was going to bring more harm than simply the unemployment mentioned in Le Figaro.[81] Ironically, according to the newspaper, the French President of the conservative origin became Turkey's advocate in French politics. Jacques Chirac, the founder of the UMP, partially gave support to the opening of the negotiations with Turkey in 2005.[82] His pro-Turkey stand lacked a sound political and electoral basis, however, and it quickly sparked an identity debate. Especially after the constitutional referendum, a majority of the UMP headed by Alain Juppe and Nicolas Sarkozy took a stand against Turkey's accession.[83] Weeks before the beginning of the membership negotiations with Turkey, a rift within the UMP was evident according to the French media. In general terms, most of the French conservatives opposed Turkey's Europeanness by appealing to national representation, the very norm of the French Revolution.

The EU and Turkey according to the French Media and Politics

The present section details how the debate over Turkey's negotiations evolved among French political actors from September to the beginning of the accession talks, the 3rd of October. Shortly before the negotiations' debut, the French media gave space to French diplomacy on Turkey's negotiations with the EU, President Jacques Chirac's standing in favour of the candidate, and the opposition within the UMP that was led by the party president and the new Minister of Home Affairs, Nicolas Sarkozy.

---

[80] Bernard Neumann, 'Ces Français qui misent sur la Turquie', L'Expansion, June 23, 2004.
[81] 'Turquie en Europe'.
[82] Philippe Goulliaud, 'Jacques Chirac, irréductible défenseur de la cause turque', Le Figaro, October 5, 2005.
[83] Chombeau and Le Coeur, 'La droite affiche'.

The chief French newspapers reported on the disputes about Turkey's EU bid between political parties, and especially within the governing UMP. Among them, Le Monde wrote about the Turkey debate in European and French politics from the angle of Turkey's democratic issues. For an example, it gave priority to the Armenian genocide by the Ottomans, the recognition of which was considered to be a precondition by almost every political camp in France.[84] Despite that, *Le Monde* remained critical of the right-wing parties' uncompromising opposition to Turkey's EU membership. To reflect on their widespread views against the candidate, for one example, the newspaper opted for the term *hostilité* in its title.[85] In return, the conservative journals represented Turkey's compatibility with the European Union mainly from the perspectives of the political right. According to Yasri-Labrique's analysis, *Le Figaro* covered the tension that Turkey's membership evoked in French Politics with keywords like *problème*, *menace*, *blocage*, and *tension*.[86] Shortly before the negotiations' beginning, *Le Figaro* did indeed use controversial terms while reporting on Turkey. For instance, the newspaper referred to Turkey as 'the former Ottoman power' in the contemporary context.[87] In another, the newspaper wrote Turkey to be 'more than a cactus' for Jacques Chirac and Dominique de Villepin, referring to the limited support for the country by these leaders.[88] The journal in one another instance denounced the head of France lending support for Turkey's negotiations and emphasised the public opinion sceptical about the country: 'Today, it is the people to save Europe and its history: it is the only one to dare to defend what remains of European soul.'[89]

L'Express, the weekly journal from the rightist tendency, instead discussed Turkey's EU membership through its economic and political backwardness in comparison with the European standards.[90] For example, a commentary held that the country had entered a process of 'quiet revolution', a modernisation and democratisation process, ever since it received the candidate status from

---

[84] Sophie Shihab, 'Turquie : des historiens brisent le tabou sur la question arménienne', *Le Monde*, September, 26, 2005.

[85] Chombeau and Le Coeur, 'La droite affiche'. Gurrey, 'La droite française'.

[86] Eléonore Yasri-Labrique, 'Les représentations de la Turquie en France à l'aune des quotidiens nationaux. Libération, Le Monde et Le Figaro (2005–2013)', in *Médias et Pluralisme: La diversité à l'épreuve*, eds. Ksenija Djordjevic Léonard and Eléonore Yasri-Labrique (Paris: Editions des archives contemporaines, 2014), 44–46.

[87] Charles Jaigu, 'Sarkozy et VGE rouvrent le dossier turc', *Le Figaro*, September 23, 2005.

[88] Philippe Goulliaud and Bruno Jeudy, 'La Turquie, cette épine dans le flanc de Chirac et Villepin', *Le Figaro*, September 23, 2005.

[89] 'Turquie en Europe'.

[90] Laure Marchand, 'Les retards turcs', L'Express, September 22, 2005.

the EU. According to the author, the European perspective was spurring Turkey's social freedoms, the rule of law, and other improvements in its notoriously corrupt system. He then compared the European influence on Turkey to the American operation in Iraq: 'What the Americans are missing in Iraq is something Europeans' plan to succeed in Turkey – despite them (the country)'.[91] A highly orientalist view thus highlighted the Western influence over the two Eastern subjects and emphasised the latter, the EU's peaceful initiation of change in Turkey. Nevertheless, the author continued, 'the majority' of the European Union, namely France, Austria, Germany, Netherlands, and Denmark were against Turkey's membership, whereas 'only' Britain, Portugal, Spain, Italy, Sweden, and the Central and Eastern European Countries favoured its accession.[92]

From September to early October, the media covered a lively debate on Turkey's compatibility with European values, the leading actors of which were President Jacques Chirac, Prime Minister Dominique de Villepin (to a lesser extent), former president Valéry Giscard d'Estaing, and finally Nicolas Sarkozy, the Minister of Interior Affairs and the UMP's leader. In this period, De Villepin and Sarkozy had more at stake than the others in debating the candidate, as the general elections in France were due in two years, and the contest between the political leaders was already evident. Sarkozy in particular aimed to turn the Turkey-sceptic French public opinion to his advantage. As a result, he pressed for a public referendum on Turkey's negotiations and emphasised the principle of national representation in French political culture.

At the outset, Jacques Chirac's views supportive of Turkey's EU bid had ignited debates in French politics. The French president had not directly campaigned for Turkey's membership but instead openly argued that the country was eligible for membership negotiations. He had expressed many times that the accession talks with Turkey would be long, difficult, and open-ended.[93] On the next day after the accession talks started, he reminded that the outcome of the candidate's negotiations was not yet known.[94] Turkey was required to adopt EU legislation during a formidable process; the country was therefore going to need a 'major cultural revolution'.[95] In Chirac's view, the French nation was going to decide Turkey's membership in a referendum even if the applicant successfully concluded the negotiations. The accession talks were eventually

---

91 Jean-Michel Demetz, 'Turquie: le paradoxe européen', *L'Express*, October 6, 2005.
92 Ibid.
93 Goulliaud and Jeudy, 'La Turquie'.
94 'A Paris Jacques Chirac et Silvio Berlusconi defendant la candidature turque a l'UE', *Le Monde*, October 4, 2005.
95 Ibid.

going to last ten to fifteen years; in that case, nobody had any right to assume how the next generation would contemplate Turkey.[96] The French would have their last word later. He therefore attempted to win the opposition over to his approval of the accession talks with Turkey. Referring to national representation, he called for a referendum in France to be held at the end of the negotiations.

Despite this comment, Jacques Chirac also argued that Turkey and Europe shared the same values: 'This is not Europe that adheres to Turkey, it is Turkey that adheres to Europe.'[97] Given his view of Turkey, he differed from his colleagues in the UMP, as he also claimed that a Europe of humanist tradition should not reject the Turkish candidate out of hand.[98] Chirac cautioned the opposition against the possibility of leaving Turkey to the fate of religious fundamentalism, in a case of blocking the accession talks completely.[99] He stated: 'this space of peace, democracy and power requires the presence of Turkey', adding that Turks were going to bring power and a dimension that the EU needed in the future.[100] In parallel with Chirac's remarks, the French government was giving the message that they would closely follow the transition in Turkey. Prime Minister Dominique de Villepin additionally reminded them that the French public was going to determine Turkey's accession with a referendum at the end of the long, open, and conditional negotiations. The solution to the candidate's problems with Cyprus was critical to the process.[101] Meanwhile, Foreign Minister Philippe Douste-Blazy admitted that they showed a 'double-standard' to Turkey, although they allowed the applicant to begin the accession talks. He stated bluntly that it was simply a 'lie' to argue that the negotiations with Turkey had the same procedures as the earlier (Eastern European) accessions. They had already asked too much of the Turkish government for the membership negotiations' beginning, and the road to the candidate's admission would be extremely arduous.[102]

Before the negotiations' beginning, French politics brought into focus two issues to be solved within Turkey's accession process: the Cyprus conflict and recognition of the Armenian Genocide.[103] Public debates over Turkey's EU bid

---

96 Ibid.
97 Goulliaud, 'Jacques Chirac'.
98 Ibid.
99 Ibid.
100 'A Paris Jacques Chirac et Silvio Berlusconi'.
101 Ibid.
102 Gurrey, 'La droite française'.
103 De Baroches, Luc, 'Les amours clandestines de Paris et Ankara', *Le Figaro*, October 3, 2005; Alexandrine Bouilhet, 'Chypre : l'Europe met la pression sur Ankara', *Le Figaro*, September 3, 2005; Semih Vaner, 'Chypre ne doit pas être un alibi', *Le Figaro*, September 2, 2005.

largely involved the candidate's Cyprus policy. Upon the EU's request to enlarge the existing association agreement following the last enlargement (2004), Turkey had announced, on 21 September, that it would continue not to recognise Cyprus and would not open its harbours and airports to the new member. The EU immediately expressed its displeasure at this announcement, and French politicians individually declared their concerns. As *Le Monde* reported, some political camps led by French conservatives were arguing that Turkey's recognition of Cyprus should be linked to the start of accession talks.[104] Shortly before the presumed date of the beginning, the common argument in France was clearly against permitting Ankara to proceed to the membership negotiations without a change in its Cyprus policy. As the French Foreign Minister stated, 'France said its last word'.[105] In that regard, the French diplomatic reactions to Turkey's Cyprus issue received severe criticism. According to *Le Figaro*, after the failure of the constitutional referendum the French government was seeking public confidence by discussing Turkey and disapproving of its Cyprus policy.[106] Dominique de Villepin had first stated that the accession negotiations with Turkey were impossible if Turkey did not recognise the island.[107] But shortly after Villepin's warning, the French government somehow consented to the opening of the negotiations with the candidate without a solution on this matter.[108] Chirac and Villepin thus came in for criticism from their own party. The UMP's member and former minister Patrick Devedjian therefore questioned: 'Cyprus is now part of European territory, and the Turkish army occupies part of this territory. For the first time in its history, the EU is negotiating with an army of occupation! Those who recall General de Gaulle should really understand this scandal'.[109]

The Armenian question equally dominated French debates. Politicians from a broad ideological spectrum admitted that the country should recognise the Armenian Genocide by the Ottomans in 1915. *Le Monde* thus raised the common genocide argument against Turkey with examples of the Vichy Regime's role in the Holocaust, and the French policy in Algeria.[110] Similarly, members of the Socialist Party insisted that Turkey confront its past. As stated by Pierre Mos-

---

104 'Accord des Vingt-Cinq pour demander à la Turquie de reconnaître Chypre avant son adhésion à l'UE', *Le Monde*, September 20, 2005; 'L'Union européenne va adresser une "contre-déclaration" à la Turquie', *Le Monde*, September 21, 2005.
105 "Turquie en Europe".
106 Luc De Baroches, 'Les amours clandestines de Paris et Ankara', *Le Figaro*, October 3, 2005.
107 Chombeau and Le Coeur, 'La droite affiche'.
108 'Devedjian: "La Turquie n'a donné aucun gage de démocratie"', *Le Figaro*, October 4, 2005.
109 ibid.
110 Michel Rocard, 'Turquie : menaces sur les négociations', *Le Monde*, October 1, 2005.

covici, the Former Minister of European Affairs, French socialists largely saw the recognition of the Ottoman Empire's Armenian Genocide to be a precondition for Turkey's EU membership.[111] Conservative politicians argued similarly. But they were rather linking the Armenian question, among other grave matters, to the country's anti-democratic nature. To give one example, to the UMP's Patrick Devedjian Turkey was an anti-democratic country; the authoritarian state was comparable to the earlier cases from Spain, Portugal, Greece, and Croatia. And, like these applicants, the EU gave Turkey a chance for democratic transition.[112] Nevertheless, he believed that the candidate had made progress toward adopting European values in none of the relevant cases, most notably the recognition of the Armenian Genocide and the implementation of women's rights and minority rights.[113]

Among these discussions, political parties except for the socialists and communists particularly opposed Jacques Chirac and a small group of his followers in the French cabinet, who sided with the beginning of the accession talks with Turkey. It was also a matter of debate that the President of France had approved Turkey's negotiations by himself and therefore ignored, even transgressed, the will of the French nation. An opinion column published in *Le Figaro* summarised the common disagreement with Chirac:

> Never, under the Fifth Republic, French diplomacy has been so out of step with public opinion. Rarely the foreign policy of France has been so decided by one man, the president of the Republic, against the advice of his parliamentary majority. Four months after French people rejected in the referendum the European Constitutional Treaty, Paris has confirmed the green light for negotiations whose objective is the accession of Turkey to the European Union.[114]

The French government held a referendum on the EU's Constitution, but not on the accession talks with Turkey. Because presumably 70% of the French population were against Turkey's EU membership, the column claimed, starting the membership negotiations without public consent was a profound error. Despite Chirac's argument that the negotiations with Turkey would last a prolonged period and the candidate's accession would be decided by the French vote in the end, the commentary found it necessary to consult the French national will as early as before the negotiations' beginning. After all, French people were highly

---

111 'La candidature turque à l'UE'.
112 'Devedjian'.
113 'Le ministre de l'Intérieur revient à la charge sur la Turquie', *Le Figaro*, June 13, 2005.
114 Barochez, 'Les amours clandestines'.

against Turkey's accession, and the open-ended negotiation period was unlikely to change this fact.[115]

In the same commentary, Jacques Chirac was acting against the traditional French diplomacy maintaining European enlargement and integration in the same direction. Since Britain's accession, earlier French presidents had maintained the argument that each enlargement had to be balanced with a new integration treaty. 'This coupling is threatened since the funeral of the draft Constitution,' the author concluded. With the failure of the EU's Constitution, the Nice Treaty (2001), the previous agreement between EU countries, remained as the common ground. The Nice Treaty had been mainly devised for the adhesion of the Central and Eastern European countries including Cyprus and Malta, and the EU in its current state did not have the additional institutional capacity required for Turkey's accession.[116] This view surely overlooked the fact that during the lengthy period of Turkey's membership negotiations the EU was going to deepen its European institutions for new members. Indeed, during its accession talks with the candidate, the EU promulgated the Lisbon Treaty in 2009 in place of its rejected Constitution and welcomed Croatia as the 28th member in 2013.

The political right mostly shared the above points. For instance, the centre-right Union for French Democracy (UDF) released a declaration that launching the negotiations with Turkey without the public vote meant 'the denial of democracy'.[117] The French government had to seek legitimacy, at least in the French Parliament. The then president of the French Parliament, Jean-Louis Debré from the UMP, argued similarly. The Parliament had given authority to the government for the representation of the French will in diplomatic affairs. Without its consent, he said, the governmental action in critical matters like Turkey's membership negotiations was illegitimate.[118] Fifty members of the UMP and UDF therefore together penned an open letter to Chirac, stating that the French government had made a 'historic mistake', by not consulting the French national will on the accession talks with Turkey.[119]

Opposition parties from the political right denounced the French government's actions on Turkey's EU membership that were attempted without public consent. Yet the harshest criticisms arrived from within the party in power. As François Bayrou from the UDF stated, there emerged a double game in the

---

115 Ibid.
116 Ibid.
117 Gurrey, 'La droite française'.
118 'Le processus d'adhésion'.
119 Ibid.

UMP between support for and objections to the negotiations' opening.[120] On the one hand, a small group that Jacques Chirac led lent conditional support for the negotiations with Turkey; on the other, the majority of the UMP had already rejected Turkey's EU bid in earlier party meetings chaired by Alain Juppe and Nicolas Sarkozy.[121] These leaders had similarly repudiated Turkey's EU membership during their campaign for the EU's constitution the previous year.[122]

This public opposition was part of a leadership contest. *Le Monde* noted that the conservative candidates for the next presidential election were repeatedly criticising the beginning of Turkey's open-ended negotiations for their political sakes, and the journal was referring to their campaigns as '*le feuilleton*', or the 'Turkish soap opera'.[123] Sarkozy systematically raised his objection to Turkey's would-be membership as propaganda for the upcoming presidential elections.[124] He thus contradicted Prime Minister Dominique de Villepin, his arch-rival, who allegedly surrendered to Turkey and ignored the French national will on the candidate's membership.[125] Along with former UMP presidents like Valéry Giscard d'Estaing and Alain Juppe, Sarkozy was standing against his opponent de Villepin in the light of the Turkey-sceptic French public opinion.[126] In other respects, Sarkozy stated that the rejection of the EU Constitution by France revealed the question of the European Union's identity and borders. He thus called on other French politicians to rethink the European strategy of France. European integration should come to focus, in his opinion, and the first step should be setting the geographical borders of Europe. Put differently, Sarkozy had intended to exclude the 'Asian' Turkey from Europe completely. He stated that the membership of the Asian candidate overall would not contribute to the French strategy of European integration.[127] The EU had sustained the accession process of Turkey for 40 years, but 'fortunately', he stressed, never completed it. For the sake of European identity, a convenient option would rather be the privileged partnership the EU could establish with Turkey.[128]

---

120 Ibid.
121 Goulliaud and Jeudy, 'La Turquie'.
122 'Se démarquant de Jacques Chirac'.
123 'La droite française'.
124 A. Aubert, 'Sarkozy calme le jeu sur la Turquie', *Le Figaro*, September 26, 2005.
125 Jaigu, 'Sarkozy et VGE'.
126 Goulliaud and Jeudy, 'La Turquie'.
127 Philippe Ridet, 'Nicolas Sarkozy rouvre le débat sur l'adhésion de la Turquie à l'UE', *Le Monde*, September 23, 2005.
128 'Le ministre de l'Intérieur'.

Ten days before the membership negotiations with Turkey started, Sarkozy convened a party meeting with the motto 'Vision, Action, Frontiers!' in an attempt to give more weight to discussing European geography without Turkey. The rationale in particular was to review the EU's enlargement and identity after the constitutional referendum in France. These two questions were posed to delegates: 'How can we take the EU out of its stalemate?' and 'Is it possible to pursue European construction without clearly defining the borders of European space?' In other words, the convention's content was an apology for the French initiative of European integration and identity. The UMP's conceptual programme devised for the event saw the rejection of the EU Constitution as an opportunity: 'it is not rejecting the European idea but because (the French) want more Europe as it builds today'.[129] In this way, France was not a stumbling block but a pathfinder to the idea of Europe. The programme added that the EU had enlarged rapidly without institutional reforms and allowed its identity to fade dramatically. This was the prime indication that the entry of the Turkish historical 'other' to the EU would undoubtedly be unfavourable to the nature of European identity. As Sarkozy asserted during the convention, Turkey, having no place in Europe, should have received an offer of privileged partnership instead.[130]

In such a context the UMP's convention witnessed severe criticism of the official French diplomacy on Turkey's EU bid. Jacques Toubon, a representative of the European People's Party in the European Parliament and in fact Jacques Chirac's close associate, directly stood against the French government's decision to allow the start of negotiations between the EU and Turkey. The candidate's accession would be inconsistent with the EU's integration plan, he claimed. With a Turkey unready to entrust its powers to the European Union, negotiations were likely to continue forever and to menace the European project and 'pollute discussions for ten years'.[131] Next, as a former French President and drafter of the EU Constitution, Valéry Giscard d'Estaing's views were valuable for the UMP's elites. He maintained that since the EU's foundation, France had always been the pathfinder of European integration. For the first time, following the failure of the EU Constitution, France had no project for Europe.[132] The former president

---

[129] 'Sarkozy réunit une convention UMP sur l'Europe'. *Le Nouvelle Observateur*, September 24, 2005.
[130] Ibid.
[131] Philippe Ridet, 'Valéry Giscard d'Estaing dénonce l'"ambiguïté" française sur la Turquie', *Le Monde*, September 26, 2005.
[132] Antoine Guiral, 'L'UMP ronge l'os européen et charge Chirac', *Liberation*, September 26, 2005.

was also disappointed by the French policy on Turkey. The EU accession of a country geographically outside Europe would dilute the project of European political integration that France had promoted for half a century, and it would play into Eurosceptic Britain's hands.[133] He thus advocated a referendum on the beginning of the negotiations with the candidate. In his logic, a referendum in France as early as possible would result in the refusal of Turkey's EU accession by the French nation and would keep the EU intact against the influence of its historical rival.[134] Chirac had promised France a referendum at the end of the negotiations with Turkey, however, instead of its beginning; then French people would never have sufficient weight to resist the candidate after such a long and detailed process.[135] European integration in the meantime would require further institutions, and Turkey's involvement in the EU would hinder the further course of integration. Besides this, the French government was giving ambiguous messages both to the candidate and to the French public. French officials were referring to indefinite negotiation periods between ten and fifteen years.[136] Under these conditions, d'Estaing contended that France in the future of European affairs needed a new initiative from the UMP. He affirmed Nicolas Sarkozy as ready to give more clarity to the French diplomacy on Turkey's EU bid.[137] Through his speech, he expressed his vocal support for Sarkozy's candidature for the presidential elections in 2007.[138]

In summary, Chirac gave backing to Turkey's eligibility to join the European Union, and part of the French cabinet also showed conditional support for the debut of the membership negotiations.[139] In return, the majority of the UMP resisted the French approval of Turkey's accession talks, and the new chairman Sarkozy was leading this group. He was also intent on bringing this issue as an argument against his rivals before the presidential elections in 2007.[140] Among the French newspapers published shortly before the negotiations' beginning, *Le Figaro* reported on Sarkozy's statements in a particularly partisan man-

---

[133] Convention de l'UMP sur l'Europe les 23 et 24 septembre 2005, Paris, September 23–24, 2005, *Les Républicains* official website, http://soutenir.republicains.fr/sites/default/files/fichiers_joints /dates_cles/discours_valery_giscard_destaing.pdf.
[134] Judith Wintraub, 'Giscard réclame de la "clarté" sur la Turquie', *Le Monde*, September 24, 2005.
[135] 'Giscard critique Chirac', *Le Monde*, October 3, 2005.
[136] Ridet, 'Valéry Giscard d'Estaing'.
[137] Ibid; 'L'UMP débat de l'avenir de l'UE', *Le Nouvel Observateur*, September 27, 2005.
[138] Wintraub, 'Giscard réclame'.
[139] Gurrey, 'La droite française'.
[140] Ibid; 'L'UMP débat de l'avenir de l'UE'

ner. The paper announced the UMP leader to be the strongest candidate for the French presidency, depicting him as 'pro-European as much as sovereignist'.[141] In *Le Monde*'s depiction, Sarkozy was a typical populist and pro-European politician, who manipulated the dominant Turkey-pessimism of the public opinion for his candidature in the next presidential elections.[142] Specifically, the statements raised by Sarkozy and d'Estaing revealed the logical connection made between the EU Constitution and the beginning of Turkey's negotiations. These leaders and the conservative media presumed the French nation to be at the centre of European identity and integration. Through their rejection of the EU Constitution, the French nation had expressed their will against the state of the future relationship between the European Union and Turkey.

Conclusion

Under the influence of a number of historical conditions underpinning French national thinking, in the first half of 2000s French political elites represented their country with a historical emphasis: the French Republic was the pathfinder of European civilisation and its logical continuation, European integration. Two decisive factors, the principles of national representation and the pro-Europeanism promoted in French politics, clashed when the French public rejected the EU Constitution in 2005. Following this incident, French elites mainly debated France, the European Union, and Turkey through the prism of national representation, the French regime's supreme principle. In general terms, French conservatives disputed Turkey's membership by overstressing the Turkey-sceptic public opinion in France.

During the discussions about Turkey's compatibility with the European Union, the context of the Copenhagen political criteria remained important but was not the only factor. Overall, socialist and communist politicians were not as active as the conservatives in the given period; through their arguments, they conceptualised the European Union and Turkey in political terms and especially remained against the religious and geographical marginalisation of the candidate. A large part of the conservatives and the far-right, though, rejected Turkey's compatibility with Europe in political, geographical, and, at times, religious terms. Regarding their attitudes towards Turkey's EU bid, the Union for Political Movement was highly fragmented. President Jacques Chirac and

---

141 Jaigu, 'Sarkozy et VGE'.
142 Gurrey, 'La droite française'.

Prime Minister Dominique de Villepin lent conditional support to the beginning of Turkey's negotiations. In return, the party's majority led by Nicolas Sarkozy entirely repudiated the membership negotiations that would presumably lead to Turkey's accession to the EU, by labouring the point that the candidate was geographically not European. In other respects, conservative politicians kept to a minimum their arguments about a Muslim Turkey in relation to a Christian Europe, most likely as a result of the role of secularism in French politics. When they commented on religion in Turkey, they mostly pointed out the Islamisation of the country as a factor against European democracy.

Conservative elites mainly determined the direction of the Turkey debate in September. The rejection of the EU Constitution had given French conservatives an opportunity to conceptualise Europe and Turkey geographically. After France turned down the EU Constitution in 2005, the conservatives were preoccupied with making apologies for this decision, revitalising the French position in Europe, and maintaining European integration at its current pace. To this end, the UMP sought to redefine Europe in geographical terms, and Sarkozy organised a party meeting shortly before the negotiations with Turkey commenced to confer about European borders. In parallel, the debate over Turkey's accession talks was an occasion for the candidates aiming to stand for the next presidential elections, as they oriented the debate to their political interests. Notably, Sarkozy repeatedly expressed his opposition to the candidate during this pre-campaign period. The beginning of the membership negotiations with Turkey was an opportune moment for Sarkozy to demonstrate his political difference from the other opponents ahead of the elections.

6 'Is it all about Welfare?' German Debates over Turkey's EU Bid in 2005

Whilst the French government was drawn into a political controversy over Turkey and the EU Constitution, the German government was showing a definite attitude in favour of the beginning of the accession negotiations with the candidate. This attitude by Social Democratic-Green coalition was therefore publicly questioned by the Christian Democratic parties, which had long allied themselves with their French equivalents at the European level (under the European People's Party). More specifically, throughout the Turkey debate the disagreements over defining national identity, including the identity aspects of migration and integration policies, which had existed over the time of the post-war (western) Germany, had surfaced. The present chapter discusses the contestations over Turkey's EU prospects in the German media and politics in 2005, with a focus on the debates held one month prior to the presumed date of the accession talks' beginning, 3 October. In this final short timeframe, Turkey's compatibility with Europe became a much-debated issue in the shadow of the German federal elections (18 September). The first section explores the structural conditions underpinning the German contemporary national thinking about Turkey and the European Union. These factors primarily influenced German politics after the Second War, as well as the present arguments about the nation, the European integration and Turkey. The second section analyses the statements raised by the political elites in 2005. It first focuses attention on prime examples of how the German media covered Turkey's EU bid weeks before the beginning of the membership negotiations with the candidate. It then introduces German political camps' backgrounds and elaborates on their perceptions about Turkey's accession to the EU. The chapter finally examines a particular debate over Turkey's compatibility with the European Union between political actors inflamed in September and continued until the negotiations' beginning.

Throughout their debates over the beginning of the membership negotiations between the EU and the candidate in 2005, German political camps categorised Turkey and Europe through five long-term conditions. At first, Germany's welfare tradition including social protectionism profoundly affected the other factors and predominated German politics. The second condition, the ethnicity-oriented German citizenship, was discussed with migrants to the country, and only partially changed in the late 1990s. Before 2005, German conservative parties concerned about migration had opposed any modification to the citizenship regime. In 2005, they were still concerned about future migrants from Turkey and therefore repudiated the candidate's EU membership. Third, political elites and the media at times referred to Germany's earlier democratic transition from illiberal to liberal practices when discussing Turkey's reform process. Fourth, the politicised religion in Germany played a visible role in some of the exclusionary arguments about Turkey. Finally, German political parties' various long-term European policies had formative influences over the arguments about Turkey's EU membership.

The first long-term factor is the welfare tradition in Germany, including social protectionism, the key strongly connected with the other structural elements.[1] Welfare might be traced as two forms, on the one hand as the German state's function, on the other hand as a social conception. First, the German state has long been considered to be a necessary element to provide and protect citizens' welfare.[2] Origins of the German welfare state go back earlier than the other European types. Prussian kings, as claimed by Frederick the Great as early as 1742, were responsible for providing the well-being of their people, who in return gave legitimacy to the rulers.[3] In the unified Germany after 1871, welfare became a common ground between different social and ethnic classes and was seen by statesmen as the pillar of the German nation.[4] The German state was well-known in the late 19th century to be the first developer of modern social policies in Europe, and even across the world.[5]

---

[1] For the relevance of welfare to German history, see Harold A. James, *A German Identity 1770–1990* (London: Weidenfeld & Nicolson, 1990). Also see Harold James, *The End of Globalization: Lessons from the Great Depression* (Cambridge: Harvard University Press, 2002). Very briefly, social protectionism in Germany developed in the 19th century as a response to rising Socialism and its ideological variations. Hans-Peter Ullmann, *Politik im Deutschen Kaiserreich 1871–1918* (München: Oldenbourg Verlag, 2005), 18–25; Michael Balfour, *Germany: The Tides of Power* (London and New York: Routledge, 2004), 15–16. Also see, George Steinmetz, 'The Local Welfare State: Two Strategies for Social Domination in Urban Imperial Germany', American Sociological Review 55, no. 6 (December 1990): 891–911, http://www.jstor.org/stable/2095753.

[2] Gosta Esping-Andersen, *The Three Worlds of Welfare Capitalism* (Cambridge: Polity Press, 1990), 26–29.

[3] Frederick II von Hohenzollern, *Anti-Machiavel, ou Essai de critique sur le Prince de Machiavel*, published by Voltaire (Amsterdam, 1742).

[4] James, A German Identity, 217; Michael Stolleis, *Origins of the German Welfare State: Social Policy in Germany to 1945* (New York: Springer, 2013), 49; Dieter Fuchs, 'Welche Demokratie wollen die Deutschen? Einstellungen zur Demokratie im vereinigten Deutschland', in *Politische Orientierungen und Verhaltensweisen im vereinigten Deutschland*, ed. Oscar W. Gabriel (Wiesbaden: Springer, 1997), 89–90. Also see Lothar Gall, *Von der ständischen zur bürgerlichen Gesellschaft* (München: Oldenbourg Verlag, 2012).

[5] George Steinmetz, *Regulating the Social: The Welfare State and Local Politics in Imperial Germany* (Princeton: Princeton University Press, 1993), 5.

German history notably showed that when the idea of 'economic nation' failed in the country, political camps became more inclined to define the nation with cultural and ethnic traits.⁶ Following the Second World War, the modern German regime then was to adopt the policy of socio-economic development and welfare to find legitimisation at the social level and to restrain radical nationalism.⁷ With this rationale, the national cause of welfare gradually changed to being an economic power within European integration. The post-war regime constituted its backbone with welfare and social policies derived from its Basic Law in 1949. Article 20 of the Basic Law declared Germany to be a 'democratic and social federal state'.⁸ The new regime's fundamental principles, in particular humanitarian rights, federal democratic governance, and the federal and welfare state, were enacted as unalterable by the law.⁹ Meanwhile, political camps also were tailoring their political identities to the principle of social market economy and welfare.¹⁰ When the foreign labour inflow to the country began in the 1960s, the tradition of welfare and socio-economic development had already formed the lines of party politics.¹¹

---

6 Ibid, 218.
7 James, *A German Identity*, 218; Stefan Berger, *Inventing the Nation: Germany* (London and New York: Bloomsbury, 2011), 184–185; James Sperling, ed., *Germany at Fifty-five: Berlin ist Nicht Bonn?* (Manchester: Manchester University Press, 2004), 4–5; Manfred G. Schmidt, 'Germany: The Grand Coalition State', in *Comparative European Politics*, ed. Josep M. Colomer (Abingdon: Routledge, 2008), 61.
8 Peter E. Quint, 'The Constitutional Guarantees of Social Welfare in the Process of German Unification', *The American Journal of Comparative Law* 47, no.2 (Spring, 1999): 305, doi:10.2307/841042.
9 See article 79 paragraph 3, Basic Law for the Federal Republic of Germany.
10 Wolfram Kaiser, *Christian Democracy and the Origins of European Union* (Cambridge: Cambridge University Press, 2007), 307; Torsten Oppelan, 'Domestic Political Developments: 1949–1969', in *The Federal Republic of Germany since 1949: Politics, Society and Economy before and after Unification*, eds. Klaus Larres and Panikos Panayi (Abingdon and New York: Routledge, 2014), 80. See, Ahlener Programm, Zonenausschuß der CDU für die britische Zone, Ahlen, Westfalen, February 3, 1947, 17. For the SPD's focus on social welfare, Stephen Padgett, 'The SPD: the Decline of the Social Democratic Volkspartei', in *The Federal Republic of Germany since 1949: Politics, Society and Economy before and after Unification*, eds. Klaus Larres and Panikos Panayi (Abingdon and New York: Routledge, 2014), 234–235. Notably, the SPD also referred to 'Christian ethics' within their definition of socialism. See Godesberger Programm: Grundsatzprogramm der Sozialdemokratischen Partei Deutschlands, November 13–15, 1959. For the party's earlier Marxist roots, see Political manifesto of the Social Democratic Party of Germany, Hanover, May 11, 1946.
11 In addition, the working class was prominently represented in the modern German regime. The Social Democrats and Christian Democrats sustained relations with trade unions re-organ-

It also needs to remember the German welfare as a social conception, which changed in parallel with the country's economic development. Germany's industrially and financially incentive exports in its European hinterland thrived together with the EU's growing economic competence.[12] In other words, German elites conceived European integration as an instrument to sustain the country's development.[13] Economic concerns did not decline, however. The unification of the western and eastern parts of Germany (1990), during the ascendancy of the Christian Democrats, was much celebrated, but also brought a substantial economic burden to society.[14] Increasing taxes and constant unemployment rates had a decisive role in the electoral success and the ascent to power of the Social Democratic Party of Germany in 1998.[15] Under worsening economic conditions, the social policies of the German welfare state were also debated. By the time Turkey was given a candidacy status for the EU membership, the argument of the Christian Democratic opposition was to cut social funds including benefits to facilitate market growth in Germany.[16] In 2005, an important part of Turkey-scepticism among the Christian Democrats was related to their argument that more migrants coming from Turkey would have an adverse effect on welfare in the case of Turkey's accession to the EU.

The second factor is the nature of German citizenship and citizenship discussions regarding immigration. The German citizenship as we know today goes back to the nationality law in 1913, which, arguably, provided an ethnic standard

---

ised after the WWII. See Heiner Dribbusch and Peter Birke, *Trade Unions in Germany: Organisation, Environment, Challenges* (Berlin: Friedrich-Ebert-Stiftung, 2012).

12 Wolfgang Rudzio, *Das politische System der Bundesrepublik Deutschland* (Springer VS, 2015), 411.

13 Berger, *Inventing the Nation*, 184.

14 Mary M. McKenzie, 'The Origins of the Berlin Republic', in *Germany at Fifty-five: Berlin ist Nicht Bonn?* ed. James Sperling (Manchester: Manchester University Press, 2004), 71–72; Raj Kollmorgen, Frank Thomas Koch, and Hans-Liudger Dienel, 'Diskurse der deutschen Einheit: Forschungsinteressen und Forschungsperspektiven des Bandes', in *Diskurs der deutsche Einheit, Kritik und Alternativen*, eds. Raj Kollmorgen, Frank Thomas Koch, Hans-Liudger Dienel (Vs Verlag, 2011), 7–8.

15 Thomas Hanf, Reinhard Liebscher, and Heidrun Schmidtke, 'Die Wahrnehmung und Bewertung der deutschen Einheitim Spiegel von Bevölkerungsumfragen', in *Diskurs der deutsche Einheit, Kritik und Alternativen*, eds. Raj Kollmorgen, Frank Thomas Koch, and Hans-Liudger Dienel (Vs Verlag, 2011), 267–268.

16 Claus Offe, 'The German Welfare State: Principles, Performance, Prospects', in *The Postwar Transformation of Germany: Democracy, Prosperity, and Nationhood*, eds. John S. Brady, Beverly Crawford, and Sarah Elise Wiliarty (Michigan: The University of Michigan Press), 202–224.

mainly to prevent migrants from integration into the German nation.¹⁷ According to the citizenship guidelines of 1921, the criteria for German citizenship were, among other things, being ethnically German and posing no potential danger against the domestic order.¹⁸ The later Nazi government added to this ethnic conception, as it introduced a hierarchy to German citizenship, in which the superior group signified ethnic Germans. The subordinate group in return consisted of Jews and also some ethnic Germans from opposition parties.¹⁹ The post-war citizenship law in Germany essentially changed little after the migrations to the country. When the citizenship was to be reformed, it was intended that welfare remain unaffected.²⁰ The Basic Law of the Federal Republic of Germany (1949), the modern regime's foundation, added political and territorial conditions to the citizenship system. Even so, blood descent remained dominant and highly restricted the naturalisation of working migrants.²¹ The Basic Law (article 116.1) made use of the term 'German' to cover citizens of the country and ethnic Germans living in Eastern Europe. In this case, the law declared 'migrants' to be only the Germans returning to the motherland from the (former) Socialist countries. The other residents in the country were instead deemed alien (*Ausländer*).²²

---

17 William Rogers Brubaker, 'Immigration, Citizenship, and the Nation-State in France and Germany: A Comparative Historical Analysis', *International Sociology* 5, no.4 (December 1990): 396–397, doi: 10.1177/026858090005004003; Annemarie Sammartino, 'Culture, Belonging, and the Law: Naturalisations in the Weimer Republic', in *Citizenship and National Identity in Twentieth-Century Germany*, eds. Geoff Eley and Jan Palmowski (Stanford: Stanford University Press, 2008), 61–63.
18 Eli Nathans, *The Politics of Citizenship in Germany. Ethnicity, Utility and Nationalism* (New York: Berg, 2004), 202.
19 Ibid, 220.
20 Gary P. Freeman, 'Migration and the Political Economy of the Welfare State', *The Annals of the American Academy of Political and Social Science* 485, (May 1986): 53, doi: 10.1177/0002716286485001005; Andrew Geddes, *The Politics of Migration and Immigration in Europe* (London: Sage, 2003), 90–93.
21 Georg G. Iggers, 'Nationalism and Historiography, 1789–1996', in *Writing National Histories, Western Europe since 1800*, eds. Stefan Berger, Mark Donovan, and Kevin Passmore (New York: Routledge, 1999), 17; Hermann Kurthen, 'Germany at the Crossroads: National Identity and the Challenges of Immigration', *International Migration Review* 29, no.4 (Winter, 1995): 929–930, doi: 10.2307/2547732.
22 Christian Jopke, 'The Evolution of Alien Rights in the United States, Germany, and the European Union', in *Citizenship Today: Global Perspectives and Practices*, eds. Alexander T. Aleinikoff and Douglas Klusmeyer (Washington DC: Carnegie Endowment for International Peace, 2001), 44–48; Ruth Mandel, *Turkish Challenges to Citizenship and Belonging in Germany* (Durham NC: Duke University Press, 2008), 51. William Rogers Brubaker, *Citizenship and Nationhood in*

The nature of citizenship stirred much debate between political camps following the arrival of migrants, most notably Turks. In an attempt to fill the necessary labour gap for its economic development, the Federal Republic of Germany adopted the policy of employing short-term workers from abroad.[23] It established a rotation system that authorised foreign workers to work in the country for 1–2 years. From the late 1950s onwards, migrations mostly covered people from Mediterranean countries, including Turkey. Roughly 18 million workers settled in West Germany, and 4 to 5 million of that amount later gained permanent residence.[24] Facing the economic recession in 1973, the European Community introduced a regulation to restrict non-European workers. Although the new regulation limited the foreign labour residing in West Germany, the number of foreigners did not diminish due to other reasons, such as the immigration through family reunions (which became possible by law in the 1980s[25]) and the high birth rate in the foreign population.[26] Over the 1980s, a small number moved back to Turkey through some incentives of a CDU government, but many Turkish migrants chose to enjoy welfare and social policies in the hosting country and to raise future generations as German citizens.[27] In fact, even the German public had expected the return of Turkish workers to their motherland in the mid-1980s.[28] The conservative camps then represented the Turks living in Germany with terms like 'the question of guest workers', 'the army of the unemployed', or 'the flood of migrants'.[29] In time, the residents of Turkish origin became a part of German politics and provided critical support for Turkey's gains in affairs with Europe and Germany.[30] They mainly tended to

---

France and Germany (Cambridge, Massachusetts, Harvard University Press, 1992), 72; Berger, *Inventing the Nation*, 174.
23 Yasemin Karakasoglu, 'Türkische Arbeitswanderer in West-, Mittel- und Nordeuropa seit der Mitte der 1950er Jahre', eds. Klaus J. Bade, Pieter C. Emmer, Leo Lucassen und Jochen Oltmer, *Enzyklopädie Migration in Europa* (Paderborn: Ferdinand Schöningh, 2007), 1054–1057.
24 Kurthen, 'Germany at the Crossroads', 922–923.
25 Geddes, *The Politics of Migration*, 81, 83; Christian Jopke, *Immigration and the Nation-state: The United States, Germany, and Great Britain* (New York: Oxford University Press, 1999), 62–99.
26 Ibid, 923.
27 Brubaker, *Citizenship and Nationhood in France and Germany*, 180–181.
28 Haldun Gülalp and Günter Seufert, *Religion, Identity and Politics: Germany and Turkey in Interaction* (Abingdon: Routledge, 2013), 61.
29 Jochen Walter, *Die Türkei – 'Das Ding auf der Schwelle': (De-)Konstruktionen der Grenzen, (De-) Konstruktionen der Grenzen Europas* (VS Verlag für Sozialwissenschaften, 2008), 170.
30 Ziya Öniş, 'Luxembourg, Helsinki and Beyond: Towards an Interpretation of Recent Turkey-EU Relations', *Government and Opposition* 35, no. 4 (2000), 470–472. doi: 10.1111/1477-7053.00041; Joschka Fischer, 'Turkey's European Perspective: The German View', *Turkish Policy Quarterly* 3, no.3 (Fall 2004).

vote for the SPD, which favoured social and minority policies in Germany and espoused Turkey's accession to the EU. In response, the Christian Democrats campaigned for the greater socio-economic integration of migrants into German economy and society.[31]

Political parties therefore often debated the citizenship law in the context of the Turkish community in Germany. The significant and only partially successful attempt to liberalise the citizenship regime, including multiple citizenship in Germany, arrived from the ruling coalition between the Social Democrats and the Greens in 1999. The CDU/CSU fiercely opposed these attempts; in the case of the following election in the state of Hesse, they campaigned against dual citizenship and also gathered signatures in public before the local elections.[32] At the end of a decisive election victory in Hesse, the Christian Democrats repelled the proposals to enlarge the option of multiple citizenship to Turks.[33] As a result, the Social Democrats and Greens managed to enact only a limited citizenship reform.[34] On the one hand, the act brought a territorial condition to citizenship for the children of foreign parents living in the country. Children of long-term residents born in Germany from 2000, the year when the act took effect, could obtain German citizenship through this territorial condition. On the other hand, the new citizenship regime obliged these young Germans with multiple citizenships to choose one of them by the age of 23.[35] In brief, the legislative periods of Federal Germany between 1998 and 2005 dominated by the Social Democratic-Green coalition featured fierce debates on the citizenship regime concerning the existing migrants.

Mainly due to citizenship policies in Germany, only 400,000 out of the populous Turkish community were German citizens in 2005. The rest were referred to as 'Turks with German passports'.[36] The Turkish community was then forming the biggest non-German society in the country, with a population of 1,764,000

---

31 For the historical changes in the German perception of Turkish immigrants, see Gunal Incesu, *Ankara – Bonn – Brüssel: Die deutsch-türkischen Beziehungen und die Europaeische Gemeinschaft, 1959–1987* (Biefeld: Transcript Verlag, 2014), 127–171.
32 Marc Morjé Howard, 'The Causes and Consequences of Germany's New Citizenship Law', *German Politics* 17, no.1 (March 2008): 50–52, doi: 10.1080/09644000701855127.
33 Jopke, 'The Evolution of Alien Rights', 52.
34 Howard, 'The Causes and Consequences', 58; Gülalp and Seufert, *Religion, Identity and Politics*, 61.
35 Mandel, *Turkish Challenges to Citizenship*, 15, 220–221; Geddes, *The Politics of Migration*, 96.
36 Bessam Tibi, 'Europeanizing Islam or the Islamization of Europe: Political Democracy vs. Cultural Difference', in *Religion in an Expanding Europe*, eds. Timothy A., Byrnes and Peter J. Katzenstein (Cambridge: Cambridge University Press, 2006), 211–212.

in 2005.[37] The number of naturalisations of Turks in Germany was also higher than other minorities. In 1999, almost 104,000 Turks acquired German citizenship, whereas the amount was 44,400 in 2004.[38] In these premises, it was feared that the likely Turkish inflow to Germany in the case of membership would destabilise German welfare, and this caused further scepticism about the candidate's EU bid.

Another factor underpinning, at least indirectly, the contemporary German perspectives of Turkey in connection with the EU is the democratic transition in Germany from illiberal to liberal practices. This transition implied a de-concentration of political power. German history before the Second World War witnessed rising concentration of power except for the short Weimar era.[39] The worldwide repercussions of the power-concentration in Germany, especially the two world wars' impact, led the current regime to make democratic institutions immune to amendments. The Basic Law of the Federal Republic of Germany (1949) therefore established the de-concentration of power as an unalterable norm in German politics.[40] The new constitution had given substantial powers to judicial and legislative institutions to safeguard the democratic regime against any group wishing to dominate the others and alter the system. This 'self-protectionism' of the German regime was called 'militant democracy'. In the early years of the Federal Republic of Germany, scholars debated whether the militant democracy was sufficient for effective democratic consolidation.[41] How the German regime could cope with new forms of extreme ideologies also came into question.

Yet later decades showed that the democratic system in Germany worked quite fine. On the one hand, the Basic Law prioritised individual rights and liberties in society regardless of the state of citizenship. It ensured that anyone enjoyed certain freedoms according to the law. On the other hand, the regime introduced greater pluralism to the system of German governance. The Basic Law

---

37 Bundesministerium des Innern, Migrationsberichtdes Bundesamtes für Migration und Flüchtlinge im Auftrag der Bundesregierung, 2005, 171.
38 Ibid. 172.
39 Ullmann, *Politik in Deutschen Kaiserreicht*, 10. For the concentration of power before the Nazi and Weimar periods, see, Fritz Fischer, *Griff nach der Weltmacht. Die Kriegszielpolitik des kaiserlichen Deutschland 1914/1918* (Düsseldorf: Droste, 1967).
40 James Sperling, 'Berlin ist nicht Bonn? Continuity and Change in postwar Germany', in *Germany at Fifty-five: Berlin ist Nicht Bonn?* ed. James Sperling (Manchester: Manchester University Press, 2004), 12.
41 John S., Brady and Sarah Elise Wiliarty, 'From the Bonn to the Berlin Republic and Beyond: Critical Junctures and the Future of the Federal Republic', Brady, Crawford, and Wiliarty, *The Postwar Transformation of Germany*, 507–508.

regulated political parties to be unique actors within the decision-making process. However, parties needed to form coalitions to govern. The political system required governing through coalitions and therefore contributed to the further development of pluralism in Germany. Even so, the national government was not alone in governing. Local governments and state bureaucrats were responsible for individual institutions, especially in the fields of public administration and economy. Finally, the national and local governments and public institutions became bound by the regulations of the European Union.[42]

That is to say, the German democracy became consolidated after a certain period of time and incidents. It is no coincidence in the end that Germans were curious about how Turkey would be able to democratise itself throughout its relations with the EU. The conception of liberal democracy in Germany provided the motivation, among other things, to discuss Turkey's democratic transition. German politicians, intellectuals, and journalists in the 2000s critically approached democratic issues in Turkey, in particular the violations of human rights in the face of authoritarian political culture.[43] Similarly, they discussed the military's role in Turkish politics and the question of the Armenian Genocide with references to the German past.[44] As Jens Alber, German sociologist, noted, 'the German example teaches that the political culture of a country is not a matter of long-term imprints, but can change quite rapidly under the pressure of new foreign policy commitments and interdependencies. In this respect, the German example gives cause for cautious optimism also for the Europeanization of Turkey'.[45]

The fourth structural factor underpinning the contemporary German national thinking in our case is politicised religion. Religion, which was chiefly represented by the Christian Democratic camps, played a decisive part in essentialist categorisations of Germany. The Christian Democratic parties were the main conservative actors in German politics, in particular through their power between 1949–1969 and 1982–1998. The CDU/CSU, the Christian Democratic Union and its Bavaria-based partner, the Christian Social Union, developed a non-confes-

---

[42] Schmidt 'Germany', 76–78.
[43] For an example, see Heinrich August Winkler, 'Überdehntes Wir-Gefühl. Als Wertegemeinschaft kann die EU nur Nationen umfassen, die sich der politischen Kultur des Westens vorbehaltlos öffnen', *Die Welt*, 28. December 2005.
[44] See the interview with Claudia Roth, 'Interview: Türkei braucht eine glaubwürdige EU-Perspektive', *Die Zeit.de*, 03.05.2005, http://www.zeit.de/politik/dlf/2005/interview_050503 (07.09.2015).
[45] Jens Alber, 'Gehört die Türkei zu Europa? – Ein Sozialporträt der Türkei im Licht vergleichender Daten der Umfrageforschung', *Leviathan* 32, no.4 (December 2004), 464–494.

sional structure following the WWII, by maintaining traditional Catholic grassroots and maintaining a distance from certain types of nationalism.[46] They merged various ethical and political approaches, such as the Catholic social teaching, the church's relationship between the individual and society, Protestant perspectives, and the laissez-faire economy under the guidance of state.[47] Through these policies, the Christian Democrats could appeal to the large German middle class. Furthermore, the CDU/CSU in the following years adopted a greater focus on the social market economy and European integration.[48] The party additionally established a number of associations with social groups like trade unions and youth organisations.[49]

During the early decades of West Germany, the Christian Democratic leaders made vital contributions to re-introduce the idea of Germanness after the failed venture of the racial nation in the Nazi past.[50] Their attempts are argued to have increased after 1990. Following the reunification of Germany, party officials increasingly came to redefine the national identity with keywords like 'family', 'home', 'values', 'patriotism', 'language', and 'culture'.[51] A recent example was 'the patriotism debate', in which the Christian Democrats put forward essential definitions of Germanness in 2004. Former general secretary of the CDU Laurenz Meyer first used the term 'patriotism' in an interview and stated that they needed 'a bit of self-confidence' for Germany.[52] Although he added that his conception was not nationalistic and that 'any Turk living in Germany could also become patriotic', his argument quickly stirred debates. Party elites of the CDU/CSU, as well as those of the Free Democratic Party, together welcomed Meyer's patriotic argument, claiming that German patriotism denoted more than simply love of the constitution.[53] In return, the Social Democrats reiterated their belief in a nation principally defined in political and economic terms. Chancellor Gerhard

---

[46] Kaiser, *Christian Democracy and the Origins of European Union*, 173; Berger, *Inventing the Nation*, 175.
[47] Rudzio, *Das politische System der Bundesrepublik Deutschland*, 129–130.
[48] Ibid, 131; Kaiser, *Christian Democracy and the Origins of European Union*, 199.
[49] David Broughton, 'The CDU-CSU in Germany: Is There any Alternative?', in *The Christian Democracy in Europe*, ed. David Hanley (London and New York: Cassel Imprint, 1994), 106–107.
[50] Berger, *Inventing the Nation*, 177–181.
[51] Rudzio, *Das politische System der Bundesrepublik Deutschland*, 134. 'Das Jahr der Schildkröte', *Der Spiegel*, no.53 (2004), December 27, 2004; Petra Bornhöft and Ralf Neukirch, 'Spiegel-Streitgespräch, Sie legen die Axt ans Grundgesetz', *Der Spiegel*, no.50 (2004), December 6, 2004; Bernd Ulrich, 'Christlich-demokratische Verunsicherung', *Die Zeit*, December 16, 2004.
[52] 'Union: Wirtschaftsflügel wettert gegen Patriotismus-Debatte', *Der Spiegel Online*, December 6, 2004.
[53] Bornhöft and Neukirch, 'Spiegel-Streitgespräch'.

6 'Is it all about Welfare?' German Debates over Turkey's EU Bid in 2005 — 169

Schröder also replied to Meyer that welfare tradition and labour culture provided the fundamental ground for German identity.[54] In the end, the debate revealed that the Christian Democrats, who apparently found inspirations in religion, tended to frame the German 'self' in cultural terms more than they previously did over the time of West Germany.

In summary of the first four long-term factors, German political camps conceptualised their national context between political (including economic), religious, and geographical terms. Before discussing how they approached Turkey's EU membership, we also need to remember how they see the European Union. The last historical condition of the German national thinking, German political parties' European policies, therefore comes to the fore. Like their French counterparts, mainstream German parties are known to elevate national interests within the European framework.[55] But in the French case, disruptions of pro-Europeanism emerged, as the rejection of the EU Constitution by French public demonstrated in 2005. In modern Germany, the significance of European integration has instead been above politics.[56] Since 1949, article 24.2 of the Basic Law states that the Federal Republic of Germany was ready to consent to limitations over its sovereignty to join a system of security and peace in Europe and the world.[57] As such, German political elites saw joining the European integration project as a crucial instrument for finding legitimacy.[58] European integration later additionally gained a substantial economic meaning for the country. Over decades, the EU's increasing economic competence cultivated Germany's industrially and financially incentive exports in the European hinterland of the country.[59] German political parties thus did not turn aside from this course of promoting European integration in general, as much as they upheld the EU Constitution in 2005.[60]

Although they both backed European integration, the Christian Democrats and Social Democrats upheld different European policies in some fields. The

---

54 Nikolaus Blome, 'Patriotismus ist das, was ich jeden Tag tue', *Die Welt*, December 4, 2004.
55 Thomas Banchoff, 'German Identity and European Integration', *European Journal of International Relations* 5, no3 (Sept. 1999): 282, doi: 10.1177/1354066199005003001.
56 Rudzio, *Das politische System der Bundesrepublik Deutschland*, 447; Wolfram F. Hanrieder, *West German Foreign Policy, 1949–1963: International Pressure and Domestic Response* (Stanford: Stanford University Press, 1967), 95, 97–98; Michael Gehler, *Europa: Von der Utopie zur Realität* (Innsbruck-Wien: Haymon Taschenbuch, 2014), 237–248.
57 See article 24.2, Grundgesetz für die Bundesrepublik Deutschland vom 23. Mai 1949.
58 James, *A German Identity*, 218; Berger, *Inventing the Nation*, 242.
59 Rudzio, *Das politische System der Bundesrepublik Deutschland*, 411.
60 Schmidt, 'Germany', 84–86; Jeřábek Martin, *Deutschland und die Osterweiterung der Europäischen Union* (Wiesbaden: Vs Verlag fur Sozialwischenschaften, 2011), 211.

CDU/CSU overall campaigned for furthering European integration by increasing the EU's and Germany's economic competitiveness. They also prioritised European security, which entailed enhancing cooperation with the United States. Throughout the European Union's history, the Christian Democrats additionally stressed the cultural unity of Europeans, and in 2004 they enthusiastically celebrated the accession of the Central and Eastern European countries to the EU.[61] In their opinions, Turkey was quite a different story than Europe. The party remained firmly against the candidate's EU membership on the assumption that it was not European by its nature: its history, its geography, and its religion were essentially out of their cultural cosmos. Regarding the pertinent Turkey debates held in 2005, the Christian Democrats notably rejected the connection between the candidate's EU membership and European multiculturalism that Social Democrats had long backed. The main argument raised by the Social Democratic Party of Germany was that Turkey's EU membership would confirm the idea of multicultural Europe and facilitate the integration of migrants in Europe and Germany.[62] In other respects, the Social Democrats concerned themselves with European integration through implementing universal social rights and policies at the European level. The party remained critical of military developments and armaments inside the EU. Nevertheless, security in Europe and its hinterland was increasingly important, and it was partially why the Social Democrats were the advocates of the EU's promotion of peace and democracy outside Europe.[63] In order to encourage democracy, their point of emphasis was establishing political and economic relationships with the EU's neighbours. This last point was decisive in the party's open support for Turkey's accession to the EU.

In a nutshell, the long-term conditions of German national thinking about Turkey and the European Union were the country's welfare tradition, the current state of citizenship and relevant discussions concerning Turkish migrants, the democratic transition in Germany from illiberal to liberal practices, the impact of religion on politics, and, finally, political parties' European policies. Under the influence of these factors, chief political camps, as well as the media, entered a lively identity debate over Turkey's EU membership in 2005.

---

[61] Rudzio, *Das politische System der Bundesrepublik Deutschland*, 134. See Rainer Hülsse, 'Imagine the EU: The Metaphorical Construction of a Supra-nationalist Identity' *Journal of International Relations and Development* 9, (2006): 396–421, doi:10.1057/palgrave.jird.1800105.
[62] Küçük, *Die Türkei und das andere Europa*, 186–187.
[63] Rudzio, *Das politische System der Bundesrepublik Deutschland*, 134.

The EU and Turkey according to the German Media and Politics

Before analysing political and media statements, it is essential to note that German public opinion in 2005 was strongly against Turkey's European Union membership. According to a Eurobarometer poll held in the same year, Germany had the third highest popular opposition to Turkey's accession to the EU, after Austria and France. Some Germans also associated the EU Constitution with Turkey's potential membership, as a part of the French public did. If Germany had held a constitutional referendum, the poll added, 29% of citizens would have voted against the EU Constitution because of their opposition to the Turkish candidate.[64]

How did this Turkey-scepticism in society impact on the media coverage? The primary newspapers included in the present analysis are *Die Welt*, *Die Frankfurter Allgemeine Zeitung* (henceforth the *FAZ*), *Der Spiegel*, and *Die Zeit*. At first, journals associated with conservative ideology, especially *Die Welt* and the *FAZ*, dealt with the Turkish case through the country's so-called non-European character. Jochen Walter illustrated these views in his study with respect to the period before 2005. In his analysis, notably the *FAZ* published news and opinions against Turkey's EU bid. In particular, the newspaper repeatedly asserted that Turkey's candidacy since 1999 'automatically' signalled its accession to the EU.[65] Christian Democratic leaders continued to object to the negotiations with Turkey for the same reason, the so-called 'automatic' trajectory of the accession talks: once began, they claimed, the technical process was most likely to culminate in Turkey's membership despite the existing opposition in the EU.[66]

The conservative newspapers continued to raise doubts about Turkey's European nature in 2005.[67] With the negotiations' opening, op-eds published in the *FAZ* repeatedly questioned whether Turkey was essentially European. The most critical question, 'whether Turkey had a logical place in the social and cultural constitution of Europe', had remained unanswered before the beginning of the

---

64 Eurobarometer 63.4: Public Opinion in the European Union, National Report Executive Summary: Germany, Spring 2005.
65 Walter, *Die Türkei*, 187, 182–204.
66 'Merkel und Stoiber: Kanzler muß Türkei-Beitritt stoppen', *Frankfurter Allgemeine (Online)*, December 5, 2004.
67 For example, See Ernst-Wolfgang Böckenförde 'Nein zum Beitritt der Türkei', Frankfurter Allgemeine Zeitung December 9, 2004; Klaus-Dieter Frankenberger and Michael Stabenow 'Zu groß, zu arm, zu verschieden', *Frankfurter Allgemeine Zeitung*, December 15, 2004; 'Unfair, unehrlich und zynisch', *Frankfurter Allgemeine Zeitung*, December 15, 2004.

negotiations.[68] A year before the negotiations' beginning it reported on EU's Commissioner Frits Bolkestein's comments that Turkey was originally not European, making a headline with his words: 'too big, too poor, too different'.[69] In another example, the *FAZ* published an interview with Samuel Huntington with a section reserved for Turkey's EU bid. The subsection on the candidate was entitled: 'The clash of civilisations continues'. Following Huntington's comments on European culture, the interviewer posed this question: 'would the accession of Muslim Turkey to the European Union, in the face of its Christian heritage, be a perversion of the European identity – even if it (the candidate) is a secular country?'[70] As might be expected, Huntington answered that the EU with Turkey would never represent what Europe designated before. In a much similar vein, *Die Welt* revealed a rigid religious stereotype of the country, as one commentary, for example, raised the prospect that 'the more democratic Turkey becomes, the more Islamised it is'.[71] The opinion contended that Turkey's democratisation, for which the candidate's accession process paves the way, in fact strengthens tendencies to radical Islam in Turkish society and politics.

Despite their Turkey-scepticism, unlike the French reportage the conservative media in Germany generally did not give significant priority to the candidate's domestic and technical issues shortly before the start of the negotiations.[72] For example, in contrast to *Le Figaro*'s denouncement of Turkey's Cyprus policy, *Die Welt* and the *FAZ* approached the case in more technical terms.[73] Similarly, German conservative elites had not insisted on a change in Turkey's relations with Cyprus before the launch of the membership negotiations. According to them, Turkey's recognition of Cyprus was indispensable for accession but not negotiation.[74]

---

68 'Wer ist hier Stur?', *Frankfurter Allgemeine Zeitung*, September 30, 2005.
69 'Zu groß'.
70 Harald Staun, 'Interview mit Samuel P. Huntington: Das Gespenst der Immigration', *Frankfurter Allgemeine Sonntagszeitung*, October 30, 2005.
71 Christopher Caldwell, 'Die Türken vor Wien', *Die Welt*, October 4, 2005.
72 'Vor dem 3. Oktober will die EU den Druck auf die Türkei erhöhen', *Die Welt*, September 17, 2005; 'Brüssel gibt Ankara wieder nach', *Die Welt*, September 21, 2005.
73 'EU räumt der Türkei für Gespräche viel Spielraum ein', *Die Welt*, September 22, 2005; 'Brüssel gibt Ankara wieder nach', *Die Welt*, September 21, 2005; 'EU will Druck auf Türkei erhöhen', *Frankfurter Allgemeine Zeitung*, September 17, 2005.
74 Bernhard Zand, 'Scheidung vor der Hochzeit?', *Der Spiegel*, no.40 (2005), October 1, 2005; 'Merkel und Stoiber bestärken in der EU ihren Widerstand', *Frankfurter Allgemeine*, August 26, 2005.

Their coverage in September and early October 2005 suggests that *Die Zeit* and *Der Spiegel* used more objective arguments than those of *Die Welt* and *Die FAZ*. To give one example, *Die Zeit* held the EU partially responsible for the 'already-decided' negative outcome of the negotiations with Turkey. Days after the membership negotiations' opening, commentaries in this newspaper argued that EU members had changed the negotiating document and rendered the accession talks almost impossible to come to a successful end.[75] One opinion stated that the EU blocked the negotiations from the beginning and escalated a short-term anti-European and nationalist backlash in Turkey. Nevertheless, the opinion still saw the accession talks with the EU as a significant opportunity for the candidate's modernisation: 'It is quite possible, therefore, that Turkey no longer needs the catalyst Europe in ten years. With its potential, it could be a blooming tiger economy on its own. The rapprochement with the EU will help it, even though it may never get to the accession.'[76]

Der Spiegel and *Die Zeit* were also concerned about the changing attitudes in Turkey towards the EU, and critically underlined the growing nationalism and declining pro-Europeanism in the country. The uncompromising attitude shown by Turkish government and public against the recognition of the Ottomans' Armenian Genocide was especially noted, and in this case the novelist Orhan Pamuk's thought crime trial stirred many reactions.[77] Very remarkably, *Der Spiegel* then was picturing Prime Minister Recep Tayyip Erdogan as having stood against the growing nationalism and anti-Europeanism in Turkey. The newspaper reported and commended his words: 'I want to live in a Turkey where the freedom of expression applies comprehensively ... The Kurdish problem should be resolved with more democracy, more civil rights and greater prosperity.'[78] These were indeed exceptional times when part of the European media put hopes on the Turkish Prime Minister, then perceived as a liberal figure, for Turkey's expected democratisation. With regard to the declining pro-Europeanism in Turkey, how the existing Turkish migrants were integrated into German socioeconomic life had equally attracted the media's attention. The newspapers remained in close contact with the journalists and representatives of the Turkish community in Germany and covered their views on cultural differences between Germans and Turks. Among them, for example, The *FAZ* and *Der Spiegel* revealed

---

[75] 'Ihre Rede ist Jein und Nö', *Die Zeit*, October 6, 2005; Joachim Riedl, 'Haiders hässliches Erbe', *Die Zeit*, October 6, 2005.
[76] 'Ihre Rede'.
[77] Zand, 'Scheidung'; 'Der Zypern-Stachel', *Die Zeit*, September 29, 2005.
[78] Zand, 'Scheidung'.

that the lives of Germans and Turks in Germany were still two different worlds.[79] *Die Zeit* reflected rather more positively that Turkish generations managed to integrate themselves into the German multicultural society.[80] The newspaper at times pointed to Germany as a model for Turkey, which liberalised its attitude towards its history and addressed its past crimes much earlier.[81]

We may summarise this coverage by saying that the newspapers in September and early October framed their news and commentaries on Turkey's political transition in line with the long-term factor of the German transition from illiberal to liberal policies. They partially compared Turkey's expected integration into European democracy to the current Turkish residents' integration into Germany. They took note of the candidate's political modernisation and critically pointed to democracy and human rights issues in the country. To *Die Welt* and *Die FAZ*, however, its political transition would not change the fact that Turkey was culturally outside Europe. The conservative newspapers at times openly adhered to the traditional view of the Christian Democrats, that the EU membership of Turkey would diminish Europe's cultural unity.

The German media's emphasis on the long-term factor of welfare demands particular attention. As a commentary in *Der Spiegel* put it, economic prosperity and the welfare state tradition formed the common ground of the culturally and politically diverse German society.[82] The editor of *Die Welt* had written one year before the negotiations' beginning: public opinion in Germany was against Turkey because ordinary Germans were already wary of the existing Turkish residents' costs with which they were burdened.[83] These economic perceptions against the candidate did not change in the short term. Days before the negotiations' beginning, *Die Zeit*'s editor made a similar point, and added that Germany's economic performance declining during the Social Democratic and Green coalition hugely affected the German opinions about Turks:

---

79 For Example, see Seidl's remarks on Hatice Akyun's and Imran Ayata's books. Clauidius Seidl, 'Eine Türkin wie wir', *Frankfurter Allgemeine Sonntagszeitung*, September 18, 2005; 'Eine große Umwälzung in der Türkei', *Der Spiegel*, no.26 (2005), June 27, 2005.

80 Dorte Huneke and Roger Boyes, 'Islamismus: Keine Bombenwerfer', *Die Zeit*, September 22, 2005. Also see an earlier op-ed, Tina Hildebrandt and Jörg Lau, 'Patriotisch, christlich, gut?', *Die Zeit*, November 25, 2004; 'Auf dem Rücken der Türken', *Die Zeit*, September 1, 2005; Hildebrandt and Lau, 'Patriotisch'. 'Die Liebe geht durch die Verfassung', *Die Zeit*, November 11, 2004.

81 See and compare Jörg Lau, 'Deutsche Schmerztherapie', *Die Zeit*, April 21, 2005 and Interview: Türkei braucht eine glaubwürdige EU-Perspektive, *Die Zeit.de*, 03.05.2005, http://www.zeit.de/politik/dlf/2005/interview_050503 (07.09.2015).

82 Jürgen Leinemann, 'Eine Nation auf der Suche', *Der Spiegel*, no.4 (2005), April 26, 2005.

83 Roger Kuppel, 'When did you last see your fatherland?', *The Spectator*, October 30, 2004, 22.

The possible cost of Turkey's EU membership has been estimated in the German media at €40bn – plus. And here Germans are concerned about more than money. The welfare state has been a continuum in German history since Bismarck ... If there is a German identity, then its hard core is the long tradition of the untouchable welfare state. [84]

In the editor's view, German people largely considered Turkey's EU membership as a menace to their welfare state tradition, the structural factor emphasised above. Germany was already in a formidable process of economic development. It had long been suffering the economic side effects of its reunification. On top of that, the country was to shoulder migrations from the EU's Eastern Enlargement that began in 2004. Now, he added, the German public worried about a new wave of migrants occasioned by Turkey's EU membership.[85] Some economic actors in Germany were arguing in a similar manner, as they told *Die Welt* that Turkey's accession would bring an obvious burden to the EU's financial resources and, at the same time, a possible labour inflow to Germany.[86] 'Large parts of the German economy', as *Die Welt* reported, such as the Confederation of German Employers' Associations (BDA), warned against the risks of Turkey's full membership. [87] The newspaper also referred to the opinions of research centres, like those of the IFO Institute for Economic Research and the Vienna Institute for International Economic Studies. According to the common argument, the membership of Turkey, with its low-paid workers, was likely to increase unemployment in Europe and Germany. The country was too big to be subsidised and integrated into the internal market without any substantial reform in the EU.[88] Given these potential economic consequences, *Die Welt* once added that the CDU/CSU's proposal of a privileged partnership with Turkey emerges as a 'better alternative' than the candidate's membership.[89]

Given the news media's coverage before the beginning of the negotiations, most of the examples overemphasised a fear in Germany caused by Turkey's future EU membership. Which political camps attended to this fear and instrumentalised it within their negative portrayal of Turkey then comes into question. We will therefore consider general positions of political camps with regard to Turkey in 2005 and later highlight a particular debate about Turkey shortly before the negotiations. Between September and early October, German political actors con-

---

84 Joachim Fitz Vannahme, 'Germany's Turkish Angst', *Europe's World*, October 1, 2005.
85 Ibid.
86 Hannelore Crolly, '22 Milliarden Euro für türkische Bauern', *Die Welt*, October 5, 2005.
87 Stefanie Bolzen and Ansgar Graw, 'Kampf um türkischstämmige Wähler', *Die Welt*, September 16, 2005.
88 Hannelore Crolly, 'Knackpunkt Finanzen', *Die Welt*, October 4, 2005.
89 Bolzen and Graw, 'Kampf'.

structed their arguments according to the federal election and the beginning of Turkey's negotiations with the EU.

Despite the lack of public backing, some political parties espoused Turkey's EU membership primarily on the grounds of democracy and security in Europe, and maintained that the country's entry would contribute to the EU's geopolitics and strengthen the idea of Europe as a source of multiculturalism. The supporters of this view were the SPD and the Alliance '90/the Greens (henceforth only the Greens), which shared the power as coalition partners, between 1998 and 2005, despite their electoral losses in general elections in 2002. These parties were known for their open support for both the EU Constitution and Turkey's EU membership. Indeed, after coming to power in 1998, they brought a positive change to Germany and the European Union's Turkey policies.[90] The 'Red-Green Coalition' increasingly weakened as their period saw continuing economic decline including rising unemployment levels. The SPD eventually lost its legislative majority to the Christian Democrats in the local elections for North-Rhine Westphalia in May 2005. Perhaps the biggest problem the Social Democrats faced was the breakaway of a significant group from the party. In the general election held the same year, this new political formation represented in Western regions achieved more than 8% of German votes – a particular group disaffected from the SPD's electoral base. Having allied with the Electoral Alternative for Labour and Social Justice, the successor of the leftist party ruling the German Democratic Republic until 1989, the new left-wing block impacted on the political landscape and the SDP's electoral basis.[91]

The Social Democrats and the Greens formed the first camp of the Turkey debate, favouring the candidate's EU membership shortly before the accession talks. In their long-term party policies, Europe was a multicultural cosmos.[92] Turkey was eligible for this multicultural Europe, as it formed an intersection between Christianity and Islam and was already involved in European security organisations. The Social Democrats and the Greens revealed their positively religious and geographical representations of Turkey, which were mostly aligned with the country's famous 'bridge' function between many cultural and geographical components. Joschka Fischer, the then Foreign Minister of Germany and the leader of the Green Party, thus stated in 2004: 'If the modernization proc-

---

[90] Rainer Hülsse, 'When Culture Determines Politics: Wie der Deutsche Bundestag die Türkei von der EU fernhält', *WeltTrends* 12, no.45 (Winter 2004): 135.
[91] 'Die Bilanz der Schröder', *Die Welt*, September 15, 2005.
[92] Didem Ozan, *Parteiliche Kommunikation am politischen Wendepunkt: Der EU-Beitritt der Türkei in deutschen und türkischen Parlamentsdebatten* (Wiesbaden: VS Verlag für Sozialwissenschaften, 2010), 105.

ess in Turkey is successful, Turkey's much-cited function as a bridge towards the Central Asian states and to the Middle East could become a reality'.[93] He raised the same point one year later, before the beginning of the negotiations: 'The comprehensive modernization and firm anchoring of Turkey in the West is a very central issue for our safety at the intersection of Europe with the Arab world and Iran'.[94]

Through their open support, the Social Democrats and the Greens linked Turkey's modernisation to the candidate's negotiations and its EU membership. The Chancellor of Germany and SPD leader Gerhard Schröder mostly prioritised the relevance of the country's reforms to the beginning of its negotiations.[95] Following the opening of the negotiations with the country, he wrote in *Die Zeit* that 'only a reformed Turkey, which fully meets the conditions of membership, can join the EU one day'.[96] Joschka Fischer also stated that the negotiations' outcome was the country's modernisation, which would benefit both the EU and Turkey. The Europeans therefore were only opening up the negotiations with Turkey; at the end of a long term, the next generation would be decisive of the candidate's membership.[97] Similar to Jacques Chirac's statements in France in the same period, the Social Democratic and Green leaders attempted to limit the EU's negotiations with Turkey to the candidate's modernisation, an open-ended process at the end of which only EU members were to decide the accession.

The German media argued that a part of this pro-Turkey policy of the Social Democrats was linked to their strategy to gain votes of the German electors of Turkish origin. The party was reported to have lost a considerable amount of 'Turkish' votes to the new Left Party, which separated from the SPD only months before the federal election in 2005. Second, the annulment of dual citizenship in Germany received many reactions from the Turkish society.[98] Therefore, according to *Der Spiegel*, Gerhard Schröder attempted to improve the party's declining popularity within the Turkish community through his campaign in favour of Turkey's EU membership. The Chancellor stated in his meeting with Turkish media

---

93 Fischer, 'Turkey's European Perspective.
94 Eckart Lojse, Markus Wehner, 'Fischer im Interview. Mehr Dylan weniger Marx', *Frankfurter Allgemeine Sonntagszeitung*, September 4, 2005.
95 'Gerhard Schröder stärkt Tayyip Erdogan den Rücken', *Die Zeit*, May 11, 2005.
96 Gerhard Schröder, 'Auf die Kleinen ist Verlass', *Die Zeit*, October 20, 2005.
97 'Schröder: Stoiber überschätzt sich in Türkei-Debatte', *Frankfurter Allgemeine Zeitung(Online)*, December 13, 2004, http://www.faz.net/aktuell/politik/eu-beitritt-schroeder-stoiber-ueberschaetzt-sich-in-tuerkei-debatte-1195701.html#/elections (13.02.2015)
98 Ferda Ataman, 'Türkische Wähler: Wo die CDU unter fünf Prozent liegt', *Spiegel Online*, September 13, 2005, http://www.spiegel.de/politik/deutschland/tuerkische-waehler-wo-die-cdu-unter-fuenf-prozent-liegt-a-374502.html (15.02.2015).

representatives: 'Turkey has fulfilled the conditions for receiving EU membership, and I say this not only on behalf of the German, but of all governments in Europe.'[99] He was confident in Turkey's success at the end of the accession negotiations.

In a nutshell, in 2005 the Social Democrats and the Greens assumed a favourable attitude towards Turkey in line with their long-term European policies. They traditionally advocated the EU's promotion of democracy in Europe and outside to establish a zone of peace and security. In their viewpoint, Europe was a multicultural cosmos, in which the Turkish candidate could permanently take part. The candidate was on a democratic track that they believed would continue during the membership negotiations. As a result, to the Social Democrats and the Greens, Turkey deserved a clear membership perspective in 2005.

In complete contrast to the Social Democrats and Greens, the Christian Democrats persistently rejected Turkey's EU membership. The union between the CDU and CSU, the partnership between the Christian Social Union in Catholic Bavaria and the Christian Democratic Union in other German states, entered the 2000s as the main opposition. The significance of the CDU/CSU was the ability to represent a large economic middle class between different religious faiths since 1945. It still would not be categorically wrong to argue the Christian Social Union from the Catholic Bavaria region to be more Eurosceptic, regionalist, and religious than the CDU.[100] In this regard, during the debates on Turkey the CSU's elites showed nuances in their statements in comparison with their sister party, as the below section highlights. That aside, the Christian Democrats, reminiscent of their conservative counterparts in France, upheld the EU's privileged partnership with Turkey, during the 2000s, which involved cooperation with a non-European country in some areas, instead of its membership.

The Christian Democrats and the Free Democratic Party (the smaller coalition partner of the CDU/CSU for most of the modern German history) therefore made up the camp against Turkey's EU membership. The CDU/CSU primarily objected to the negotiations with the candidate until 3 October. The Christian Democrats argued in their election programme (for the federal elections on 18 September) that the EU had already given Turkey a sort of privileged partnership through economic and security organisations.[101] According to their common argument, Germany and the EU could gain benefits from, and at the same time pre-

---

99 Ibid.
100 Schmidt, 'Germany', 66, Ozan, *Parteiliche Kommunikation*, 106.
101 CDU/CSU, 'Deutschlands Chancen nutzen. Wachstum. Arbeit. Sicherheit', Regierungsprogramm 2005–2009, Berlin, July 11, 2005, 36.

vent economic risks of, the future relationship with Turkey only through a privileged partnership with the candidate instead of its full EU membership.[102] With this argument the party made considerable efforts to block the negotiations' opening. The Free Democratic Party of Germany rather indirectly mentioned privileged partnership in its election document: it favoured the beginning of the open-ended negotiations with Turkey but also sustained a suggestion for different alternatives other than the membership.[103]

In accord with their long-term party policy on Europe, the Christian Democrats commonly raised their stance against Turkey's EU membership on religious and geographical grounds.[104] Despite that, it could also be argued that there were slight differences between the vocabularies the CDU and CSU employed while discussing Turkey. In comparison with the CDU, the Christian Social Union from Catholic Bavaria is generally characterised as more Eurosceptic, regionalist, and religious. In that vein, the party's leader Edmund Stoiber many times openly disqualified Turkey because of the country's 'difference' from Europe. To him, the EU should not embrace Asia by welcoming Turkey.[105] He contended that the EU's subjects gathered around a known history, common Christian and Judaic roots, widespread secular processes, and the same cosmopolitan values of human dignity, justice, and equality. He similarly conceived Germany as a Christian club; their responsibility was to safeguard their 'community of Christian fate'.[106] Turkey's membership in return would dilute the economic, political, and cultural integration of Europe and Germany, which built on these historical values. The real option could then only be a privileged partnership between the EU and the candidate.[107] Statements of the CDU's leader Angela Merkel were less straightforward, more practical. To Merkel, Turkey's admission would overwhelm the EU in economic and cultural terms. The EU was to make a historic decision to either remain a political union with shared values or deteriorate through admitting Turkey and thereby turning to a simple free-trade area.

---

102 Ozan, *Parteiliche Kommunikation*, 107.
103 'FDP beharrt auf Steuerentlastung', *Die Welt*, September 12, 2005; 'Mister Mittelmaß', Der Spiegel, no.37 (2005), September 12, 2005. Also see, Wahlprogrammzur Bundestagswahl 2005 der Freien Demokratischen Partei, 'Arbeit hat Vorfahrt. Deutschlandprogramm 2005', Berlin, 2005.
104 Hülsse, 'When Culture Determines Politics', 135–146.
105 'Union bleibt bei Nein zu türkischem EU-Beitritt', *Frankfurter Allgemeine (Online)*, February 14, 2004, http://www.faz.net/aktuell/politik/europawahl-union-bleibt-bei-nein-zu-tuerkischem-eu-beitritt-1146987.html#/elections (25.03.2015).
106 Hildebrandt and Lau, 'Patriotisch'.
107 'EU-Beitritt Merkel für einen "dritten Weg" mit der Türkei', *Frankfurter Allgemeine Zeitung*, February 16, 2004.

For Merkel the Christian Democrats did not reject Turkey's contributions to Europe, as they shared the view that the country should become an example of compatibility between Islam and democracy. They were backing the EU's rationale to transform the country and to connect it to the West, but not through membership.[108]

Earlier leaders of the CDU similarly expressed their arguments against Turkey with geographical and economic characters other than the religious ones. Wolfgang Schäuble rejected the allegation that the Christian Democrats saw Europe as a Christian Club. In his opinion, Europeans were rejecting the integration of Turkey into the EU's free movement regime mainly because the country was adjacent to Iran and Syria.[109] Turkey's membership would mainly bring economic and security risks to the EU. Helmut Kohl similarly claimed that those who backed Turkey's accession already knew that they could never find public consent in Europe. Kohl did not expect Turkey to meet the Copenhagen Criteria for the accession. Through the lengthy negotiation process, European public opinion would be further distanced from the candidate. He also argued that the EU had reached its maximum enlargement with Romania and Bulgaria. Despite saying that, the former chancellor additionally suggested that the EU take Ukraine into consideration for future enlargements, as the country was bearing geostrategic importance for the European Union.[110]

In summary, the Christian Democrats on the whole rejected Turkey's accession to the European Union on geographical, political (mostly economic), and, sometimes, religious grounds. They emphasised the long-term welfare tradition in Germany, and argued that Turkey's EU membership would destabilise Germans' economic well-being. Second, the Christian Democrats, in particular the members of the Christian Social Union, pointed out the religious commonalities of Europe while discussing their difference than Turkey and its culture. Their arguments were in line with their tradition of seeing Europe as a source of cultural unity in which Turkey has no room.

Stoiber had declared in late 2004 that the Christian Democrats were ready to try all necessary means to rule out Turkey's EU membership.[111] However, although the Christian Democrats overtly rejected Turkey's EU membership publicly, during the Brussels European Council of December 2004, they could not hold

---

[108] 'Union bleibt bei Nein zu türkischem EU-Beitritt'.
[109] Wolfgang Schauble and David L. Phillips, 'Talking Turkey', *Foreign Affairs* 83, no.6 (November/December 2004).
[110] 'Unfair, unehrlich.
[111] 'Schröder: Stoiber überschätzt'.

other European actors back from setting a target date for the negotiations' opening, 3 October 2005. The party then followed various strategies until the beginning of the negotiations. First, they centred their federal election campaign, among other things, on Turkey's EU bid.[112] The *FAZ* reported that the expectation on the side of the CDU/CSU was to win the next general election and, together with the conservative government in France, to keep Turkey out of the EU.[113] Second, until the opening of the negotiations the Christian Democrats were to lobby in Germany and Europe against Turkey, declaring that most of the Europeans were sceptical of the candidate.[114] Their strategy to win over the pro-Turkey politicians through the negative public opinion against the candidate was therefore reminiscent of those of the French conservative parties. The aim of the CDU/CSU was to turn the current situation into a privileged partnership scenario, as stated by Hans Poettering, the EPP's leader in the European Parliament. According to him, many European politicians in fact implied a privileged partnership with Turkey behind their statements about anchoring the country in the European structures.[115]

The debate between the Social Democrats, Greens, and the Christian Democrats grew in time into a polemic and was addressed by the politicians in September 2005, weeks before the presumed beginning date of the accession talks with Turkey. As the beginning, a live discussion between the leaders of the SPD and CDU/CSU took place on 4 September upon a number of matters including Turkey's accession to the EU. Gerhard Schröder during the debate generally pointed out the country's geostrategic significance for the continent. In his opinion, the EU should understand Turkey's geopolitical contribution that could be achieved only through the full membership of the candidate. Angela Merkel in return argued that the West had already confirmed Turkey's strategic importance by granting it NATO membership. The Christian Democrats were instead offering the prospect of privileged partnership in order to continue to benefit from the candidate's geostrategic position. Merkel also stated why they included Turkey in their election campaign; to the Christian Democrats, German citizens needed to know the EU's new frontiers in the possible case of Turkey's accession.[116] The

---

112 Ibid.
113 Ibid.
114 'Eine Art Kriegserklärung', *Frankfurter Allgemeine Zeitung (Online)*, October 11, 2004, http://www.faz.net/aktuell/politik/ausland/union-unterschriftenaktion-eine-art-kriegserklaerung-1193138.html (22.02.2015).
115 'Annäherung in der EU über türkischen Beitritt', *Frankfurter Allgemeine Zeitung*, December 10, 2004.
116 'Wo die Kontrahenten punkten konnten', *Die Welt*, September 6, 2005.

two speeches heralded contrasting images of Europe and Turkey: in the first example the candidate's geography was European; in the latter, Turkey was merely the EU's neighbour.

In the mid-September, a surprising opposition to the Social Democrats' Turkey policy emerged from their former leader. In his interview with *Die Zeit*, former German chancellor Helmut Schmidt repudiated Turkey's membership on political and religious grounds. Contrary to the Social Democrats' and Greens' expectations about a more democratic Turkey, to Schmidt the country was being re-Islamised, and it would likely to export about 10 millions of its subjects to Germany in the case of accession. He contended that Turkey's membership was nonsense, as it had a culture entirely foreign to the Europeans, and stated: '(with the candidate) economic cooperation, yes, customs union, yes, free trade zone, yes. But (I say) no to the freedom of movement leading to the population excesses stemming from Turkey'.[117] He therefore concurred with the mainstream Christian Democratic viewpoint on Turkey's cultural difference than the Europeans and a potential overflow of Turks into Europe in the future.

In September 2005, the conservative opposition leaders and the press were together denouncing the SPD's election campaign especially favouring the Turkish community living in Germany. They called it the predominance of Turks over German public interests. The former CDU leader Wolfgang Schäuble had argued earlier that the Social Democrats seemed to be committed to Turkey's accession to the EU in an attempt to ignite the interests of German-Turkish voters.[118] The Christian Democrats sustained this reproach until the federal election. In particular, they construed Gerhard Schröder's insistence on Turkey's EU membership to be a strategy to win Turkish votes.[119] *Die Welt* was covering CDU member Roland Koch's criticisms of Schröder's rhetoric: although the chancellor had previously cautioned political actors against a cultural conflict, he now intended to manipulate cultural groups.[120] Therefore, the Christian Democrats in this period were additionally emphasising their long-term cultural concerns about Germany's integration, which were manifest during the earlier citizenship discussions mentioned above. Conservative newspapers also declared the SPD's pro-Turkey position to be somewhat of an election promise given to the voters of Turkish ori-

---

[117] Giovanni di Lorenzo and Jan Ross, 'Interview: Kommen Sie uns nicht mit 1945!', *Die Welt*, September 15, 2005.
[118] Hartmut Palmer and Christoph Schult, 'Ein verlorenes Jahr', *Der Spiegel*, no.50 (2004), December, 6, 2004.
[119] Ibid.
[120] Bolzen, Graw, 'Kampf'.

gin. The *Bild* showed a remarkable example. According to polls, only 4.8% of the Turkish voters sided with the Christian Democrats, and the rest were inclined to vote for the Social Democrats and the Greens.[121] According to a commentary published in the tabloid, Schröder and Fischer were aiming at 'selling German interests to the 600-thousand Turkish votes'. It deplored the situation: 'How miserable he could be' when Schröder 'begged' for any favour from the 'purchased German-Turks' against his own countrymen.[122] Another commentary published on the *Bild* also denounced the Greens' election documents distributed in the Turkish language in some areas. It proclaimed the Social Democratic and Green voters as 'exploited', and concluded: 'the Turkish-born are no Germans, they are and will remain Turks.'[123] From *Die Welt*'s point of view, in a similar vein, the German chancellor's affinity with the politicians from Turkey, just because they have contacts with Turks in Germany, was misleading and against the nature of integration in Germany. Through this strategy, *Die Welt* added, the SPD spoke to around 77% of Turkish voters in Germany.[124] The newspaper commented that the chancellor's close connection with ethnic Turkish electors was likely to harm the aspiration of an integrated Germany. The *FAZ*, on the other hand, pointed to the new citizenship code that weakened the Turkish community's voting force in Germany. In line with the current German integration policy, thousands of Turks were not able to vote because they had lost their German nationality with the new law ending their multiple citizenships.[125]

The general election in Germany was eventually held on 18 September and resulted in the success of the CDU/CSU as anticipated. However, contrary to the public surveys their victory was not a landslide; the Christian Democrats reached 35%, only 1 per cent ahead of the SPD's vote rate. This result relieved Turkish observers in the short term. Journalist Mehmet Ali Brand wrote in *Die Zeit*: 'had the CDU/CSU clearly won the elections with Chancellor Merkel, that would have been a disaster for the Turks'.[126] Indeed, following the elections the Christian Democrats had to form a grand coalition with the Social Democrats. In other words, although the Social Democrats were slightly defeated,

---

121 'Schröder kämpft um 600.000 Stimmen: Entscheiden Türken die Wahl?', *Bild Zeitung*, September 14, 2005.
122 Ibid. Also see, Bolzen and Graw, 'Kampf'.
123 'Entscheiden Türken'.
124 Bolzen and Graw, 'Kampf'.
125 '20 500 Deutschtürken dürfen nicht wählen', *Frankfurter Allgemeine Zeitung*, September 17, 2005.
126 Mehmet Ali Birand, 'Merkels Niederlage lässt die Türken aufatmen', *Die Zeit*, September 22, 2005.

they still held on to political power through the new coalition. The German diplomacy on Turkey's EU membership also continued, at least partially, since Gerhard Schröder assumed the foreign ministry in the new cabinet. Although the policy on Turkey's EU perspective was a stumbling block between two mainstream parties, the new government under the leadership of Angela Merkel did not show a dramatic change in Germany's diplomacy to the candidate. As might be expected, this outcome contrasted with the French foreign policy, which was dramatically altered by the victory of a Turkey-sceptic Nicolas Sarkozy at the end of the 2007 general elections in France.

The Christian Democrats were still against Turkey's EU membership in principle, however. The leaders of the CDU/CSU continued their lobbying strategy in Europe against the beginning of the negotiations. In late September they found a critical opportunity when the conservative government of Austria asked to renegotiate the terms of the accession talks with Turkey. As the term president of the Council of the EU, Britain gathered an informal EU meeting on 2 and 3 October in Brussels to discuss with Austria and the other Turkey-sceptic members the beginning of the membership negotiations with the candidate. Before the event, the CDU and CSU leaders sent the conservative governments of Europe, and additionally the British Labour government, a letter encouraging the privileged partnership with Turkey. Merkel and Stoiber there stated straightforwardly: 'we are convinced that Turkey's entry into the EU will overburden and endanger European integration politically, economically, and socially'.[127] European actors then had to reflect on the consequences of the negotiating framework and consider other alternatives. In other respects, Merkel and Stoiber acknowledged in their letter that establishing stronger connections with Turkey was of the EU's interest.

Until the EU's informal summit, the leaders of the CDU/CSU were concerned about a *fait accompli* of Turkey's accession, which they reject resolutely.[128] The previous enlargements had shown that any candidate commencing the accession talks had been eventually welcomed to the EU. At the end of the EU's informal summit resulting in the new negotiating framework for Turkey, the conservative politicians and the media were yet largely satisfied with the new conditions stipulated to the candidate. According to the FAZ, the lengthy negotiations with the candidate without an accession date gave Germans and Europeans

---

127 'Merkel und Stoiber bestärken'.
128 'Merkel und Stoiber: Kanzler'.

an opportunity to discuss the geographical end of Europe.[129] The reference to the EU's 'absorption capacity' within the negotiating document was equally approved.[130] To the *FAZ* and *Die Welt*, it became possible to finalise the long-lasting debates among EU actors only when the pro-Turkey factions agreed to Austria's conditions. Owing to the efforts of the Austrian delegation, the EU's absorption capacity was introduced to a negotiating document for the first time. The Austrian foreign minister also stated that they inserted the EU's absorption capacity to the negotiations framework and therefore managed to set out an additional condition intrinsic to Turkey's membership.[131]

German political leaders expressed contradictory opinions at the end of the informal summit. On the one hand, the Social Democrats and the Greens welcomed the beginning of the negotiations with Turkey and repeated their positive geographical and religious arguments about the candidate. Schröder noted that the EU was about to keep the promise it gave the country more than 40 years ago. In return, he expected Turkey to stay committed to a substantial reform process. The membership negotiations would be a long and formidable process, he added, at the end of which the EU would benefit from Turkey's economic and social contributions. He thus held: 'Turkey, which shows that Islam and the values of the European Enlightenment can be consistent, will bring a huge increase in stability and security in Europe and beyond'.[132] Joschka Fischer similarly affirmed the negotiations' opening as a historic step and claimed that Europe won the day. According to him, the negotiations signified an invaluable opportunity for both sides, and a means for Europe to safeguard its security interests in the 21st century.[133]

The beginning of the negotiations caused some controversy on the Christian Democratic side. Leaders of the Christian Social Union were mostly not content with the decision. Michael Glos, the CSU's leader at the German Parliament, declared the opening of the negotiations with Turkey to be 'a black day', and accused the German Foreign Minister Joschka Fischer of being in a 'state of mad-

---

129 'Zu spät?' *Frankfurter Allgemeine Zeitung*, September 28, 2005; Bacia Horst, 'Wieder einmal heißt es: Weiterstrampeln', *Frankfurter Allgemeine Zeitung*, October 4, 2005.
130 Joachim Riedl, 'Haiders hässliches Erbe', Die Zeit, October 6, 2005.
131 Reinhard Olt, 'Stolz in Wien', *Frankfurter Allgemeine Zeitung*, October 5, 2005; Petra Stuiber, 'Wolfgang Schüssel: Allein gegen alle', *Die Welt*, October 4, 2005.
132 'Ein schwarzer Tag für Europa', *Frankfurter Allgemeine (Online)*, October 4, 2005, http://www.faz.net/aktuell/politik/inland/tuerkei-verhandlungen-ein-schwarzer-tag-fuer-europa-1255987.html (18.02.2015).
133 Ibid.

ness'.[134] He held the foreign minister the chief responsible for this decision, as he acted against the European and German will on Turkey's EU membership. Despite his negative comments on Turkey, Glos did welcome the beginning of the negotiations with Croatia. The CSU's party leader Edmund Stoiber rather cautiously commented on the negotiations' beginning. He claimed that Austria took important steps by bringing preconditions to Turkey's EU membership and thus making the negotiations more precise. The EU's absorption capacity should also remain a condition concerning the future enlargements. Should the accession talks fail, Stoiber added, Turkey had to remain 'a close friend and partner' of the EU. The CDU's former president Wolfgang Schäuble similarly held that the beginning of the negotiations did not automatically mean Turkey's accession. He argued that future referendums in member countries were likely to turn Turkey's membership bid into a privileged partnership with the EU.[135] Therefore, as he added, the new government led by the Christian Democrats was going to remain loyal to the accession talks with the candidate, for the moment.

In summary of the period from September to early October, political camps in Germany discussed Turkey in consideration of two events, the federal elections on 18 September and the EU's unofficial summit, which was held on 2 and 3 October to discuss the beginning of the negotiations with the candidate. Until the national elections, German political elites involved in their election campaigns the arguments about Turkey's accession to the EU. Among the mainstream political camps, the Social Democrats and the Greens on the whole adhered to a conception of Europe inclusive of a democratic and modernised Turkey. They also remained in contact with the Turkish community residing in Germany, which in the end came in for conservatives' criticisms. In contrast to the Social Democratic and Green opinions, the CDU/CSU opposed the candidate, arguing that it was inherently not European. On that account, before the federal elections the Christian Democrats brought into discussion the indefinite frontiers of Eastern Europe, mirroring the conservative camp in France that gathered a party convention to discuss the same issue. Shortly before the presumed beginning date of the membership negotiations, they chose to lobby in Europe against Turkey and based their arguments on the negative public opinion about the candidate in Germany and Europe.

---

134 Ibid.
135 Ibid.

Conclusion

A number of structural factors exerted stark influences over the German national thinking about Turkey in relation to the European Union. Among them, welfare almost always remained a part of the political debate over Turkey's accession to the EU in 2005. Political elites and the news media mostly aligned their perceptions of Turkey, positive or negative, with Germany's long-term welfare tradition. In parallel, they referred to the candidate's EU membership and Turkish migrations together, and discussed whether Turkey's EU membership and future migrants from the country would put a major strain on the German and European economic well-being. In particular, the conservative newspapers discussed in detail the economic repercussions of Turkey's membership. European policies of German political camps were also decisive over the perceptions about the candidate. Overall, the political parties that championed the multicultural aspect of Europe welcomed Turkey's membership negotiations with the EU; at least they did not estrange the candidate in exclusionary terms.

The federal election on 18 September was the decisive event for German politics in 2005, and it also impacted on the debate over the beginning of the membership negotiations with Turkey. Political parties therefore instrumentalised the current Turkey debate within their election campaigns. Among them, the Social Democrats approached Turkey with their long-term European policy, which included an emphasis on the promotion of democracy and peace in Europe and beyond. The Social Democrats thus gave open support for the beginning of the negotiations with the candidate, which they believed to result in its political modernisation in liberal characters. Second, the multicultural idea of Europe was at the forefront of the Social Democrats and the Greens that affirm Turkey's path to the accession. In their opinion, a more democratic Turkey, with its 'bridge' function between many geographical and cultural regions, could better contribute to the European zone of peace and democracy. In addition to all these conditions, it was an assertion by the conservative politics and press that the Social Democrats and the Greens showed their public backing to Turkey in an attempt to appeal to their electorates of Turkish origin. In brief, they positively conceptualised the candidate in political and geographical terms of Europe.

The Christian Democrats in general disaffirmed Turkey's EU membership in political, geopolitical, and religious terms. In the political context, the long-term factor of welfare remained effective over the Christian Democratic views about Turkey. Members of the CDU/CSU argued that Turkey's EU membership would occasion a massive migrant inflow from the country and hence was likely to weaken the German welfare system. In the religious and geographical contexts, the Christian Democrats' and most notably the Christian Social Union's traditional stress on religion and their exclusionary EU vision played prominent roles in their negative conceptualisations of Turkey. They essentially excluded the candidate from Europe on the assumption that it was geographically and religiously not European. As a result, the German and French cases in 2005 bore similarities with regard to conservative parties' Turkey-scepticism. In the British context that the next chapter discusses, however, political parties including the conservative camp showed attitudes profoundly different from the European opinions on Turkey's compatibility with European values in the same period.

7 The Struggle against European Political Integration: British Debates over Turkey's EU Bid in 2005

Right after the beginning of the membership negotiations with Turkey, an opinion column published in *The Guardian* pointed out the mainstream views on the candidate in Britain and France: 'Roughly speaking, the British hated the (EU) constitution because they thought it would create a French Europe, while the French hate enlargement because they think it will create a British Europe.'[1] With the EU Constitution's rejection, surprisingly due to the French (and Dutch) votes, the EU's enlargement case with Turkey stood out, and many of the European conservative camps believed it would dilute the already-fragile integration project and play into Eurosceptic Britain's hands. As opposed to Europe's Turkey-sceptic conservative governments, on 3 October Britain played a decisive role in the start of the accession negotiations between the EU and Turkey. The present chapter discusses British conceptualisations of Turkey in relation to the European Union, and it mirrors the methodology of the previous two chapters. It analyses statements about Turkey's EU membership raised by British political elites and reported by the media in 2005, and in particular during the same period from September until the beginning of the membership negotiations between the European Union and Turkey.

Three historical factors exerted strong influences over the contemporary British opinions on the European Union and Turkey. First, the religious policy of Britain gave rise to the overall scepticism about European integration and has historical relevance to the contemporary national thinking. Second, British citizenship, which was first designed with colonialist aspirations, changed, in scope and essence, in the face of the migrations to the country. The amendments made to British citizenship law in the second half of the 20th century are noteworthy in that they demonstrate the Conservative Party's backlash against growing immigration. The third and final structural factor is the political parties' European policies. Political integration of Europe has traditionally been opposed in Britain, although slight differences between political camps' European policies exist.

The first long-term factor is the religious policy in Britain, which partially prompted the country's political distance from Europe historically, and also af-

---

1 Timothy Garton Ash, 'How the Dreaded Superstate Became a Commonwealth', *The Guardian*, October 6, 2005.

fected the debates surrounding Turkey's compatibility with European values in religious terms. In 2005, British politics was quite a secular case, especially in comparison with Germany, in which religion remained politicised, not least because contemporary British history notably featured budding non-conformism against Church authority. But detachment from church affairs should not mean that religion is entirely unpoliticized in Britain. When it comes to the state's involvement in religious matters, for instance, the country allowed certain autonomy to faith communities in its history and thus contrasted with France, where religion was, and still is, kept under strict state control.[2]

Religion played a historical part in Britain's relationship with Europe. Since the foundation of the Anglican Church of England, religious policies of England and then Great Britain were instrumental in preserving the country from Roman Catholic influence, and in particular French influence.[3] Despite the Catholic sympathies of a few monarchs, the state remained Anglican on religious and political grounds.[4] At least until the early 19th century, England and then Great Britain defined its regime with an individual religious identity throughout its political rivalry with Catholic Europe.[5] The Church of England over the centuries provided the religious motive of the state's breakaway from the Catholic realm, but it did not find agreement everywhere in the United Kingdom. Religious struggle with Scotland and Ireland resulted in the founding treaties of 1707 and 1921, which recognised a multi-sectarian religious environment in regions outside England dominated by local churches.[6] In time, the British regime also managed to channel autonomous churches to its colonialist cause. In the 19th century, for example, not only the Church of England but also local institutions like the Protestant Church of Scotland or the Catholic Church of Ireland were active missionaries

---

[2] Joe Casanova, 'Religion, European Secular Identities, and European Integration', in *Religion in an Expanding Europe*, eds. Timothy Byrnes and Peter J. Katzenstein (Cambridge: Cambridge University Press, 2006), 75.

[3] Richard Bonney and David J.B. Trim, 'Introduction', in *The Development of Pluralism in Modern Britain and France*, eds. Richard Bonney and David J.B. Trim (Bern: Peter Lang, 2007), 49–63; Smith Anthony D., '"Set in the Silver Sea": English National identity and European Integration', *Nations and Nationalism* 12, no.3 (2006): 447–448; Also see Jason White, *Militant Protestantism and British Identity*, 1603–1642 (London: Pickering and Chatto, 2012).

[4] It is meant here the Stuart royal family, their religious belief, and their influence on British foreign policy. Roger Lockyer, *Tutor and Stuart Britain 1485–1714* (Abingdon: Routledge, 2013), 408–409.

[5] Smith, '"Set in the Silver Sea"', 444.

[6] Krishan Kumar, *The Making of English National Identity* (Cambridge, Cambridge University Press, 2003), 150.

abroad.⁷ Faith communities of Britain together incorporated their religious zeal and a sense of belonging in their colonial propaganda.⁸

Nevertheless, Britain was turning out to be a more secular example during the 20th century. The era saw the demise of religion in British social life and politics, which Simon Green neatly explains with reference to three conditions. First, religious tension between Protestant Britain and its Catholic subjects began to decline with an independent Ireland in 1922. Following (Southern) Ireland's separation, led by a separatist movement spurred by Roman Catholicism, religious conflicts abated on the British island, and never again became a serious issue. The second reason was the nonconformist Protestant movement in Britain, especially in Wales, which lessened the hegemony of the Church of England. Finally, the nature of British politics became decidedly more secular with the rise of the Labour party and its non-religious political programme.⁹ Under these conditions, the Conservative Party, which already lacked official links with the Church of England, further secularised its party cadres in the 20th century.¹⁰ The breakaway from religious identity was thus a continuous process in Britain. In the end, this non-conformism had an effect on contemporary arguments that discarded religious exclusions of Turkey from Europe and Britain.

The second long-term characteristic underpinning British national thinking about Europe and Turkey is the changing nature of citizenship in relation to migrations to the country. The rationale of political citizenship in Britain corresponded to the regime's colonial policies until the 20th century. The *jus soli* principle, in which any person born on the British soil was granted citizenship, allowed the kingdom to run, arguably, overseas colonies without religious and ethnic discrimination. Therefore, the terms "British subject" and "Commonwealth citizen" could be used interchangeably for a long time. The Nationality Act adopted in 1948 maintained this tradition.¹¹ In the face of rising migration, Britain gradually abandoned this practice throughout the second half of the 20th century. This period saw migration from the Commonwealth regions as well as Communist Vietnam. Encouraged at the time to provide cheap labour, the

---

7 Hillary M. Carey, *God's Empire. Religion and Pluralism in the British World, c. 1801–1908* (New York: Cambridge University Press, 2011), 73–83.
8 Ibid., 81–82.
9 S.J.D., Green, *The Passing of Protestant England, Secularisation and Social Change c. 1920–1960* (New York: Cambridge University Press, 2011), 35–48.
10 Peter Catterall, 'The Party and Religion', Anthony Seldon and Stuart Ball, *Conservative Century: The Conservative Party since 1900* (New York: Oxford University Press, 2011).
11 Andrew Geddes, *The Politics of Migration and Immigration in Europe* (London: Sage, 2003), 32.

West Indians, Ugandan and Kenyan Asians, and the Vietnamese arrived. Then followed a steady trickle from Pakistan, Bangladesh, and a few other countries, which affected the political culture. In the 1970s, especially the British Conservatives were worried about the British welfare.[12] Conservative elites were also arguing that the migrations from former colonies around the world could change the cultural, even racial composition of Britain.[13] To cite a provocative example, Margaret Thatcher was quite preoccupied with British culture, as she stated in an interview in 1979: 'People are really rather afraid that this country might be rather swamped by people with a different culture.'[14] In later decades Thatcher maintained her hardline attitude towards migration.

The Conservatives had been the most prominent opponents of immigration, and in their fierce opposition, they had employed essentialist and even, sometimes, racist terms.[15] They found an opportunity to change citizenship law after assuming power in 1979 elections. The new Nationality Act in 1981 then replaced the traditional *jus soli* principle of British citizenship with a mixed system, which brought certain limitations to the British overseas territories. British citizenship since then has not been through a fundamental change, and migration to Britain continued from the members of the European Union, primarily from Eastern Europe, up to the UK's decision to leave the European Union in 2016. Until the Brexit referendum, the Conservatives maintained their discourse against the continuous migrant inflow. For one example, the British Secretary of Defence had stated, in 2014, that 'British towns are being swamped', in a similar fashion to Margaret Thatcher's earlier statement.[16] The Conservative politician added his economic and social concerns: 'In some areas of the UK, down the east coast, towns do feel under siege, large numbers of migrant workers and people claiming benefits.'[17] In brief, the Conservative Party has traditionally op-

---

[12] Christina Julios, *Contemporary British Identity: English Language, Migrants and Public Discourse* (Cornwall: Ashgate, 2008), 86–87.
[13] Geddes, *The Politics of Migration*, 33–46.
[14] Jon Swaine, 'Margaret Thatcher Complained about Asian Immigration to Britain', *The Telegraph*, December 30, 2009.
[15] Adrian Favell, *Philosophies of Integration: Immigration and the idea of citizenship in France and Britain* (Palgrave Macmillan, Basingstoke, 2001), 108–110; James Hampshire, *Citizenship and Belonging: Immigration and the Politics of Demographic Governance in Postwar Britain* (Hampshire: Palgrave Macmillan, 2005), 180–185; Randall Hansen, *Citizenship and Immigration in Post-war Britain* (New York: Oxford University Press, 2000), 207–209.
[16] Stuart Jeffries, '"Swamped" and "riddled": the Toxic Words that Wreck Public Discourse', *The Guardian*, October 27, 2014.
[17] Ibid.

posed migration, and they are almost always the principal actors making British citizenship more exclusive.

The third long-term factor is Britain's policy against European political integration. The UK in the previous centuries unvaryingly maintained the policy of preventing any power from altering the balance between European states.[18] The EU project in the beginning was no exception. The country did not change its policy of remaining distant from but attentive to European affairs in the early years of the European Union. Churchill expressed the traditional British attitude to European integration in 1953:

> We are not members of the European Defence Community, nor do we intend to be merged in a Federal European system. We feel we have a special relation to both. This can be expressed by prepositions, by the preposition 'with' but not 'of' – we are with them, but not of them.

Through his speech, Churchill hinted at Britain's long-term conditions in international relations. The country following the Second World War was reshaping its European policy between its own (commercial) interests in Europe, its leadership position in the Commonwealth, and finally its strategic partnership with the United States. Under these conditions, British political actors remained faithful to the approach that Churchill briefed above: being selective in the course of co-operation with European countries.[19]

Political camps later shaped their European approaches in accord with Britain's traditional foreign policy. They contributed much to the recognition of Euroscepticism since the 1980s. The term 'Euroscepticism' is linked to a wide array of approaches, from leaving the European Union to remaining a member of the EU with a certain distance from common fiscal and visa policies. In particular, British Euroscepticism stood for a set of political behaviours and discourses of political actors in Britain in the second half of the 20th century.[20] It first appeared in the 1950s when Britain rejected participation in the European project. In 1973,

---

[18] Pail W. Scroeder, 'The 19th-Century International System: Changes in the Structure', *World Politics* 39, no.1 (October 1986): 16–17, doi: 10.2307/2010296; J. Samuel Barkin, Bruce Cronin, 'The State and the Nation: Changing Norms and the Rules of Sovereignty in International Relations', *International Organisation* 48, no.1, (December 1994): 120, doi: 10.1017/S0020818300000837.
[19] Andrew Geddes, *Britain and the European Union* (Basingstoke: Palgrave Macmillan, 2013), 29–31.
[20] Menno Spiering, 'British Euroscepticism', in *Euroscepticism: Party Politics, National Identity and European Integration*, eds. Robert Harmsen and Menno Spiering (Amsterdam and New York: Rodopi B.V.,2004), 131–134.

the Conservatives advocating limited cooperation with the EC in economic fields finalised the UK's entry into the organisation. As a response, Labour politicians promised a referendum on Britain's EC membership (which resulted in Britain's remaining) and continued to campaign against specific supranational policy fields. With the 1980s, the Conservative Party was turning into the main opposition camp to the European integration. In particular, the Conservative government under Margaret Thatcher became growingly sceptical about the EU after the signing of the European Single Act in 1986.[21] The Labour Party in return adhered to European economic integration in the late 1980s, although it remained sceptical of forming a political union. In a nutshell, throughout the development of monetary policies in the European Community (EC), Euroscepticism became consolidated among British parties.[22]

In the 1990s and 2000s, the British Conservatives mostly spearheaded the Eurosceptic camp. The Conservative Party, along with nationalist parties in Wales, remained the prime Eurosceptics of Britain. Margaret Thatcher stated in 1997 at the Conservative Congress in the United States:

> The main challenges to our British identity, however, are directly related to our powers of self-government, now under attack from European federalism. The current preoccupation in European capitals with the proposed single currency and its appalling implications for participants and non-participants alike should not for a moment distract our attention from the fact that this is, and always has been, not an economic but a political project.[23]

Thatcher directed her speech at the ever-closer European Union. She declared that European political integration, which was always a political project, was posing a growing threat to the British national identity. The Conservatives remained primarily attached to the viewpoint she summarised.

On the other hand, the attitude towards European integration of the Labour Party in the early 2000s was somewhat different from both their former position and that of the Conservatives. Tony Blair's speeches revealed their contemporary

---

[21] Anthony Forster, *Euroscepticism in Contemporary British Politics: Opposition to Europe in the British Conservative and Labour Parties Since 1945* (London: Routledge, 2002), 63–67.

[22] David Baker, Andrew Gamble, Nick Randall, and David Seawright, 'Euroscepticism in the British Party System: "A Source of Fascination, Perplexity, and Sometimes Frustration"', in *Opposing Europe? The Comparative Party Politics of Euroscepticism, Volume 1: Case Studies and Country Surveys*, eds. Aleks Szczerbiak and Paul Taggart (Oxford: Oxford University Press, 2008), 96, 98.

[23] See Margaret Thatcher's speech, 'Speech to The First International Conservative Congress', September 28, 1997, www.margaretthatcher.org/document/108374. (10.10.2015).

standing, as he was arguing that the UK had to stay an EU member in order to maintain its economic growth and keep up with globalisation.[24] European integration, in his terms, was in Britain's interests. He stated in his opening speech at the European Parliament (2005): 'I believe in Europe as a political project. I believe in Europe with a strong and caring social dimension. I would never accept a Europe that was simply an economic market.'[25]

It might at first seem that the prime minister unconditionally backed European integration including its political side. Yet he was not content with the current pace of the European integration, which he thought to benefit the EU's founding members rather than Britain. He stated in the same speech that the reason for the EU Constitution's rejection in France and the Netherlands was the mismatch between the political and economic parts of European integration:

> it is not a crisis of political institutions, it is a crisis of political leadership. People in Europe are posing hard questions to us. They worry about globalisation, job security, about pensions and living standards ... People say: we need the budget to restore Europe's credibility. Of course we do. But it should be the right budget.[26]

According to Blair, the constitution was rejected because Europe was economically inadequate. To him, a new budget was necessary to make the first step ahead. Britain in those years was against the current budgetary order that was then to the advantage of the other great European powers. Indeed, in a European summit held a month later, the Prime Minister asked for an update on the EU's budget system and entered into an intense debate with the French president. In brief, the Labour Party led by Tony Blair did not champion European integration, and if anything they lobbied against its current pace that did not favour British interests as they expected.

In Britain during the 2000s, the Conservative Party strictly opposed any sort of European integration, whereas the Labour Party was concerned with turning it to Britain's advantage. The most pro-European political camp in the country, though, was the Liberal Democrats, who advocated European integration and claimed during the general elections in 2005 that 'the UK should be at the centre of the European Union.'[27] They laid stress on common political values of Europe as the foundations of the EU and European integration. Despite their pro-Euro-

---

[24] Pauline Schnapper, 'The Labour Party and Europe from Brown to Miliband: Back to the Future?', *Journal of Common Market Studies* 53, no.1 (2015): 160–161, doi: 10.1111/jcms.12209.
[25] 'Full text: Tony Blair's Speech to the European Parliament', *The Guardian*, June 23, 2005.
[26] Ibid.
[27] See, The Liberal Democrats The Real Alternative Election Manifesto, 2005.

pean views, the Liberal Democrats were still considered to be sceptical of European political integration, partially because they campaigned for increasing Britain's leverage within the EU.[28] In a similar vein, their stand favouring European integration was argued to be somewhat moderate since their voters were as Eurosceptic as the other British citizens.[29]

In summary, the historical role of religion, the evolution of British citizenship in the face of immigration, and British parties' scepticism about the EU's political integration exerted obvious influence on the British national thinking about Turkey and the European Union. In view of these long-term factors, the section below discusses British statements about Turkey reported by the media before the beginning of the negotiations between the EU and the candidate. In the period between early September and the 3rd of October, the beginning of the negotiations with Turkey came to the forefront as a priority of British foreign policy. Despite that, election campaigns held months before this period had demonstrated that political camps were also concerned about the continuing migration to Britain. Then, the question remains how political camps approached Turkey's accession to the EU, as an 'other', a potential source of further immigration, or an opportunity, with which Britain can realise its interests in a politically divided European organisation.

The EU and Turkey according to the British Media and Politics

The news media, in the present context specifically the Guardian, *the Independent*, *the Telegraph* (*the Telegraph Online*, *the Daily Telegraph*, and *the Sunday Telegraph*), *the Times*, *the Financial Times*, and *the Economist*, gave a fair overview of Turkey's accession process. While sympathizing with Turkey's EU bid, they remained critical of the country's issues with democracy, especially the situation of minority rights, the denial of the Armenian genocide, torture and ill-treatment by the state, and violations of freedom of thought.[30]

---

28 See, Liberal Democrat General Election Manifesto: Freedom, Justice, Honesty, 2001.
29 Geddes, *Britain and the European Union*, 102, 243.
30 For example, see Amberin Zaman and Tony Peterson, 'Trial of Novelist "Shows Turkey Not Ready for EU"', *The* Sunday *Telegraph*, September 11, 2005; Jonathan Power, 'How Turkey Fails Its Kurds', *International Herald Tribune*, September 21, 2005; Vincent Boland, 'Doubts over Turkish Justice Cast Shadow on EU Accession Talks', *Financial Times*, September 26, 2005; Ben Macintyre, 'Brutality, poverty and religion stand between Turkey and EU', *The Times*, September 30, 2005; Ian Traynor and Ewen MacAskill, 'Torture Claims Threaten Turkey's Bid to Join EU', *The*

Despite their remarks on democratic deficits in Turkey, the news media in Britain generally pointed out the strategic importance of the candidate's membership for the EU and the UK for peaceful relationships with the Middle East. For example, the Economist revealed the common strategic approach in favour of Turkey's accession, which was shared by British and American political camps:

> After September 11th, taking Turkey into the club is no longer just a question of helping a big and strategically important country to modernise. It is a test of whether the EU, and the West as a whole, has any role in encouraging moderate and democratic Islam.[31]

In other words, Turkey's EU membership was presumed to be a key to settling religious conflicts in Europe and in its hinterland. Years after the September 11 attacks in the United States, in the aftermath of the American and British war on Iraq (2003), and in the face of the terrorist assaults in Europe and the UK, the British public had begun to speak of the outbreak of a 'clash of civilisations' between cultural domains. Then, many agreed that EU membership of Turkey, a predominantly Muslim and secular country, was a great opportunity to de-escalate strained relations between various religious communities.[32] The Economist, therefore, symbolised the overall view in Britain at that time, which geographically and religiously favoured a progressive construction of Turkey through the term 'democratic/moderate Islam'.

In comparison with France and Germany, Britain, therefore, was the only case in which newspapers of different ideological origins sided with Turkey's EU bid and criticised several EU members for their growing opposition to the candidate. They accused Europeans of bringing idiosyncratic preconditions to the negotiations with Turkey.[33] In that sense, British newspapers mostly ques-

---

Guardian, September 28, 2005; Helena Smith, 'European Mission Unearths Torture Claims in Turkey', *The Guardian*, October 10, 2005; 'Turkey Must Relent', *The Spectator*, September 10, 2005; 'Turkey Must Recognize Genocide', *The Telegraph*, September 28, 2005.
31 'When to talk Turkey', *The Economist, Europe Edition*, September 15, 2005.
32 Sevilay Aksoy, 'The Prospect of Turkey's EU Membership as Represented in the British Newspapers The Times and The Guardian, 2002–2005', *Journal of European Studies* 39, no.4 (2009): 476, doi: 10.1177/0047244109344801; Derek Bryce, 'The Generous Exclusion of Ottoman-Islamic Europe: British Press Advocacy of Turkish EU Membership', *Culture and Religion* 10, no.3 (2009): 311–312, doi: 10.1080/14755610903279721.
33 See, Nicholas Watt, 'Austria Blocks Turkey's Road to EU membership', *The Guardian*, September 14, 2005, 'When to Talk Turkey'.

tioned Europe's latent Islamophobia directed against Turkey.³⁴ As the Independent commented, following the 11 September attacks Turkey's Islamic character translated to 'the opportunity for Europe to embrace the Muslim world and for individual EU states to bridge divisions with their own Muslim communities.'³⁵ Commentaries like those of the Guardian, therefore, called on the EU to keep the promise it gave the candidate 40 years ago, especially since Turkey was now striving to become an example of both an Islamic country and liberal democracy.³⁶ In another instance, the Spectator stated very similarly: 'while Turkey is far from a perfect democracy, and still falls short of the standards we have come to expect of Western European nations, it is essentially a benign country travelling in the right direction.'³⁷

Shortly before the beginning of the negotiations with Turkey, the British media were mostly concerned with Turkey-sceptic public opinion and political attitudes in Germany, France, and Austria.³⁸ The declining public support for Turkey in these countries was an issue for Britain's pro-Turkish European policy. The British media accused these countries' Turkey policies of being 'Turcophobic' or 'hostile'.³⁹ The German elections on 14 September 2005 in this case leap to the eye. The newspapers interpreted the Christian Democrats' election victory in Germany to be an adverse change against Turkey's EU bid. The Independent, for example, first mentioned Angela Merkel's pro-American standing in international relations, and then criticised her vision of Europe excluding Turkey. It stated: 'Her populist opposition to Turkey's entry to the EU is no less objectionable than Mr Schröder's opposition to the Iraq war was in the last election.'⁴⁰ In the final example, an op-ed in the Times illustrated popular stereotypes in Europe against Turkey with the words of William Ewart Gladstone,

---

34 Ibid; 'Now make Turkey's case', *the Economist*, October 6, 2005. For an earlier example, see, 'It Is in Europe's Best Interests that Turkey's Hopes are not Betrayed', *The Independent*, December 18, 2004.
35 'It Is in Europe's best interests that Turkey's hopes are not Betrayed'.
36 Ash, 'How the Dreaded'. See Andrew Finkel's book review, Andrew Finkel, 'Turkish Delight', *The Guardian*, October 8, 2005.
37 'Turkey Must Relent', *The Spectator*, September 10, 2005.
38 David Rennie, 'Chirac on Collision Course with Blair over Turkey in EU', *The Telegraph*, August 27, 2005; Colin Randall, 'Turkey's Membership of Europe Cast Long Shadow over French Poll', *The Telegraph*, May 30, 2005; 'Emergency Talks to Save Turkey EU Entry', *The Telegraph*, September 30, 2005; Luke Harding and Nicholas Watt, 'Turkey's EU Dream Dealt Double Blow as Chirac and Merkel Raise Doubts', *The Guardian*, August 27, 2005.
39 'When to Talk Turkey'. Also see Yusuf Devran, 'The Portrayal of Turkey in the British Media: Orientalism Resurfaced', *Insight Turkey* 9, no.4 (2010): 113.
40 'Germany needs change', *The Telegraph*, September 18, 2005.

Prime Minister of Britain in the late 19th century, which had reprimanded the violent and corrupt Ottomans. Gladstone, as Prime Minister, voiced the common prejudice back then against a corrupt and violent Turkey allegedly threatening Europe's very existence: 'From the black day they entered Europe, the one great anti-human specimen of humanity.'[41]

In summary, the shared argument in the British media was that European politicians overlooked, or even marginalised, Turkey's accession process in many terms. In the economic field, British politicians and the media were also disagreeing with the Europeans. On the one hand, the British press initially acknowledged the European fear that Turkish workers might overwhelm the European (and consequently British) labour market.[42] On the other hand, it was known that the UK most of the time primarily conceived the EU as an international organization of economic privileges, and British diplomats usually aimed to keep these rights on a commercial basis. Throughout Britain's membership in the EU, British elites were mostly intent on exploiting the Union's historical function of being a trade zone. Turkey's EU membership would then strengthen the EU's commercial capacity and halt or perhaps overturn European political integration, all in Britain's interests.[43] Shortly before the negotiations' beginning, Jack Straw reportedly claimed: 'stopping enlargement would only weaken Europe's ability to compete with emerging Asian economies.'[44] As a commentary held in the Spectator, Turkey's international role was serving the British aspiration of transforming the EU into a trade zone.[45]

Following the beginning of the accession talks with the candidate, the former French president Giscard d'Estaing reportedly argued that Britain would succeed in turning the EU into a large, free market zone with the start of Turkey's membership negotiations.[46] The Economist later discussed d'Estaing's speech and pointed out how he could be right in fact, and how Turkey's accession to the EU might indeed alter French, and also German, plans of transforming the European Union:

---

41 Macintyre, 'Brutality, poverty and religion'.
42 Ibid.
43 Antonio V Menéndez-Alarcón, *The Cultural Realm of European Integration: Social Representations in France, Spain, and the United Kingdom*, (Westport: Praeger, 2004), 127.
44 Graham Bobley, 'EU divided on talks for Turkey', *International Herald Tribune*, September 9, 2005.
45 Matthew Parris, 'The Riots May Be Just What the French Economy Needs', *The Spectator*, November 12, 2005.
46 'Barroso Fires EU Warning to Turkey' *The Guardian*, October 4, 2005.

> So France's ex-president, Valéry Giscard d'Estaing, is right to say that an EU including Turkey will be a looser grouping than some people desire. The Turks may well wreck things for any state or pair of states which still hope the EU as a whole will act as a mouthpiece for their own political, or geopolitical, ideas; or that the Union will turn into a super-state with one or two of its current members in charge....[47]

In other words, d'Estaing had revealed that Turkey's accession to the EU could play into the hands of Britain. Timothy Garton Ash from the Guardian agreed:

> Roughly speaking, the British hated the constitution because they thought it would create a French Europe, while the French hate enlargement because they think it will create a British Europe. Thus Giscard laments that these further enlargements 'are obviously going to transform Europe into a large free-trade zone'. That is what continental Europeans classically charge the British with wanting.[48]

Turkey's accession was believed to help to undermine the current European venture of forming a political union, which had re-emerged with the debates surrounding the EU Constitution in the early 2000s. The same commentary celebrated the beginning of the negotiations with Turkey on the pre-given date, 3 October 2005: 'this week, the European Union did something remarkable. It chose to become an all-European commonwealth, not the part-European superstate of Tory nightmares.'[49]

In general terms, the British media employed highly technical language in dealing with Turkey-related matters in the EU.[50] Compared to the French and German media, the British approached the EU more as a loosely-structured international organisation. Especially the British media's reportage of Turkey's Cyprus policy reflected this viewpoint.[51] First, Britain prioritised the beginning of the membership negotiations with Turkey and matters such as the candidate's problematic relations with Cyprus should not impede the process. As commentaries in the Guardian and Independent revealed, the British government did

---

[47] 'Now Make Turkey's Case', *The Economist*, October 6, 2005.
[48] Ash, 'How the Dreaded'.
[49] Ibid.
[50] See Daniel Dombey, 'Deal Boosts Turkish Hopes on Start of EU Accession Talks', *Financial Times*, September 12, 2005; 'EU remains divided over Turkey's refusal to recognize Cyprus', *Daily Star*, September 15, 2005.
[51] David Rennie, 'Threats and Bickering as the EU Ministers Meet to Talk Turkey', *The Telegraph*, September 2, 2005.

not see Turkey's recognition of Cyprus as a precondition to the negotiations.[52] As the media noted that the British government officially backed Turkey on the issue before the beginning of the accession talks, a diplomat spoke to the Financial Times that Britain was too preoccupied with securing Turkey's negotiations 'at the expense of (losing) an EU member', which was Cyprus.[53] Second, the British media additionally approached the Cyprus conflict by referring to the reasons for Turkey's refusal to recognise the country.[54] The common argument in politics and the media was that the EU should also bear responsibility for ending the isolation of the Turkish Cypriots on the island.[55]

To sum up, British newspapers wrote about Britain's long-term foreign policy against European political integration, linking Turkey's EU membership to the British strategy against the formation of a European superstate. While reporting on Turkey, they generally did not evoke the long-term British opposition to migration, or at least the British Conservatives' disapproval of migration. British newspapers, in addition, did not cover economic consequences of Turkey's EU membership as much as the French and German ones did. If anything, news and commentaries largely argued that the deliberate attempts of EU members to prevent Turkish workers' integration into Europe were against the nature of EU enlargement. For an earlier example, after the Brussels European Council in 2004 the Independent had questioned the conditions introduced only to Turkey's negotiating document, most notably the 'permanent safeguard clauses against Turkey', in an attempt to protect labour markets of member states.[56] This was, to the common assumption, against the nature of the EU as a common market.

In the French and German political landscapes discussed in previous chapters, a substantial amount of people connected the EU Constitution with Turkey's future accession and therefore opposed both proposals. British public opinion, while firmly rejecting the EU Constitution, instead partially supported Turkey

---

[52] Harding and Watt, 'Turkey's EU Dream'. 'Deal on Turkish Membership of EU Saved by Compromise over Cyprus', *The Independent*, December 18, 2004; Collin Randall, 'Turkey's Membership of Europe Cast Long Shadow over French Poll', *The Telegraph*, May 30, 2005.
[53] Daniel Dombey, 'Time Runs Short for EU Deal on Turkey Talks', *Financial Times*, September 18, 2005.
[54] Graham Bobley, 'EU Divided on Talks for Turkey', *International Herald Tribune*, September 9, 2005.
[55] For example, see House of Commons Hansard Debates, Debates and Oral Answers 437, October 11, 2005, Column 157, 6.
[56] 'EU Leaders to Offer Turkey Deal on Membership Talks', The *Independent*, December 16, 2004; 'It Is in Europe's Best Interests that Turkey's Hopes Are not Betrayed', *The Independent*, December 18, 2004.

with a significant percentage. According to the Eurobarometer, 45 % of British backed Turkey's EU membership, a value much higher than the support for the candidate in France and Germany.[57] Surveys also showed that only 20 % would have approved the EU Constitution in a possible constitutional referendum in the UK.[58] These polls then suggest that other conditions than Turkey's EU membership played roles in the high opposition to the EU Constitution in 2005. Admittedly, half of the British people reportedly thought that the EU Constitution meant the loss of their political sovereignty.[59] Referendum polls outside England pointed to the same attitude; in Scotland, for example, the dominant trend had been equally against European integration. As studies showed, in 2005 only a minority in Scotland welcomed the idea of promoting European integration through the EU Constitution.[60]

British political parties similarly debated the EU Constitution without associating it with Turkey's EU membership. Among them, the Labour Party entered the 2000s as the ruling party of Britain under the leadership of Tony Blair. As discussed above, the Labour Party under Blair, from 1997, had advocated a limited level of pro-Europeanism. On the one hand, the party claimed that Britain could best uphold its national interests inside an integrated European Union. On the other, they maintained their Eurosceptic emphasis on the empowerment of national parliaments vis-à-vis the EU's supranational institutions. The Labour Party therefore backed the EU's enlargement and the EU Constitution for economic reasons, as they revealed through their manifesto for the 2005 general elections.[61] Meanwhile, the Labour government in Scotland equally supported the EU Constitution, believing that it would strengthen the country's role in the EU's decision-making.[62]

---

[57] Eurobarometer 63.4, Public Opinion in the European Union, Executive Summary: Turkey, European Commission Public Opinion Analysis 63, no.4 (Spring 2005), 8, http://ec.europa.eu/public_opinion/archives/eb/eb63/eb63_exec_tr.pdf (08.03.2015).
[58] Special Eurobarometer 214, The Future Constitutional Treaty, European Commission Public Opinion Analysis 214, March 2005, 17, http://ec.europa.eu/public_opinion/archives/ebs/ebs_214_en.pdf (12.03.2015).
[59] Ibid., 28.
[60] Carine Berberi, 'Scotland's Attitude to the European Constitution: The End of the Pro-European Era?', in *Scotland and Europe, Scotland in Europe*, ed. Gilles Leydier (Newcastle: Cambridge Scholars Publishing, 2007), 287–290; Mahendran Kesi and Iain McIver, 'Attitudes towards the European Union & the Challenges in Communicating "Europe": Building a Bridge between Europe and its Citizens Evidence', Review Paper 2, (Scottish Executive Social Research, 2007), 8.
[61] 'Britain Forward not Back', The Labour Party Manifesto 2005, 82–83.
[62] Berberi, 'Scotland's Attitude', 280–291; Alan Crawford, 'McConnell and Barroso Hit It off', *The Sunday Herald*, April 3, 2005.

Within this period, the Labour Party declared firm support for Turkey's accession to the EU and in particular for the opening of the negotiations with the candidate. Its election manifesto stated: 'During Britain's EU presidency this year, we will work to ... bring closer EU membership for Turkey, the Balkans and Eastern Europe.'[63] Indeed, as early as December 2004, the time of the Brussels European Council, the British delegation had started lobbying to lead the other EU actors into a decision favourable to Turkey that would keep the candidate on track.[64] Tony Blair celebrated the Council's decision that named an opening date for Turkey's negotiations, 3 October 2005. He stated: 'It (the summit) shows that those who believe that there is some fundamental clash of civilisations between Christians and Muslims are actually wrong.'[65] In this speech, he implicitly categorised Europe and Turkey in religious terms but added that there could be a common ground between the two domains. He asserted:

> the fact that Turkey is a Muslim country does not mean it should be barred from the European Union. On the contrary, if it fulfils the same principles of democracy and human rights, then Muslim and Christian can work together. That is a very, very important signal right across the world.[66]

Through his references to the candidate, Tony Blair presented Turkey as a remarkable example of moderate Islam and argued that the EU could incorporate Turkey provided the applicant complied with the EU's accession criteria. Jack Straw, the foreign secretary of the Labour government, similarly argued that the EU membership of a democratic Turkey would demonstrate that 'Islam is compatible with the values of liberal democracy, which form the bedrock of the European Union'.[67] Days after the beginning of Turkey's membership negotiations and amidst the prolonged identity discussions Straw made his point once again:

> By welcoming Turkey, with its large Muslim population, we are embarking on a new era in which it is manifest that the European Union and Europe is not just an exclusive Christian club, at best cold to its neighbours, at worst actively hostile. Instead, we are able to show

---

[63] 'Britain Forward', 84.
[64] 'Deal on Turkish membership'.
[65] Ambrose Evans-Prichard and Andrew Sparrow, 'EU Offer to Turkey 'a Triumph for Tolerance and World Peace', *The Telegraph*, September 18, 2004.
[66] Ibid.
[67] House of Commons Hansard Debates 436, July 30, 2005, Column 1452, 9.

that what binds this modern Europe together is a set of fundamental rights and freedoms combined with a common purpose, regardless of race or religion.[68]

According to Straw, the best way to show that the European Union was built on political values was welcoming a predominantly Muslim country. He associated Europeanness essentially with political traits and implied the importance of Turkey's modernisation/Europeanization in order for the EU to avert the clash of civilisations.

At the same time, though, Labour Party members remained critical of the slow pace of Turkey's democratic change. The candidate was slowing down the necessary reforms and lagging behind in its modernisation process. In reply to these judgments, the government pointed out Turkey's entire reform performance up to that point. For example, a parliamentarian of the Labour Party asked whether the British government would take action against the violations of human rights in Turkey. Tony Blair replied accordingly:

> It is important, if Turkey wants to become a member of the EU, that it abide by the criteria for membership, including the criterion on freedom of expression. I hope, however, that my hon. Friend would also agree that Turkey has gone a considerable way down the path of reform over the past few years. I hope that these issues will also be dealt with as part of future reforms so that Turkey can proceed to EU membership, which I believe is in the interests of Turkey, Europe and the wider world.[69]

The Prime Minister showed his confidence that the candidate would settle its political issues later during its membership negotiations. In this instance, it would not be wrong to argue that the Labour government prioritised Turkey's negotiations rather than its sluggish reform process; at the beginning of the accession talks, the British statesmen tended not to mention common problems in Turkey.

In summary, the Labour Party first and foremost backed Turkey's EU membership on account of the long-term policy of turning European integration to Britain's advantage. Second, the party approached Turkey's accession process with political terms originated in the EU's accession criteria. Third, Labour politicians emphasised Turkey's possible contribution to the EU as a remedy to the clash of civilisations between European and Islamic domains. Only in this final justification did the Labour Party categorise the candidate in explicitly religious terms.

---

[68] House of Commons Hansard Debates 437, October 11, 2005, Column 157, 6.
[69] House of Commons Hansard Debates 439, November 23, 2005, Column 1507, 3

The British Conservative Party led the main opposition in 2005. Throughout its long history, the party became known for its emphases on the free market economy, national interest, national security, and restricting migration. The British Conservatives, who by far made the most significant contribution to the United Kingdom's long-term Eurosceptic image until the 2000s, had an unbending opposition to the EU Constitution in 2005. Before the parliamentary election in May, its then-president Michael Howard pledged to reclaim the responsibilities given to the European Union by the Labour government.[70] The Conservative election programme included: 'We will settle our relationship with the European Union by bringing powers back from Brussels to Britain.'[71] In contrast to the Labour Party, therefore, the Conservatives campaigned against the EU Constitution with their argument that Britain could best preserve its interests outside an integrated EU. The party's disapproval of European integration was much connected with their long-term stand against the current migration to Britain. Instead of the ruling party's encouraging policy on migration, they raised the concept of 'controlled immigration' in their election programme.[72] Howard also vowed to struggle with the current migration to Britain and entered into a debate with his social democrat and liberal counterparts before the election. Against his accusations of racism, Howard maintained his position to be 'common sense' and defended limiting migration to Britain 'for good community relations, national security and the management of public services.'[73]

Despite their committed opposition to the Labour Party on certain points, the Conservatives shared the same view with the government over Turkey's accession to the EU. The Conservative Party's election manifesto promised to 'build on the success of enlargement, making Europe more diverse by working to bring in more nations, including Turkey'.[74] Michael Howard had also publicly confirmed the official policy of Britain, and welcomed an earlier compromise reached at the Brussels European Council (December 2004) thanks to the efforts of the British delegation:

> I welcome the agreement that was reached on the membership negotiations and the prospect of Turkey providing an invaluable bridge between the rest of Europe and the Islamic world. Does that not lay to rest any claim that the European Union, or the west as a whole,

---

70 Duncan Watts, British *Government and Politics: A Comparative Guide* (Edinburgh: Edinburgh University Press, 2006), 237, 239–240.
71 'It's Time for Action', Conservative Election Manifesto 2005, 1.
72 Ibid., 19.
73 Patrick Hennessy, 'Howard Puts Immigration at Heart of Election Battle', *The Telegraph*, January 23, 2005.
74 Ibid., 26.

is in any way anti-Islamic in nature? And should it not be seen as a very positive development for that reason alone? The Prime Minister was quite right to pay tribute to Prime Minister Erdogan for the reforms that have been introduced under his leadership and for the progress that has been made. I very much hope that those negotiations will reach a successful conclusion and that Turkey will, in due course, become a full member of the EU.[75]

Like Tony Blair, Michael Howard characterised Turkey's accession process as a solution to the potential clash of civilisations. He thus employed the 'bridge' function of the candidate, the term reflecting the relationship between 'the rest of Europe and Islamic world'. He not only stated his party's positive attitude towards Turkey's modernisation process but also his confidence in it. Likewise, the Conservatives' election campaign presented only months later would involve positive mentions on Turkey's EU bid. There were, however, some Conservatives becoming more sceptical about it due to the rising terrorism in Europe and the UK. Under the shadow of terrorist attacks in London in July 2005, a conservative politician questioned the free movement of Turks in the event of Turkey's EU membership.[76] Despite his party's known backing of the candidate, Michael Portillo wrote his misgivings about Turkey:

> As a former Defence Secretary I am very much swayed by the strategic arguments for Turkish accession ... But now the context in which we consider the Turkish application has been altered because of Islamic terror. The EU has become much more culturally diverse ... I believe that Europe has benefited from that change. But it has also brought a danger that not many foresaw. Today a few of our citizens are intent on destroying us in the name of Islam ... That hugely complicates the issue of Turkish EU membership.[77]

In his commentary Portillo associated, although indirectly, Turkey's membership with Islamic terrorism. He first questioned the cultural composition of the European Union becoming more diverse with the enlargement, and argued that this diversity made Europe more susceptible to Islamic terrorism. Turkey's EU membership could augment the already dangerous situation, as he wrote, especially if the country were 'ruled by an extremist Islamic regime hostile to the West'.[78] In the face of the terrorist attacks in Britain and Europe, the likelihood of rising fundamentalism in Turkey apparently concerned him. A similar counter-argument to the applicant's accession perspective would later emerge, in 2016, at a time when

---

75 House of Commons Hansard Debates 428, December 20, 2004, Column 1921, 10.
76 Aksoy, 'The Prospect of Turkey's EU Membership', 493–494.
77 Michael Portillo, 'The Land of Promise and Danger at the EU's Door', *The Sunday Times*, September 4, 2005.
78 Ibid.

some conservatives were intent on mobilising votes towards leaving the European Union. Ahead of the Brexit Referendum, the Brexiteers from the British Conservatives and the UK Independence Party created the bogeyman of Turkey, claiming that the country's presumed entry would produce an influx of immigrants and help radical Islam flourish.[79]

Despite these comments ascribing labour migration, Islamism, and religious terrorism to Turkey's future EU membership, in 2005 the Conservative Party largely remained in favour of the candidate's accession. The Conservatives supported it as a result of their long-term policy against European integration. After all, as a commentary claimed shortly after the beginning of the membership negotiations, the candidate's membership would have a high potential to end 'the part-European superstate of Tory nightmares'.[80] The party officially approached Turkey's accession process using political terms from the EU's political accession criteria, and largely agreed with Labour Party politicians on the country's would-be role, the example of 'democratic Islam', in the EU's peaceful relations with the Islamic world.

The Liberal Democrats forming another opposition party also deserve attention since they critically emphasised Turkey's human rights issues during this period. The Liberal Democrats backed both European enlargement and the EU Constitution in 2005, and, in line with Britain's commonly acknowledged Eurosceptic position, they additionally campaigned for empowering national parliaments inside the EU.[81] In agreement with their political identity dedicated to the promotion of liberal values, the Liberal Democrats highlighted democratic problems in Turkey and attached importance to its democratic transition for EU accession. They argued in the House of Commons many times that the human rights violations considering the Kurdish minority in the country continued despite the candidate's membership aspiration.[82] A member expressed shortly after the negotiations' beginning: 'As for Turkey itself, I hope that we will make it clear from the outset that economic qualification is not enough, and that pluralism, the rule of law and freedom of speech must be realities, not merely aspirations.'[83]

---

[79] James Ker-Lindsay, 'Turkey's EU Accession as a Factor in the 2016 Brexit Referendum', Turkish Studies 19, no.1 (2018): 1–22, doi: https://doi.org/10.1080/14683849.2017.1366860.
[80] Ash, 'How the Dreaded'.
[81] 'Liberal Democrats: The Real Alternative', Election Manifesto 2005, 13.
[82] For example, see House of Commons Hansard Debates 436, July 19, 2005, 2; House of Commons Hansard Debates 438, November 1, 2005, Columns 714–715, 3.
[83] House of Commons, Hansard Debates 437, October 11, 2005, Column 162, 7.

Their political backgrounds and statements suggest that Britain's major parties showed open support for Turkey at the beginning of its negotiations with the EU. In this direction, Britain's successive governments reiterated their support following the start of the accession talks at times, at least until the time of Brexit.[84] In 2005, however, the harshest reactions to this common position arrived from the far-right, which was then a relatively weak political group in Britain. To take one example, Nigel Farage, a member of the European Parliament from the UK Independence Party back then, rejected the other parties' election campaigns favouring the candidate's accession. He slammed the Conservative Party's recent election document involving Turkey's EU prospect with these words: 'This is a bogus general election campaign! ... Disgusting! ... And now they want Turkey to join the EU! We have simply got to say enough is enough!'[85] Farage had also told earlier that the government's pro-Turkey policy had not any support in the British public. He had thus attacked Britain's involvement in the Turkey debate between EU members: 'This is undemocratic, it's anti-democratic, and it's damned dangerous.'[86] UKIP members were then publicly praising their party for being the only British faction repudiating Turkey's entry to the EU.[87]

In summary, British political camps, except for the extreme right, seemed in accord on backing the EU's enlargement with Turkey and commencing the membership negotiations in 2005. The idea of a European Turkey found approval on a larger scale in Britain, as the stances of these parties suggest, in comparison with the favouring opinions in continental Europe. Thus, a commentator argued in Spectator that 'in Britain, happily, this (Turkey's membership perspective) is one European issue where the acrimonious EU divisions between Labour and the Conservatives play no part'.[88] The period shortly before the beginning of the accession talks then saw an almost uniform British argument in favour of the Turkish candidate. The debate from September to early October between the British government and conservative governments of Europe over the beginning of the negotiations eminently exemplifies this argument.

---

[84] See, House of Commons Foreign Affairs Committee, *UK-Turkey Relations and Turkey's Regional Role: Twelfth Report of Session 2010–12* (London: The Stationery Office limited, 2012), 73–86.
[85] Oliver Burkeman, 'Wandering in the Wilderness – How Tories stole Ukip's political clothes', *The Guardian*, April 29, 2005.
[86] Keith B. Richburg, 'E.U., Turkey Agree To Membership Talks', *The Washington Post*, December 18, 2004.
[87] See, Gerard Batten's address, Debate on Croatia: progress report 2008 – Turkey: progress report 2008 – Former Yugoslav Republic of Macedonia: progress report 2008, March 11 2009, Strasbourg.
[88] 'Why Turkey is Good for Europe', *Spectator*, February 21, 2004.

At the outset, Britain assumed the term presidency at the Council of the European Union months before the pre-given date of the EU's negotiations with Turkey, which gave them the advantage of overseeing the start of the accession talks. As the Telegraph stated, the Labour government had two main tasks to follow during its term leadership: securing the EU budget in favour of British interests and ensuring the start of the accession talks with Turkey despite opposition in Europe.[89] A British diplomat told the Financial Times: 'Ever since the UK assumed the presidency in July, their priority has been to make sure that Turkey does not walk away.'[90]

Over this period, European bureaucrats were restating the negotiations with Turkey to be open-ended; as the President of the European Commission reminded, the candidate's accession was 'neither guaranteed nor automatic'.[91] Yet British actors were instead implying that the negotiations were most likely to lead to a successful end. Tony Blair stated a week before the pre-given date of the negotiations: 'I sincerely believe that EU membership is Turkey's future ...We shall work towards achieving that.'[92] Jack Straw pointed out the security consequences of an outcome other than the candidate's accession: 'Bringing Turkey in is a way of binding Europe. We are concerned about a so-called clash of civilisations ... We need to see Turkey in the European Union and not pushed the other way.'[93] In the foreign minister's statement, the country was still positioned within another cultural category. But his conceptualisation of Europe was open-ended, progressive, and convenient for merging with other cultures within a project against cultural conflicts. Stephen Twigg from the Labour Party similarly cautioned against neglecting the Turkish ally, adding that millions of Turks were already in Europe. He said: 'what will future generations say about us if we turn our backs now ... on the best Muslim friend we have?'[94]

The negotiations with Turkey were expected to start on 3 October on the basis of the promising conclusions of the Brussels European Council held the previous year. The optimism, however, was to change in September 2005, when the Austrian government asked to re-negotiate the terms of the accession

---

89 'Britain Persuades the EU to Talk Turkey', *The Daily Telegraph*, October 4, 2005.
90 Dombey, Daniel, 'Time Runs Short for EU Deal on Turkey Talks', *Financial Times*, September 18, 2005.
91 'Barroso Fires EU Warning to Turkey', *The Guardian*, October 4, 2005.
92 Mark Oliver, 'Turkey's Future Lies in EU, Says Blair', *The Guardian*, September 30, 2005.
93 Justin Stares and Nick Holdsworth, 'Europe "Faces Disaster" If It Spurns Turkey', *The Telegraph*, October 2, 2005. Also see, 'Straw: We Must not Push Turkey Away', *The Telegraph*, October 2, 2005.
94 Stares and Holdsworth, 'Europe "Faces Disaster"'.

talks. The Telegraph commented that this latest move had the sole aim of 'sabotaging Turkey's accession talks'.[95] The governing Austrian People's Party was primarily against the accession negotiations' direction, which then intrinsically signified a clear membership scenario for the candidates. Instead, Vienna raised the alternative of a privileged partnership with Turkey, which German and French conservative parties had long been insisting on. The common fear between these parties and the Austrian government was that the membership negotiations would inevitably result in Turkey's EU accession unless any other precondition was stipulated beforehand.[96]

The second goal of the Austrian government was aligning the beginning of Turkey's accession talks with those of Croatia, another membership candidate and Austria's critical ally in the Balkans. The EU had previously specified a condition for Croatia's starting the negotiations that it had to cooperate with the United Nations in the investigation of crimes committed by Croatian warlords during the Yugoslavian Civil War. The Austrian delegation then hinted that they were ready to give the green light to Turkey's accession talks if the EU removed this condition and affirmed the beginning of the negotiations also with Croatia.[97] Austria's intransigence in return drew reactions from the British media and political actors. The Economist, for instance, called the renegotiations between European countries and Britain over Turkey's accession talks as a 'Bazaar Bargaining'.[98] Daniel Hannan, British Conservative and member of the European Parliament, reacted that there was a price to pay if Turkey was set aside from the course of EU accession:

> We risk creating the very thing we fear: a Turkey oriented towards Mecca ... Today, Turkey is an inspiration to Muslims everywhere who believe in democracy. Ten years from now, we may have turned a loyal ally into a snarling rival, an Iran on our doorstep. We are stumbling towards a truly epochal mistake.[99]

The Conservative deputy argued that Turkey's democratic lifestyle was an example to the Islamic world. He associated the opposite of this image with a different, violent kind of Islam, which was accordingly conceptualised with Iran, and,

---

[95] 'Austria Sabotages Turkish EU Talks', *The Telegraph*, September 30, 2005.
[96] Ibid.
[97] Ibid. David Rennie, 'Britain Faces Showdown over Turkey', *The Telegraph*, September 28, 2005.
[98] 'Bazaar Bargaining', *The Economist*, September 1, 2005.
[99] Daniel Hannan, 'A Cynical Comedy that is Likely to End in Ironic Tragedy', *The Telegraph*, October 2, 2005.

surprisingly, Mecca, a city bearing no political but a central religious meaning for Muslims. Hannan urged Europeans to start the accession talks without degrading their goal into an alternative other than full membership, so that the Turkish ally would not change sides and turn to traditional Islam, the epicentre of antagonisms to Europe. He thus religiously categorised Turkey as currently pro-European but at the same time a volatile actor that could be drawn to anti-European cultural domains.

All in all, the general argument backed in British politics in this period was that Turkey was transforming itself through the EU's membership leverage; should the EU ever turn its back on the candidate, it would mean undermining the applicant's modernisation, losing a prominent ally, and missing an opportune moment to prevent the clash of civilisations. The British government's official stance was expressed by Jack Straw: 'We are concerned about this theological-political divide, which could open up even further down the boundary between so-called Christian-heritage states and those of Islamic heritage.'[100] He also stated in the House of Commons:

> By standing by our promise to Turkey, we will make the European Union stronger, safer and more competitive ... We have to show that the greatest threat to our European culture and heritage comes not from opening our doors to a vibrant, secular nation such as Turkey, but from closing in on ourselves and allowing Europe to stagnate in the face of global competition.[101]

Seeing that the candidate's negotiations were at risk, Britain, the term president of the Council of the EU, convened an unofficial meeting a day before the scheduled opening of the negotiations, where Britain and Austria bargained to start the accession talks with Turkey and Croatia together. In the end, the EU started the membership negotiations with the two candidates on the same date, 3 October 2005. As implied by the British media, during this unofficial bargain Austria represented the overall Turkey-sceptic European conservatives whereas Britain challenged the idea of a strict political union in Europe.[102]

---

100 'Straw: We must not'.
101 House of Commons Hansard Debates 437, October 11, 2005, Column 177, 6. Also see House of Commons, Hansard Debates 438, November 1, 2005, 3.
102 'Britain persuades the EU'.

Conclusion

In 2005, Britain had by far the most decisive role in ensuring the start of the accession negotiations, and historical factors embedded in British politics help to explain this role. Rising scepticism in British public and politicians about the ever-closer European Union was the dominant factor, as traditional European policies of British political parties structured the perceptions about Turkey's accession to the European Union in 2005. In a similar vein, the media's coverage suggests that the overall Euroscepticism mostly strengthened pro-Turkish statements. The media, at times, openly commented that the government's support for the candidate was in agreement with the long-term British policy of opposing European political integration. The country's prime goal was diluting the integration plans that were vaguely discussed in Europe during 2005, especially when the EU Constitution was being rejected in parts of the continent. The membership of culturally and geographically 'different' Turkey would play into Britain's hands in this way. The examples from the British press between September and early October cited this strategy, especially during Britain's term presidency in the Council of the European Union.

Election campaigns and parliamentary debates in 2005 suggest that British parties approached the candidate in terms of their programmes, which were mostly against the EU's current political integration but in favour of its enlargement, and, as the Conservatives' election manifesto proclaimed, making the EU more diverse. British political camps then debated Turkey's EU membership mainly in the political terms derived from the EU's accession criteria, and most of them agreed on the view that Turkey should accede to the EU once it is politically modernised/westernised at the end of its negotiation process. Moreover, British political elites conceptualised the candidate specifically in religious and geographical terms and saw it as an example of moderate/democratic Islam and a "bridge" between the European and Islamic domains. Turkey as a member of the EU was argued to play a significant part in the solution to a potential clash of civilisations. The opportunity of making the European Union more pluralist and tolerant through the country's membership was also in harmony with the long-term British policy against European political integration. As a result, the British government and political parties together advocated Turkey's EU perspective with political, religious, and geographical grounds during a lively debate against the conservative European governments shortly before the negotiations' beginning.

During the relevant process, the government's most influential supporter was perhaps the British Conservative Party. In keeping with their traditional Eurosceptic position, the British Conservatives fiercely opposed the Labour Party on its 'pro-European' policy and also repudiated the EU Constitution and freedom of movement. Yet the Tories seemed almost in full agreement with the Labour Party on Turkey's political, religious, and geographical contributions to the European Union, and thus differed remarkably from most of their European counterparts, who, as the previous chapters indicated, stigmatised the candidate with non-European traits in the same period. This outcome can solely be explained by the British Conservatives' priority in 2005 of interfering with the trajectory of the European integration towards a federal state.

8 Conclusion

The European Union inaugurated the accession talks with Turkey on 3 October 2005. On the day of the negotiations' opening, Jack Straw stated his confidence in the candidate's success during the future accession process. Almost 250 years after the Ottoman Empire was first referred to as the 'sick man' in European (British) literature and diplomacy,[1] a British politician was saluting Europeans for their decision about Turkey's compatibility with Europe,

> This is a further key step on the road to full membership ... It will strengthen the European Union. It means now that we are an EU founded on values, not on history ... Turkey has always been a European country. We are showing tonight that it's not about religion and religious differences, it's about values.[2]

The British Foreign Minister construed 'values' as the political principles underlying the European Union. In his hopeful address, Europeans apparently adhered to this conception and were putting aside their concerns rooted in historical strife with Turkey. However, the following years proved the contrary: Europeans continued to discuss the candidate's compatibility with what they presented as European values with references to history. As the previous chapters have shown, Turkey remained a subject of controversy between European political camps during its membership negotiations until the late 2000s. The present study has attempted to demonstrate the connection between representations of history and the debates over Turkey's EU membership in a limited timeframe. It therefore addressed the question: *To what extent and by what historical values did the European political camps conceptualise Turkey in relation to the European Union during the accession talks in the 2000s?*

The second and third chapters discussed the historical relationship between Europe and Turkey, and also traced the origins of political, religious, and geographical concepts, which are part of the contemporary European language about the candidate. The pertinent question then was how focal values of Europeanness from the 18th century onwards determined the relationship with the Ottoman Empire and later with modern Turkey. At least until the 17th century, the

---

[1] Although attributed to a statement made by Tsar Nikolas in 1853, the practice of crediting the Ottoman Empire with being the 'sick man' goes back to George Lindsay Crawford's depiction in 1769. Asli Cirakman, *From the 'Terror of the World' to the 'Sick Man of Europe': European Images of Ottoman Empire and Society from the Sixteenth Century to the Nineteenth* (New York: Peter Lang Publishing, 2005), 164.

[2] 'EU opens historic talks with Turkey', Philippine Daily, October 5, 2005, 12.

time of the Westphalian peace, religious terms had dominated descriptions of Europeans and outsiders. To Europeans, the Ottoman Empire was then a barbaric realm intent on struggling with Christian Europe. It can be argued that the secularisation of European social and political life later dissolved such firm categorisations, and Europeans approached the declining Ottomans as an object of European power politics.

With the waning influence of religion over politics and diplomacy, political terms came to predominate in European and national thinking about Turkey. The roots of today's political values lie in the intellectual and political movements of the 18th and 19th centuries. The Enlightenment and political revolutions generated political terms, such as republican values or individual rights, which were applicable across Western Europe and therefore considered to be cosmopolitan. Meanwhile, national politics and public opinion were increasingly considered to be the source of political legitimacy. As a consequence, political and religious values throughout Western Europe led Europeans to primarily portray the Ottoman Empire with dichotomous terms and stereotypes. Rising colonialist aspirations in this age also added a pragmatic character to the arguments. The second chapter located examples in the statements by the notable figures of the English and French literature and diplomacy from the 18th and 19th centuries. In a nutshell, these names mostly argued that Ottoman Turkey was irredeemably opposed to modern European values or that it should be aligned with these values under the influence of European powers.

In this regard, modernisation was a familiar concept between debates over the Ottoman Empire and those about modern Turkey. The country's long march towards political modernisation bridged the gap between European descriptions of the Ottoman Empire and Turkey. It can be argued, in a nutshell, that the country's transition was shaped by the late Ottoman modernisation, republican Turkey, and then Turkey's candidacy for EU membership. Over this long period, European statesmen and intellectuals saw Turkey's modernisation as a set of attempts to reform underdeveloped governance, to orient foreign policy into the West, and to internalise minority rights in the Ottoman Empire or modern Turkey. In the late Ottoman era, the empire's salvation entailed modernisation under European conditions. Inspired by the French nation state, which was a typical example to 19th century Europe, Ottoman bureaucrats strived to modernise the state and politics in order to emerge from under western supremacy. Although European actors in return mentioned these attempts, they also noted the continuing collapse of the Ottoman state. They regarded the empire's last decades as a process of minorities' liberation from a 'corrupted' authority. Then the birth and progress of the Turkish Republic as a result of its modernisation venture brought a sharp change to the country's international image. Europeans expressed approval of the revolutionary changes in Turkish social and political life, including the birth of secularism. In particular, European intellectuals largely celebrated the empowerment of women, an area in which Turkey performed more progressively than quite a few European states. All these changes in the country aside, international conditions became more favourable to modern Turkey's recognition, especially compared with the previous century. Throughout most of the 20th century, the decline of colonialist Europe and the rise of the Soviet Union had rendered the modernising Turkey essential for the West in security terms. Europeans, especially during the Cold War, attached high importance to the country's contribution to the western security bloc.

The European terms of conceptualising Turkey acquired an official character with Turkey's association with the European Community from 1963 and its candidacy for membership from 1999. Through these relations, Europeans systematically discussed the candidate in political, religious, and geographical terms. Following its official application in 1987, Turkey was considered to be geographically European and thus eligible to apply for the accession. Later, Europeans institutionalised the political terms of forthcoming enlargements. In 1993, the European Union introduced the Copenhagen criteria, with which the applicant countries of Central and Eastern Europe were required to comply. The EU's legislation therefore primarily implied shared European political values while discussing any candidate. Turkey has also been subject to the same accession criteria ever since it became a candidate for EU membership in 1999. Nevertheless, European political camps in the 2000s remained in disagreement on Turkey's compatibility with Europeanness. Political camps which visualise Europe as a cultural cosmos with common religious and geographical characteristics next to shared political values began to dominate European politics. In particular, the conservative and nationalist parties that gained significant electoral support in post-war Europe uncompromisingly rejected Turkey's accession perspective on the assumption that the candidate was not European in religious and geographical terms.

Western Europe had largely internalised political values after the Second World War as the European Union's legislation enshrined them. But religious and geographical values always retained their importance in national politics. In the 1990s and 2000s, political camps represented Europe and European values with these dichotomous values. As Turkey made progress in its EU accession process, political parties began to discuss in parallel whether the country conformed to their conceptions of European values. In particular, the mainstream conservative and far-right political parties of continental Europe rejected the candidate's EU membership not only on political grounds but also in religious and geographical terms. Europe's political camps thus remained divided about

Turkey's EU membership even at the beginning of the membership negotiations. However, while discussing Turkey, they had to take into consideration the 'European language' justified by EU legislation and, most importantly, the accession criteria. Throughout Turkey's negotiation process, political actors in the European Parliament principally oriented their political, religious, and geographical categories to the Copenhagen criteria. In other words, political parties in various cases attempted to legitimise their essentially dichotomous arguments about Turkey and the European Union using the accession conditions.

Within the European Parliament, members of the Party of European Socialists, the European Green Party, the European Left, and the Alliance of Liberals and Democrats for Europe discussed Turkey's compliance with European values on the basis of the political accession criteria. They mostly rejected other preconditions. In other words, these camps principally conceptualised the candidate in political terms. In religious terms, they again discussed the situation of religious freedoms and minorities in Turkey in relation to the political accession criteria. When it comes to geographical constructions, these camps presumed Turkey's location to be complementary to the European Union. They used the term 'bridge' in order to signify the candidate's geostrategic contribution to the EU. In contrast, members of the European People's Party and the far-right tended to discuss Turkey's accession to the EU in terms that went beyond the Copenhagen criteria. They, at times, stereotyped the candidate using religious and geographical terms that did not have origins in the EU's legislation.

European conservative political camps claimed that it was a grave mistake to declare Turkey's candidacy in 1999 and to begin negotiations with it in 2005 because the EU had thereby made an official commitment to Turkey's accession. Many believed Turkey's negotiations would automatically lead to the candidate's accession despite their opposition. Conservative parties in national and European politics were obviously worried about such an outcome. In order to avert Turkey's foreseen membership, conservative elites in European politics then attached additional conditions to the existing accession criteria. In particular, the EPP made use of the European Union's 'absorption capacity' as a precondition for Turkey's membership. Conservative members would thus be able to block Turkey's accession at the end of the long negotiation process on the grounds that the European Union was not ready to absorb the candidate. Next, they attempted to introduce alternative scenarios to Turkey's membership, in case the candidate ever fulfilled the existing accession criteria. EPP members and other conservative parliamentarians, except those from Britain, therefore strongly advocated the privileged partnership with Turkey.

In addition to the political camps given above, members of the British Conservative Party (which was an ally of the European People's Party in until 2009) acted remarkably differently from their right-wing European counterparts. In general terms, they supported Turkey's EU membership at the end of the negotiations period and tended to discuss the candidate's compatibility with European values solely through the accession criteria. What had led them to approach Turkey in primarily political terms, unlike the European conservatives? In fact, it is implausible to ground the British Conservatives' apparently 'pro-Turkish' approach merely on statements at the European Parliament. We may assume, rather, that the Tories' position was related to the overall British view, which was critical of European integration but in favour of Turkey's membership. In other words, MEPs also conceptualised the candidate according to their national contexts. As might be expected, the EU's accession criteria had less effect on political discussions about Turkey's EU membership in national politics than in the European Parliament.

Like Britain, France has been influenced in its attitudes to the Turkish candidacy by its unique national characteristics. The French regime since the late 18th century has generated five long-term conditions, which underpin French national thinking about Europe and Turkey. The prime influence of the French Revolution has been the idea of national sovereignty and its legitimising function in French politics. French political actors, whether emperors after the *ancien régime* or republicans of modern France, have often sought to legitimise their power with national elections. The nation has been the pillar of French politics. In 2005, it was once again considered to be the source of legitimacy when most French conservatives campaigned against Turkey's EU membership with references to public opinion. Second, French citizenship was constructed with political means that were aligned with earlier colonialist policies. In the face of immigration, the citizenship law was partially changed in the 1990s but remained an example of the *jus soli* principle. In the 2000s, the conservative and far-right camps were concerned about the labour inflow from Eastern Europe and any future immigration following Turkey's EU membership. Third, the French *laïcité*, the strict type of secularism that the republican regime adopted in history, ultimately constrained the role of religion in politics. It was then not surprising to see that religious conceptualisations about Turkey were relatively restricted in French politics. That being said, arguments linked to *laïcité* also disapproved of the active role of religion in Turkish politics. The next factor was the depiction of France as the origin and pathfinder of European civilisation. The fifth and final factor was the French concern with geopolitics in Europe, which, together with the previous element, led to the French elite having a traditional pro-European position.

In line with these structural factors, a historical argument has marked French politics ever since the establishment of the European Union: The French Republic represented the drive for European integration that was imbued with

French political virtues. However, this traditional standpoint came into question when French voters rejected the proposed EU Constitution on 29 May 2005. The legacies of two structural factors, the priority of national representation and the pro-Europeanism of French political elites, came into conflict with each other after the constitutional referendum. Under these conditions, the pre-given date for membership negotiations with Turkey caused much concern within the French conservatives.

After the constitutional referendum, the French political elites entered a heated debate on whether the EU should begin the accession talks with Turkey. Shortly before the negotiations opened, the French conservatives were discussing the European Union and Turkey on the basis of the principle of national representation, always a prerequisite for the French regime. The conservatives argued that French politicians had to heed public opinion against Turkey's membership before making their arguments about the candidate. They also insisted on a referendum for the beginning of the EU's negotiations with Turkey, since the French nation had rejected the EU Constitution months ago in a similar poll.

Party-based disagreements on Turkey's accession were quite noticeable in French politics. The Socialist Party of France and the Communist Party mostly discussed Turkey in political terms and emphasised the European Union's multi-cultural nature and the candidate's political modernisation. They remained critical of Turkey's progress on a number of matters, including its denial of the Armenian genocide and its problematic relations with Cyprus, yet they favoured Turkey's accession on the assumption that membership would deconstruct the EU's image of being a 'Christian Club'.

The Union for Political Movement (UMP) similarly criticised Turkey's reform process in political terms. But there was more. The conservative ruling party was quite divided on the Turkey debate until the negotiations began. In general terms, the French President Jacques Chirac suggested 'giving a chance to the candidate' although his minister of internal affairs and the leader of the UMP, Nicolas Sarkozy, led the bulk of party members against Turkey's membership. In addition to their political terms, this huge group within the UMP characterised the candidate in geographical and, sometimes, religious terms. In this regard, the rejection of the EU Constitution gave Nicolas Sarkozy the opportunity to propagate his own geographical categorisations of Europe and Turkey. After France rejected the EU Constitution in 2005, the UMP leader concerned himself with maintaining the pace of European integration. In the aftermath of the constitutional failure, the UMP sought to redefine Europe by redrawing its Eastern frontiers and their geographical conception of Europe that a priori excluded Turkey. Finally, Sarkozy and his followers opposed the beginning of the negotiations with Turkey on the grounds that the French public opinion was against the candidate. In the end, despite the opposition and the negative public opinion in France, the French delegation in Europe, under the 'pro-Turkish' President Chirac's leadership, agreed to give the green light to the beginning of the negotiations with the candidate. The friction in France was thus between two mainstream arguments: the first that Turkey should be aligned with European values by means of the membership negotiations with the European Union, the civilisation project led by the French Republic, and the second that Turkey essentially had no place in the European Union.

German perceptions about Turkey in relation to the European Union in 2005 were considered in terms of five conditions. At first, Germany's welfare tradition including social protectionism profoundly influenced the other structural factors and dominated the German politics in this period. Members of the Christian Democratic Union and the Christian Social Union (CDU/CSU) both argued that Turkey's membership would jeopardise German welfare. The second factor, the ethnicity-oriented German citizenship, had been much discussed as a result of immigration to the country and only partially resolved in the 1990s. Until the 2000s, these citizenship debates had partially evolved around the situation of the large existing Turkish migrants in Germany, and the conservatives viewed Turkey's potential EU membership with one eye on the potential for further migration from the candidate. Economic protectionism, one of the primary rationales of German citizenship, therefore emerged, as Turkey-sceptical camps argued that a possible inflow of Turkish migrants would destabilise the German economy, including employment levels and welfare conceptions. Third, the democratic transition in Germany from a totalitarian state to a liberal democracy after 1945 also shaped contemporary political conceptualisations of Turkey's candidature. The press and politicians sometimes made references to Germany's past when discussing Turkey's democratic issues, raising the role of the military in Turkish politics and the need for Turkey to accept responsibility for the Armenian Genocide. Fourth, the politicised nature of religion in Germany also played a role in generating more essentialist conceptualisations of Turkey. Discussions about Turkey's religious differences from the EU were more noticeable in Germany than in France or Britain. Finally, the various European policies of German political parties had formative influences over the arguments about Turkey's EU membership.

The prime examples of the German press in the period shortly before the negotiations' beginning mostly discussed Turkey with regard to the long-term factor of German welfare. They brought to the fore the costs of Turkey's membership and future immigrants from the country. In addition, they reflected on the candidate's democratic issues in the process of implementing EU reforms. Through their statements on the situation of human rights in Turkey, the media highlighted Germany's earlier political transition as a model. Newspapers also pointed at social and political parallelisms between Turkey's integration into the European Union and the integration of the existing Turkish immigrants into Germany. Finally, the traditional premise, that Turkey was not European by its nature, was occasionally mentioned in Germany's conservative newspapers.

Similar arguments occurred within German politics. The federal election on 18 September defined the German political agenda in 2005, and political parties expressed their opinions on Turkey's EU membership within these election debates. The elites of the SPD and Green Party (Alliance '90/The Greens) discussed the candidate from the position of their long-term European policy. The Social Democrats had traditionally advocated promoting democracy and peace in Europe and beyond. Turkey's candidacy was an opportunity to further that aim. They backed the beginning of the membership negotiations with Turkey, which they believed to hasten the candidate's political modernisation. Along with its strategic location, a more democratic Turkey had the potential to play a particular role in the progress of the European zone of peace and democracy. The Social Democrats in Germany tend to see Europe as a multicultural cosmos, which should, categorically, embrace a modernised Turkey. Another consideration for the Social Democrats and the Greens was to attract or retain Turkish voters before the German federal election. Throughout 2005, and particularly in the period before the federal election and the negotiations, the then-coalition between the SPD and the Green Party represented the candidate positively in political, religious, and geographical terms.

By contrast, the Christian Democrats tended to use political, geopolitical, and religious terms in order to marginalise Turkey. In political terms, they linked Turkey's potential membership of the EU to domestic welfare issues. Members of the CDU/CSU insisted that Turkey's EU membership and a possible immigrant inflow from the country would put a major strain on the German welfare system. The party's uncompromising public stand against further immigrants from Turkey seemed to be a logical extension of its earlier anti-immigration policies. The essentially religious and geographical arguments against Turkey that they deployed in 2005 were also not new. The party's traditional stress on religion and its EU vision influenced the Christian Democrats' stance towards Turkey. Their assumptions of Turkey's non-European nature, which they largely linked to its location and Islamic character, inherently excluded the country. In this respect, there were many similarities between the approach adopted towards Turkey by the German and French conservative parties in 2005. In summary, the mainstream arguments during the discussions in Germany were, on one side that Turkey can make a crucial contribution to the European Union's peace and security, and on the other, that the country is essentially not European, and its membership would undermine German and European welfare.

Britain, the term president of the Council of the European Union at that time, was, more than any other EU member, responsible for the beginning of Turkey's membership negotiations on 3 October 2005. British politicians and the public gave remarkable support to the candidate in the 2000s as a result of a number of long-term factors. These factors underpinned a historically distinct national identity of Britain against Europe and exerted strong influences over arguments about Turkey. The first factor was the role of religion in British politics. Religion had a historical significance, as the state for centuries distinctively categorised itself in a religious manner and made use of its official belief in European power politics. At least until the 19th century first England and then Britain instrumentalised its Protestant identity in interfering European affairs against the French rival and preserving the island from Roman Catholic control. Despite this, religion gradually took a back seat in British politics as the 20th century progressed. As a result, very limited references to religion appeared amongst discussions on Turkey's compatibility with European values. Religion did play a role in British categorisations of the candidate when political camps considered the Muslim, yet secular, Turkey to be a model for resolving potential conflicts between religious domains. The second long-term factor, British citizenship, which was first designed with colonialist aspirations, also changed in the face of migration. Amendments to the rules for British citizenship introduced in the late 20th century were mainly the results of the Conservative Party's firm opposition to immigration. This leads us to ask whether the British Conservatives raised the potential immigration issue in 2005 while discussing Turkey. The final structural factor underpinning perceptions about the EU and Turkey was the European policies of the British regime and political parties. Many British actors in 2005 were highly sceptical towards the EU's further political integration, in line with the United Kingdom's traditional foreign policy. It was thus believed that the accession of Turkey would hamper the EU's integration process and this would be in Britain's interests.

The British press mostly reflected this last point. The leading newspapers between September and early October explicitly stated that the British government's support for Turkey's EU bid was in agreement with the long-term British opposition to European political integration. News and commentaries published in this term highlighted, together, the growing Euroscepticism in Britain, the country's term presidency at the Council of the European Union, and the British government's commitments to secure the pre-given date for Turkey's membership negotiations. The British press largely welcomed the accession talks' beginning on 3 October, although they were also critical of the current pace of the candidate's political modernisation.

British political elites expressed similar characteristics to the media. Political camps first of all prioritised their long-term European policies, rather than common 'European values', in their attitudes towards Turkey. British parties that contain a broad spectrum of Euroscepticism pragmatically approached and welcomed the idea of the EU's enlargement with Turkey. The two primary examples were the Labour Party and the British Conservative Party, which were at odds with each other on the EU Constitution but concurred on Turkey's EU membership. Party elites discussed Turkey in the political terms originating from the EU's accession criteria. Politicians from both parties argued that European actors should not impose any further conditions on the candidate other than the existing accession criteria. The membership negotiations with Turkey would bind the candidate closer to Europe's common political standards and would foster its political modernisation, a process that British politicians saw as of strategic importance for the European Union. In this regard, British politicians conceptualised Turkey's modernisation in political, religious and geographical terms. Turkey was commonly described as being an example of 'moderate/democratic' Islam and acting as a 'bridge' between various religious and geographical domains. A modernised Turkey, as an EU member, could play a role in resolving the 'clash of civilisations'. Between September and early October, the British government and political parties backed Turkey's EU candidature from these perspectives and engaged in a lively debate with European conservative governments. In a nutshell, a mainstream argument emerged in Britain in 2005, and shortly before the negotiations' beginning: Turkey, at the end of its modernisation, can contribute to the European Union's peace and security, and its membership would play into British interests in Europe. With these justifications, the British government backed the beginning of the accession talks with Turkey during their term presidency and stood against the conservative Austrian government, which aimed to block the negotiations' beginning.

Similarities and differences between French, German, and British public opinions on Turkey's EU bid entail also demand attention. In France and Germany, conservative parties added geographical and religious terms to the political vocabulary when discussing Turkey. In Britain, the conservatives focused more on the EU's accession criteria and publicly supported the candidate. Given their pro-Turkish statements at the European Parliament, it appears that the British Conservatives strongly approved of the candidate in both European and national politics; their stance was in contrast with French and German conservatives. This can be explained by long-term conditions within British politics.

The national contexts of France, Germany and Britain affected the accession debates in ways unique to those countries. The dominant factor in French politics in 2005 was the republican ideology long represented by the regime. Shortly before the beginning of the membership negotiations with Turkey, French conservatives argued against the candidate on the principle of national representation. They called for a referendum on the start of the membership negotiations with Turkey, in both France and Europe, where the majority were against the candidate. It was a similar case in Germany. German conservative leaders campaigned against the beginning of the membership negotiations by pointing out the Turkey-sceptic public opinion in Germany and Europe. The ruling factor in German politics was the welfare system, which the conservatives considered to be under threat from Turkey's EU membership. In Britain, welfare also had a general importance for the British Conservative Party, as their economic concerns were one factor responsible for their long-term anti-immigration stance. Despite this, welfare considerations did not influence British conservatives' opinion about Turkey's EU membership. Instead, the historically important factor, Britain's scepticism towards the EU's political integration, was at the forefront of the British conservatives' overt and pragmatic support for Turkey's EU membership. In parallel, as German and French political camps prioritised their conceptions of 'common European values' while discussing Turkey's EU membership, in 2005, the British rather pragmatically approached the candidate in line with their long-term attitude against the ever-closer European Union.

Structural factors also influenced the media coverage of Turkey in the three countries between September and early October 2005. The conservative media in France and Germany commonly stood against Turkey's EU membership. Economic concerns and questions about Turkey's European nature were the prime factors here. News and commentaries published in Le Figaro, a leading conservative paper in France, uncompromisingly disapproved the beginning of the membership negotiations with Turkey. In Germany, reports published in the conservative Die Welt and Die Frankfurter Allgemeine Zeitung similarly opposed Turkey's EU membership negotiations. They sometimes described Turkey with the presumption that it was not essentially European. The French press also argued that recognition of the Armenian Genocide should be a precondition for the candidate's accession. The German media paid more attention to the economic impacts of Turkey's membership. In contrast to the French and German press, British journals in their reporting on Turkey were almost unanimous that the candidate deserved to start membership negotiations. News and commentaries published in the British press media during the period explicitly justified their support for Turkey's membership as being in Britain's interests against further European political integration.

Turkey's membership bid influenced the election debates in all three countries. Political camps, officially or unofficially, drew arguments about Turkey's EU membership into the federal election campaign in Germany, the parliamentary election in Britain (both in 2005) and the presidential election in France (two years later). In Britain, both the Labour and the Conservative Parties declared their open support for Turkey's EU membership prior to the parliamentary election on 5 May 2005. In Germany, Turkey's membership application was more than a matter concerning European affairs. The Social Democratic Party and the Green Party both hoped to maintain their traditional support from the voters of Turkish origin. In this case, the Christian Democrats and conservative press in Germany claimed that the two parties were publicly backing Turkey's EU membership in order to lure these voters. On the other hand, the Christian Democrats' election campaign wholly opposed Turkey's accession bid. Conservative election candidates justified their opposition by arguing that Germans needed to know more about the new European Union after Turkey's accession. In France, the next poll was the presidential election in 2007, but this was also linked to the earlier debate about Turkey. The competition between presidential candidates impacted on the discussions about Turkey shortly before the accession talks' beginning. The French party leaders that stood for the presidential election publicly discussed the issue of Turkey's EU membership and used it to further their political interests. In particular, Nicolas Sarkozy regarded uncertainty about Europe's eastern borders as an issue that required resolving and, in this regard, expressed his opposition to Turkey's EU membership in geographical terms during his pre-campaign term.

Election campaigns suggest that the concerns about immigration were common among conservative and nationalist politicians in all three countries in 2005. For decades these camps had been claiming that immigration posed a threat to their national economies. In 2005, when the EU's accession talks with Turkey were about to start, they linked the candidate's membership to the immigration issue. In France, it was mostly the National Front who campaigned against the prospect of migration from Turkey. In Germany, the Christian Democrats claimed that any further Turkish migration would harm the German welfare system and cited the poor social and economic integration of the existing Turkish community within Germany. In Britain, the British Conservatives had been opposed to immigration for decades but peculiarly did not focus much on migration issues that might stem from Turkey's future EU membership. This was to change remarkably in 2016, ahead of the Brexit referendum, when parts of conservative camps in Britain, spearheaded by the UK Independence Party and a minority in British Conservative Party, used migration from Turkey as an object of fear, in an attempt to mobilise masses to vote no in the referendum. But at least in 2005, the conventional attitudes of the conservatives against migration did not dominate British politics favouring Turkey's EU bid.

Finally, two themes appeared to be commonly discussed in both countries. At first, political camps that favoured Turkey's accession stressed the country's security contribution to Europe with its famous bridge function. *Bridge* was a concept that appeared during plenaries in the European Parliament and was also used in national politics. Politicians supporting Turkey's accession bid used the term to conceptualise the candidate positively in geographical and religious terms. The concept 'bridge' had two connotations: on the one hand, it referred to Turkey's strategic location, straddling Europe and the Islamic world. Yet, there was also a religious implication of a Turkey: The country dominated by Islamic belief was categorically secular. In this respect, the candidate could become a model of democracy for its Muslim neighbours. Furthermore, the most likely alternative to Turkey's secularism would be Islamic extremism. British pro-Turkish politicians were highly concerned about the possibility of Turkey's further Islamisation if the EU put the accession talks on hold.

A related theme was Turkey's modernisation. Socialists in France and Germany and the mainstream parties in the United Kingdom all contended that the EU's membership negotiations would help accelerate Turkey's political modernisation. In France, this transition signified the extension of European and, essentially, French historic political values. German actors described Turkey's modernisation as a necessary transition to European values from the present illiberal practices that were nationally and religiously motivated. They held up Germany, which underwent a similar political change after the Second World War, as a model country. In Britain, Turkey's modernisation was more seen as having a cultural significance; its political transition could provide the linkage between Islam, on the one hand, and western-type democracy and religious pluralism, on the other. In the British view, Turkey's modernisation and EU membership could be a strategic benefit to the EU by helping to prevent a potential clash of civilisations in Europe. In summary, the political actors in national politics who mentioned Turkey's 'bridge function' and political modernisation tended to see the European Union as a source of multiculturalism, which Turkey's accession could potentially strengthen in political, religious, and geographical terms.

In 2005 Europeans entered a lively debate over Turkey's EU bid, or more strictly speaking, Turkey's compatibility with European values, in terms that originated from two sources: EU legislation, in particular the accession criteria, and the national politics of member states. Political actors at the European level largely discussed the issue of Turkey's compatibility with European values on the basis of the accession criteria, and members of the European Parliament mostly used a language justified by EU legislation. Still, there were many instances in which deputies revealed the influences of their national contexts. They conceptualised the EU and Turkey using values constructed in history, together with their national interests, even if they made references to the accession criteria. Second, the political elites in France, Germany, and Britain formed their arguments about Turkey around a number of decisive historical factors, most notably public opinion (and the principle of national representation), conceptions of welfare, and the political parties' European policies (being pro-European or Euro-sceptic). In France, the Turkey-sceptic conservatives mostly raised political and geographical arguments, and also religious arguments to a lesser extent, and claimed that the French nation was already against the candidate's EU membership with the same arguments. In Germany, the conservatives excluded Turkey from Europe in political, religious, and geographical terms and added that its accession to the EU would destabilise German welfare. In Britain, the conservatives instead joined the social democrats in backing Turkey's EU membership, which they believed to play into the long-term British interests in Europe.

A particular aspect of the prolonged contestations over Turkey's EU bid is the historical images of the candidate understood in Europe. How these images contributed to the fading accession prospects of Turkey remains in question today. This book has pointed out the importance of historical inquiries to the contemporary Turkey-EU relationship and attempted to shed light on the role of history in a political debate provoked by the start of the membership negotiations. But the later period begs the same question, how the old stereotypes exacerbated the relations between Turkey and the EU that were persistently strained after 2005. This raises the question of how Turkey and the EU estranged themselves throughout the accession talks and how the accession prospects of Turkey abated in time.[3] True, Turkey is responsible for the failing negotiation process due to its disinclination to democratise and to comply with the EU's accession criteria. But European conservative parties should also be held responsible, for their fierce oppositions to the candidate and their moves to marginalise it religiously and geographically still had a role in this outcome. All in all, Turkey's past has undeniably strong relevance to its conceptualisations in contemporary European politics, and, as this book suggests, further historical insights into this relevance should be provided.

---

3 For example, see Paul Levin, 'Who Lost Turkey? The Consequences of Writing an Exclusionary European History', in *History and Belonging: Representations of the Past in Contemporary European Politics*, eds. Caner Tekin and Stefan Berger (New York: Berghahn Books, 2018), 152–173.

Bibliography

Documents of European Institutions

Adonnino, Pietro. A People's Europe, Reports from the Ad Hoc Committee, Bulletin of the European Communities, no.7, 1985.

Agreement, Establishing an Association between the European Economic Community and Turkey (signed at Ankara, 12 September 1963), Official Journal of European Communities O.J. C113, December 24, 1973.

Commission of European Communities, 2004 Regular Report on Turkey's Progress towards Accession, Brussels, SEC(2004)1201, Brussels, October 06.

Commission of European Communities, Communication from the Commission to the Council and the Parliament on the Association Agreements with the countries of Central and Eastern Europe, Com(90) 398 Final, August 27, 1990.

Commission of European Communities, Negotiating Framework, Luxembourg, October 3, 2005.

Commission of European Communities, Opinion on Greek application for membership (transmitted to the Council by the Commission on 29 January 1976, Bulletin of the European Communities, no.2, February 1976.

Commission of European Communities, Progress report of Turkey, SEC(2005)1426, November 9, 2005.

Commission of European Communities, Turkey 2005 Progress Report, Brussels, SEC(2005) 1426, Brussels, November 9, 2005, 33. Turkey 2006 Progress Report, SEC(2006) 1390, Brussels, November 8, 2006.

Commission of European Communities, Turkey 2005 Progress Report, Brussels, SEC(2005) 1426, Brussels, November 9, 2005.

Commission of European Communities. Communication from the Commission to the Council and the European Parliament, Recommendation of the European Commission on Turkey's Progress towards Accession, COM(2004) 656 final. Brussels, October 6, 2004.

Commission of the European Communities, Commission Opinion on Turkey's Request for Accession to the Community, SEC(89), 2290 final 1989.

Commission of the European Communities, European Union Report by Leo Tindemans to the European Council, Bulletin of the European Communities, Supplement 1/76, 1975.

Commission of the European Communities, Negotiating Framework, Luxembourg, October 3, 2005.

Commission of the European Communities, Recommendation of the Commission on Turkey's Progress Towards Accession, 8, 10.

Commission of the European Communities, Recommendation of the Commission on Turkey's Progress Towards Accession, Com2004 0656, 2004.

Consolidated Versions of the Treaty on European Union, Official Journal of European Union 55, C326, 2012.

Consolidated Versions of the Treaty on European Union, Official Journal of European Union 55, C326, 2012.

Consolidated Versions of the Treaty on European Union, Official Journal of European Union 55, C326, 2012.

Council of the European Union, Enlargement: Turkey. Declaration by the European Community and its Member States, Document 12541/05, September 21, 2005.
Council of the European Union, Presidency Conclusions, Brussels European Council, 14/15.12.2006, 16879/1/06 REV 1 CONCL 3, Brussels, February 12, 2007.
Council of the European Union, Presidency Conclusions, Copenhagen European Council, 21–22 June, 1993, SN 180/1/93.
Council of the European Union, Presidency Conclusions, Helsinki European Council, Press Release, Brussels, December 11, 1999, 0300/99.
Council of the European Union, Presidential Conclusions, The Luxembourg European Council, December 12–13, 1997.
Enlargement Report for Turkey, European Parliament Resolution on the 2011 Progress Report on Turkey, P7_TA(2012)0116 B7–0189/2012, March 29, 2012.
Europe Agreement Establishing an Association between the European Communities and their Member States, of the One Part, and the Republic of Poland, of the Other Part, Official Journal of the European Communities O.J. L348, December 16, 1991.
European Commission Directorate General for Enlargement, Good to Know about EU Enlargement (Brussels: Publication Office, 1999).
European Commission. Commission of the European Communities, The 2004 Progress Report on Bulgaria's Progress Towards Accession, SEC(2004) 1199, October 6, 2004.
European Community, Declaration on Democracy, Bull. EC 3–1978.
European Council, Solemn Declaration on European Union, Bulletin of the European Communities, no.6 June 1983.
European Parliament, Amendments 1–343 for Draft Report on Turkey's progress towards Accession 2006, PE 376.373v02–00, July 4, 2006.
European Parliament Resolution of 21 May 2008 on Turkey's 2007 Progress Report, P6_TA(2008)0224, A6–0168/2008 Strasbourg, May 21, 2008.
European Parliament, Amendments, 1–151, on Croatia's 2006 Progress Report, PE 384.604v01–00, March 1, 2007.
European Parliament, Amendments 1–156, for the 2006 Progress Report on the Former Yugoslav Republic of Macedonia, PE 388.550v01–00, May 11, 2007.
European Parliament, Amendments 1–236 for the Draft Motion for a Resolution, PE393.947v02–00, September 25, 2007.
European Parliament, Amendments 1–184, on the 2007 Progress Report on the Former Yugoslav Republic of Macedonia, 2007/2268(INI), February, 12, 2008.
European Parliament, Amendments 1–162 for the Draft Motion for a Resolution, PE404.587v01–00, April 7, 2008.
European Parliament, Amendments 1–188 for the Draft Motion for Resolution, PE416.543v01–00, January 7, 2009.
European Parliament, Amendments 1–149 for the Draft Motion for Resolution, PE430.291v01–00, November 9, 2009.
European Parliament, Amendments 1–243 for the Draft Motion for a Resolution, PE431.004v02–00, January 1, 2010.
European Parliament, Amendments 1–315 for the Draft Motion for a Resolution, PE456.654v02–00, January 25, 2011.
European Parliament, Amendments 1 – 461 for the Draft Motion for a Resolution on the 2011 Progress Report on Turkey, PE478.719v01–00, February 1, 2012.

European Parliament, Amendments 1–207 for the Draft Motion for Resolution on the 2012 Progress Report of Turkey, PE504.377v01–00, February 12, 2013.

European Parliament, Amendments 208–415 for the Draft Motion for Resolution on the 2012 Progress Report of Turkey, Part II, PE.504.402v01–00, February 12, 2013.

European Parliament, Amendments 1–200 for Draft motion for a resolution on the 2013 Progress Report on Turkey, PE526.229v01–00, January 13, 2014.

European Parliament, Resolution on a Political Solution to the Armenian Question, Official Journal of the European Communities, Doc. A2, July 7, 1987.

European Parliament, Report of the Committee on External Economic Relations on a General Outline for Association Agreements with the Countries of Central and Eastern Europe. Session Documents 1991, A3–0055/91, March 13, 1991.

European Parliament, Draft Report on Turkey's progress towards accession, PE 374.360v03–00, A6–0269/2006, September 13, 2006.

European Parliament, European Parliament Critical of Slowdown in Turkey's Reform Process, Press Service 20060922IPR10896, September 27, 2006.

European Parliament, European Parliament Resolution on Turkey's Progress towards Accession, P6_TA(2006)0381, Strasbourg, September 27, 2006.

European Parliament, Motion for a Resolution on EU-Turkey Relations, PE 396.011v01–00, B6–0376/2007, October 15, 2007.

European Parliament, Report On Turkey's Progress 2007 Progress Report, PE 402.879v02–00, A6–0168/2008, April 28, 2008.

European Parliament, Motion for Resolution on Turkey's Progress Report 2009, PE430.695v02–00, December 8, 2009.

European Parliament, European Parliament Resolution of 9 March 2011 on Turkey's 2010 Progress Report, P7_TA(2011)0090, March 9, 2011.

European Parliament, European Parliament Resolution of 29 March 2012 on the 2011 Progress Report on Turkey, P7_TA(2012)0116, Brussels, March 29, 2012.

European Parliament, European Parliament resolution of 10 February 2010 on Turkey's progress report 2009, P7_TA(2010)0025, B7–0068/2010, February 10, 2010.

European Parliament, European Parliament, European Parliament resolution on the 2004 regular report and the recommendation of the European Commission on Turkey's progress towards accession, P6_TA(2004)0096, A6–0063/2004, December 15, 2004.

The Charter of the Fundamental Rights of the European Union, Official Journal of European Union 55, C326, 2012.

The Council of the European Union, Corrigendum to Council Regulation (EC) No 866/2004 of 29 April 2004: on a regime under Article 2 of Protocol 10 to the Act of Accession, Official Journal of the European Union, L 161 (30.04.2004).

The European Community, Agreement Establishing an Association between the European Economic Community and Turkey, (signed at 12.09.1963), Official Journal of the European Communities, vol.16.c113, December 24, 1973.

'Document on the European Identity Published by the Nine Foreign Ministers, Copenhagen, 14 December 1973', European Political Cooperation Fifth Edition (Bonn: Press and Information Office, 1988).

'Overview ECHR 1959–2016', European Court of Human Rights Public Relations Unit, March 2017, available from www.echr.coe.int/Documents/Overview_19592016_ENG.pdf (12.08.2017).

Election Programmes and other Documents of pan-European and National Political Parties

Alternative Für Deutschland, Programm für Deutschland. Das Grundsatzprogramm der Alternative für Deutschland.
Christian Democratic Union, Ahlener Programm, Zonenausschuß der CDU für die britische Zone, Ahlen, Westfalen, February 3, 1947.
Convention de l'UMP sur l'Europe les 23 et 24 septembre 2005, Paris, September 23–24, 2005, Les Républicains official website, http://soutenir.republicains.fr/sites/default/files/fichiers_joints /dates_cles/discours_valery_giscard_destaing.pdf.
EU Democrats. Political Demands for EU Reform, June, 2007.
European Alliance for Freedom. Political Party Manifesto, European Elections 2014
European Democratic Party. From the Crisis in Europe to Renewed European Hope Time for Rebuilding, Manifesto of the European Democratic Party, February 28, 2014.
European Liberal Democrat and Reform Part.y European Liberals' Top 15 for EP Elections, ELDR Manifesto for the European Elections 2009.
European Liberal Democrat and Reform Party. ELDR Manifesto 2004 European Parliamentary Elections, Amsterdam, November 14, 2003.
European Liberal Democrat and Reform Party. ELDR Manifesto for the European Elections 2009, Stockholm, October 31, 2008.
European Liberal Democrat and Reform Party. ELDR Manifesto, 2004 European Parliamentary Elections, Approved in Amsterdam, November 14, 2003
European Liberal, Democrat and Reform Party, European Liberals' Top 15 for EP Elections, Manifesto for the European Elections 2009, Adopted at the Stockholm Congress, October 31, 2008.
European People's Party. A Europe of Opportunities, EPP Election Manifesto, 1999. European People's Party, The EPP: Your Majority in Europe, EPP Election Manifesto, February 4–5, 2004.
European People's Party. EPP Action Programme: 2014–2019.
European People's Party. Strong for the People, EPP Manifesto-European Elections, 2009.
European People's Party. Why Vote for the Political Family of the European People's Party? EPP Manifesto, May 22–24, 2014.
European People's Party. 'A Union of Values', Basic Document Adopted by the Fourteenth EPP Congress in Berlin on 11–13 January 2001, cited in Jansen, At Europe's Service.
Free Democratic Party, Wahlprogrammzur Bundestagswahl 2005 der Freien Demokratischen Partei, 'Arbeit hat Vorfahrt. Deutschlandprogramm 2005', Berlin, 2005.
Le Front national. Programme électoral du Front national aux élections européennes 2004, May 26, 2004.
Party of European Socialists. Manifesto for Elections, June 2009.
Party of the European Left. The Statue of the Party of the European Left, adopted at the Founding Congress of the European Left in Rome, September 5, 2014, with the amendments approved by the 2nd Congress in Prague, November 23–25, 2007, and by the 3rd Congress in Paris, December 5, 2010.
Party of the European Left. Together for Change in Europe, Manifesto for European Elections, October 28, 2009.
Party of the European Left. United for a Left Alternative in Europe, European Left Election Manifesto, 2004.

Schuman, Robert, Schuman Declaration, June 9, 1950.
Scottish Liberal Democrats. Stronger Together Poorer Apart, The Liberal Democrat Manifesto for the 2009 Elections to the European Parliament, 2009.
Social Democratic Party of Germany, Godesberger Programm: Grundsatzprogramm der Sozialdemokratischen Partei Deutschlands, November 13–15, 1959.
Social Democratic Party of Germany, Political manifesto of the Social Democratic Party of Germany, Hanover, May 11, 1946.
The British Conservative Party. Vote for Change: European Election Manifesto, Manifesto for European Elections, 2009. Liberal Democrats, Stronger Together Poorer Apart.
The Conservative and Unionist Party. 'It's Time for Action', Conservative Election Manifesto 2005.
The European Green Party. Manifesto for the 2004 European Elections, Fourth European Greens Congress, Rome, 20–22 February, 2004.
The Labour Party. 'Britain Forward not Back'. Manifesto 2005.
The Liberal Democrats. Liberal Democrat General Election Manifesto: Freedom, Justice, Honesty, 2001.
The Liberal Democrats. The Real Alternative Election Manifesto, 2005.
UK Independence Party, 'Create an Earthquake'. UKIP Manifesto 2014.
United Green Parties of Europe. A Green New Deal for Europe, Manifesto for the European Election Campaign, 2009. European Green Party, Change Europe, Vote Green, the Common Manifesto, 2014.

Debates in the European Parliament

Debate on Accession Partnership with Turkey, Strasbourg, February 14, 2001.
Debate on Turkey's Application for EU Membership, Strasbourg, July 4, 2003.
Debate on Turkey's Progress towards Accession, Strasbourg, December 13, 2004.
Debate on Opening of Negotiations with Turkey – Additional Protocol to the EEC-Turkey Association Agreement, Strasbourg, September 28, 2005.
Debate on Turkey's Progress Towards Accession, Strasbourg, September 26, 2006.
Debate on Women in Turkey, Strasbourg, February 12, 2007.
Debate on EU-Turkey Relations, Strasbourg, October 24, 2007
Debate on Turkey's 2007 Progress Report, Strasbourg, May 21, 2008.
Debate on 2009 Progress Report on Croatia, 2009 Progress Report on the Former Yugoslav Republic of Macedonia – 2009 Progress Report on Turkey, Strasbourg, February 10, 2010
Debate on Democratic Process in Turkey, Strasbourg, May 5, 2009.
Debate on Croatia: progress report 2008 – Turkey: progress report 2008 – Former Yugoslav Republic of Macedonia: progress report 2008, Strasbourg, May 11, 2009.
Debate on Enlargement Strategy 2009 Concerning the Countries of the Western Balkans, Iceland and Turkey, Strasbourg, November 25, 2009.
Debate on Democratization in Turkey, Strasbourg, January 20, 2010.
Debate on 2010 Progress Report on Turkey, Strasbourg, May 8, 2011.
Debate on 2020 perspective for women in Turkey, Strasbourg, May 21, 2012.
Debate on Enlargement report for Turkey, Brussels, March 28, 2012.
Debate on Situation in Turkey, Strasbourg, June 12, 2013.

Debate on 2012 Progress Report on Turkey, Strasbourg, April 18, 2013.
Debate on 2013 Progress Report on Turkey, Strasbourg, March 11, 2014.
Debate on 2013 progress report on Turkey, Strasbourg, March 12, 2014

Speeches

Franco Maria Malfatti, President of the European Commission, at the Signing of the Acts of Accession. Brussels, 22 January 1972. Bulletin of the European Communities, The Enlarged Community: Outcome of the Negotiations with the Applicant States, Supplement 1, 1972.
Helmut Kohl, Address given by Helmut Kohl to the Bundestag, Bonn, 13 December 1991, Centre Virtuel de la Connaissance sur l'Europe, http://www.cvce.eu/obj/address_given_by_helmut_kohl_on_the_outcome_of_the_maastricht_european_council_bonn_13_december_1991-en-12090399-dc71-42ee-8a3d-daf2420c0a9a.html (12.06.2017).
Margaret Thatcher, 'Speech to The First International Conservative Congress', September 28, 1997, www.margaretthatcher.org/document/108374. (10.10.2017).
Olli Rehn, Strategy Paper at EP Plenary, Strasbourg, November 25, 2009, Speech/09/555.
Romano Prodi, Speech in the European Parliament: 2000–2005: Shaping the New Europe, European Parliament, Strasbourg, 15 February, 2000, SPEECH/00/41
Tony Blair, 'Full text: Tony Blair's Speech to the European Parliament', The Guardian, June 23, 2005.

Opinion Polls

European Commission, Eurobarometer 56 Public Opinion in the European Union October-November 2001
European Commission, Eurobarometer 56.2: Radioactive Waste, Demographic Issues, the Euro, and European Union Enlargement, October-November 2001.
European Commission, Eurobarometer 63.4: Public Opinion in the European Union, National Report Executive Summary: Germany, Spring 2005.
European Commission, Eurobarometer 63.4, Public Opinion in the European Union, Executive Summary: Turkey, European Commission Public Opinion Analysis 63, no.4 Spring 2005.
European Commission, Special Eurobarometer 214, The Future Constitutional Treaty, European Commission Public Opinion Analysis 214, March 2005.
Eurobarometer 64: Public Opinion in the European Union, Autumn 2005.
European Commission, *Eurobarometer 69: 1. Values of Europeans*, November 2008.

Other Documents

l'Assemblée nationale, Déclaration des droits de l'homme et du citoyen du 26 août 1789.

Cairo Declaration on Human Rights in Islam, August 5, 1990, U.N. GAOR, World Conference on Humanitarian Rights, 4th Session, Agenda Item 5, U.N. Doc. A/CONF.157/PC/62/Add.18, 1993.
Grundgesetz für die Bundesrepublik Deutschland vom 23. Mai 1949.
House of Commons Hansard Debates 428, December 20, 2004.
House of Commons Hansard Debates 436, July 19, 2005.
House of Commons Hansard Debates 436, July 30, 2005.
House of Commons, Hansard Debates 437, October 11, 2005.
House of Commons Hansard Debates 438, November 1, 2005.
House of Commons Hansard Debates 439, November 23, 2005.
Le Gouvernement provisoire de la République française, Ordonnance du 9 août 1944 relative au rétablissement de la légalité républicaine sur le territoire continental, JORF (d'Alger), no. 65, August 10, 1944.
Public disclosure to North Atlantic Organization: 'Statement by M. Guy Mollet On Algeria', Item RDC(57)15, January 10, 1957.
Transparency International, Transparency International Corruption Perceptions Index 2012.

Bibliography

A. R. Gibb, Hamilton, *Studies on the Civilization of Islam*. Boston: Beacon Press, 1968.
Adamson, Fiona B. 'Democratization and the Domestic Sources of Foreign Policy: Turkey in the 1974 Cyprus Crisis'. *Political Science Quarterly* 116, no.2 (2001): 295–296, 297, doi:10.2307/798062.
Adanir, Fikret. 'Turkey's Entry into the Concert of Europe'. *European Review* 13, no.4 (2005): 395–417, doi:10.1017/S1062798705000530.
Agathocleous, Tanya. *Urban Realism and the Cosmopolitan Imagination in the Nineteenth Century: Visible City, Invisible World.* New York: Cambridge University Press, 2011.
Agnew, John. *Geopolitics: Re-Visioning World Politics.* London and New York: Routledge, 1998.
Agoston, Gabor, and Bruce Masters. *Encyclopedia of the Ottoman Empire.* New York: Facts on File, 2009.
Aksoy, Sevilay. 'The Prospect of Turkey's EU Membership as Represented in the British Newspapers The Times and The Guardian, 2002–2005', *Journal of European Studies* 39, no.4 (2009): 469–506, doi: 10.1177/0047244109344801.
Aksu, Esref. 'Perpetual Peace: A Project by Europeans for Europeans?' *Peace & Change: A Journal of Peace Research* 33, no:3 (2008): 368–387, doi: http://10.1111/j.1468–0130.2008.00503.x.
Alexander, John T. Catherine the Great: Life and Legend. New York: Oxford University Press, 1989.
Alexandrova Petya, and Arco Timmermans. 'National Interest versus the Common Good: The Presidency in European Council Agenda Setting'. *European Journal of Political Research* 52, no.3 (May 2013): 316–338, doi: http://10.1111/j.1475–6765.2012.02074.x.
Anastasakis, Othon. 'The EU's Political Conditionality in the Western Balkans: Towards a More Pragmatic Approach'. *South East European and Black Sea Studies* 8, no.4 (December 2008): 365–377, doi:10.1080/14683850802556384.

Andersen, Niels Åkerstrøm. *Discoursive Analytical Strategies: Understanding Foucault, Koselleck, Laclau, Luhmann*. Bristol: The Policy Press, 2003.

Anderson, Benedict. *Imagined Communities: Reflections on the Origin and Spread of Nationalisms*. New York: Verso, 1991.

Arikan, Harun. *Turkey and the EU: An Awkward Candidate for Membership?* Hampshire: Ashgate Publishing Limited, 2006.

Arts, Will, and Loek Halman, eds. *European Values at the Turn of the Millennium*. Leiden: Brill, 2004.

Arts, Will, and Loek Halman. *Value Contrasts and Consensus in Present-Day Europe*. Leiden: Brill, 2014.

Arts, Will, Jacques Hagenaars, and Loek Halman, eds. *The Cultural Diversity of European Unity: Findings, Explanations and Reflections from the European Values Study*. Leiden: Brill, 2003.

Arvanitopoulos, Constantine. *Turkey's Accession to the European Union: An Unusual Candidacy*. Heidelberg: Springer Verlag, 2009.

Aybet, Gulnur, and Meltem Muftuler Bac, 'Transformations in Security and Identity after the Cold War: Turkey's Problematic Relationship with the EU'. *International Journal* 55, no.4 (Autumn, 2000): 567–582, doi:10.2307/40203501.

Aydin, Ali Ihsan. 'Imagining the EU in the Turkish Mirror'. In *Turkey's Accession to the European Union: An Unusual Candidacy*, ed. Constantine Arvanitopoulos, 171–182. Berlin and Heidelberg: Springer, 2009.

Aydin-Duzgit, Senem. *Constructions of European Identity, Debates and Discourses on Turkey and the EU*. Basingstoke: Palgrave Macmillan, 2012.

Baker, David, Andrew Gamble, Nick Randall, and David Seawright. 'Euroscepticism in the British Party System: "A Source of Fascination, Perplexity, and Sometimes Frustration"'. In *Opposing Europe? The Comparative Party Politics of Euroscepticism*, eds. Aleks Szczerbiak and Paul Taggart, 93–116. Oxford: Oxford University Press, 2008.

Balfour, Michael. *Germany: The Tides of Power*. London and New York: Routledge, 2004.

Banchoff, Thomas. 'German Identity and European Integration'. *European Journal of International Relations* 5, no3 (Sept. 1999): 259–289, doi: 10.1177/1354066199005003001.

Banchoff, Thomas. 'German Policy towards the European Union: The Effects of Historical Memory'. *German Politics* 6, no.1 (1997): 60–76, doi: 10.1080/09644009708404464.

Barkin, J. Samuel, and Bruce Cronin. 'The State and the Nation: Changing Norms and the Rules of Sovereignty in International Relations'. *International Organization* 48, no.1 (December 1994): 107–130, http://www.jstor.org/stable/2706916.

Barnard, F. M. 'National Culture and Political Legitimacy: Herder and Rousseau'. *Journal of the History of Ideas* 44, no.2 (April-June 1983): 231–253, doi:10.2307/2709138.

Barysch, Katinka. *What Europeans Think about Turkey and Why*. London: Centre for European Reform, 2007.

Berberi, Carine. 'Scotland's Attitude to the European Constitution: The End of the Pro-European Era?' In *Scotland and Europe, Scotland in Europe*, ed. Gilles Leydier, 270–292. Newcastle: Cambridge Scholars Publishing, 2007.

Berger, Stefan. *The Search for Normality: National Identity and Historical Consciousness in Germany Since 1800*. Oxford: Berghahn Books, 1997.

Berger, Stefan. ed. *Writing National Histories: Western Europe since 1800*. London: Routledge, 1999.
Berger, Stefan. ed. *A Companion to the 19th Century Europe*. Oxford: Blackwell Publishing, 2006.
Berger, Stefan. 'National Historiographies in Transnational Perspective Europe in the Nineteenth and Twentieth Centuries', *Storia Della Storiografia*, no.50 (2006): 3–26.
Berger, Stefan. 'Introduction: Towards a Global History of National Historiographies'. In *Writing the Nation: A Global Perspective*, ed. Stefan Berger, 1–29. Hampshire, Palgrave Macmillan, 2007.
Berger, Stefan. Inventing the Nation: Germany. London and New York: Bloomsbury, 2011.
Berger, Stefan, Mark Donovan, and Kevin Passmore. 'Apologias for the Nation State in Western Europe since 1800'. In *Writing National Histories: Western Europe since 1800*, eds. Stefarn Berger, Mark Donovan, and Kevin Passmore, 3–14. London: Routledge, 1999.
Berger, Stefan, and A. Miller. 'Nation-Building and Regional Integration, C. 1800–1914: The Role of Empires'. *European Review of History: Revue Europeenne d'Historie* 15, no.3 (June 2008): 317–330, doi: 10.1080/13507480802082649.
Berlin, Isaah. *Vico and Herder: Two Studies in the History of Ideas*. London: Chatto &Vindus, 1976.
Bevir, Mark. 'The Errors of Linguistic Contextualism'. *History and Theory* 31, no.3 (1992): 276–298, doi:10.2307/2505371.
Bevir, Mark. 'Mind and Method in the History of Ideas'. *History and Theory* 36, no.2 (1997): 167–189, http://www.jstor.org/stable/2505336.
Bevir, Mark. 'The Role of Contexts in Understanding Explanation'. *Human Studies* 23, (2000): 395–411, doi: 10.1023/A:1005636214102.
Bevir, Mark. 'Contextualism: From Modernist Method to Post-Analytic Historicism'. *Journal of the Philosophy of History* 3, (2009): 211–224, doi: 10.1163/187226309X461506.
Bevir, Mark. 'The Contextualist Approach'. In *The Oxford Handbook of the History of the Modern Philosophy*, ed. George Klosko, 11–23. New York: Oxford University Press, 2009.
Beyers, Jan, and Guido Dierickk. 'The Working Groups of the Council of the European Union: Supranational or Intergovernmental Negotiations?'. *Journal of Common Market Studies* 36, no.3 (September 1998): 289–317, doi: 10.1111/1468–5965.00112.
Biedenkopf, Kurt, Bronislaw Geremek, and Krzysztof Michaleski. *The Spiritual and Cultural Dimension of Europe: Reflection Group Concluding Remarks*. Luxembourg: Office for Official Publications of the European Communities, 2005.
Bilgin, Pinar. 'A Return to 'Civilisational Geopolitics' in the Mediterranean? Changing Geopolitical Images of the European Union and Turkey in the Post-Cold War Era'. *Geopolitics* 9, no.2 (2004): 269–291, doi: 10.1080/14650040490442863.
Bisaha, Nancy. *Creating East and West: Renaissance Humanists and Ottoman Turks*. Philadelphia: University of Pennsylvania Press, 2004.
Blanchard, Pascal, Nicolas Bancel, and Sandrine Lemaire. *La fracture coloniale: La société française au prisme de l'héritage colonial*. Paris: Editions La Découverte, 2006.
Blommaert, Jan. *Discourse: A Critical Introduction*. New York: Cambridge University Press, 2005.

von Bogdandy, Armin. 'Founding Principles of EU Law: A Theoretical and Doctrinal Sketch'. *European Law Journal* 16, no.2 (March,2010): 95–111, doi: http://10.1111/j.1468–0386. 2009.00500.x.

Bogdani, Mirela. *Turkey and the Dilemma of EU Accession: When Religion Meets Politics*. London: Tauris, 2011.

Bohler, Philip, Jacques Pelkmans, and Can Selcuki. 'Who Remembers Turkey's Pre-accession?'. Centre for European Policy Studies Special Report, no.74 (December 2012).

Bohman James, and Matthias Lutz-Bachmann. 'Introduction'. In *Perpetual Peace: Essays on Kant's Cosmopolitan Ideal*, eds. Bohman, James and Matthias Lutz-Bachmann, 1–22. Cambridge: MIT Press, 1997.

Bolukbasi, Deniz, *Turkey and Greece: the Aegean Disputes: A Unique Case in International Law*. London: Cavendish Publishing, 2004.

Bonney, Richard, and David J.B. Trim. 'Introduction'. In *The Development of Pluralism in Modern Britain and France*. eds. Richard Bonney and David J.B. Trim, 15–67. Bern: Peter Lang, 2007.

Bottger, Katrin, and Eva-Maria Maggi. 'German Perceptions'. *Turkey Watch: EU Member States' Perceptions on Turkey's Accession to the EU*, eds. Sait Aksit, Ozgehan Senyuva, and Cigdem Ustun, 22–33. Ankara: Zeplin Iletisim, 2010.

Brady, John S., and Sarah Elise Wiliarty. 'From the Bonn to the Berlin Republic and Beyond: Critical Junctures and the Future of the Federal Republic'. In *The Postwar Transformation of Germany: Democracy, Prosperity, and Nationhood*, eds. John S. Brady, Beverly Crawford, and Sarah Elise Wiliarty, 503–518. Michigan: The University of Michigan Press, 1999.

Brandsma, Gijs Jan and Jens Blomhansen. 'The EU Comitology System: What Role for the Commission?', *Public Administration* 88, no.2 (2010): 496–512, doi: 10.1111/j.1467–9299.2010.01819.x.

Braudel, Fernand. *A History of Civilizations*. Trans. Richard Mayne. New York: Penguin Press, 1994.

Braudel, Fernand. 'Histoire et Science Sociales, la longue durée'. *Annales. Économies, Sociétés, Civilisations* 13, no.4 (1958): 725–753.

Breeze, Ruth. 'Critical Discourse Analysis and its Critics'. *Pragmatics* 21, no.4 (2011): 493–525, doi: 10.1075/prag.21.4.01bre.

Broberg, Morten P. 'Don't Mess with the Missionary Man! On the Principle of Coherence, the Missionary Principle, and the European Union's Development Policy'. In *EU External Relations Law and Policy in the Post-Lisbon Era*, ed. Paul James Cardwell, 181–197. Hague: T.M.C. Asser Press 183, 2012.

Broughton, David. 'The CDU-CSU in Germany: Is There any Alternative?'. In *The Christian Democracy in Europe*, ed. David Hanley, 101–120. London and New York: Cassel Imprint, 1994.

Brubaker, William Rogers. 'The French Revolution and the Invention of Citizenship'. *French Politics and Society* 7, no.3 (1989): 10–49.

Brubaker, William Rogers. 'Immigration, Citizenship, and the Nation-State in France and Germany: A Comparative Historical Analysis'. *International Sociology* 5, no.4 (December 1990), 379–407, doi: 10.1177/026858090005004003.

Brubaker, William Rogers. *Citizenship and Nationhood in France and Germany*. Cambridge, Massachusetts, Harvard University Press, 1992.

Brubaker, William Rogers. *Nationalism Refrained: Nationhood and the National Question in the New Europe*. Cambridge: Cambridge University Press, 1996.
van der Brug, Wouter, and Anthony Mughan. 'Charisma, Leader Effects and Support for Right-wing Populist Parties', *Party Politics* 13, no.1 (2007): 29–51, doi: 10.1177/1354068806071260.
van der Brug, Wouter, Meindert Fennema, and Jean Tillie. 'Anti-immigrant Parties in Europe: Ideological or Protest Vote?' *European Journal of Political Research*, no.37 (2000): 77–102, doi: 10.1111/1475–6765.00505.
Bruter, Michael. *Citizens of Europe: the Emergence of a Mass European Identity*. Hampshire and New York: Palgrave Macmillan, 2005.
Burgh, Hélène de. Sex, Sailors and Colonies: Narratives of Ambiguity in the Works of Pierre Loti. Bern: Peter Lang, 2005.
Burke, Edmund. *The Works of the Right Honourable Edmund Burke: with a Portrait and Life of the Author*. London: Thomas M'lean Haymarket, 1823.
Burke, Edmund. Further Reflections on the Revolution in France. Indianapolis: Liberty Fund, 2012.
Bürgin, Alexander. 'Cosmopolitan Entrapment: The Failed Strategies to Reverse Turkey's EU Membership Eligibility'. *Perspectives* 18, no.2 (2010): 38–50, http://www.jstor.org/stable/ 23616117.
Calligaro, Oriane. *Negotiating Europe: Promotion of Europeanness since the 1950s*. New York: Palgrave Macmillan, 2013.
Campbell, David. *Writing Security: United States Foreign Policy and the Politics of Identity*. Manchester: Manchester University Press, 1992.
Campbell, David. *National Deconstruction: Violence, Identity, and Justice in Bosnia*. Minneapolis, London: University of Minnesota Press, 1998.
Canan-Sokullu, Ebru S, and Cigdem Kentmen. 'Public Opinion Dimension: Turkey in the EU? An Empirical Analysis of European Public Opinion on Turkey's "Protracted" Membership'. In *Fifty Years of EU-Turkey Relations: A Sisyphean Story*, ed. Armagan Emre Cakir, 104–135. Oxon: Routledge, 2011.
Capelo, Roberta. 'Cohesion Policies and the Creation of a European Identity: The Role of Territorial Identity', *Journal of Common Market Studies* 56, no. 3 (2018): 489–502, doi: 10.1111/jcms.12611
Carey, Hillary M. God's Empire. *Religion and Pluralism in the British World, c. 1801–1908*. New York: Cambridge University Press, 2011.
Carey, Seen. 'Undivided Loyalties: Is National Identity an Obstacle to European Integration?' *European Union Politics* 3, no.4 (2002): 387–413, doi: 10.1177/1465116502003004001.
Carr, E.H. *The Twenty Years Crisis*. London: Palgrave, 2001.
Carter, April. *The Political Theory of Global Citizenship*. London and New York: Routledge, 2001.
Casanova, José. 'Religion, European Secular Identities, and European Integration', in *Religion in an Expanding Europe*, eds. Timothy Byrnes and Peter J. Katzenstein, 65–92. New York: Cambridge University Press, 2006.
Casanova, José. 'The Long, Difficult and Torturous Journey of Turkey into Europe and the Dilemmas of European Civilization', *Constellations* 13, no.3 (2006): 234–247, doi: 10.1111/j.1351–0487.2006.00453.x.

Castiglione, Dario. 'Political Identity in a Community of Strangers'. In *European Identity*, eds. Jeffrey T. Checkel and J. Peter Katzenstein, 29–51. New York: Cambridge University Press, 2009.
Castoriadis, Cornelius. *The Imaginary Institution of Society*. Cambridge: Polity Press, 1997.
Catterall, Peter. 'The Party and Religion'. In, Conservative Century: The Conservative Party since 1900, eds. Anthony Seldon and Stuart Ball, 637–670. New York: Oxford University Press, 2011.
Cerutti, Furio. 'Why Political Identity and Legitimacy Matter in the European Union'. In *The Search for a European Identity: Values, Principles, and Legitimacy of the European Union*, eds. Furio Cerutti and Sonia Lucarelli, 3–22. London and New York: Routledge, 2008.
Chadbourne, Richard M. *Ernest Renan*. New York: Twayne Publishers, 1968.
Charles-Louis de Secondat, Baron de La Brède et de Montesquieu. *Persian Letters*, trans. Margaret Mouldon. New York: Oxford University Press, 2008.
Chartier, Roger. *Les origines culturelles de la Révolution française*. Paris, Seuil, 1990.
Chateaubriand, M. Le Vicomt, *Itinéraire de Paris à Jérusalem, Volume I*. Paris: Libraire de Firmin Didot Freres, 1852.
Checkel, Jeffrey T. 'The Europeanization of Citizenship'. In *Transforming Europe, Europeanization and Domestic Change*, eds. Maria Green Cowles, James A. Caporaso, and Thomas Risse-Kappen, 180–197. Ithaca: Cornell University Press, 2001.
Checkel Jeffrey T., and J. Peter Katzenstein. 'Politicization of European Identities'. In *European Identity*, eds. Jeffrey T. Checkel and J. Peter Katzenstein, 1–25. New York: Cambridge University Press, 2009.
Christian, Jorerges, and Jurgen Neyer, 'Transforming Strategic Interaction into Deliberative Problem-Solving: European Comitology in the Foodstuff's Sector'. *European Journal of Public Policy* 4, no.4 (1997): 609–625, doi: 10.1080/135017697344091.
Chryssochoou, Dimitris N. 'Civic Competence and Identity in the European Polity', in *Making European Citizens: Civic Inclusion in a Transnational Context*, eds. Richard Bellamy, Dario Castiglione, and Jo Shaw, 219–237. London and New York: Palgrave Macmillan, 2006.
Churchill, Winston S. *A History of the English-Speaking Peoples: The Great Democracies*. New York: Dodd, Mead, 1958.
Cirakman, Asli. 'From Tyranny to Despotism: The Enlightenment's Unenlightened Image of the Turks'. *International Journal of Middle East Studies* 33, no.3 (2001): 49–68.
Casanova, José. *From the 'Terror of the World' to the 'Sick Man of Europe': European Images of Ottoman Empire and Society from the Sixteenth Century to the Nineteenth*. New York: Peter Lang Publishing, 2005.
Clayton, C. D. *Britain and the Eastern Question: Missolonghi to Gallipoli*. London: University of London Press, 1971.
Clémentin-Ojha, Catherine, and Pierre-Yves Manguin. *A Century in Asia: The History of the École Française D'Extrême-Orient, 1898–2006*. Singapore: Editions Didier Millet, 2007.
Cohen, Joshua. 'Structure, Choice, and Legitimacy: Locke's Theory of the State'. In *The Social Contract Theorists: Critical Essays on Hobbes, Locke, and Rousseau*, ed. Christopher W. Morris, 143–166. Lanham: Rowman Littlefield, 1999.
Cole, Alexandra. 'Old Right or New Right? The Ideological Positioning of Parties of the Far Right'. *European Journal of Political Research*, no.44 (2005): 203–230, doi: 10.1111/j.1475-6765.2005.00224.x.

Conklin, Alice L., Sarah Fishman, and Robert Zaretsky. *France and Its Empire Since 1870.* New York: Oxford University Press, 2011.
Connolly, William E. *Identity/Difference: Democratic Negotiations of Political Paradox.* Minneapolis: University of Minnesota Press: 1991.
Crombez, Christophe. 'Legislative Procedures in the European Parliament'. *British Journal of Political Science* 26, no.2 (1996): 199–228, doi: 10.1017/S0007123400000429.
Croxton, Derek. 'The Peace of Westphalia of 1648 and the Origins of Sovereignty'. *The International History Review* 21, no.3 (1999): 569–591, http://www.jstor.org/stable/ pdf/40109077.pdf?acceptTC=true.
Curtis, Michael. *Orientalism and Islam: Thinkers on the Muslim Government in the Middle East and India.* New York: Cambridge University Press, 2009.
D. Smith, Anthony. *Chosen Peoples: Sacred Sources of National Identity.* New York: Oxford University Press, 2003.
Darling, L.T. 'Ottoman Politics through British Eyes: Paul Rycaut's "The Present State of the Ottoman Empire"'. *Journal of World History* 5, no.1 (1994 Spring): 71–97, http://www.jstor.org/stable/20078582.
Davison, Roderic H. *Essays in Ottoman and Turkish History, 1774–1923: The Impact of the West.* Texas: University of Texas Press, 1990.
Deflem, Matheu, and Fred C. Pampel. 'The Myth of Postnational Identity: Popular Support for Unification'. *Social Forces* 75, no.1 (September 1996): 119–143, doi: 10.2307/2580759.
Delanty, Gerard. Inventing Europe: Idea, Identity, Reality. London: Palgrave Macmillan, 1995.
Delanty, Gerard. 'Fear of Others: Social Exclusion and the European Crisis'. *Social Policy & Administration* 42, no.6 (December 2008): 676–690, doi: 10.1111/j.1467-9515.2008.00631.x.
Delanty, Gerard. *Formations of European Modernity: A Historical and Political Sociology of Europe.* Cham: Palgrave Macmillan, 2019.
Delanty, Gerard, and Chris Rumford. Re*thinking Europe: Social Theory and Implications of Europeanization.* London: Routledge, 2005.
Denitch, Bogdan. *End of Cold War: European Unity, Socialism and the Shift in Global Power.* Minneapolis: University of Minnesota Press, 1990.
Derrida, Jacques. *The Other Heading: Reflections on Today's Europe.* Bloomington, Indianapolis: Indiana University Press, 1992.
Derrida, Jacques. 'Différance'. In *Identity: A reader*, eds. Paul Du Gay, Jessica Evans, and Peter Redman, 87–93.London: Sage Publications, 2000.
Devran, Yusuf. 'The Portrayal of Turkey in the British Media: Orientalism Resurfaced', Insight Turkey 9, no.4 (2010).
Diez, Thomas. 'Europe's Others and Return of Geopolitics'. *Cambridge Review of International Affairs* 17, no.2 (2004): 319–335, doi: 10.1080/0955757042000245924.
Diez, Thomas. 'Constructing the Self and Changing Others: Reconsidering "Normative Power Europe"'. *Millennium-Journal of International Studies* 33, no.3 (2005): 613–636, doi:10.1177/03058298050330031701.
Diez, Thomas. 'Ethical Dimension: Promises, Obligations, Impatience and Delay: Reflections on the Ethical Aspects of Turkey-EU Relations'. In *Fifty Years of EU-Turkey Relations: A Sisyphean Story*, ed., Armagan Emre Cakir, 158–175. Oxon: Routledge, 2011.

Diez, Thomas, and Ian Manners. 'Reflecting on Normative Power Europe', in *Power in World Politics*, eds. Felix Berenskoetter and M.J. Williams, 173–188. London, New York: Routledge, 2007.
van Dijk, Pieter, Godefridus J. H. Hoof, and G. J. H. Van Hoof, *Theory and Practice of the European Convention on Human Rights*. The Hague: Kluwer Law International, 1998.
van Dijk, Teun A., ed., *Discourse Studies: A Multidisciplinary Introduction*. London: Sage Publishing, 2011.
Dittmer, Jason. 'Textual and Discourse Analysis'. In T*he Sage Handbook of Qualitative Geography*, eds. Dydia Delyser, Steve Herbert, Stuart Aitken, Mike Crang, and Linda McDowell, 274–286. London: Sage, 2010.
Donelly, Jack. *Universal Human Rights in Theory and Practice*. Ithaca: Cornell University Press 2013.
Dosemeci, Mehmet. *Debating Turkish Modernity: Civilization, Nationalism, and the EEC*. New York: Cambridge University Press, 2013.
Dribbusch, Heiner, and Peter Birke. *Trade Unions in Germany: Organisation, Environment, Challenges*. Berlin: Friedrich-Ebert-Stiftung, 2012.
Duchêne, Francois. 'Europe's role in world peace'. In *Europe Tomorrow: Sixteen Europeans Look Ahead*, ed. R. Mayne, 32–47. London: Fontana, 1972.
Dudley, Will. *Understanding German Idealism*. London and New York: Routledge, 2007.
Eder, Klaus. 'Remembering National Memories Together: The Formation of a Transnational Identity in Europe'. In *Collective Memory and European Identity: The Effects of Integration and Enlargement*, eds. Klaus Eder and Willfried Spohn, 187–220. Aldershot: Ashgate, 2005.
Egle, Christoph. 'The SPD's Political Preference on European Integration: Always One Step Behind?' In Soc*ial Democracy and European Integration: The Politics of Preference Formation*, ed., Dionyssis G. Dimitrakopoulos 23–50. London and New York: Routledge, 2011.
van Elsuwege, Peter. *From Soviet Republics to EU Member States, A Legal and Political Assessment of the Baltic States' Accession to the EU*. Leiden: Martinus Nishoff, 2008.
Emerson, Michael, Senem Aydin, Julia de Clerck-Sachsse, and Gergana Noutcheva. 'Just What is this Absorption Capacity of the European Union?'. Center for European Policy Studies Policy Brief, no.113 (2006).
Eralp, Atilla. 'The Role of Temporality and Interaction in the Turkey-EU Relationship'. *New Perspectives on Turkey*, no. 40 (2009): 147–168, doi:10.1017/S0896634600005252.
Eriksen, Erik Oddvar. 'The EU: A Cosmopolitan Polity?' *Journal of European Public Policy* 13, no.2 (2006): 252–269, doi: 10.1080/13501760500451683.
Ertuğrul, Kürşad, and Öznur Akcalı Yılmaz, 'The Otherness of Turkey in European Integration'. *Turkish Studies* 19, no.1 (2018): 48–71, doi: 10.1080/14683849.2017.1396895.
Esping-Andersen, Gosta. *The Three Worlds of Welfare Capitalism*. Cambridge: Polity Press, 1990).
Fabbrini, Sergio. 'The European Union and the Puzzle of Parliamentary Government'. *Journal of European Integration* 37, no.5 (2015): 571–586, doi: 10.1080/07036337.2015.1019877.
Fairclough, Norman, Jane Mulderrig, and Ruth Wodak. 'Critical Discourse Analysis'. In *Discourse Studies: A Multidisciplinary Introduction*, ed. Teun A. Van Dijk, 357–378. London: Sage Publishing, 2011.
Faroqhi, Suraiya. Geschichte des Osmanischen Reiches. Munich: C.H. Beck Verlag, 2000.

Faroqhi, Suraiya. *Approaching Ottoman History: An Introduction to the Sources.* Cambridge: Cambridge University Press, 2004.
Faroqhi, Suraiya. *The Ottoman Empire and the World Around It.* London: Tauris, 2006.
Faucompret, Eric, and Jozef Konings. *Turkish Accession to the EU: Satisfying the Copenhagen Criteria.* London and New York: Routledge, 2008.
Favell, Adrian. *Philosophies of Integration: Immigration and the idea of citizenship in France and Britain.* Palgrave Macmillan, Basingstoke, 2001.
Fernández Sebastian, Javiér, and Juan Francisco Fuentes. 'Conceptual History, Memory, and Identity: an Interview with Reinhart Koselleck'. *Contributions to the History of Concepts* 2, no.1 (2006): 99–127.
Feyzioglu, Turhan. *Un Libérateur et Un Modernisateur Génial: Kemal Atatürk.* Ankara: Centre des Recherches Atatürk, 1987.
Fischer, Fritz. *Griff nach der Weltmacht. Die Kriegszielpolitik des kaiserlichen Deutschland 1914/1918.* Düsseldorf: Droste, 1967.
Fischer, Joschka. 'Turkey's European Perspective: The German View'. *Turkish Policy Quarterly* 3, no.3. Fall 2004.
Fligstein, Neil, Alina Polyakova, and Wayne Sandholtz. 'European Integration, Nationalism and European Identity'. *JCMS: Journal of Common Market Studies* 50, no.8 (March 2012): 106–122, doi: http://10.1111/j.1468–5965.2011.02230.x.
Fligstein, Neil. *Euro-clash: the EU, European Identity, and the Future of Europe.* New York: Oxford University Press, 2008.
Forster, Anthony. *Euroscepticism in Contemporary British Politics: Opposition to Europe in the British Conservative and Labour Parties Since 1945.* London: Routlege, 2002.
France, John. *The Crusades and the Expansion of Catholic Christendom, 1000–1714.* London and New York: Routledge, 2005.
Franck, Raphael. 'Why did a majority of French voters reject the European Constitution?'. *European Journal of Political Economy* 21, no.4 (2005): 1071–1076, doi:10.1016/j.ejpoleco.2005.09.004.
Frederick II Von Hohenzollern, *Anti-Machiavel, ou Essai de critique sur le Prince de Machiavel*, published by Voltaire. Amsterdam, 1742.
Freeman, Gary P. 'Migration and the Political Economy of the Welfare State'. *The Annals of the American Academy of Political and Social Science 485*, (1986): 51–63, doi: 10.1177/0002716286485001005.
Freitag, Jason. *Serving Empire, Serving Nation: James Tod and the Rajputs of Rajasthan.* Leiden: Brill, 2011.
Fsadni, Ranier. 'The Debate's Impact on Europe'. In *Turkey's Accession to the European Union: An Unusual Candidacy*, ed. Constantine Arvanitopoulos, 159–170. Berlin and Heidelberg: Springer, 2009.
Fuchs, Dieter. 'Welche Demokratie wollen die Deutschen? Einstellungen zur Demokratie im vereinigten Deutschland'. In *Politische Orientierungen und Verhaltensweisen im vereinigten Deutschland*, ed. Oscar W. Gabriel, 81–113. Wiesbaden: Springer, 1997.
Furet, François. *Penser la Révolution française.* Paris: Gallimard, 1983.
Gagatek, Wojciech, Alexander H. Trechsel, and Fabian Breuer. 'Preface: Bringing the European Parliament Election Results Closer to the Citizens'. In *2009 Elections to the European Parliament, Country Reports*, ed. Wojciech Gagatek XI-XII. Florance: European University Institute, 2010.

Gall, Lothar. *Von der ständischen zur bürgerlichen Gesellschaft*. München: Oldenbourg Verlag, 2012.

Garcia, Bouza Louis. 'European Political Elites' Discourses on the Accession of Turkey to the EU: Discussing Europe through Turkish Spectacles?'. *European Perspectives – Journal on European Perspectives of the Western Balkans* 3, no.2 (October 2011): 53–73.

Gaulis, Berthe Georges. *La Nouvelle Turquie*. Paris: Colin, 1924.

Geddes, Andrea M. *Promoting Unity, Preserving Diversity? Member-State Institutions and European Integration*. Oxford: Lexington Books, 2006.

Geddes, Andrew. *The Politics of Migration and Immigration in Europe*. London: Sage, 2003.

Geddes, Andrew. *Britain and the European Union*. Basingstoke: Palgrave Macmillan, 2013.

Geertz, Clifford. *The Interpretation of Cultures*. New York: Basic Books, 1973.

Gehler, Michael. *Europa: Von der Utopie zur Realität*. Innsbruck-Wien: Haymon Taschenbuch, 2014.

Gehler, Michael, and Wolfram Kaiser. *Christian Democracy in Europe since 1945: Volume 2*. New York: Routledge, 2004.

Gemie, Sharif. 'Revolutions and Revolutionaries: Histories, Concepts, and Myths'. In *A Companion to the 19th Century Europe*, ed. Stefan Berger, 125–136. Oxford: Blackwell Publishing, 2006.

Giannakopoulos, Angelos. *Europa-Türkei-Identität Der 'ewige Kandidat' und die EU seit der Zollunion*. Wiesbaden: Springer, 2012.

Gladstone, Right Hone W. E., *Bulgarian Horrors and the Question of the East*. London: J. Murray, 1876.

Goffman Daniel. *The Ottoman Empire and Early Modern Europe*. Cambridge: Cambridge University Press, 2002.

Grabbe, Heather. 'European Union Conditionality and the "Acquis Communautaire"'. *International Political Science Review / Revue Internationale De Science Politique* 23, no.3 (July 2002): 249–268, http://www.jstor.org/stable/1601310.

Green, S.J.D. *The Passing of Protestant England, Secularisation and Social Change c. 1920–1960*. New York: Cambridge University Press, 2011.

Greenblatt, Spethen. *Renaissance Self-Fashioning: From Moore to Shakespeare*. Chicago: The University of Chicago Press, 2005.

Grumeza, Ion. *The Roots of Balkanization: Eastern Europe C.E. 500–1500*. Lanham: University Press of America, 2010.

Güney, Aylin. 'Imagining "Europe as an Empire": Competing/converging Geopolitical Imaginations and EU Enlargements'. In *Revisiting the European Union as an Empire*, eds. Hartmut Behr and Yannis A. Stivachtis 96–114. Abingdon and New York: Routledge, 2016.

Göçek, Fatma Müge. *East Encounters the West: France and the Ottoman Empire in the 18th Century*. New York: Oxford University Press, 1987.

Gürkan, Seda. 'The Role of the European Parliament in Turkey-EU Relations: A Troublemaker or a Useful Normative Actor?' *Southeast European and Black Sea Studies* 18, no.1 (2018): 107–125, doi: 10.1080/14683857.2018.1431515.

Gülalp, Haldun, and Günter Seufert. *Religion, Identity and Politics: Germany and Turkey in Interaction*. Abingdon: Routledge, 2013.

Habermas Jurgen, and Jacques Derrida. 'February 15, or What Binds Europeans Together: A Pleas for a Common Foreign Policy, Beginning in the Core of Europe', *Constellations* 10, no.3 (2003): 291–297, doi: 10.1111/1467–8675.00333.
Hafez, Farid. 'The Refugee Crisis and Islamophobia', *Insight Turkey* 17, no.14 (2015): 19–26.
Hagen, J. 'Redrawing the Imagined Map of Europe: The Rise and Fall of the Center', *Political Geography* 22, no.5 (2003): 489–517, doi: 10.1016/S0962–6298(03)00030–1.
Hainsworth, Paul. *The Extreme Right in Western Europe*. London and New York: Routledge, 2008.
Hainsworth, Paul. 'France Says No: the 29 May 2005 Referendum on the European Constitution'. *Parliamentary Affairs* 59, no: 1 (January 2006).
Hale, William. *Turkish Foreign Policy: 1774–2000*. London: Frank Cass Publishers, 2000.
Hall, Stuart. 'Ethnicity: Identity and Difference' In *Becoming National: A Reader*, eds. Geoff Eley and Grigor Suny, 339–349. New York: Oxford University Press, 1996.
Hall, Stuart. 'Introduction: Who Needs identity?' In *Questions of Cultural Identity*, eds. Stuart Hall and Paul du Gay, 1–17. London: Sage Publications, 1996.
Hampshire, James. *Citizenship and Belonging: Immigration and the Politics of Demographic Governance in Postwar Britain*. Hampshire: Palgrave Macmillan, 2005.
Hanf, Thomas, Reinhard Liebscher, and Heidrun Schmidtke. 'Die Wahrnehmung und Bewertung der deutschen Einheitim Spiegel von Bevölkerungsumfragen'. In *Diskurs der deutsche Einheit, Kritik und Alternativen*, eds. Raj Kollmorgen, Frank Thomas Koch, and Hans-Liudger Dienel, 249–300. VS Verlag für Sozialwissenschaften, 2011.
Hanrieder, Wolfram F. *West German Foreign Policy, 1949–1963: International Pressure and Domestic Response*. Stanford: Stanford University Press, 1967.
Hansen, Randall. *Citizenship and Immigration in Post-war Britain*. New York: Oxford University Press, 2000.
Harvey, David. *Cosmopolitanism and the Geographies of Freedom*. New York: Colombia University Press, 2009.
Heller, Peggy. 'Derrida and the Idea of Europe'. *Dalhousie French Studies* 82, (2008): 93–106, http://www.jstor.org/stable/40838450.
Hermann, Richard, and Marilynn B. Brewer. 'Identities and Institutions: Becoming European in the EU'. In *Transnational Identities: Becoming European in the EU*, eds. Richard Hermann, Thomas Risse-Kappen, and Marilynn B. Brewer, 1–22. Lanham: Rowman& Littlefield Publishers, 2004.
Herrmann, Richard K., Thomas Risse-Kappen, and Marilynn B. Brewer, eds. *Transnational Identities: Becoming European in the EU*. Lanham: Rowman Littlefield Publishers Inc., 2004.
Hildermeier, Manfred. *Geschichte der Sowjetunion 1917–1991: Entstehung und Niedergang des ersten sozialistischen Staates*. Munich: C.H. Beck, 1998.
Hillion, Christophe. 'The Copenhagen Criteria and their Progeny'. In *EU Enlargement: A Legal Approach*, ed. Christophe Hillion, 1–22. Oregon: Hart Publishing, 2004.
Hix, Simon. 'Legislative Behaviour and Party Competition in the European Parliament: An Application of Nominate to the EU'. *Journal of Common Market Studies* 39, no.4 (November 2001): 663–688, doi: 10.1111/1468–5965.00326.
Hix, Simon. *The Political System of the European Union*. New York: Palgrave Macmillan, 2005.
Hix, Simon, Tapio Raunio, and Roger Scully. An Institutional Theory of Behaviour in the European Parliament. European Parliament Research Group Working Paper, No. 1 (1999):

8, http://www.lse.ac.uk/government/ research/resgroups/EPRG/pdf/workingPaper1.pdf (12.10.2017).

Hix, Simon, Abdul Noury, and Gérard Roland. 'Dimensions of Politics in the European Parliament'. *American Journal of Political Science* 50, no.2 (April 2006): 494–520, doi: 10.1111/j.1540–5907.2006.00198.x.

Hobsbawm, Eric J. 'The Social Function of the Past: Some Questions'. *Past & Present*, no. 55 (May, 1972): 3–17, doi:10.1093/past/55.1.3.

Hix, Simon. *The Age of Empire 1875–1914*. New York: Vintage Books, 1989.

Hix, Simon. *Nations and Nationalism Since 1780: Programme, Myth, Reality*. Cambridge: Cambridge University Press, 1992.

Hix, Simon. *The Age of Revolution: 1789–1848*. New York: Vintage Books, 1996.

Hooghe, Liesbet, and Gary Marks. 'The Making of a Polity: The Struggle over European Integration', Social Science Research Network, European Integration Online Papers 1, no.4, http://ssrn.com/abstract=302663 (05.02.2015).

Hooghe, Liesbet. 'Supranational Activists or Intergovernmental Agents? Explaining the Orientations of Senior Commission Officials Toward European Integration'. *Comparative Political Studies* 32, no.4 (1999): 435–463, doi: 10.1177/0010414099032004002.

Holzhacker, Ronald, and Marek Neuman. 2019. 'Framing the Debate: The Evolution of the European Union as an External Democratization Actor Democracy Promotion and the Normative Power Europe Framework' in *The European Union in South Eastern Europe, Eastern Europe, and Central Asia*, ed. Marek Neuman, 13–36. Cham: Springer.

Horkheimer, Max, and Theodor W. Adorno, *Dialectic of Enlightenment: Philosophical Fragments*, ed. Gunzelin Schmid Noerr, trans. Edmund Jephcott. Stanford: Stanford University Press, 2002.

Howard, Marc Morjé. 'The Causes and Consequences of Germany's New Citizenship Law'. *German Politics* 17, no.1 (March 2008): 41–62, doi: 10.1080/09644000701855127.

Hughes, James, Gwendolyn Sasse, and Claire Gordon. 'Conditionality and Compliance in the EU's Eastern Enlargement: Regional Policy and Reform of Sub-National Government'. *Journal of Common Market Studies* 42, no.3 (2004): 523–551, doi: http://10.1111/j. 0021–9886.2004.00517.x.

Huntington, Samuel. *The Clash of Civilizations and the Remaking of World Order*. New York: Simon & Schuster, 1996.

Hülsse, Rainer. 'When Culture Determines Politics: Wie der Deutsche Bundestag die Türkei von der EU fernhält', *WeltTrends* 12, no.45 (Winter 2004): 135–146.

Hülsse, Rainer. 'Imagine the EU: The Metaphorical Construction of a Supra-nationalist Identity'. *Journal of International Relations and Development* 9, no.4 (2006): 407, doi:10.1057/palgrave.jird.1800105.

Ichijo, Atsuko, and Willfried Spohn. 'Introduction', in *Identities: Nations and Europe*, eds. Atsuko Ichijo and Willfried Spohn, 1–18. Aldershot: Ashgate, 2005.

Ifversen, Jan. 'Text, Discourse, Concept: Approaches to Textual Analysis'. *Kontur*, no.7 (2003).

Ifversen, Jan. 'About Key Concepts and How to Study Them'. *Contributions to the History of Concepts* 6, no.1 (2011): 65–88, doi: http://dx.doi.org/10.3167/choc.2011.060104.

Iggers, Georg G. 'Nationalism and Historiography, 1789–1996'. In *Writing National Histories, Western Europe since 1800*, eds. Stefan Berger, Mark Donovan, and Kevin Passmore, 15–29. New York: Routledge, 1999.

Ignatieff, Michael. *Human Rights as Politics and Idolatry*. Princeton: Princeton University Press, 2001.
Inalcik, Halik. *Turkey and Europe in History*. Istanbul: Eren, 2006.
Incesu, Gunal. *Ankara-Bonn-Brusel: Die deutsch-türkischen Beziehungen und die Beitrittsbemühungen der Türkeiin die Europäische Gemeinschaft, 1959–1987*. Bielefeld: Transcript Verlag, 2014.
Insel, Ahmet. 'Boasting Negotiations with Turkey: What Can France Do?' In *Global Turkey in Europe*, eds. Senem Aydin Duzgit, Anne Duncker, Daniela Huber, E. Fuat Keyman, and Nathalie Tocci, 49–58. Roma: Edizioni Nuova Cultura, 2013.
Inthorn, Sanna. 'What Does It Mean to Be an EU Citizen? How News Media Construct Civic and Cultural Concepts of Europe'. Westminster Papers in Communication and Culture 3, no.3 (2006), doi: http://doi.org/10.16997/wpcc.60.
Irwin, Robert. *For Lust of Knowing: The Orientalists and Their Enemies*. London: Allen Lane, 2006.
James, Harold A. *A German Identity 1770–1990*. London: Weidenfeld & Nicolson, 1990.
James, Harold A. *The End of Globalization: Lessons from the Great Depression*. Cambridge: Harvard University Press, 2002.
James, Stephen. *Universal Human Rights: Origins and Development*. New York: LFB Scholarly Publishing, 2007.
Jansen, Thomas, and Steven Van Hecke. *At Europe's Service: The Origins and Evolution of the European People's Party*. Heidelberg: Springer, 2011.
Jennings, Jeremy. 'Citizenship, Republicanism and Multiculturalism in Contemporary France'. British Journal of Political Science 30, no.4 (October 2000): 575–598, http://www.jstor.org/stable/194286.
Johanson, Jonna. *Learning to be a Good European, A Critical Analysis of the Official European Union Discourse on European Identity and Higher Education*. Linköping: Linköping University Press, 2008.
Jones, H. S. *The French State in Question: Public Law and Political Argument in the Third Republic*. Cambridge: Cambridge University Press, 1993.
Jopke, Christian. *Immigration and the Nation-state: The United States, Germany, and Great Britain*. New York: Oxford University Press, 1999.
Jopke, Christian. 'The Evolution of Alien Rights in the United States, Germany, and the European Union'. In *Citizenship Today: Global Perspectives and Practices*, eds. Alexander T. Aleinikoff and Douglas Klusmeyer, 36–62. Washington DC: Carnegie Endowment for International Peace, 2001.
Jordheim, Holge. 'Against Periodization: Koselleck's Theory of Multiple Modernities'. *History and Theory* 51, (2012): 151–171, doi: 10.1111/j.1468–2303.2012.00619.x.
Juergensmeyer, Mark. *The New Cold War? Secular Nationalism Confronts the Secular State*. Berkeley and Los Angeles: University of California Press, 1993.
Julios, Christina. *Contemporary British Identity: English Language, Migrants and Public Discourse*. Cornwall: Ashgate, 2008.
Kafadar, Cemal. 'A Rome of One's Own: Reflections on Cultural Geography and Identity in the Lands of Rum'. In *History and Ideology: Architectural Heritage of the 'Lands of Rum'*, eds. Julia Bailey, Sibel Bozdoğan, and Gülru Necipoğlu, 7–26. Leiden: Brill, 2007.
Kaiser, Wolfram. *Christian Democracy and the Origins of European Union*. Cambridge: Cambridge University Press, 2007.

Kalyvas, Stathis N. *The Rise of Christian Democracy in Europe*. Ithaca: Cornell University Press, 1996.
Karakasoglu, Yasemin. ' Türkische Arbeitswanderer in West-, Mittel- und Nordeuropa seit der Mitte der 1950er Jahre'. In *Enzyklopädie Migration in Europa*, eds. Klaus J. Bade, Pieter C. Emmer, Leo Lucassen und Jochen Oltmer, 1054–1060. Paderborn: Ferdinand Schöningh, 2007.
Karpat, Kemal. *The Politicization of Islam: Reconstructing Identity, State, Faith, and Community in the Late Ottoman State*. New York: Oxford University Press, 2001.
Katz, Richard S. 'Representation, the Locus of Democratic Legitimation, and the Role of the National Parliaments in the European Union'. In *The European Parliament, the National Parliaments, and European Integration*, eds. Richard S. Katz and Bernhard Wessels, 21–44. Oxford: Oxford University Press, 1999.
Katzenstein, Peter. 'Multiple Modernities as Limits to Secular Europeanization?' In *Religion in an Expanding Europe*, eds. Timothy Byrnes and Peter J. Katzenstein, 1–33. New York: Cambridge University Press, 2006.
Kaufmann, Eric P. 'The Rise of Cosmopolitanism in the 20th Century West: A Comparative-historical Perspective on the United States and European Union'. *Global Society* 17, no.4 (2003): 359–383, doi:10.1080/1360082032000132144.
Kaya, Ayhan. 'Citizenship and the Hyphenated Germans: German Turks'. In *Citizenship in a Global World, European Questions and Turkish Experiences*, eds. Fuat Keyman and Ahmet Icduygu, 219–241. London and New York: Routledge, 2005.
Kaya, Ayhan and Ayse Tecmen, 'Europe versus Islam?: Right-Wing Populist Discourse and the Construction of a Civilizational Identity'. *The Review of Faith & International Affairs* 17, no.1 (2019): 49–64, doi: 10.1080/15570274.2019.1570759.
Kedourie, Elie. 'Islam and Orientalists: Some Recent Discussions'. *The British Journal of Sociology* 7, no.3 (Sep. 1956): 217–225, doi:10.2307/587993.
Kedourie, Elie. *Nationalism*. Oxford and Massachusetts: Blackwell Publishing, 1993.
Ker-Lindsay, James. 'Turkey's EU Accession as a Factor in the 2016 Brexit Referendum'. *Turkish Studies* 19, no.1 (2018): 1–22, doi: https://doi.org/10.1080/14683849.2017.1366860.
Keitner, Chimène J. *The Paradoxes of Nationalism: The French Revolution and its Meaning for Contemporary Nation-Building*. Albany: State University of New York Press, 2007.
Kesi, Mahendran, and Iain McIver. 'Attitudes towards the European Union & the Challenges in Communicating "Europe": Building a Bridge between Europe and its Citizens Evidence'. Review Paper 2. Scottish Executive Social Research, 2007.
Keyman, E. Fuat, and Ziya Öniş. 'Helsinki, Copenhagen and beyond Challenges to the New Europe and the Turkish state'. In *Turkey and European Integration: Accession Prospects and Issues*, eds. Mehmet Ugur and Nergis Canefe, 173–193. London: Routledge, 2004.
Kochenov, Dimitry. *EU Enlargement and the Failure of Conditionality*. Kluwer Law International, 2008.
Koenig, Thomas, Sabina Mihelj, John Downey, and Mine Gencel Bek. 'Media Framings on the Issue of Turkish Accession to the EU, a European or National Process?' *Innovation: the European Journal of Science Research* 19, no.2 (2006): 149–169, doi: 10.1080/13511610600804240.
Kohn, Hans. 'The Paradox of Fichte's Nationalism'. *Journal of the History of Ideas* 10, no.3 (Jun. 1949): 319–343, doi:10.2307/2707040.

Koselleck, Reinhart. *Critique and Crisis: Enlightenment and the Pathogenesis of Modern Society*, trans. Thomas McCarthy. Cambridge, Massachusetts: MIT Press, 1988.
Koselleck, Reinhart. *The Practice of Conceptual History: Timing History, Spacing Concepts*, trans. Todd Presner. Stanford, Stanford University Press, 2002.
Koselleck, Reinhart. *Begriffsgeschichten*. Frankfurt: Suhrkamp Verlag, 2006.
Kramer, Heinz, and Maurus Reinkowski. *Die Türkei und Europa: eine wechselhafte Beziehungsgeschichte*. Stuttgart: W. Kohlhammer, 2008.
Kraus, Peter. *A Union of Diversity Language, Identity, and Polity-Building in Europe*. New York: Cambridge University Press, 2008.
Krell, Christian. *Sozialdemokratie und Europa: Die Europapolitik von SPD, Labour Party und Parti Socialiste*. Wiesbaden: Verlag für Sozialwissenschaften. 2009.
Krzyzanowski, Michal. *The Discursive Construction of European Identities: A Multi-level Approach to Discourse and Identity in the Transforming European Union*. Bern: Peter Lang, 2010.
Kumar, Krishan. *The Making of English National Identity*. Cambridge, Cambridge University Press, 2003.
Kumar, Krishan. 'Themed Section on Varieties of Britishness: English and French National Identity: Comparisons and Contrasts'. *Nations and Nationalism* 12, no.3 (2006): 413–432, doi: 10.1111/j.1469–8129.2006.00247.x.
Kurthen, Hermann. 'Germany at the Crossroads: National Identity and the Challenges of Immigration'. *International Migration Review* 29, no.4 (Winter, 1995): 914–938, doi: 10.2307/2547732.
Kürti, László. 'Globalization and the Discourse of 'Otherness' in the New Eastern and Central Europe'. In *The Politics of Multiculturalism in the New Europe: Racism, Identity and Community*, eds. Tariq Modood and Pnina Werbner, 29–53. New York: Zed Books, 1997.
Küçük, Bülent. *Die Türkei und das andere Europa: Phantasmen der Identität im Beitrittsdiskurs*. Bielefeld: Transcript Verlag, 2008.
Laclau, Ernesto, and Chantal Mouffe. *Hegemony and Socialist Strategy*. Verso, 2002.
Laclau, Ernesto. 'Universalism, Particularism and the Question of Identity'. In *The Politics of Difference, Ethnic Premises in a World of Power*, eds. Edwin Wilmsen and Patrick McAllister, 45–58. Chicago and London: The University of Chicago Press, 1996.
Ladrech, Robert. 'Political parties in the European Parliament'. In *Political Parties and the European Union*, ed. John Gaffney, 291–307. New York: Routledge, 1996.
Lamartine, Alphonse de. *A Pilgrimage to the Holy Land, Comprising, Recollections, Sketches, and Reflections, Made During a Tour in the East in 1832–1833, Volume 2*. London: Rayner and Hodges, 1835.
Lavenex, Sandra, and Frank Schimmelfennig. *EU Democracy Promotion in the Neighbourhood: From Leverage to Governance?* Abingdon: Routledge, 2013.
Laçiner, Sedat. 'France, Asia Minor and Mind Minor'. *Turkish Weekly*, September 22, 2007.
Leffler, Melvyn P. 'Strategy, Diplomacy, and the Cold War: The United States, Turkey, and NATO, 1945–1952'. *The Journal of American History* 71, no.4 (1985): 807–825, doi:10.2307/1888505.
Leino, Päivi, and Roman Petrov. 'Between "Common Values" and Competing Universals—The Promotion of the EU's Common Values through the European Neighbourhood Policy'. *European Law Journal* 15, no.5 (September 2009): 654–671, doi: 10.1111/j.1468–0386.2009.00483.x.

Leonhard, Jorn. 'The Rise of the Modern Leviathan, State Functions and State Features'. In *A Companion to the 19th Century Europe*, ed. Stefan Berger, 137–148. Oxford: Blackwell Publishing, 2006.

Lexutt, Athina. *Luther und der Islam, Spiegel der Forschung*, no. 2 (2011): 61–71.

Levin, Paul T. *Turkey and the European Union: Christian and Secular Images of Islam*. New York: Palgrave Macmillan, 2011.

Levin, Paul T. 'Who Lost Turkey? The Consequences of Writing an Exclusionary European History', in *History and Belonging: Representations of the Past in Contemporary European Politics*, eds. Caner Tekin and Stefan Berger, 152–173. New York: Berghahn Books, 2018.

Lewis, Bernard. *The Emergence of Modern Turkey*. New York: Oxford University Press, 1968.

Lewis, Bernard. *A Middle Eastern Mosaic*. New York: Random House, 2000.

Lewis, Reina. *Rethinking Orientalism: Women, Travel, and the Ottoman Harem*. New Brunswick: Rutgers University Press, 2004.

Lieberman, Sarah, and Tim Gray. 'The so-called "Moratorium" on the Licensing of New Genetically Modified (GM) Products by the European Union 1998–2004: A Study in Ambiguity'. *Environmental Politics* 25, no.4 (2006): 592–609, doi: 10.1080/09644010600785218.

Lipset, Seymour Martin, and Stein Rokkan. *Cleavage Systems. Party Systems, and Voter Alignments: Cross-national Perspectives*. New York : Free Press, 1967.

Liu, James H., and Denis J. Hilton. 'How the Past Weighs on the Present: Social Representations of History and Their Role in Identity Politics'. *British Journal of Social Psychology* 44, no.4 (2005): 537–556, doi: 10.1348/014466605X27162.

Lock, F.P. *Edmund Burke: Volume II*. Oxford: Clarendon Press, 2006.

Locke, John. *Two Treaties of Government*. London: Harvard College Library, 1824.

Locke, John. *A Letter Concerning Religious Toleration, and Other Writings*, ed. Mark Goldie. Indianapolis: Liberty Fund, 2010.

Lockyer, Roger. *Tutor and Stuart Britain 1485–1714*. Abingdon: Routledge, 2013.

Lucarelli, Sonia, and Ian Manners, eds., *Values and Principles in European Union Foreign Policy*. London and New York: Routledge, 2006.

Lucarelli, Sonia. 'European Political Identity, Foreign Policy, and the Other's Image: an Underexplored Relationship'. In *The Search for a European Identity: Values, Principles, and Legitimacy of the European Union*, eds. Furio Cerutti and Sonia Lucarelli, 23–42. London and New York: Routledge, 2008.

Luitwieler, Sander. *The Treaty of Lisbon from a Christian-social Perspective, ECPM Publication*, Amersfoort, March 2009.

Lénárt, Levente. 'Sir Winston Spencer Churchill and the Movement of the Unification of Europe'. *European Integration Studies* 2, no.2 (2003).

Mackenzie, John M. 'Edward Said and the Historians'. In *Edward Said, Vol.3: Cultural Forms, Disciplinary Boundaries*, ed. Patrick Williams, 127–143. London: Sage Publications, 2001.

Macmillan, Catherine. *Discourse, Identity and the Question of Turkish Accession to the EU: Through the Looking Glass*. Surrey: Ashgate, 2013.

Madeker, Ellen. *Türkei und europäische Identität Eine wissenssoziologische Analyse der Debatte um den EU-Beitritt*. Wiesbaden: VS Verlag für Sozialwissenschaften, 2007.

Mahn, Kaur Churnjeet. 'The Sculpture and the Harem: Ethnography in Felicia Skene's Wayfaring Sketches'. In *Women Writing Greece: Essays on Hellenism, Orientalism and Travel*, eds Va Vassiliki Kolocotroni, Efterpi Mitsi, 97–112. Amsterdam: Editions Rodopi B.V., 2008.

Malouf, Amin. *In the name of Identity: Violence and the Need to Belong*. New York: Arcade Publishing, 2001.

Mandel, Ruth. *Turkish Challenges to Citizenship and Belonging in Germany*. Durham NC: Duke University Press, 2008.

Manners, Ian. 'Normative Power Europe: A Contradiction in Terms?' *Journal of Common Market Studies* 40, no.2 (2002): 235–258, doi: 10.1111/1468-5965.00353.

Manners, Ian. 'The Constitutive Nature of Values, Images and Principles in the European Union'. In *Values and Principles in European Union Foreign Policy*, eds. Sonia Lucarelli and Ian Manners, 19–41. London and New York: Routledge, 2006).

Manners, Ian. 'The European Union as a Normative Power: A Response to Thomas Diez'. *Millennium* 35, no.1 (2006): 167–180, doi: 10.1177/03058298060350010201.

Manners, Ian. 'The Normative Ethics of the European Union'. *International Affairs* 84, no.1 (January 2008): 45–60, doi:10.1111/j.1468-2346.2008.00688.x.

Marcussen, Martin, Thomas Risse, Daniela Engelmann-Martin, Hans Joachim Knopf, and Klaus Roscher. 'Constructing Europe? The Evolution of French, British and German Nation State Identities'. *Journal of European Public Policy* 6, no.4 (1994): 614–633, doi: 10.1080/135017699343504.

Marcussen, Martin, Thomas Risse, Daniela Engelmann-Martin, Hans-Joachim Knopf, and Klaus Roscher. 'Constructing Europe? The Evolution of Nation State Identities'. In *The Social Construction of Europe*, eds. Thomas Christiansen, Knud Erik Jørgensen, and Antje Wiener, 101–120. London: Sage Publications, 2001.

Mardin, Serif. 'Power, Civil Society and Culture in the Ottoman Empire'. *Comparative Studies in Society and History* 11, no.3 (June 1969): 258–281, doi:10.1017/S0010417500005338.

Mardin, Serif. 'Oryantalizmin Hasıraltı Ettikleri'. *Dogu Bati*, no.20 'Oryantalizm-1' (2005).

Mardin, Serif. *Religion, Society, and Modernity in Turkey*. Syracuse, New York: Syracuse University Press, 2006.

Mariott, J. A. R. *The Eastern Question: An Historical Study*. Oxford: Cralendon Press, 1917.

Martin, Jeřábek. *Deutschland und die Osterweiterung der Europäischen Union*. Wiesbaden: Vs Verlag fur Sozialwischenschaften, 2011.

Marx, Karl, and Frederick Engels. Manifesto of The Communist Party. February 1848.

Maull, Hans W. 'Europe and the New Balance of Global Order'. *International Affairs* 81, no.4 (July 2005): 775–799, doi: 10.1111/j.1468-2346.2005.00484.x.

Maurer, Kathrin. *Visualizing the Past, the Power of the Image in German Historicism*. Berlin: Walter de Gruyter, 2013.

Mayall, James. 'Sovereignty, Nationalism, and Self-determination'. *Political Studies* 47, no.3 (1999): 474–502, doi: 10.1111/1467-9248.00213.

McCrea, Ronan. *Religion and Public Order in the European Union*. New York: Oxford University Press, 2010.

Mckay, Donald Vernon. 'The French in Tunisia'. *Geographical View* 35, no.3 (July 1945): 368–390.

McKenzie, Mary M. 'The Origins of the Berlin Republic'. In *Germany at Fifty-five: Berlin ist Nicht Bonn?* ed. James Sperling, 58–79. Manchester: Manchester University Press, 2004.
McKitterick, Rosamond. *Charlemagne: The Formation of a European Identity*. Cambridge: Cambridge University Press, 2008.
McLaren, Lauren M. 'Explaining Opposition to Turkish Membership of EU'. *European Union Politics* 8, no.2 (2007): 252–278, doi. 10.1177/1465116507076432.
Medrano, Juan Diez. 'The Public Sphere and the European Union's Political Identity'. In *European Identity* eds. Jeffrey T. Checkel and Peter J. Katzenstein, 81–110. New York: Cambridge University Press, 2009.
Meindert, Fennema. 'Some Conceptual Issues and Problems in the Comparison of Anti-Immigrant Parties in Western Europe'. *Party Politics* 3, no.4 (October 1997): 473–492, doi: 10.1177/1354068897003004002.
Menéndez-Alarcón, Antonio V. *The Cultural Realm of European Integration: Social Representations in France, Spain, and the United Kingdom*. Westport: Praeger, 2004.
Miller, M. A. *The Ottoman Empire: 1801–1913*. Cambridge: Cambridge University Press, 1913.
Milner, Henry. '"YES to the Europe I want; NO to this one." Some Reflections on France's Rejection of the EU Constitution'. *Political Science & Politics* 39, no. 2 (April 2006): 257–260, http://www.jstor.org/stable/20451732.
Mole, Richard C.M. *Discursive Constructions of Identity in European Politics*. Hampsire and New York: Palgrave Macmillan. 2007.
Monceau, Nicolas. 'French Perceptions'. In *Turkey Watch: EU Member States' Perceptions on Turkey's Accession to the EU*, eds. Sait Aksit, Ozgehan Senyuva, and Cigdem Ustun, 9–21. Ankara: Zeplin Iletisim, 2010.
Moravcsik, Andrew. 'The Origins of Human Rights Regimes: Democratic Delegation in Post-War Europe'. *International Organization* 54, no.2 (March 2000): 217–252, doi:10.1162/002081800551163.
Moravcsik, Andrew. 'Reassessing Legitimacy in the European Union'. *Journal of Common Market Studies* 40, no.4 (November 2002): 603–624, doi: 10.1111/1468–5965.00390.
Moravscik, Andrew, and Frank Schimmelfennig. 'Liberal Intergovernmentalism'. In *European Integration Theory*, eds. Antje Wiener and Thomas Diez, 67–90. Oxford: Oxford University Press, 2009.
Muller, Jan-Werner. 'The End of Christian Democracy'. *Foreign Affairs*, July 15, 2014.
Muntigl, Peter, Gilbert Weiss, and Ruth Wodak. *European Union Discourses on Unemployment: An inter-disciplinary Approach to Employment Policy-Making and Organizational Change*. John Benjamins Publishing Company, 2000.
Mörth, Ulrika. 'Europeanization as Interpretation, Translation, and Editing of Public Policies'. in *The Politics of Europeanization*, eds. Kevin Featherstone and Claudio M. Radaelli, 159–178. New York: Oxford University Press, 2003.
Müftüler-Baç, Meltem. 'The Never-Ending Story: Turkey and the European Union'. *Middle Eastern Studies* 34, no.4 (October 1998): 240–258, http://www.jstor.org/stable/4283976.
Müftüler-Baç, Meltem. 'Turkey's Political Reforms and the Impact of the European Union'. South European Society and Politics 10, no.1 (2005): 17–31, doi:10.1080/13608740500037916.

Müftüler-Baç, Meltem. 'The European Union's Legitimacy Crisis and the Final Frontiers of Europe'. In *European Integration from Rome to Berlin, 1957–2007: History, Law and Politics*, eds. Julio Baquero Cruz and Carlos Closa, 263–280. Brussels: Peter Lang, 2009.

Müftüler-Baç, Meltem. 'Turkey's Accession to the European Union: The impact of the EU's internal dynamics'. *International Studies Perspectives* 9, No.2 (2011): 201–219, doi: http://10.1111/j.1528-3585.2008.00327.x.

Nash, Geoffrey. 'New Orientalisms for old Articulations of the East in Raymond Schwab, Edward Said, and the Nineteenth-century French Orientalists'. In *Orientalism Revisited: Art, Land and Voyage*, ed. Netton Richard, 87–97. London and New York: Routledge, 2013.

Nathans, Eli. *The Politics of Citizenship in Germany. Ethnicity, Utility and Nationalism.* New York: Berg, 2004.

Necipoglu, Gülru. 'Süleyman the Magnificent and the Representation of Power in the Context of Ottoman- Hapsburg-Papal Rivalry', *Art Bulletin* 71, no.3 (Sep. 1989).

Neill, Edmund. 'Political Ideologies, Liberalism, Conservatism and Socialism'. In *A Companion to the 19th Century Europe*, ed. Stefan Berger, 211–223. Oxford: Blackwell Publishing, 2006.

Nerval, Gerard M. *Voyage en Orient*, Troisième Édition. Paris: Charpentiere Libraire Éditeur, 1851.

Nettl, J. P. 'State as a Conceptual Variable'. *World Politics* 20, no.4 (July 1968): 559–592, http://www.jstor.org/stable/2009684.

Neumann, Iver B., and Jennifer Welsh. 'The Other in European Self-Definition: An Addendum to the Literature on International Society'. *Review of International Studies* 17, no.4 (Oct 1991): 327–348, http://www.jstor.org/stable/20097270.

Neumann, Iver B., and Jennifer Welsh. *Uses of Other: The East in European Identity Formation.* Minneapolis: University of Minnesota Press, 1999.

Neumann, Iver B., and Jennifer Welsh. 'European Identity, EU Expansion, and the Integration/Exclusion Nexus'. In *Constructing Europe's Identity: The External Dimension*, ed. Lars-Erik Cederman, 141–164. Colorado and London: Lynne Rienner Publishers, 2001.

Nussbaum, Marta C. 'Kant and Stoic Cosmopolitanism'. *The Journal of Political Philosophy* 5, no.1 (1997): 1–25, doi: 10.1111/1467-9760.00021.

Oakes, Augustus, and R. B. Mowat, eds. *The Great European Treaties of the Nineteenth Century.* London: Oxford University Press, 1918.

Odysseos, Louiza. *The Subject of Coexistence, Otherness in International Relations.* Minneapolis, London: University of Minnesota Press, 2007.

Offe, Claus. 'The German Welfare State: Principles, Performance, Prospects'. *Thesis Eleven* 63, no.1 (November 2000): 11–37, doi: doi: 10.1177/0725513600063000003.

Oppelan, Torsten. 'Domestic Political Developments: 1949–1969'. In *The Federal Republic of Germany since 1949: Politics, Society and Economy before and after Unification*, eds. Klaus Larres and Panikos Panayi, 74–99. Abingdon and New York: Routledge, 2014.

Ortayli, Ilber. *Avrupa ve Biz.* Istanbul: Türkiye İş Bankası Yayınları, 2000.

Ostergren, Robert Clifford, and Mathias Le Bossé. *The Europeans: A Geography of People, Culture, and Environment.* New York: The Guilford Press, 2011.

Ozan, Didem. *Parteiliche Kommunikation am politischen Wendepunkt: Der EU-Beitritt der Türkei in deutschen und türkischen Parlamentsdebatten*. Wiesbaden: VS Verlag für Sozialwissenschaften, 2010.

Ozbudun, Ergun. 'Democratization Reforms in Turkey 1993–2004'. *Turkish Studies* 8, no.2 (2007): 179–196, doi: 10.1080/14683840701312195.

Öniş, Ziya. 'Luxembourg, Helsinki and Beyond: Towards an Interpretation of Recent Turkey-EU Relations'. *Government and Opposition* 35, no.4 (October 2000): 463–483, doi: 10.1111/1477-7053.00041.

Padgett, Stephen. 'The SPD: the Decline of the Social Democratic Volkspartei'. In *The Federal Republic of Germany since 1949: Politics, Society and Economy before and after Unification*, eds. Klaus Larres and Panikos Panayi, 230–253. Abingdon and New York: Routledge, 2014.

Pagden, Anthony. 'Europe: Conceptualizing a Continent'. In *The Idea of Europe: From Antiquity to the European Union*, ed. Anthony Pagden, 33–54. New York: Cambridge University Press, 2002.

Pasture, Patrick. *Imagining European Unity since 1000 AD*. Basingstoke: Palgrave, 2015.

Pattison, Robert. *The Great Dissent: John Henry Newman and the Liberal Heresy*. New York: Oxford University Press, 1991.

Pelinka, Anton. 'Right-Wing Populism: Concept and Typology'. In *Right-Wing Populism in Europe: Politics and Discourse*, eds. Ruth Wodak, Majid Khosravinik, and Brigitte Mral, 3–22. London: Bloomsburry Academic, 2013.

Penn, William. *A Collection of the Works of William Penn. To Which is Prefixed a Journal of his Life, with Many Original Letters and Papers not before Published*. Volume 2. London: J. Sowle, 1726.

Perry, Marvin, Myrna Chase, James R. Jacob, Margaret C. Jacob, and Theodore Von H. Laue. *Western Civilization, Ideas, Politics, and Society, Vol. II: From the 1600s*. Boston: Wadsworth, 2012.

Petithomme, Mathieu. 'La candidature Turque et la construction subjective d'un "autre" à la communauté des européens: une analyse systématique des discours de la presse en France, en Belgique et en Grande-Bretagne', *REVUE Asylon(s)*, no.4 (May 2008), http://www.reseau-terra.eu/article752.html.

Pichler, Florian. 'Cosmopolitan Europe: Views and Identity'. *European Societies* 11, no.1 (2009): 3–24, doi: 10.1080/14616690802209697.

Pocock, J.G.A. *Virtue, Commerce, and History, Essays on Political Thought and History Chiefly in the 18th Century*. Cambridge: Cambridge University Press, 1985.

Pocock, J.G.A. 'Concepts and Discourses: A Difference in Culture? Comment on a Paper by Melvin Richter'. In *The Meaning of Historical Terms and Concepts New Studies on Begriffsgeschichte*, eds. Hartmut Lehmann and Melvin Richter, German Historical Institute Washington, D.C. Occasional Paper No. 15, 1996.

Pocock, J.G.A. *Barbarism and Religion, Vol. 5: The First Triumph*. Cambridge: Cambridge University Press, 2010.

Polo, Marco. *The Travels of Marco Polo: The Complete Yule-Cordier Edition Volume 1*. Toronto: General Publishing Company, 1993.

Porter, James. *Turkey: Its History and Progress*. London: Hurst and Blackett Publishers, 1854.

Pourchot, Georgeta. 'EU's "Eastern Empire"'. In *Revisiting the European Union as an Empire*, eds. Hartmut Behr and Yannis A. Stivachtis, 17–31. Abingdon and New York: Routledge, 2016.

Prasad, Pratima. *Colonialism, Race, and the French Romantic Imagination*. London and New York: Routledge, 2009.

Proksch, Sven-Oliver, and Jonathan B. Slapin, 'Position Taking in European Parliament Speeches'. *European Union Politics* 11, no.3 (2009): 587–611, doi:10.1017/S0007123409990299.

Proudhon, Pierre Joseph. *General Idea of the Revolution in the Nineteenth Century*. Trans. John Beverley Robinson. New York: Haskell House Publishers, 1969.

Quataert, Donald. *The Ottoman Empire: 1700–1922*. New York: Cambridge University Press, 2005.

Quint, Peter E. 'The Constitutional Guarantees of Social Welfare in the Process of German Unification'. *The American Journal of Comparative Law* 47, no.2 (Spring, 1999): 303–326, doi:10.2307/841042.

Raj Kollmorgen, Frank Thomas Koch, and Hans-Liudger Dienel, 'Diskurse der deutschen Einheit: Forschungsinteressen und Forschungsperspektiven des Bandes', in *Diskurs der deutsche Einheit, Kritik und Alternativen*, eds. Raj Kollmorgen, Frank Thomas Koch, Hans-Liudger Dienel, 7–23. Wiesbaden: VS Verlag für Sozialwissenschaften, 2011.

von Ranke, Leopold. *The Secret of World History: Selected Writings on the Art and Science of History*, ed. trans. Roger Wines. New York: Fordham University Press, 1981.

Reisigl, Martin, and Ruth Wodak. *Discourse and Discrimination: Rhetorics of Racism and Antisemitism*. London: Routledge, 2001.

Renan, Ernest. *L'Islamisme et la science; conférence faite à la Sorbonne, le 29 mars 1883*. Paris: C. Levy, 2005.

Risse, Thomas, Stephen C., Ropp, and Kathryn Sikkink, eds. *The Power of Human Rights: International Norms and Domestic Change*. Cambridge: Cambridge University Press, 1999.

Risse, Thomas. *A Community of Europeans? Transnational Identities and Public Spheres*. Ithaca: Cornell UniversityPress, 2010.

Risse, Thomas. 'Identity Matters: Exploring the Ambivalence of EU Foreign Policy'. *Global Policy* 3, no.1 (2012): 87–95, doi: 10.1111/1758–5899.12019.

Risse, Thomas. 'Nationalism and Collective Identities: Europe versus the Nation-state?'. In *Developments in West European Politics* 2, eds. Paul Heywood, Erik Jones, and Martin Rhodes, 77–93. Basingstoke: Palgrave Macmillan, 2002.

Risse, Thomas. 'A European Identity? Europeanization and Evolution of a Nation-State Identities'. In *Transforming Europe, Europeanization and Domestic Change*, eds. Maria Green Cowles, James A. Caporaso, and Thomas Risse-Kappen, 198–216. Ithaca: Cornell University Press, 2001.

Roads, Murphey. 'Bigots or Informed Observers? A Periodization of Pre-Colonial English and European Writing on the Middle East'. *Journal of the American Oriental Society* 110, no.2 (April-June 1990): 291–303, doi: 10.2307/604532.

Robins, Kevin. 'Interactive Identities: Turkey/Europe'. In *Questions of Cultural Identity*, eds. Stuart Hall and Paul du Gay, 61–86. London: Sage Publications, 1996.

Roessler, Shirley Elson. *Out of Shadows: Women and Politics in the French Revolution, 1789–1895*. P.Lang, 2006.

Rousseau, Jean Jacques. *The Social Contract: And, The First and Second Discourses*. Vail-Ballau Press, New York, 2002.
Rowen, Herbert H. '"L'Etat c'est moi": Louis the XIV and the State'. *French Historical Studies* 2, no.1 (Spring, 1961): 83–98, do: 10.2307/286184.
Rudzio, Wolfgang. *Das politische System der Bundesrepublik Deutschland*. Springer VS, 2015.
Rumelili, Bahar, and Didem Cakmakli. '"Culture" in EU-Turkey Relations'. In *Culture and External Relations: Europe and Beyond*, eds. Jozef Bátora and Monika Mokre, 99–118. Burlington: Ashgate, 2011.
Rumelili, Bahar. 'Negotiation Europe: EU-Turkey Relations from an Identity Perspective'. *Insight Turkey* 10, no.1 (2008).
Rustow, Dankwart A. 'The Military: Turkey', in *Political Modernization in Japan and Turkey*, eds. Robert E. Ward and Dankwart Rustow, 352–388. Princeton: Princeton University Press, 1964.
Ruth Woodsmall, Francess. *Women in the Changing Islamic System*. Delhi: Bilma Pulishing House, 1936.
Ruß-Sattar, Sabine. 'Building Borders on a Bias: The Culturalist Perception of Turkish Migrants in France and Germany and the Debate'. In *New Border and Citizenship Politics*, eds. Helen Schwenken and Sabine Ruß-Sattar. New York, London: Palgrave Macmillan, 2014.
Saatcioglu, Beken. 'The EU's 'Rhetorical Entrapment' in Enlargement Reconsidered: Why Hasn't it Worked for Turkey?'. *Insight Turkey* 14, no.3 (2012).
Saatcioglu, Beken. 'Turkey-EU Relations from 1960s to 2012: A Critical Overview'. In *Turkey's Accession to the European Union: Political and Economic Challenges*, eds. Belgin Akcay, Bahri Yilmaz, 3–24. Lenham MD: Lexington Books, 2013.
Said, Edward W. *Orientalism*. New York: Vintage Books, 1978.
Said, Edward W. 'The Clash of Ignorance'. *The Nation*, October 22, 2001.
Saint Augustine, *City of God*. Trans. Marcus Dods. Massachusetts: Hendrickson Publishers, 2009.
Salama, Mohammed. *Islam, Orientalism, and Intellectual History: Modernity and the Politics of Exclusion since Ibn Khaldun*. London: Tauris & Co Ltd, 2001.
Sammartino, Annemarie. 'Culture, Belonging, and the Law: Naturalisations in the Weimer Republic'. In *Citizenship and National Identity in Twentieth-Century Germany*, eds. Geoff Eley and Jan Palmowski, 57–72. Stanford: Stanford University Press, 2008.
Sasatelli, Monica. 'Imagined Europe: The Shaping of a European Cultural Identity Through EU Cultural Policy'. *European Journal of Social Theory* 54, (2002): 435–451, doi: 10.1177/136843102760513848.
Schildberg, Cäcilie. *Politische Identität und Soziales Europa*. Wiesbaden: VS Verlag für Sozialwissenschaften, 2010.
Schimmelfennig, Frank, and Hanno Scholtz. 'EU Democracy Promotion in the European Neighbourhood: Political Conditionality, Economic Development and Transnational Exchange'. *European Union Politics* 9, no.2 (2008): 187–215, doi: 10.1177/1465116508089085.
Schimmelfennig, Frank, and Ulrich Sedelmeier, eds. *The Europeanization of Central and Eastern Europe*. Ithaca: Cornell University Press, 2005.
Schimmelfennig, Frank, and Ulrich Sedelmeier. 'Introduction: Conceptualizing the Europeanization of Central and Eastern Europe'. In *The Europeanization of Central and*

Eastern Europe, eds. Frank Schimmelfennig and Ulrich Sedelmeier, 1–28. New York: Cornell University Press, 2005.

Schimmelfennig, Frank. 'Liberal Identity and Postnationalist Inclusion: The Eastern Enlargement of the European Union'. In *Constructing Europe's Identity: the External Dimension*, ed. Lars-Erik Cederman, 165–186. Boulder, Colo: Lynne Rienner Publishers, 2001.

Schimmelfennig, Frank. 'The Community Trap: Liberal Norms, Rhetorical Action, and the Eastern Enlargement of the European Union'. *International Organization* 55, no.1 (2001): 47–80, doi: 10.1162/002081801551414.

Schimmelfennig, Frank. Entrapped Again: The Way to EU Membership Negotiations with Turkey. UCD Dublin European Institute Working Paper, August 8, 2008.

Schlesinger, Philip. 'On National Identity: Some Conceptions and some Misconceptions Criticised'. *Social Sciences Information* 26, no. 2 (1987): 219–264, doi: 10.1177/053901887026002001.

Schmidt, Manfred G. 'Germany: The Grand Coalition State'. In *Comparative European Politics*, ed. Josep Colomer, 58–93. Abingdon: Routledge, 2008.

Schmidt, Royal J. 'Cultural Nationalism in Herder'. *Journal of the History of Ideas* 17, no.3 (1956): 407–417, doi:10.2307/2707552.

Schnapper, Pauline. 'The Labour Party and Europe from Brown to Miliband: Back to the Future?', *Journal of Common Market Studies* 53, no.1 (2015): 160–161, doi: 10.1111/jcms.12209.

Schuman, Robert. 'France in Europe'. *Foreign Affairs*, April, 1953.

Schwan, Gesine, Birgit Schwelling, Gesine Schwan, Jerzy Holzer, Marie-Claire Lavabre, and Birgit Schwelling, eds. *Demokratische politische Identität: Deutschland, Polen und Frankreich im Vergleich*. Wiesbaden: VS Verlag für Sozialwissenschaften, 2006.

Schwoebel, Robert. *The Shadow of the Crescent: The Renaissance Image of the Turk, 1453–1517*. New York: St Martin Press, 1967.

Scott, Haine. *The History of France*. Westport: Greenwood Publishing Group, 2000.

Scott, Joan Wallach. 'French Feminists and the Rights of "Man": Olympe de Gouges's Declarations'. *History Workshop*, no.28 (1989): 1–21.

Scroeder, Pail W. 'The 19th-Century International System: Changes in the Structure'. *World Politics* 39, no.1 (October 1986): 16–17, doi: 10.2307/2010296.

Sedelmeier, Ulrich. *European Enlargement, Identity, and the Analysis of European Foreign Policy: Identity Formation through Policy Practice*. Robert Schuman Centre for Advanced Studies, no.2003/13. 2003.

Sending, Jacob Ole. 'Constitution, Choice and Change: Problems with the Logic of Appropriateness and its Use in Constructivist Theory'. *European Journal of International Relations* 8, (2002): 443–470, doi: 10.1177/1354066102008004001.

Shaw, Jo. *The Transformation of Citizenship in the European Union: Electoral Rights and the Re-structuring of the Political Space*. Cambridge: Cambridge University Press, 2007.

Shaw, Stanford J., and Ezel Kural Shaw. *History of the Ottoman Empire and Modern Turkey, Volume II: Reform, Revolution, and Republic. The Rise of Modern Turkey 1808–1975*. New York: Cambridge University Press, 1977.

Shepard, Todd. *The Invention of Decolonization: The Algerian War and the Remaking of France*. Ithaca: Cornell University Press, 2006.

Shilliam, Robert. 'The "Other" in Classical Political Theory: Re-Contextualizing the Cosmopolitan/Communitarian Debate'. In *Classical Theory in International Relations*, ed. Jahn Beate, 207–232. Cambridge: Cambridge University Press, 2006.

Shore, Chris. 'Inventing the "People's Europe": Critical Approaches to European Community "Cultural Policy"'. *Man* 28, no.4 (December 1993): 779–800, doi:10.2307/2803997.

Shore, Chris. *Building Europe: The Cultural Politics of European Integration*. London-New York: Routledge, 2000.

Sjursen, Helene. 'Why Expand? The Question of Legitimacy and Justification in the EU's Enlargement Policy'. *Journal of Common Market Studies* 40, no.3 (2002): 491–513, doi: 10.1111/1468–5965.00366.

Sjursen, Helene. 'Introduction: Enlargement and the Nature of the EU Polity'. In *Questioning EU Enlargement: Europe in Search of Identity*, ed. Helene Sjursen, 1–15. New York and London: Routledge, 2006.

Sjursen, Helene. 'The European Union between Values and Rights'. In *Questioning EU Enlargement: Europe in Search of Identity*, ed. Helene Sjursen (New York and London: Routledge, 2006), 203–215. Macmillan, Discourse, Identity and the Question of Turkish Accession to the EU.

Slade, Adolphus. *Turkey, Greece and Malta Volume 1*. London: Saunders and Otley, 1837.

Slapin, Jonathan B., Sven-Oliver Proksch, 'Look Who's Talking: Parliamentary Debate in the European Parliament'. *European Union Politics* 11, no.3 (2010): 333–357, doi: 10.1177/1465116510369266.

Smith, Anthony D. *National Identity*. London: Penguin Books, 1991.

Smith, Anthony D. 'National Identity and the Idea of Unity'. *International Affairs, (Royal Institute of International Affairs 1944-)* 68, no.1 (1992), 55–76, doi:10.2307/2620461.

Smith, Anthony D. '"Set in the Silver Sea": English National identity and European Integration'. *Nations and Nationalism* 12, no.3 (2006): 433–452.

Smith, Julie. *Europe's Elected Parliament*. Sheffield: Sheffield Academic Press, 1999.

Sperling, James, ed. *Germany at Fifty-five: Berlin ist Nicht Bonn?* Manchester: Manchester University Press, 2004.

Sperling, James. 'Berlin ist nicht Bonn? Continuity and Change in postwar Germany', in *Germany at Fifty-five: Berlin ist Nicht Bonn?* ed. James Sperling, 3–36. Manchester: Manchester University Press, 2004.

Spiering, Menno. 'British Euroscepticism'. In *Euroscepticism: Party Politics, National Identity and European Integration*, eds. Robert Harmsen and Menno Spiering, 127–150. Amsterdam and New York: Rodopi B.V., 2004.

Stan Lavinia, and Lucian Turcescu. *Church, State, and Democracy in Expanding Europe*. New York: Oxford University Press, 2011.

Statham, Paul. 'What Kind of Europeanized Public Politics?' In *The Making of a European Public Sphere: Media Discourse and Political Contention*, eds. Ruud Koopmans and Paul Statham, 277–306. New York: Cambridge University Press, 2010.

Stein, Peter. *Roman Law in European History*. Cambridge: Cambridge University Press, 1999.

Steinmetz, George. *Regulating the Social: The Welfare State and Local Politics in Imperial Germany*. Princeton: Princeton University Press, 1993.

Steinmetz, George. 'The Local Welfare State: Two Strategies for Social Domination in Urban Imperial Germany', *American Sociological Review* 55, no. 6 (December 1990): 891–911, http://www.jstor.org/stable/2095753.

Stelzenmüller, Constanze. 'Turkey's EU Bid: A View from Germany'. In *Conditionality, Impact and Prejudice in EU-Turkey Relations*, ed. Nathalie Tocci, IAI-TEPAV Report July 2007.

Steunenberg, Bernard, Simay Petek, and Christiane Rüth. 'Between Reason and Emotion: Popular Discourses on Turkey's Membership of the EU'. *South European Society and Politics* 11, no.3 (2011): 449–468, doi: 10.1080/13608746.2011.598361.

Stolleis, Michael. *Origins of the German Welfare State: Social Policy in Germany to 1945*. New York: Springer, 2013.

Strath, Bo. 'European Identity: To the Historical Limits of a Concept', *European Journal of Social Theory* 5, no.4 (November 2002): 387–401, doi: 10.1177/136843102760513965.

Strath, Bo. 'Insiders and Outsiders: Borders in 19th Century Europe'. In *A Companion to the 19th Century Europe*, ed. Stefan Berger, 3–10. Oxford: Blackwell Publishing, 2006.

Strauman, Benjamin. 'The Peace of Westphalia as a Secular Constitution'. *Constellations* 15, no.2 (2008): 173–188.

Sutherland, Peter D. 'Europe: Values and Identity'. *Studies: An Irish Quarterly Review* 99, no.396 (Winter 2010): 415–426, doi: http://www.jstor.org/stable/27896508.

Taylor, Charles. 'The Politics of Recognition'. In *Multiculturalism: Examining the Politics of Recognition*, ed. Amy Gutmann, 25–74. Princeton: Princeton University Press, 1994.

Tekin, Ali. 'Future of EU-Turkey Relations: A Civilizational Discourse'. *Futures* 37, (2005): 287–302, doi: 10.1016/j.futures.2004.07.008.

Tekin, Beyza C. *Representations and Othering in Discourse: The Construction of Turkey in the EU Context*. Amsterdam: John Benjamins Publishing Company, 2010.

Tekin, Beyza C. 'The Construction of Turkey's Possible EU Membership in French Discourse'. *Discourse & Society* 19, no.6 (November 2008): 727–763, doi: 10.1177/0957926508095891.

The Annual Register or a View of the History Politics and Literature of the Year 1758, Ninth Edition. London: R. and J. Dodsley, 1758.

The Annual Register, or a View of the History, Politics, and Literature of the Year 1826. London: Pater-noster-row Press, 1827.

Thränhardt, Dietrich. *Europe, a New Immigration Continent: Policies and Politics in Comparative Perspective*. Munster: LIT Verlag, 1996.

Tibi, Bessam. 'Europeanizing Islam or the Islamization of Europe: Political Democracy vs. Cultural Difference'. In *Religion in an Expanding Europe*, eds. Timothy A., Byrnes and Peter J. Katzenstein, 204–224. Cambridge: Cambridge University Press, 2006.

Tocci, Nathalie. 'Report Unpacking European Discourses: Conditionality, Impact and Prejudice in EU-Turkey Relations'. In *Conditionality, Impact and Prejudice in EU-Turkey Relations*, ed. Nathalie Tocci, IAI-TEPAV Report July 2007.

Toynbee, Arnold. *A Study of History: Volume I: Abridgement of Volumes 1–6*. New York: Oxford University Press, 1947.

Trechsel, Alexander H. 'How Much 'Second-order' were the European Parliament Elections 2009?'. In *2009 Elections to the European Parliament, Country Reports*, ed. Wojciech Gagatek, 3–12. Florance: European University Institute, 2010.

Tsakonas, Panayotis J. 'How Can the European Union Transform the Greek-Turkish Conflict?', in *Turkey's Accession to the European Union: An Unusual Candidacy*, ed. Constantine Arvanitopoulos, 107–120. Heidelberg: Springer Verlag, 2009.

Tsebelis George, and Geoffrey Garrett. 'The Institutional Foundations of Intergovernmentalism and Supranationalism in the European Union'. *International Organization* 55, no.2 (Spring 2001): 357–390, http://www.jstor.org/stable/3078635.

Turhan, Filiz. *The Other Empire: The British Romantic Writings about the Ottoman Empire.* New York and London: Routledge, 2003.

Ugur, Mehmet. *The European Union and Turkey: an Anchor/credibility Dilemma.* Aldershot: Ashgate, 1999.

Ugur, Mehmet. 'Testing Times in EU–Turkey Relations: the Road to Copenhagen and Beyond'. *Journal of Southern Europe and the Balkans* 5, no.2 (2003): 165–183, http://doi.10.1080/1463319032000097923.

Ugur, Mehmet. 'Open-Ended Membership Prospect and Commitment Credibility: Explaining the Deadlock in EU–Turkey Accession Negotiations'. *Journal of Common Market Studies* 48, no.4 (2010): 967–991, doi: http://10.1111/j.1468–5965.2010.02082.x.

Ullmann, Hans-Peter. *Politik im Deutschen Kaiserreich 1871–1918.* München: Oldenbourg Verlag, 2005.

Velley, Serge. *Histoire constitutionalle francaise de 1789 a nos jours.* Paris: Elipses, 2009.

Verney, Susannah. 'Justifying the Second Enlargement: Promoting interests, Consolidating Democracy or Returning to the Roots?'. In *Questioning EU Enlargement: Europe in Search of Identity*, ed. Helene Sjursen, 19–43. Oxon: Routledge, 2006.

Visier, Claire. 'La Turquie: instrument de politisation, objet de politisation'. *European Journal of Turkish Studies*, no. 9 (2009), http://ejts.revues.org/3709.

Walter, Jochen. *Die Türkei – 'Das Ding auf der Schwelle': (De-)Konstruktionen der Grenzen Europas.* Wiesbaden: VS Verlag für Sozialwissenschaften, 2008.

Watson, Peggy. 'Eastern Europe's Silent Revolution: Gender'. *Sociology* 27, no.3 (August 1993): 471–487, http://www.jstor.org/stable/42855234.

Watts, Duncan. *British Government and Politics: A Comparative Guide.* Edinburgh: Edinburg University Press. 2006).

Weatherill, Stephen. *Cases and Materials in EU Law.* Oxford: Oxford University Press, 2012.

Wells, Robin Headlam, Glen Burgess, and Rowland Wymer. 'Introduction', in *Neo-historicism, Studies in Renaissance Literature, History and Politics*, eds. Robin Headlam Wells, Glen Burgess, and Rowland Wymer, 1–28. Cambridge: DS Brewer, 2000.

Whelan, F. 'Oriental Despotism: Anquetil-Duperron's Response to Montesquieu'. *History of Political Thought* 22, no.4 (2001): 619–647.

White, Jason. *Militant Protestantism and British Identity, 1603–1642.* London: Pickering and Chatto, 2012.

White, Jenny B. 'State Feminism, Modernization, and the Turkish Republican Woman'. *NWSA Journal* 15, no.3 Gender and Modernism between the Wars, 1918–1939 (Autumn, 2003): 145–159.

de Wilde, Pieter, and Tapio Raunio, 'Redirecting national parliaments: Setting Priorities for Involvement in EU Affairs'. *Comparative European Politics* 16, no.2 (2018): 310–329, doi: 10.1057/cep.2015.28.

Willaime, Jean Paul. 'Religion et Politique en France: Dans le Contexte de la Construction Européenne'. *French Politics, Culture & Society* 25, no.3 (Winter 2007): 37–61, http://www.jstor.org/stable/42843513.

Winnacker, Rudolph A. 'Elections in Algeria and the French Colonies under the Third Republic'. *The American Political Science Review* 32, no.2 (April 1938): 261–277, doi: 10.2307/1948669.

Wodak, Ruth, Rudolf de Cecilia, Martin Reisigl and Karin Liebhart. *The Discursive Construction of National Identity*. Edinburgh: Edinburgh University Press, 2009.

Wodak, Ruth. 'The Discourse-Historical Approach'. In *Methods of Critical Discourse Analysis: Introducing Qualitative Methods*, eds. Ruth Wodak and Michael Meyer, 63–94. London: Sage Publications, 2001.

Wolff, Larry. *Inventing Eastern Europe: The Map of Civilization in the Minds of the Enlightenment*. Stanford, Stanford University Press, 1994.

Wright, Gordon. *France in Modern Times: From the Enlightenment to the Present*. Chicago: Rand McNally, 1960.

Yasri-Labrique, Eléonore. 'Les représentations de la Turquie en France à l'aune des quotidiens nationaux. Libération, Le Monde et Le Figaro (2005–2013)'. In *Médias et Pluralisme: La diversité à l'épreuve*, eds. Ksenija Djordjevic Léonard and Eléonore Yasri-Labrique, 33–61. Paris: Editions des archives contemporaines, 2014.

Yegenoglu, Meyda. *Islam, Migrancy, and Hospitality in Europe*. New York: Palgrave Macmilla, 2012.

Yilmaz, Hakan. 'Turkish Identity on the Road to the EU: Basic Elements of the French and German Discourses'. *Journal of Southern Europe and the Balkans* 9, no.3 (December 2007): 293–305, doi: 10.1080/14613190701689993.

Yilmaz, Hakan. 'Turkish Identity on the Road to the EU: Basic Elements of French and German Oppositional Discourses'. In *Turkey's Road to European Union Membership: National Identity and Political Change*, eds. Susannah Verney and Kostas Ifantis, 79–92. London and New York: 2009.

Zachary, Lockman. *Contending Visions of Middle East: The History and Politics of Orientalism*. New York: Cambridge University Press, 2010.

Zepp-La Rouche, Helga. 'The Empire is Crumbling: Future of Europe's Nations is with the Silk Road'. *Executive Intelligence Review*, June 6, 2014.

Zürcher, Erik J. *Turkey: A Modern History*. London and New York: I.B. Tauris, 2007.

Zürcher, Erik J. *The Young Turk Legacy and Nation Building*. London: Tauris, 2010.

Öniş, Ziya. 'Luxembourg, Helsinki and Beyond: Towards an Interpretation of Recent Turkey-EU Relations'. *Government and Opposition* 35, no.4 (2000): 463–483, doi: 10.1111/1477-7053.00041.

Öniş, Ziya. 'Domestic Politics, International Norms and Challenges to the State, Turkey-EU Relations in the post-Helsinki Area'. *Turkish Politics* 4, no.1 (2003): 9–34, doi: 10.1080/714005718.

'Talking Turkey', by Wolfgang Schauble and David L. Phillips. *Foreign Affairs* 83, no.6 (November/December 2004).

News Media

'Mister Mittelmaß'. *Der Spiegel*, no.37 (2005), September 12, 2005.

Ash, Timothy Garton. 'How the Dreaded Superstate Became a Commonwealth'. *The Guardian*, October 6, 2005.

Ataman, Ferda. 'Türkische Wähler: Wo die CDU unter fünf Prozent liegt'. *Spiegel Online*, September 13, 2005, http://www.spiegel.de/politik/deutschland/tuerkische-waehler-wo-die-cdu-unter-fuenf-prozent-liegt-a-374502.html (15.02.2015).
Aubert, A. 'Sarkozy calme le jeu sur la Turquie'. *Le Figaro*, September 26, 2005.
Avril, Pierre, 'Pour ou contre l'adhésion: cinq questions en débat'. *Le Figaro*, December 16, 2004.
de Baroches, Luc. 'Les amours clandestines de Paris et Ankara'. *Le Figaro*, October 3, 2005.
Birand, Mehmet Ali. 'Merkels Niederlage lässt die Türken aufatmen'. *Die Zeit*, September 22, 2005.
Blome, Nikolaus. 'Patriotismus ist das, was ich jeden Tag tue'. *Die Welt*, December 4, 2004.
Bobley, Graham. 'EU Divided on Talks for Turkey'. *International Herald Tribune*, September 9, 2005.
de Boissieu, Laurent. 'Europe: la Turquie cherche l'appui de la Francemardi'. *Le Figaro*, July 20, 2004.
Boland, Vincent. 'Doubts over Turkish Justice Cast Shadow on EU Accession Talks'. *Financial Times*, September 26, 2005.
Bolzen, Stefanie, and Ansgar Graw. 'Kampf um türkischstämmige Wähler', *Die Welt*, September 16, 2005.
Bornhöft, Petra, and Ralf Neukirch. 'Spiegel-Streitgespräch, Sie legen die Axt ans Grundgesetz'. *Der Spiegel*, no.50 (2004), December 6, 2004.
Bouilhet, Alexandrine. 'Bruxelles dédramatise l'adhésion de la Turquie'. *Le Figaro*, September 29, 2004.
Bouilhet, Alexandrine. 'La Commission fait l'éloge de l'adhésion turque'/ *Le Figaro*, October 1, 2004.
Bouilhet, Alexandrine. 'Bruxelles garde le cap avec Ankara'. *Le Figaro.* June 29, 2005.
Bouilhet, Alexandrine. 'Chypre : l'Europe met la pression sur Ankara'. *Le Figaro*, September 3, 2005.
Burkeman, Oliver. 'Wandering in the Wilderness – How Tories stole Ukip's political clothes'. *The Guardian*, April 29, 2005.
Béatrice Gurrey, 'La droite française, hostile à l'entrée de la Turquie, en fait un enjeu présidentiel pour 2007'. *Le Monde*, October 3, 2005.
Böckenförde, Ernst-Wolfgang. 'Nein zum Beitritt der Türkei'. *Frankfurter Allgemeine Zeitung*, December 9, 2004.
Caldwell, Christopher. 'Die Türken vor Wien'. *Die Welt*, October 4, 2005.
Chombeau, Christiane and Philippe Le Coeur. 'La droite affiche son hostilité à l'adhésion de la Turquie'. *Le Monde*, September 30, 2005.
Crawford, Alan. 'McConnell and Barroso Hit It off'. *The Sunday Herald*, April 3, 2005.
Crolly, Hannelore. '22 Milliarden Euro für türkische Bauern'. *Die Welt*, October 5, 2005.
Crolly, Hannelore. 'Knackpunkt Finanzen'. *Die Welt*, October 4, 2005.
Demetz, Jean-Michel. 'Turquie: le paradoxe européen'. L'Express, October 6, 2005.
Dombey, Daniel. 'Deal Boosts Turkish Hopes on Start of EU Accession Talks'. *Financial Times*, September 12, 2005.
Dombey, Daniel. 'Time Runs Short for EU Deal on Turkey Talks', Financial Times, September 18, 2005.
Erlanger, Steven. 'Sarkozy's Union of the Mediterranean Falters'. *New York Times*, June 6, 2008.

Evans-Prichard, Ambrose, and Andrew Sparrow. 'EU Offer to Turkey a Triumph for Tolerance and World Peace'. *The Telegraph*, September 18, 2004.
Finkel, Andrew. 'Turkish Delight', *The Guardian*, October 8, 2005.
Fischer, Joschka. 'Turkey's European Perspective: The German View', *Turkish Policy Quarterly* 3, no.3 (Fall 2004).
Gordon, Phil. 'Europe's Helsinki Summit: Now Make Turkey a Serious Offer'. *International Herald Tribune*, October 12, 1999.
Goulliaud, Philippe, and Bruno Jeudy. 'La Turquie, cette épine dans le flanc de Chirac et Villepin'. *Le Figaro*, September 23, 2005.
Goulliaud, Philippe, and Bruno Jeudy. 'Jacques Chirac, irréductible défenseur de la cause turque'. *Le Figaro*, October 5, 2005.
Guiral, Antoine. 'L'UMP ronge l'os européen et charge Chirac'. *Liberation*, September 26, 2005.
Hannan, Daniel. 'A Cynical Comedy that is Likely to End in Ironic Tragedy'. *The Telegraph*, October 2, 2005.
Harding, Luke, and Nicholas Watt. 'Turkey's EU Dream Dealt Double Blow as Chirac and Merkel Raise Doubts'. *The Guardian*, August 27, 2005.
Hennessy, Patrick. 'Howard Puts Immigration at Heart of Election Battle', The Telegraph, January 23, 2005.
Hildebrandt, Tina and Jörg Lau. 'Patriotisch, christlich, gut?'. *Die Zeit*, November 25, 2004.
Horst, Bacia. 'Wieder einmal heißt es: Weiterstrampeln'. *Frankfurter Allgemeine Zeitung*, October 4, 2005.
Huneke, Dorte, and Roger Boyes. 'Islamismus: Keine Bombenwerfer'. *Die Zeit*, September 22, 2005.
Jaigu, Charles. 'Sarkozy et VGE rouvrent le dossier turc'. *Le Figaro*, September 23, 2005.
Jean-Baptiste De Montvalon, 'La tentation du populisme'. *Le Monde*, July 19, 2005.
Jeffries, Stuart. '"Swamped" and "riddled": the Toxic Words that Wreck Public Discourse', *The Guardian*, October 27, 2014.
Kinzer, Stephen. 'Europeans Shut the Door on Turkey's Membership in Union'. *The New York Times*, May 27, 1997.
Kuppel, Roger. 'When did you last see your fatherland?' *The Spectator*, October 30, 2004, 22.
Lau, Jörg. 'Deutsche Schmerztherapie'. *Die Zeit*, April 21, 2005
Leinemann, Jürgen. 'Eine Nation auf der Suche'. *Der Spiegel*, no.4 (2005), April 26, 2005.
Lohse, Eckart and Wehner, Markus. 'Fischer im Interview. Mehr Dylan weniger Marx'. *Frankfurter Allgemeine Sonntagszeitung*, September 4, 2005.
di Lorenzo, Giovanni, and Jan Ross. 'Interview: Kommen Sie uns nicht mit 1945!', Die Welt, September 15, 2005.
Lyttelton, Alfred. 'Women at Istanbul'. *The Spectator*, May 2, 1935.
Macintyre, Ben. 'Brutality, poverty and religion stand between Turkey and EU'. *The Times*, September 30, 2005.
Marchand, Laure. 'Les retards turcs'. *L'Express*, September 22, 2005.
Neumann, Bernard. 'Ces Français qui misent sur la Turquie'. *L'Expansion*, June 23, 2004.
Nuttall, Chris and Ian Traynor. 'Kohl Tries To Cool Row with Ankara'. *The Guardian*, March 7, 1997.
Oliver, Mark. 'Turkey's Future Lies in EU, Says Blair'. *The Guardian*, September 30, 2005.
Olt, Reinhard. 'Stolz in Wien'. *Frankfurter Allgemeine Zeitung*, October 5, 2005.

Stuiber, Petra. 'Wolfgang Schüssel: Allein gegen alle'. *Die Welt*, October 4, 2005.
Palmer, Hartmut, and Christoph Schult. 'Ein verlorenes Jahr'. *Der Spiegel*, no.50 (2004), December, 6, 2004.
Parris, Matthiew. 'The Riots May Be Just What the French Economy Needs'. *The Spectator*, November 12, 2005.
Pognon, Olivier. 'Simone Veil dit non à l'entrée d'Ankara dans l'Union européenne'. *Le Figaro*, May 12, 2005.
Portillo, Michael. 'The Land of Promise and Danger at the EU's Door'. *The Sunday Times*, September 4, 2005.
Power, Jonathan. 'How Turkey Fails Its Kurds', International Herald Tribune, September 21, 2005.
Randall, Colin. 'Turkey's Membership of Europe Cast Long Shadow over French Poll'. *The Telegraph*, May 30, 2005.
Randall, Collin. 'Turkey's Membership of Europe Cast Long Shadow over French Poll'. *The Telegraph*, May 30, 2005.
Rehn, Olli. 'Donnons sa chance à la Turquie'. *Le Monde*, September 1, 2005.
Rennie, David. 'Chirac on Collision Course with Blair over Turkey in EU'. *The Telegraph*, August 27, 2005.
Rennie, David. 'Threats and Bickering as the EU Ministers Meet to Talk Turkey'. *The Telegraph*, September 2, 2005.
Rennie, David. 'Britain Faces Showdown over Turkey'. *The Telegraph*, September 28, 2005.
Richburg, Keith B. 'E.U., Turkey Agree To Membership Talks'. *The Washington Post*, December 18, 2004.
Ridet, Philippe. 'Nicolas Sarkozy rouvre le débat sur l'adhésion de la Turquie à l'UE'. *Le Monde*, September 23, 2005.
Ridet, Philippe. 'Valéry Giscard d'Estaing dénonce l'"ambiguïté" française sur la Turquie'. *Le Monde*, September 26, 2005.
Riedl, Joachim. 'Haiders hässliches Erbe'. *Die Zeit*, October 6, 2005.
Robert-Diard, Pascale, and Daniel Vernet. 'Lionel Jospin veut faire l'Europe de demain "sans défaire la France"'. *Le Monde*, May 29, 2001.
Rocard, Michel. 'Turquie : menaces sur les négociations'. *Le Monde*, October 1, 2005.
Schröder, Gerhard. 'Auf die Kleinen ist Verlass'. *Die Zeit*, October 20, 2005.
Seidl, Clauidius. 'Eine Türkin wie wir'. *Frankfurter Allgemeine Sonntagszeitung*, September 18, 2005.
Shihab, Sophie. 'Turquie : des historiens brisent le tabou sur la question arménienne'. *Le Monde*, September, 26, 2005.
Smith, Helena. 'European Mission Unearths Torture Claims in Turkey'. *The Guardian*, October 10, 2005.
Stares, Justin, and Nick Holdsworth. 'Europe "Faces Disaster" If It Spurns Turkey', The Telegraph, October 2, 2005.
Staun, Harald. 'Interview mit Samuel P. Huntington: Das Gespenst der Immigration'. *Frankfurter Allgemeine Sonntagszeitung*, October 30, 2005.
Swaine, Jon. 'Margaret Thatcher Complained about Asian Immigration to Britain'. *The Telegraph*, December 30, 2009.
Time, 'Mustafa Kemal Pasha', *Time* 1, no.4, March 24, 1923.
Toynbee, Arnold. 'The Savior of Turkey'. *The Spectator*, November 18, 1938.

Traynor, Ian, and Ewen MacAskill. 'Torture Claims Threaten Turkey's Bid to Join EU'. *The Guardian*, September 28, 2005.
Ulrich, Bernd .'Christlich-demokratische Verunsicherung'. *Die Zeit*, December 16, 2004.
Vaner, Semih. 'Chypre ne doit pas être un alibi'. *Le Figaro*, September 2, 2005.
Vannahme, Joachim Fitz. 'Germany's Turkish Angst'. *Europe's World*, October 1, 2005.
Watt, Nicholas. 'Early French Vote on EU Constitution'. *The Guardian*, February 28, 2005.
Watt, Nicholas. 'Austria Blocks Turkey's Road to EU membership'. *The Guardian*, September 14, 2005.
Wintraub, Judith. 'Giscard réclame de la "clarté" sur la Turquie'. Le Monde, September 24, 2005.
Wrench, Evelyn. 'A Country Without God'. *The Spectator*, November 22, 1935.
Zaman, Amberin, and Tony Peterson, 'Trial of Novelist "Shows Turkey Not Ready for EU"'. *The Sunday Telegraph*, September 11, 2005.
Zand, Bernhard. 'Scheidung vor der Hochzeit?' *Der Spiegel*, no.40 (2005), October 1, 2005.
'20 500 Deutschtürken dürfen nicht wählen'. *Frankfurter Allgemeine Zeitung*, September 17, 2005.
'A Paris Jacques Chirac et Silvio Berlusconi defendant la candidature turque a l'UE'. *Le Monde*, October 4, 2005.
'A Prized Area Divided Within, Beset from without and Jealous of its Own Heritage'. *Life*, March 26, 1956.
'Accord des Vingt-Cinq pour demander à la Turquie de reconnaître Chypre avant son adhésion à l'UE'. *Le Monde*, September 20, 2005.
'Annäherung in der EU über türkischen Beitritt'. *Frankfurter Allgemeine Zeitung*, December 10, 2004.
'Auf dem Rücken der Türken'. *Die Zeit*, September 1, 2005.
'Austria Sabotages Turkish EU Talks'. *The Telegraph*, September 30, 2005.
'Barroso Fires EU Warning to Turkey'. *The Guardian*, October 4, 2005.
'Bazaar Bargaining'. *The Economist*, September 1, 2005.
'Britain Persuades the EU to Talk Turkey'. *The Telegraph*, October 4, 2005.
'Brüssel gibt Ankara wieder nach'. *Die Welt*, September 21, 2005.
'Das Jahr der Schildkröte'. *Der Spiegel*, no.53 (2004), December 27, 2004
'Deal on Turkish Membership of EU Saved by Compromise over Cyprus'. *The Independent*, December 18, 2004.
'Der Zypern-Stachel'. *Die Zeit*, September 29, 2005.
'Devedjian: "La Turquie n'a donné aucun gage de démocratie"'. *Le Figaro*, October 4, 2005.
'Die Bilanz der Schröder'. *Die Welt*, September 15, 2005.
'Die Liebe geht durch die Verfassung'. *Die Zeit*, November 11, 2004.
'EU Leaders to Offer Turkey Deal on Membership Talks'. *The Independent*, December 16, 2004.
'EU President: Herman Van Rompuy Opposes Turkey Joining'. *The Telegraph*, September 19, 2009.
'EU remains divided over Turkey's refusal to recognize Cyprus'. *Daily Star*, September 15, 2005.
'EU räumt der Türkei für Gespräche viel Spielraum ein'. *Die Welt*, September 22, 2005.
'EU will Druck auf Türkei erhöhen'. *Frankfurter Allgemeine Zeitung*, September 17, 2005.

'EU-Beitritt Merkel für einen "dritten Weg" mit der Türkei'. *Frankfurter Allgemeine Zeitung*, February 16, 2004.
'Ein schwarzer Tag für Europa'. *Frankfurter Allgemeine Zeitung* (Online), October 4, 2005, http://www.faz.net/aktuell/politik/inland/tuerkei-verhandlungen-ein-schwarzer-tag-fuer-europa-1255987.html (18.02.2015).
'Eine Art Kriegserklärung', *Frankfurter Allgemeine Zeitung* (Online), October 11, 2004, http://www.faz.net/aktuell/politik/ausland/union-unterschriftenaktion-eine-art-kriegserklaerung-1193138.html (22.02.2015).
'Eine große Umwälzung in der Türkei'. *Der Spiegel*, no.26 (2005), June 27, 2005.
'Emergency Talks to Save Turkey EU Entry'. *The Telegraph*, September 30, 2005.
'FDP beharrt auf Steuerentlastung'. *Die Welt*, September 12, 2005.
'Full text: Tony Blair's Speech to the European Parliament'. *The Guardian*, June 23, 2005.
'Gerhard Schröder stärkt Tayyip Erdogan den Rücken'. *Die Zeit*, May 11, 2005.
'Germany needs change'. *The Telegraph*, September 18, 2005.
'Giscard critique Chirac'. *Le Monde*, October 3, 2005.
'Ihre Rede ist Jein und Nö'. *Die Zeit*, October 6, 2005.
'Interview: Türkei braucht eine glaubwürdige EU-Perspektive'. *Die Zeit.de*, 03.05.2005, http://www.zeit.de/politik/dlf/2005/interview_050503 (07.09.2015).
'It Is in Europe's Best Interests that Turkey's Hopes Are not Betrayed'. *The Independent*, December 18, 2004.
'L'UMP débat de l'avenir de l'UE'. *Le Nouvel Observateur*. September 27, 2005.
'La candidature turque à l'UE a-t-elle des chances d'aboutir?'. *Le Monde*, October 3, 2005.
'Le ministre de l'Intérieur revient à la charge sur la Turquie'. *Le Figaro*, June 13, 2005.
'Le processus d'adhésion de la Turquie à l'UE avive les tensions au PS et à droite'. *Le Monde*, September 30, 2005.
'Les Français contre l'entrée de la Turquie'. *Le Nouvel Observateur*, October 3, 2005.
'Les Français réfractaires au processus d'adhésion de la Turquie à l'UE'. *Le Figaro*, January 26, 2014.
'Lord Curzon's Mission'. *The Spectator*, September 22, 1922.
'L'Union européenne va adresser une "contre-déclaration" à la Turquie'. *Le Monde*, September 21, 2005.
'Merkel und Stoiber bestärken in der EU ihren Widerstand', *Frankfurter Allgemeine* Zeitung, August 26, 2005.
'Merkel und Stoiber: Kanzler muß Türkei-Beitritt stoppen', *Frankfurter Allgemeine Zeitung* (Online), December 5, 2004, https://www.faz.net/-gpf-pkxs?GEPC=s3 (17.08.2018)
'Mitterrand Backs European Integration'. *New York Times*, August 12, 1989.
'Now Make Turkey's Case'. *The Economist*, October 6, 2005.
'Pour ou contre l'adhésion de la Turquie à l'Union européenne'. *Le Monde*, November 8, 2002.
'Sarkozy réunit une convention UMP sur l'Europe'. *Le Nouvelle Observateur*. September 24, 2005.
'Schröder kämpft um 600.000 Stimmen: Entscheiden Türken die Wahl?'. *Bild Zeitung*, September 14, 2005.
'Schröder: Stoiber überschätzt sich in Türkei-Debatte', *Frankfurter Allgemeine Zeitung* (Online), December 13, 2004, http://www.faz.net/aktuell/politik/eu-beitritt-schroeder-stoiber-ueberschaetzt-sich-in-tuerkei-debatte-1195701.html#/elections (13.02.2015)

'Se démarquant de Jacques Chirac, l'UMP prend position contre l'entrée de la Turquie dans l'UE'. *Le Monde*, April 9, 2004.
'Straw: We Must not Push Turkey Away'. *The Telegraph*, October 2, 2005.
'The Turkish Empire'. *The Spectator*, November 28, 1840.
'Turkey Must Recognize Genocide'. *The Telegraph*, September 28, 2005.
'Turkey Must Relent'. *The Spectator*, September 10, 2005.
'Turquie en Europe: "le coût du mépris"'. *Le Figaro*, October 7, 2005.
'Turquie: les britanniques passent en force', *Le Figaro*, October 5, 2005.
'Unfair, unehrlich und zynisch'. *Frankfurter Allgemeine Zeitung*, December 15, 2004.
'Union bleibt bei Nein zu türkischem EU-Beitritt', *Frankfurter Allgemeine Zeitung* (Online), February 14, 2004, http://www.faz.net/aktuell/politik/europawahl-union-bleibt-bei-nein-zu-tuerkischem-eu-beitritt-1146987.html#/elections (25.03.2015).
'Union: Wirtschaftsflügel wettert gegen Patriotismus-Debatte'. *Der Spiegel Online*, December 6, 2004, https://spon.de/abyjr (15.03.2015)
'Vor dem 3. Oktober will die EU den Druck auf die Türkei erhöhen'. *Die Welt*, September 17, 2005.
'Wer ist hier Stur?' *Frankfurter Allgemeine Zeitung*, September 30, 2005.
'When to talk Turkey'. *The Economist, Europe Edition*, September 15, 2005.
'Why Turkey is Good for Europe'. *Spectator*, February 21, 2004.
'Wo die Kontrahenten punkten konnten'. *Die Welt*, September 6, 2005.
'Zu groß, zu arm, zu verschieden'. *Frankfurter Allgemeine Zeitung*, December 15, 2004.
'Zu spät?' *Frankfurter Allgemeine Zeitung*, September 28, 2005.

Index

Absorption Capacity (Integration Capacity) 79, 83, 90, 106, 109–113, 185f., 217
Accession criteria (Copenhagen criteria) 6, 24, 26, 37, 74, 78, 80f., 83f., 89, 96, 98, 100, 105, 131, 146, 203f., 207, 212, 216–218, 223, 227
Accession talks (See, Negotiations) 1, 5, 21f., 40, 91, 93, 97, 101, 104, 106–110, 116, 124–126, 132, 142, 147, 149–153, 156, 158f., 171, 173, 176, 181, 184, 186, 196, 199–201, 204, 208–211, 214, 219, 222f., 225–227
– Chapters 6, 22, 33f., 38, 40, 97, 118, 130f., 189, 201, 213f.
Acquis Communautaire (EU Legislation) 1, 16, 83
Additional Protocol 75, 102f., 108f., 114, 116, 124
AFET (Committee on Foreign Affairs) 6, 39, 97, 101
AKP (Justice and Development Party) 121
Alevi Minority 73, 123
Alliance of Liberals and Democrats for Europe (ALDE) 98, 102, 105, 217
Anderson, Benedict 7
Anglican 43, 190
Ankara Agreement (Association Agreement) 75
Armenian Genocide 64, 71, 113, 145, 148, 150–152, 167, 173, 196, 219f., 224
Atatürk (Mustafa Kemal) 65f., 66, 71

Basic Law (of Germany) 161, 163, 166, 169
Blair, Tony 194f., 202–204, 206, 209
Bodin, Jean 53
Brexit 12, 26, 30, 95, 192, 207f., 225
Britain 7, 14, 16, 28–30, 36, 38, 40, 48, 50, 54, 57f., 73, 89, 103, 107, 131, 140f., 146, 149, 156, 164, 184, 189–205, 207–212, 217f., 220, 222, 224, 227
– British Empire 73
– England 45, 190f., 202, 222

British Conservative Party (British Conservatives) 104, 106f., 116, 205, 212, 217, 223–225
Burke, Edmund 46, 50f., 53f., 60
Byron, George Gordon 57

Catherine, the Great 48
CEE (Central and Eastern European Countries) 21, 84f., 88, 106
Central and Eastern European Countries (CEE Countries) 1, 10, 84f., 149, 153, 170
Cevdet, Abdullah 62
de Chateaubriand, François-Rene 55, 56
Chirac, Jacques 93, 132, 142, 147–150, 152–154, 157, 177, 219
Christian Democratic Union (CDU) 130, 167, 178, 220
Christian Democrats 31, 92f., 98, 102–105, 108f., 111, 115, 117f., 124, 161f., 165, 168–170, 174, 176, 178–184, 186f., 198, 221, 225
– Christianity 19, 34, 44, 56, 98, 128, 176
Christian Social Union (CSU) 167, 178–180, 185, 187, 220
Church of England 43, 57, 190f.
Citizenship 17, 29, 38, 41, 46f., 78, 80f., 134, 136–138, 159, 162–166, 170, 177, 182f., 189, 191–193, 196, 218, 220, 222
– In Britain 12, 26, 31, 40, 47, 91, 122, 139, 189–191, 193–195, 197, 199, 206, 208, 222–227
– In France 12, 24f., 29, 31, 36, 38, 40, 46f., 49, 53f., 89, 94, 132, 135–137, 140–144, 146, 148–151, 155–157, 163f., 177f., 181, 184, 186, 192, 195, 199, 202, 220, 223–227
– In Germany 7, 26, 28–31, 36, 40, 47, 92, 95, 130, 146, 160, 162–168, 170, 172–175, 177, 180–184, 186, 198, 220f., 224f., 227
Cold War 8f., 12, 18f., 23, 26, 39, 68f., 74f., 80, 92f., 96f., 127, 216
Community of Union and Progress (CUP) 71

Compte, August 63
Congress of Vienna 55
– Concert of Europe 48
Copenhagen criteria 20, 24, 37, 80–83, 85, 87–90, 101, 104–106, 109, 111, 113, 117, 119f., 122f., 146, 180, 216f.
Copenhagen European Council 81, 83, 88, 92, 100f., 110
– in 1973 70, 164, 193
– in 1978 76, 81, 100
– in 2002 145, 176
Council of Europe 69f.
Craven, Elizabeth 56
Cyprus 21, 70, 73–75, 83–85, 87f., 90, 106, 113–116, 150f., 153, 172, 200f., 219

Declaration of the Rights of the Man and Citizen 135, 137
Declaration on Democracy (1978) 76f., 81, 100
Declaration on European Identity (1973) 76, 81
Der Spiegel (magazine) 168, 171–174, 177, 179, 182
Devedjian, Patrick 151f.
Die Bild (newspaper)
Die Welt (newspaper) 167, 169, 171–176, 179, 181–183, 185, 224
Die Zeit (newspaper) 167f., 171, 173f., 177, 182f., 185
Douste-Blazy, Philippe 150
Duff, Andrew 118f.

Economist (newspaper) 196–200, 210
EEC (See, European Economic Community) 15f, 74–79, 102f., 108f., 114, 116, 124
– Treaty of Rome 78, 80f., 127
Ellison, Grace 67
Enlargement 1–4, 7, 9–12, 19–25, 27–30, 33, 37, 39, 76–79, 81–85, 88, 90–92, 94f., 97–99, 101–106, 108, 110–112, 114f., 117–119, 124, 127, 129, 134, 142, 146, 151, 153, 155, 175, 180, 184, 186, 189, 199–202, 205–208, 212, 216, 223
Enlightenment 13, 19, 25, 34, 38, 41, 45f., 51f., 92, 103, 122, 133, 135f., 185, 215
Erdogan, Recep Tayyip 173

d'Estaing, Valery Giscard 18
– and Sarkozy 149, 158
EU Constitution 12, 25f., 29, 40, 94, 132, 142–144, 146, 154f., 157–159, 169, 171, 176, 189, 195, 200–202, 205, 207, 212f., 219, 223
EU Legislation (Acquis Communautaire) 1f., 4, 6–8, 16–18, 20–22, 24, 34f., 40, 83, 86, 88, 123, 149, 217, 226
Eurobarometer 25, 91, 171, 202
European Commission (EC) 2–4, 19f., 22, 24f., 76–80, 83, 85f., 89, 97, 101, 106, 108–110, 112, 114, 116f., 120f., 123, 141, 146, 202, 209
– Directorate for Education and Culture 2
– Directorate General for Research 4
European Conservatives 125, 211, 218
European Court of Human Rights (ECHR) 70
European Democrats 107, 116, 124
European Economic Community (See, EEC) 15, 74f., 77, 79f., 84, 114, 127
European Green Party 102, 105, 119, 126, 217
European Left 102, 105, 107, 112f., 117, 217
European Parliament (EP) 1, 5–7, 22f., 35, 37–40, 71, 77–80, 82, 85f., 90–92, 96–99, 101f., 105–108, 110–124, 127, 155, 181, 195, 208, 210, 217f., 223, 226, 232
European People's Party (EPP) 92, 98, 102f., 124, 142, 159, 217
European Single Act 141, 194
European Union 1–6, 8f., 11–20, 22f., 25–28, 30–35, 37–40, 64, 66, 69f., 72–74, 78, 80–88, 90–102, 104f., 107–109, 116, 119, 124f., 127, 129f., 132, 134, 139–143, 148f., 152, 154–157, 159, 161, 163, 167–172, 176, 180, 187, 189, 192–196, 199f., 202–207, 209, 211–214, 216–221, 223–226
– Council of the European Union 74, 78f., 83, 86f., 89, 101, 110, 115, 209, 212, 222
European values 1, 4–6, 14, 16–19, 24, 33, 35, 37f., 49, 59, 66, 76, 82, 84, 97f., 100–105, 117f., 124f., 127, 130f., 149,

152, 188, 190, 214–218, 220, 222–224, 226
– Lisbon Treaty   8f., 112, 127, 153
– the Accession criteria   5, 20, 39, 74, 77, 86f., 96, 98, 101–106, 110, 112f., 116, 120, 130f., 217f., 226f.
Euroscepticism   30, 94, 193f., 212, 222f.

Farage, Nigel   208
Fikret, Tevfik   62
Financial Times (newspaper)   196, 200f., 209
Fischer, Joschka   87, 164, 176f., 185
Frankfurter Allgemeine Zeitung (FAZ)   6, 171f., 177, 179, 181, 183, 185, 224
French Revolution   34, 39, 41, 46f., 51, 91, 133–136, 147, 218
– French Declaration of the Rights of Man and Citizen   47
– National Assembly   135f.
– Republicanism   34, 46, 134, 137f.
Furet, François   13, 45, 134

Gaulis, Berthe Georges   66
de Gaulle, Charles   136, 140f.
Geertz, Clifford   34, 42, 97
Germany   28f., 31, 36, 38, 40, 65, 80, 91, 94f., 110, 124, 130, 132, 136f., 139f., 149, 159–171, 174–179, 182f., 187, 190, 197f., 202, 220f., 223–227
– Federal Republic of Germany   161, 163f., 166, 169
Gibb, Rosskeen   67
Gladstone, William Ewart   58, 198
Gökalp, Ziya   63
Greece   10, 49, 51, 54, 56f., 70, 73–75, 77f., 83, 87, 115, 120, 152
– Greek revolts   56
Green Party   176, 221, 225
– Alliance '90/the Greens   176
– Greens   87, 93, 102, 104f., 107, 115, 117, 126, 130, 165, 176–178, 181–183, 185–187, 221
– See, European Green Party
Grotius, Hugo   44
Guardian   3, 92, 143, 189, 192, 195–200, 208f.

Helsinki European Council (1999)   83, 87, 91, 106, 113
Hobsbawm, Eric   13, 41, 47, 135
Hollande, François   143
Howard, Michael   205f.
Hugo, Victor   13, 49

Independent   33, 103, 191, 196, 198, 200f.
Integration Capacity (Absorption Capacity)   79, 90, 105, 112f.
Islam   14f., 18, 27f., 37, 43, 50, 56–59, 62f., 67f., 72, 121–125, 128, 137, 165, 172, 180, 185, 197, 203, 206f., 210–212, 223, 226
– Islamic culture   50, 68
– Islamic Slavery   56
– Islamophobia   18, 122, 198

Justice and Development Party (AKP)   121, 123, 125

Karlowitz   43
Kemalism   122
Kohl, Helmut   10, 92, 180
Kosselleck, Reinhart   36
– Conceptual History (Beggriffgechichte)   36f., 42
– Kurdish   73, 117, 173, 207

Labour Party   108, 143, 191, 194f., 202–205, 207, 209, 212f., 223
Lady Craven   56
Laïcité (See, Secularism)   134, 137, 218
de Lamartine, Alphonse   50, 59
Le Figaro (newspaper)   89, 144–148, 150–152, 154, 156, 172, 224
Le Monde (newspaper)   142f., 145f., 148f., 151, 154–157
Lewis, Bernard   15, 41, 68
L'Express (newspaper)   148
Liberal Democrats   106, 195f., 207
L'Institute nationale des langues et civilizations   49
Locke, John   52
Loti, Pierre   59
Luther, Martin   43

Luxembourg European Council (1997)   85f., 91
Lyttelton, Alfred   67

Maastricht Treaty (Treaty on EU)   80
Mariott, J.A.R.   64
Marshall Plan   70
Merkel, Angela   179, 181, 184, 198
Migration   5, 11, 30, 91, 94f., 110, 127, 142, 159, 163–166, 175, 187, 189, 191–193, 196, 201, 205, 207, 220, 222, 225f.
– Migrants   29, 94f., 146, 159, 162–165, 170, 173, 175, 187, 192, 220
Military   61, 63–66, 69–72, 75, 77–79, 91, 113, 115, 117, 122, 139, 167, 170, 220
– civil-military relations   70
– Coup   71, 75
Miller, William   64
Millet System   72
Minority   20, 24, 34, 61f., 65, 70, 72f., 88, 113, 117, 122, 152, 165, 196, 202, 207, 215, 225
Mitterrand, François   10, 29, 141
Montesquieu   50–54, 59f., 65

Napoleon   6, 135–137
National Front   95, 143–146, 225
National Representation   134, 136–139, 147, 149f., 157, 219, 224, 227
NATO (North Atlantic Organization)   69f., 107, 115, 181
Negotiations (See, Accession Talks)   5–7, 21f., 31, 33, 35f., 39f., 44, 65, 76, 78f., 84–86, 88–91, 93, 96f., 102–104, 106–111, 113–116, 118–121, 124, 129f., 132, 144–159, 171–179, 181, 184–187, 189, 196–201, 203–212, 214, 217–224, 226f.
Nerval, Gerard   50, 56, 59
Newman, John Henry   50, 57f.
North Atlantic Treaty Organisation (NATO)   69

Organisation of the Islamic Conference (OIC)   125
Orden, Geoffrey   107, 116

Orientalism   13f., 16, 32, 43, 49f., 52f., 57, 61, 67f., 198
Ottoman Empire   5f., 13–16, 35, 38f., 41–45, 48–50, 53–56, 58–66, 68f., 71, 113, 122, 126, 152, 214f.
Ottoman/Turkish Modernisation   41, 61, 69

Pamuk, Orhan   173
– Paris Peace Conference   16, 57, 62
Party of European Socialists (PES)   98, 102–104, 143, 217
Penn, William   43f.
Poettering, Hans-Gert   108f., 128
Polo, Marko   43
Porter, James   50, 60
Privileged Partnership   108f., 128, 131, 154f., 175, 178f., 181, 184, 186, 210, 217

Referendum   12, 26, 30, 94f., 132, 136, 139, 142–144, 147, 149–152, 155f., 171, 186, 192, 194, 202, 207, 219, 224–226
Reform Act (1856)   62
Renan, Ernest   50, 57
Riza, Ahmed   63
Romantics   13, 50, 51, 54–57, 59
Rousseau, Jean-Jacques   135
Russia   16, 48, 55, 57, 60–62, 69, 73
– Turco-Russian War(s)   48, 62
Rycaut, Paul   52

Said, Edward   13f., 32
Sarkozy, Nicolas   132, 142, 147, 149, 154, 156, 158, 184, 219, 225
Schäuble, Wolfgang   182, 186
Schengen Agreement   78
Schmidt, Helmut   182
Schröder, Gerhard   169, 177, 181f., 184
Schulz, Martin   103
Schuman Declaration   134, 140
Schuman, Robert   140, 141
Second World War (WWII)   5, 68f., 74, 140, 161, 166, 193, 216, 226
Secularism (See, Laïcité)   19, 123, 134, 158, 216, 218, 226
Self-determination   59, 137–139
Seljuk Turks   42f.
Skene, James   57

Slade, Adolphus 51, 63
Social Democratic Party of Germany (SPD) 161f., 170
Socialist Party of France (PS) 219
Soviet Union 69, 216
State 2–5, 8f., 11, 14–16, 18, 20–22, 28, 30f., 33f., 39, 44–48, 51f., 55f., 58, 61–64, 66–70, 72, 74, 76–79, 81–83, 85–88, 90, 93, 95, 98f., 101, 107, 115, 119, 123, 125, 127, 131, 133–141, 143, 152f., 157, 160–170, 174f., 177f., 185, 190, 193f., 196–198, 200f., 211, 213, 215f., 220, 222, 226
– French conception of 133, 135
Stoiber, Edmund 179, 186
Straw, Jack 199, 203, 209, 211, 214

Tanzimat Act (1839) 61
Telegraph (newspaper) 124, 192, 196–198, 200f., 203, 205, 209f.
Thatcher, Margaret 192, 194
The Porte 55, 61, 65
Times (newspaper) 3, 5, 41, 50, 61, 84, 86, 93, 102, 110, 115, 124, 129, 133, 136f., 141, 149, 157, 160, 173f., 179, 196–198, 206–208, 212, 217
Toynbee, Arnold 15, 66f.
Treaty of Lausanne 73
Treaty of Lisbon 1, 17, 33, 80, 82, 97, 100
Treaty of Sevres 65
Treaty of Versailles 65
Treaty of Westphalia 44
Treaty on EU (Maastricht Treaty) 98, 101
Tyranny 52, 55f., 64

UK Independence Party (UKIP) 95, 119, 131, 207f., 225
Union for Popular Movement (UMP) 142f.

Van Rompuy, Herman 124
de Villepin, Dominique 148–151, 154, 158

Welfare 5, 29, 40, 95, 159–164, 166, 169f., 174f., 180, 187, 192, 220–222, 224f., 227
Wrench, Evelyn 72
WWII (Second World War) 69, 136, 162, 168

www.ingramcontent.com/pod-product-compliance
Lightning Source LLC
Chambersburg PA
CBHW031803220426
43662CB00007B/513